Python® for Data Science

3rd Edition

by John Paul Mueller and Luca Massaron

for
dummies®
A Wiley Brand

Python® for Data Science For Dummies®, 3rd Edition

Published by: **John Wiley & Sons, Inc.**, 111 River Street, Hoboken, NJ 07030-5774, www.wiley.com

Copyright © 2024 by John Wiley & Sons, Inc., Hoboken, New Jersey

Media and software compilation copyright © 2023 by John Wiley & Sons, Inc. All rights reserved.

Published simultaneously in Canada

For general information on our other products and services, please contact our Customer Care Department within the U.S. at 877-762-2974, outside the U.S. at 317-572-3993, or fax 317-572-4002. For technical support, please visit https://hub.wiley.com/community/support/dummies.

Wiley publishes in a variety of print and electronic formats and by print-on-demand. Some material included with standard print versions of this book may not be included in e-books or in print-on-demand. If this book refers to media such as a CD or DVD that is not included in the version you purchased, you may download this material at http://booksupport.wiley.com. For more information about Wiley products, visit www.wiley.com.

Library of Congress Control Number: 2023946155

ISBN 978-1-394-21314-6 (pbk); ISBN 978-1-394-21308-5 (ebk); ISBN ePDF 978-1-394-21309-2 (ebk)

SKY10056117_092523

Contents at a Glance

Table of Contents

Introduction

The growth of the internet has been phenomenal. According to Internet World Stats (https://www.internetworldstats.com/emarketing.htm), 69 percent of the world is now connected in some way to the internet, including developing countries. North America has the highest penetration rate 93.4 percent, which means you now have access to nearly everyone just by knowing how to manipulate data. Data science turns this huge amount of data into capabilities that you use absolutely every day to perform an amazing array of tasks or to obtain services from someone else.

You've probably used data science in ways that you never expected. For example, when you used your favorite search engine this morning to look for something, it made suggestions on alternative search terms. Those terms are supplied by data science. When you went to the doctor last week and discovered that the lump you found wasn't cancer, the doctor likely made the prognosis with the help of data science.

In fact, you may work with data science every day and not even know it. Even though many of the purposes of data science elude attention, you have probably become more aware of the data you generate, and with that awareness comes a desire for control over aspects of your life, such as when and where to shop, or whether to have someone perform the task for you. In addition to all its other uses, data science enables you to add that level of control that you, like many people, are looking for today.

Python for Data Science For Dummies, 3rd Edition not only gets you started using data science to perform a wealth of practical tasks but also helps you realize just how many places data science is used. By knowing how to answer data science problems and where to employ data science, you gain a significant advantage over everyone else, increasing your chances at promotion or that new job you really want.

About This Book

The main purpose of *Python for Data Science For Dummies*, 3rd Edition, is to take the scare factor out of data science by showing you that data science is not only really interesting but also quite doable using Python. You may assume that you need to be a computer science genius to perform the complex tasks normally associated with data science, but that's far from the truth. Python comes with a host of useful libraries that do all the heavy lifting for you in the background. You don't even realize how much is going on, and you don't need to care. All you really need to know is that you want to perform specific tasks, and Python makes these tasks quite accessible.

Part of the emphasis of this book is on using the right tools. You start with either Jupyter Notebook (on desktop systems) or Google Colab (on the web) — two tools that take the sting out of working with Python. The code you place in Jupyter Notebook or Google Colab is presentation quality, and you can mix a number of presentation elements right there in your document. It's not really like using a traditional development environment at all.

You also discover some interesting techniques in this book. For example, you can create plots of all your data science experiments using Matplotlib, and this book gives you all the details for doing that. This book also spends considerable time showing you available resources (such as packages) and how you can use Scikit-learn to perform some very interesting calculations. Many people would like to know how to perform handwriting recognition, and if you're one of them, you can use this book to get a leg up on the process.

Of course, you may still be worried about the whole programming environment issue, and this book doesn't leave you in the dark there, either. At the beginning, you find complete methods you need to get started with data science using Jupyter Notebook or Google Colab. The emphasis is on getting you up and running as quickly as possible, and to make examples straightforward and simple so that the code doesn't become a stumbling block to learning.

This third edition of the book provides you with updated examples using Python 3.x so that you're using the most modern version of Python while reading. In addition, you find a stronger emphasis on making examples simpler, but also making the environment more inclusive by adding material on deep learning. More important, this edition of the book contains updated datasets that better demonstrate how data science works today. This edition of the book also touches on modern concerns, such as removing personally identifiable information and enhancing data security. Consequently, you get a lot more out of this edition of the book as a result of the input provided by thousands of readers before you.

To make absorbing the concepts even easier, this book uses the following conventions:

>> Text that you're meant to type just as it appears in the book is in **bold**. The exception is when you're working through a list of steps: Because each step is bold, the text to type is not bold.

>> When you see words in *italics* as part of a typing sequence, you need to replace that value with something that works for you. For example, if you see "Type *Your Name* and press Enter," you need to replace *Your Name* with your actual name.

>> Web addresses and programming code appear in monofont. If you're reading a digital version of this book on a device connected to the internet, note that you can click the web address to visit that website, like this: `http://www.dummies.com`.

>> When you need to type command sequences, you see them separated by a special arrow, like this: File ⇨ New File. In this example, you go to the File menu first and then select the New File entry on that menu.

Foolish Assumptions

You may find it difficult to believe that we've assumed anything about you — after all, we haven't even met you yet! Although most assumptions are indeed foolish, we made these assumptions to provide a starting point for the book.

You need to be familiar with the platform you want to use because the book doesn't offer any guidance in this regard. (Chapter 3 does, however, provide Anaconda installation instructions, which supports Jupyter Notebook, and Chapter 4 gets you started with Google Colab.) To provide you with maximum information about Python concerning how it applies to data science, this book doesn't discuss any platform-specific issues. You really do need to know how to install applications, use applications, and generally work with your chosen platform before you begin working with this book.

You must know how to work with Python. This edition of the book no longer contains a Python primer because you can find a wealth of tutorials online (see `https://www.w3schools.com/python/` and `https://www.tutorialspoint.com/python/` as examples).

This book isn't a math primer. Yes, you do encounter some complex math, but the emphasis is on helping you use Python and data science to perform analysis tasks rather than teaching math theory. Chapters 1 and 2 give you a better understanding of precisely what you need to know to use this book successfully.

This book also assumes that you can access items on the internet. Sprinkled throughout are numerous references to online material that will enhance your learning experience. However, these added sources are useful only if you actually find and use them.

Icons Used in This Book

As you read this book, you come across icons in the margins, and here's what those icons mean:

TIP

Tips are nice because they help you save time or perform some task without a lot of extra work. The tips in this book are time-saving techniques or pointers to resources that you should try in order to get the maximum benefit from Python or in performing data science–related tasks.

WARNING

We don't want to sound like angry parents or some kind of maniacs, but you should avoid doing anything that's marked with a Warning icon. Otherwise, you may find that your application fails to work as expected, or you get incorrect answers from seemingly bulletproof equations, or (in the worst-case scenario) you lose data.

TECHNICAL STUFF

Whenever you see this icon, think advanced tip or technique. You may find that you don't need these tidbits of useful information, or they could contain the solution you need to get a program running. Skip these bits of information whenever you like.

REMEMBER

If you don't get anything else out of a particular chapter or section, remember the material marked by this icon. This text usually contains an essential process or a morsel of information that you must know to work with Python or to perform data science–related tasks successfully.

Beyond the Book

This book isn't the end of your Python or data science experience — it's really just the beginning. We provide online content to make this book more flexible and better able to meet your needs. That way, as we receive email from you, we can address questions and tell you how updates to either Python or its associated add-ons affect book content. In fact, you gain access to all these cool additions:

» **Cheat sheet:** You remember using crib notes in school to make a better mark on a test, don't you? You do? Well, a cheat sheet is sort of like that. It provides you with some special notes about tasks that you can do with Python, IPython, IPython Notebook, and data science that not every other person knows. You can find the cheat sheet by going to www.dummies.com and entering *Python for Data Science For Dummies, 3rd Edition* in the search field. The cheat sheet contains neat information such as the most common programming mistakes, styles for creating plot lines, and common magic functions to use in Jupyter Notebook.

» **Updates:** Sometimes changes happen. For example, we may not have seen an upcoming change when we looked into our crystal ball during the writing of this book. In the past, this possibility simply meant that the book became outdated and less useful, but you can now find updates to the book by searching this book's title at www.dummies.com.

In addition to these updates, check out the blog posts with answers to reader questions and demonstrations of useful book-related techniques at http://blog.johnmuellerbooks.com/.

» **Companion files:** Hey! Who really wants to type all the code in the book and reconstruct all those plots manually? Most readers would prefer to spend their time actually working with Python, performing data science tasks, and seeing the interesting things they can do, rather than typing. Fortunately for you, the examples used in the book are available for download, so all you need to do is read the book to learn *Python for Data Science For Dummies* usage techniques. You can find these files at www.dummies.com/go/pythonfordatasciencefd3e. You can also find the source code on author John's website at http://www.johnmuellerbooks.com/source-code/.

Where to Go from Here

It's time to start your *Python for Data Science For Dummies* adventure! If you're completely new to Python and its use for data science tasks, you should start with Chapter 1 and progress through the book at a pace that allows you to absorb as much of the material as possible.

If you're a novice who's in an absolute rush to use Python with data science as quickly as possible, you can skip to Chapter 3 (desktop users) or Chapter 4 (web browser users) with the understanding that you may find some topics a bit confusing later. More advanced readers can skip to Chapter 5 to gain an understanding of the tools used in this book.

Readers who have some exposure to Python and know how to use their development environment can save reading time by moving directly to Chapter 6. You can always go back to earlier chapters as necessary when you have questions. However, you should understand how each technique works before moving to the next one. Every technique, coding example, and procedure has important lessons for you, and you could miss vital content if you start skipping too much information.

1

Getting Started with Data Science and Python

Chapter 1

Discovering the Match between Data Science and Python

Data science may seem like one of those technologies that you'd never use, but you'd be wrong. Yes, data science involves the use of advanced math techniques, statistics, and big data. However, data science also involves helping you make smart decisions, creating suggestions for options based on previous choices, and making robots see objects. In fact, people use data science in so many different ways that you almost can't look anywhere or do anything without feeling the effects of data science on your life. In short, data science is the person behind the partition in the experience of the wonderment of technology. Without data science, much of what you accept as typical and expected today wouldn't even be possible. This is the reason that being a data scientist is one of the most interesting jobs of the 21st century.

REMEMBER

To make data science doable by someone who's less than a math genius, you need tools. You could use any of a number of tools to perform data science tasks, but Python is uniquely suited to making it easier to work with data science. For one thing, Python provides an incredible number of math-related libraries that help you perform tasks with a less-than-perfect understanding of precisely what is going on. However, Python goes further by supporting multiple coding styles (programming paradigms) and doing other things to make your job easier. Therefore, yes, you could use other languages to write data science applications, but Python reduces your workload, so it's a natural choice for those who really don't want to work hard, but rather to work smart.

This chapter gets you started with Python. Even though this book isn't designed to provide you with a complete Python tutorial, exploring some basic Python issues will reduce the time needed for you to get up to speed. (If you do need a good starting tutorial, please get *Beginning Programming with Python For Dummies*, 3rd Edition, by John Mueller (Wiley)). You'll find that the book provides pointers to tutorials and other aids as needed to fill in any gaps that you may have in your Python education.

Understanding Python as a Language

This book uses Python as a programming language because it's especially well-suited to data science needs and also supports performing general programming tasks. Common wisdom says that Python is interpreted, but as described in the blog post at `http://blog.johnmuellerbooks.com/2023/04/10/compiling-python/`, Python can act as a compiled language as well. This book uses Jupyter Notebook because the environment works well for learning, but you need to know that Python provides a lot more than you see in this book. With this fact in mind, the following sections provide a brief view of Python as a language.

Viewing Python's various uses as a general-purpose language

Python isn't a language just for use in data science; it's a general-purpose language with many uses beyond what you need to perform data science tasks. Python is important because after you have built a model, you may need to build a user interface and other structural elements around it. The model may simply be one part of a much larger application, all of which you can build using Python. Here are some tasks that developers commonly use Python to perform beyond data science needs:

>> Web development

>> General-purpose programming:

- Performing Create, Read, Update, and Delete (CRUD) operations on any sort of file

- Creating graphical user interfaces (GUIs)
- Developing application programming interfaces (API)s

» Game development (something you can read about at https://realpython.com/tutorials/gamedev/)

» Automation and scripting

» Software testing and prototyping

» Language development (Cobra, CoffeeScript, and Go all use a language syntax similar to Python)

» Marketing and Search Engine Optimization (SEO)

» Common tasks associated with standard applications:

- Tracking financial transactions of all sorts
- Interacting with various types of messaging strategies
- Creating various kinds of lists based on environmental or other inputs
- Automating tasks like filling out forms

The list could be much longer, but this gives you an idea of just how capable Python actually is. The view you see of Python in this book is limited to experimenting with and learning about data science, but don't let this view limit what you actually use Python to do in the future. Python is currently used as a general-purpose programming language in companies like the following:

Amazon	Dropbox	Facebook
Google	IBM	Instagram
Intel	JP Morgan Chase	NASA
Netflix	PayPal	Pinterest
Reddit	Spotify	Stripe
Uber	YouTube	

Interpreting Python

You see Python used in this book in an interpreted mode. There are a lot of reasons to take this approach, but the essential reason is that it allows the use of literate programming techniques (https://notebook.community/sfomel/ipython/LiterateProgramming), which greatly enhance learning and significantly reduce the learning curve. The main advantages of using Python in an interpreted mode are that you receive instant feedback, and fixing errors is significantly easier. When combined with a notebook environment, using Python in an interpreted mode also makes it easier to create presentations and reports, as well as to create graphics that present outcomes of various analyses.

Compiling Python

Outside this book, you may find that compiling your Python application is important because doing so can help increase overall application speed. In addition, compiling your code can reduce the potential for others stealing your code and make your applications both more secure and reliable. You do need access to third-party products to compile your code, but you'll find plenty of available products discussed at https://www.softwaretestinghelp.com/python-compiler/.

Defining Data Science

At one point, the world viewed anyone working with statistics as a sort of accountant or perhaps a mad scientist. Many people consider statistics and analysis of data boring. However, data science is one of those occupations in which the more you learn, the more you want to learn. Answering one question often spawns more questions that are even more interesting than the one you just answered. However, the thing that makes data science so interesting is that you see it everywhere and used in an almost infinite number of ways. The following sections provide more details on why data science is such an amazing field of study.

Considering the emergence of data science

Data science is a relatively new term. William S. Cleveland coined the term in 2001 as part of a paper entitled "Data Science: An Action Plan for Expanding the Technical Areas of the Field of Statistics." It wasn't until a year later that the International Council for Science actually recognized data science and created a committee for it. Columbia University got into the act in 2003 by beginning publication of the *Journal of Data Science.*

REMEMBER

However, the mathematical basis behind data science is centuries old because data science is essentially a method of viewing and analyzing statistics and probability. The first essential use of statistics as a term comes in 1749, but statistics are certainly much older than that. People have used statistics to recognize patterns for thousands of years. For example, the historian Thucydides (in his *History of the*

Peloponnesian War) describes how the Athenians calculated the height of the wall of Plataea in fifth century BC by counting bricks in an unplastered section of the wall. Because the count needed to be accurate, the Athenians took the average of the count by several solders.

The process of quantifying and understanding statistics is relatively new, but the science itself is quite old. An early attempt to begin documenting the importance of statistics appears in the ninth century when Al-Kindi wrote *Manuscript on Deciphering Cryptographic Messages*. In this paper, Al-Kindi describes how to use a combination of statistics and frequency analysis to decipher encrypted messages. Even in the beginning, statistics saw use in practical application of science to tasks that seemed virtually impossible to complete. Data science continues this process, and to some people it may actually seem like magic.

Outlining the core competencies of a data scientist

As is true of anyone performing most complex trades today, the data scientist requires knowledge of a broad range of skills to perform the required tasks. In fact, so many different skills are required that data scientists often work in teams. Someone who is good at gathering data may team up with an analyst and someone gifted in presenting information. It would be hard to find a single person with all the required skills. With this in mind, the following list describes areas in which a data scientist could excel (with more competencies being better):

>> **Data capture:** It doesn't matter what sort of math skills you have if you can't obtain data to analyze in the first place. The act of capturing data begins by managing a data source using database management skills. However, raw data isn't particularly useful in many situations — you must also understand the data domain so that you can look at the data and begin formulating the sorts of questions to ask. Finally, you must have data-modeling skills so that you understand how the data is connected and whether the data is structured.

>> **Analysis:** After you have data to work with and understand the complexities of that data, you can begin to perform an analysis on it. You perform some analysis using basic statistical tool skills, much like those that just about everyone learns in college. However, the use of specialized math tricks and algorithms can make patterns in the data more obvious or help you draw conclusions that you can't draw by reviewing the data alone.

>> **Presentation:** Most people don't understand numbers well. They can't see the patterns that the data scientist sees. It's important to provide a graphical presentation of these patterns to help others visualize what the numbers mean and how to apply them in a meaningful way. More important, the presentation must tell a specific story so that the impact of the data isn't lost.

Linking data science, big data, and AI

Interestingly enough, the act of moving data around so that someone can perform analysis on it is a specialty called Extract, Transformation, and Loading (ETL). The ETL specialist uses programming languages such as Python to extract the data from a number of sources. Corporations tend not to keep data in one easily accessed location, so finding the data required to perform analysis takes time. After the ETL specialist finds the data, a programming language or other tool transforms it into a common format for analysis purposes. The loading process takes many forms, but this book relies on Python to perform the task. In a large, real-world operation, you may find yourself using tools such as Informatica, MS SSIS, or Teradata to perform the task.

REMEMBER

Data science isn't necessarily a means to an end; it may instead be a step along the way. As a data scientist works through various datasets and finds interesting facts, these facts may act as input for other sorts of analysis and AI applications. For example, consider that your shopping habits often suggest what books you may like or where you may like to go for a vacation. Shopping or other habits can also help others understand other, sometimes less benign, activities as well. *Machine Learning For Dummies*, 2nd Edition and *Artificial Intelligence For Dummies*, 2nd Edition, both by John Mueller and Luca Massaron (Wiley) help you understand these other uses of data science. For now, consider the fact that what you learn in this book can have a definite effect on a career path that will go many other places.

EXTRACT, LOAD, AND TRANSFORM (ELT)

You may come across a new way of working with data called ELT, which is a variation of ETL. The article "Extract, Load, Transform (ELT)" (https://www.techtarget.com/searchdatamanagement/definition/Extract-Load-Transform-ELT), describes the difference between the two. This different approach is often used for nonrelational and unstructured data. The overall goal is to simplify the data gathering and management process, possibly allowing the use of a single tool even for large datasets. However, this approach also has significant drawbacks. The ELT approach isn't covered in this book, but it does pay to know that it exists.

Creating the Data Science Pipeline

Data science is partly art and partly engineering. Recognizing patterns in data, considering what questions to ask, and determining which algorithms work best are all part of the art side of data science. However, to make the art part of data science realizable, the engineering part relies on a specific process to achieve specific goals. This process is the data science pipeline, which requires the data scientist to follow particular steps in the preparation, analysis, and presentation of the data. The following list helps you understand the data science pipeline better so that you can understand how the book employs it during the presentation of examples:

>> **Preparing the data:** The data that you access from various sources doesn't come in an easily packaged form, ready for analysis. The raw data not only may vary substantially in format but also need you to transform it to make all the data sources cohesive and amenable to analysis.

>> **Performing exploratory data analysis:** The math behind data analysis relies on engineering principles in that the results are provable and consistent. However, data science provides access to a wealth of statistical methods and algorithms that help you discover patterns in the data. A single approach doesn't ordinarily do the trick. You typically use an iterative process to rework the data from a number of perspectives. The use of trial and error is part of the data science art.

>> **Learning from data:** As you iterate through various statistical analysis methods and apply algorithms to detect patterns, you begin learning from the data. The data may not tell the story that you originally thought it would, or it may have many stories to tell. Discovery is part of being a data scientist. If you have preconceived ideas of what the data contains, you won't find the information it actually does contain.

>> **Visualizing:** Visualization means seeing the patterns in the data and then being able to react to those patterns. It also means being able to see when data is not part of the pattern. Think of yourself as a data sculptor, removing the data that lies outside the patterns (the outliers) so that others can see the masterpiece of information beneath.

>> **Obtaining insights and data products:** The data scientist may seem to simply be looking for unique methods of viewing data. However, the process doesn't end until you have a clear understanding of what the data means. The insights you obtain from manipulating and analyzing the data help you to perform real-world tasks. For example, you can use the results of an analysis to make a business decision.

Understanding Python's Role in Data Science

Given the right data sources, analysis requirements, and presentation needs, you can use Python for every part of the data science pipeline. In fact, that's precisely what you do in this book. Every example uses Python to help you understand another part of the data science equation. Of all the languages you could choose for performing data science tasks, Python is the most flexible and capable because it supports so many third-party libraries devoted to the task. The following sections help you better understand why Python is such a good choice for many (if not most) data science needs.

Considering the shifting profile of data scientists

Some people view the data scientist as an unapproachable nerd who performs miracles on data with math. The data scientist is the person behind the curtain in an Oz-like experience. However, this perspective is changing. In many respects, the world now views the data scientist as either an adjunct to a developer or as a new type of developer. The ascendance of applications of all sorts that can learn is the essence of this change. For an application to learn, it has to be able to manipulate large databases and discover new patterns in them. In addition, the application must be able to create new data based on the old data — making an informed prediction of sorts. The new kinds of applications affect people in ways that would have seemed like science fiction just a few years ago. Of course, the most noticeable of these applications define the behaviors of robots that will interact far more closely with people tomorrow than they do today.

From a business perspective, the necessity of fusing data science and application development is obvious: Businesses must perform various sorts of analysis on the huge databases it has collected — to make sense of the information and use it to predict the future. In truth, however, the far greater impact of the melding of these two branches of science — data science and application development — will be felt in terms of creating altogether new kinds of applications, some of which aren't even possibly to imagine with clarity today. For example, new applications could help students learn with greater precision by analyzing their learning trends and creating new instructional methods that work for that particular student. This combination of sciences may also solve a host of medical problems that seem impossible to solve today — not only in keeping disease at bay, but also by solving problems, such as how to create truly usable prosthetic devices that look and act like the real thing.

Working with a multipurpose, simple, and efficient language

Many different ways are available for accomplishing data science tasks. This book covers only one of the myriad methods at your disposal. However, Python represents one of the few single-stop solutions that you can use to solve complex data science problems. Instead of having to use a number of tools to perform a task, you can simply use a single language, Python, to get the job done. The Python difference is the large number scientific and math libraries created for it by third parties. Plugging in these libraries greatly extends Python and allows it to easily perform tasks that other languages could perform, but with great difficulty.

TIP

Python's libraries are its main selling point; however, Python offers more than reusable code. The most important thing to consider with Python is that it supports four different coding styles:

>> **Functional:** Treats every statement as a mathematical equation and avoids any form of state or mutable data. The main advantage of this approach is having no side effects to consider. In addition, this coding style lends itself better than the others to parallel processing because there is no state to consider. Many developers prefer this coding style for recursion and for lambda calculus.

>> **Imperative:** Performs computations as a direct change to program state. This style is especially useful when manipulating data structures and produces elegant, but simple, code.

>> **Object-oriented:** Relies on data fields that are treated as objects and manipulated only through prescribed methods. Python doesn't fully support this coding form because it can't implement features such as data hiding. However, this is a useful coding style for complex applications because it supports encapsulation and polymorphism. This coding style also favors code reuse.

>> **Procedural:** Treats tasks as step-by-step iterations where common tasks are placed in functions that are called as needed. This coding style favors iteration, sequencing, selection, and modularization.

Learning to Use Python Fast

It's time to try using Python to see the data science pipeline in action. The following sections provide a brief overview of the process you explore in detail in the rest of the book. You won't actually perform the tasks in the following sections. In fact, you don't install Python until Chapter 3, so for now, just follow along in the text. This book uses a specific version of Python and an IDE called Jupyter Notebook, so please wait until Chapter 3 to install these features (or skip ahead, if you insist, and install them now). (You can also use Google Colab with the source code in the book, as described in Chapter 4.) Don't worry about understanding every aspect of the process at this point. The purpose of these sections is to help you gain an understanding of the flow of using Python to perform data science tasks. Many of the details may seem difficult to understand at this point, but the rest of the book will help you understand them.

REMEMBER

The examples in this book rely on a web-based application named Jupyter Notebook. The screenshots you see in this and other chapters reflect how Jupyter Notebook looks in Chrome on a Windows 10/11 system. The view you see will contain the same data, but the actual interface may differ a little depending on platform (such as using a notebook instead of a desktop system), operating system, and browser. Don't worry if you see some slight differences between your display and the screenshots in the book.

TIP

You don't have to type the source code for this chapter in by hand. In fact, it's a lot easier if you use the downloadable source (see the Introduction for details on downloading the source code). The source code for this chapter appears in the P4DS4D3_01_Quick_Overview.ipynb source code file.

Loading data

Before you can do anything, you need to load some data. The book shows you all sorts of methods for performing this task. In this case, Figure 1-1 shows how to load a dataset called California Housing that contains housing prices and other facts about houses in California. It was obtained from StatLib repository (see https://www.dcc.fc.up.pt/~ltorgo/Regression/cal_housing.html for details). The code places the entire dataset in the housing variable and then places parts of that data in variables named X and y. Think of variables as you would storage boxes. The variables are important because they make it possible to work with the data. The output shows that the dataset contains 20,640 entries with eight features each. The second output shows the name of each of the features.

Training a model

Now that you have some data to work with, you can do something with it. All sorts of algorithms are built into Python. Figure 1-2 shows a linear regression model. Again, don't worry precisely how this works; later chapters discuss linear regression in detail. The important thing to note in Figure 1-2 is that Python lets you perform the linear regression using just two statements and to place the result in a variable named hypothesis.

Learning to Use Python Fast

Loading data

```
In [1]: from sklearn.datasets import fetch_california_housing
        housing = fetch_california_housing()
        X, y = housing.data,housing.target
        print("The size of the data set is {}".format(X.shape))
        print("The names of the data columns are {}", housing.feature_names)

        The size of the data set is (20640, 8)
        The names of the data columns are {} ['MedInc', 'HouseAge', 'AveRooms', 'AveBed
        rms', 'Population', 'AveOccup', 'Latitude', 'Longitude']
```

FIGURE 1-1: Loading data into variables so that you can manipulate it.

Training a model

```
In [2]: from sklearn.linear_model import LinearRegression
        hypothesis = LinearRegression()
        hypothesis.fit(X,y)

Out[2]: LinearRegression()
```

FIGURE 1-2: Using the variable content to train a linear regression model.

Viewing a result

Performing any sort of analysis doesn't pay unless you obtain some benefit from it in the form of a result. This book shows all sorts of ways to view output, but Figure 1-3 starts with something simple. In this case, you see the coefficient output from the linear regression analysis. Notice that there is one coefficient for each of the dataset features.

Viewing a result

```
In [3]: print(hypothesis.coef_)

        [ 4.36693293e-01  9.43577803e-03 -1.07322041e-01  6.45065694e-01
         -3.97638942e-06 -3.78654265e-03 -4.21314378e-01 -4.34513755e-01]
```

FIGURE 1-3: Outputting a result as a response to the model.

TIP

One of the reasons that this book uses Jupyter Notebook is that the product helps you to create nicely formatted output as part of creating the application. Look again at Figure 1-3, and you see a report that you could simply print and offer to a colleague. The output isn't suitable for many people, but those experienced with Python and data science will find it quite usable and informative.

Chapter **2**

Introducing Python's Capabilities and Wonders

All computers run on just one kind of language — machine code. However, unless you want to learn how to talk like a computer in 0s and 1s, machine code isn't particularly useful. You'd never want to try to define data science problems using machine code. It would take an entire lifetime (if not longer) just to define one problem. Higher-level languages make it possible to write a lot of code that humans can understand quite quickly. The tools used with these languages make it possible to translate the human-readable code into machine code that the machine understands. Therefore, the choice of languages depends on the human need, not the machine need. With this in mind, this chapter introduces you to the capabilities that Python provides that make it a practical choice for the data scientist. After all, you want to know why this book uses Python and not another language, such as Java or C++. These other languages are perfectly good choices for some tasks, but they're not as suited to meet data science needs.

The chapter begins with some simple Python examples to give you a taste for the language. As part of exploring Python in this chapter, you discover all sorts of interesting features that Python provides. Python gives you access to a host of libraries that are especially suited to meet the needs of the data scientist. In fact, you use a number of these libraries throughout the book as you work through the coding examples. Knowing about these libraries in advance will help you understand the programming examples and why the book shows how to perform tasks in a certain way.

REMEMBER

Even though this chapter shows examples of working with Python, you don't really begin using Python in earnest until Chapter 6. This chapter offers an overview so that you can better understand what Python can do. Chapter 3 shows how to install the particular version of Python used for this book. Chapters 4 and 5 are about tools you can use, with Chapter 4 emphasizing Google Colab, an alternative environment for coding. In short, if you don't quite understand an example in this chapter, don't worry: You get plenty of additional information in later chapters.

Working with Python

This book doesn't provide you with a full Python tutorial. (However, you can get a great start with *Beginning Programming with Python For Dummies,* 3rd Edition, by John Paul Mueller (Wiley)). For now, it's helpful to get a brief overview of what Python looks like and how you interact with it, as in the following sections.

TIP

You don't have to type the source code for this chapter manually; using the downloadable source a lot easier (see the Introduction for details on downloading the source code). The source code for this chapter appears in the P4DS4D3_02_Using_Python.ipynb file.

Contributing to data science

Because this is a book about data science, you're probably wondering how Python contributes to better data science and what the word *better* actually means in this case. Knowing that a lot of organizations use Python doesn't help you because it doesn't really say much about how they use Python, and if you want to match your choice of language to your particular need, understanding how other organizations use Python becomes important.

One such example appears at https://www.datasciencegraduateprograms. com/python/. In this case, the article talks about Forecastwatch.com (https:// forecastwatch.com/), which actually does watch the weather and try to make predictions better. Every day, Forecastwatch.com compares 36,000 forecasts with the weather that people actually experience and then uses the results to create better forecasts. Trying to aggregate and make sense of the weather data for 800 U.S. cities is daunting, so Forecastwatch.com needed a language that could do these tasks with the least amount of fuss. Here are the reasons Forecast.com chose Python:

>> **Library support:** Python provides support for a large number of libraries, more than any one organization will ever need. According to https://www.python.org/about/success/forecastwatch/, Forecastwatch.com found the regular expression, thread, object serialization, and gzip data compression libraries especially useful.

>> **Parallel processing:** Each of the forecasts is processed as a separate thread so that the system can work through them quickly. The thread data includes the web page URL that contains the required forecast, along with category information, such as city name.

>> **Data access:** This huge amount of data can't all exist in memory, so Forecast.com relies on a MySQL database accessed through the MySQLdb (https://sourceforge.net/projects/mysql-python/) library, which is one of the few libraries that hasn't moved on to Python 3.x yet. However, the associated website promises the required support soon. In the meantime, if you need to use MySQL with Python 3.x, then using mysqlclient (https://pypi.org/project/mysqlclient/) will be a good replacement because it adds Python 3.x support to MySQLdb.

>> **Data display:** Originally, the PHP scripting language produced the Forecastwatch.com output. However, by using Quixote (https://www.mems-exchange.org/software/quixote/), which is a display framework, Forecastwatch.com was able to move everything to Python. (An update of this framework is DurusWorks, at https://www.mems-exchange.org/software/DurusWorks/.)

Getting a taste of the language

Python is designed to provide clear language statements but to do so in an incredibly small space. A single line of Python code may perform tasks that another language usually takes several lines to perform. For example, if you want to display something on-screen, you simply tell Python to print it, like this:

```
print("Hello There!")
```

The point is that you can simply tell Python to output text, an object, or anything else using a simple statement. You don't really need too much in the way of advanced programming skills. When you want to end your session using a command line environment such as IDLE, you simply type quit() and press Enter. This book relies on a much better environment, Jupyter Notebook (or Google Colab

Understanding the need for indentation

Python relies on indentation to create various language features, such as conditional statements. One of the most common errors that developers encounter is not providing the proper indentation for code. You see this principle in action later in the book, but for now, always be sure to pay attention to indentation as you work through the book examples. For example, here is an if statement (a conditional that says that if something meets the condition, perform the code that follows) with proper indentation.

```
if 1 < 2:
    print("1 is less than 2")
```

WARNING

The print statement must appear indented below the conditional statement. Otherwise, the condition won't work as expected, and you may see an error message, too.

Working with Jupyter Notebook and Google Colab

The vast majority of this book relies on Jupyter Notebook (with code also tested using Google Colab), which is part of the Anaconda installation you create in Chapter 3. Jupyter Notebook is used in Chapter 1 and again later in the book. The presentation for Google Colab is similar to, but not precisely the same as, Jupyter Notebook, and you see Google Colab in detail in Chapter 4. The purpose behind using an Integrated Development Environment (IDE) such as Jupyter Notebook and Google Colab is that they help you create correct code and perform some tasks, such as indentation, automatically. An IDE can also give your code a nicer appearance and give you a means for making report-like output with graphics and other noncode features.

Performing Rapid Prototyping and Experimentation

Python is all about creating applications quickly and then experimenting with them to see how things work. The act of creating an application design in code without necessarily filling in all the details is *prototyping*. Python uses less code than other languages to perform tasks, so prototyping goes faster. The fact that many of the actions you need to perform are already defined as part of libraries that you load into memory makes things go faster still.

Data science doesn't rely on static solutions. You may have to try multiple solutions to find the particular solution that works best. This is where experimentation comes into play. After you create a prototype, you use it to experiment with various algorithms to determine which algorithm works best in a particular situation. The algorithm you use varies depending on the answers you see and the data you use, so there are too many variables to consider for any sort of canned solution.

TECHNICAL STUFF

The prototyping and experimentation process occurs in several phases. As you go through the book, you discover that these phases have distinct uses and appear in a particular order. The following list shows the phases in the order in which you normally perform them.

1. **Building a data pipeline.** To work with the data, you must create a pipeline to it. It's possible to load some data into memory. However, after the dataset gets to a certain size, you need to start working with it on disk or by using other means to interact with it. The technique you use for gaining access to the data is important because it impacts how fast you get a result.

2. **Performing the required shaping.** The shape of the data — the way in which it appears and its characteristics (such as data type), is important in performing analysis. To perform an apples-to-apples comparison, like data has to be shaped the same. However, just shaping the data the same isn't enough. The shape has to be correct for the algorithms you employ to analyze it. Later chapters (starting with Chapter 7) help you understand the need to shape data in various ways.

3. **Analyzing the data.** When analyzing data, you seldom employ a single algorithm and call it good enough. You can't know which algorithm will produce the most useful results at the outset. To find the best result from your dataset, you experiment on it using several algorithms. This practice is emphasized in the later chapters of the book when you start performing serious data analysis.

4. **Presenting a result.** A picture is worth a thousand words, or so they say. However, you need the picture to say the correct words or your message gets lost. Using the MATLAB-like plotting functionality provided by the Matplotlib library, you can create multiple presentations of the same data, each of which describes the data graphically in different ways. (MATLAB, found at https://www.mathworks.com/products/matlab.html, is a widely used mathematical modeling program; see *MATLAB For Dummies*, 2nd Edition, by John Paul Mueller and Jim Sizemore [Wiley] for more details.) To ensure that your meaning really isn't lost, you must experiment with various presentation methods and determine which one works best.

Considering Speed of Execution

Computers are known for their prowess in crunching numbers. Even so, analysis takes considerable processing power. The datasets are so large that you can bog down even an incredibly powerful system. In general, the following factors control the speed of execution for your data science application:

» **Dataset size:** Data science relies on huge datasets in many cases. Yes, you can make a robot see objects using a modest dataset size, but when it comes to making business decisions, larger is better in most situations. The application type determines the size of your dataset in part, but dataset size also relies on the size of the source data. Underestimating the effect of dataset size is deadly in data science applications, especially those that need to operate in real time (such as self-driving cars).

» **Loading technique:** The method you use to load data for analysis is critical, and you should always use the fastest means at your disposal, even if it means upgrading your hardware to do so. Working with data in memory is always faster than working with data stored on disk. Accessing local data is always faster than accessing it across a network. Performing data science tasks that rely on internet access through web services is probably the slowest method of all. Chapter 6 helps you understand loading techniques in more detail. You also see the effects of loading technique later in the book.

» **Coding style:** Some people will likely try to tell you that Python's programming paradigms make writing a slow application nearly impossible. They're wrong. Anyone can create a slow application using any language by employing coding techniques that don't make the best use of programming language functionality. To create fast data science applications, you must use best-of-method coding techniques. The techniques demonstrated in this book are a great starting point.

» **Machine capability:** Running data science applications on a memory-constrained system with a slower processor is an extremely painful process akin to sitting in the dentist's chair for a root canal without Novocain. The system you use needs to have the best hardware you can afford. Given that data science applications are both processor and disk bound, you can't really cut corners in any area and expect great results.

» **Analysis algorithm:** The algorithm you use determines the kind of result you obtain and controls execution speed. Many of the chapters in the latter parts of this book demonstrate multiple methods to achieve a goal using different algorithms. However, you must still experiment to find the best algorithm for your particular dataset.

REMEMBER

A number of the chapters in this book emphasize performance, most notably speed and reliability, because both factors are critical to data science applications. Even though database applications tend to emphasize the need for speed and reliability to some extent, the combination of huge dataset access (disk-bound issues) and data analysis (processor-bound issues) in data science applications makes the need to make good choices even more critical.

Visualizing Power

Python makes it possible to explore the data science environment without resorting to using a debugger or debugging code, as would be needed in many other languages. The print()function and dir() function let you examine any object interactively. In short, you can load something up and play with it for a while to see just how the developer put it together. Playing with the data, visualizing what it means to you personally, can often help you gain new insights and create new ideas. Judging by many online conversations, playing with the data is the part of data science that its practitioners find the most fun.

To get an idea of how the print() and dir() functions work, you can try the following code that appears in the downloadable source:

```
from sklearn.utils import Bunch
items = dir(Bunch)
for item in items:
    if 'key' in item:
        print(item)
```

Don't worry if you don't understand this code, you'll discover more about it later. Beginning with Chapter 4, you start to play with code more, and the various sections give you more details. You can also obtain the book *Beginning Programming with Python For Dummies*, 3rd Edition, by John Paul Mueller (Wiley) if you want a more detailed tutorial. Just follow along with the concept of playing with data for now. You see the following output when you run this code:

```
fromkeys
keys
```

Scikit-learn datasets appear within *bunches* (a bunch is a kind of data structure). When you import a dataset, that dataset will have certain functions that you can use with it that are determined by the code used to define the data structure — a bunch. This code shows which functions deal with *keys* — the data identifiers for the *values* (one or more columns of information) in the dataset. Each row in the dataset has a unique key, even if the values in that row repeat another row in the dataset. You can use these functions to perform useful work with the dataset as part of building your application.

Before you can work with a dataset, you must provide access to it in the local environment. The following code shows the import process and demonstrates how you can use the `keys()` function to display a list of keys that you can use to access data within the dataset.

```
from sklearn.datasets import fetch_california_housing
housing = fetch_california_housing()
print(housing.keys())
```

The output from this code shows that you can access a variety of information about the dataset:

```
dict_keys(['data', 'target', 'frame', 'target_names',
           'feature_names', 'DESCR'])
```

You don't have to know what all these names mean for now, but `feature_names` tells you about the data columns used in the dataset. When you have a list of keys you can use, you can access individual data items. For example, the following code shows a list of all the feature names contained in the California Housing dataset. Python really does make it possible to know quite a lot about a dataset before you have to work with it in depth.

```
print(housing.feature_names)
```

In this case, you see the following column names for the data:

```
['MedInc', 'HouseAge', 'AveRooms', 'AveBedrms',
 'Population', 'AveOccup', 'Latitude', 'Longitude']
```

Using the Python Ecosystem for Data Science

You have already seen the need to load libraries in order to perform data science tasks in Python. The following sections provide an overview of the libraries you use for the data science examples in this book. Various book examples show the libraries at work.

Accessing scientific tools using SciPy

The SciPy stack (http://www.scipy.org/) contains a host of other libraries that you can also download separately. These libraries provide support for mathematics, science, and engineering. When you obtain SciPy, you get a set of libraries designed to work together to create applications of various sorts. These libraries are

» NumPy

» SciPy

» Matplotlib

» Jupyter

» Sympy

» pandas

The SciPy library itself focuses on numerical routines, such as routines for numerical integration and optimization. SciPy is a general-purpose library that provides functionality for multiple problem domains. It also provides support for domain-specific libraries, such as Scikit-learn, Scikit-image, and statsmodels.

Performing fundamental scientific computing using NumPy

The NumPy library (http://www.numpy.org/) provides the means for performing n-dimensional array manipulation, which is critical for data science work. The California Housing dataset used in the examples in Chapters 1 and 2 is an example of an n-dimensional array, and you couldn't easily access it without NumPy functions that include support for linear algebra, Fourier transform, and random-number generation (see the listing of functions at http://docs.scipy.org/doc/numpy/reference/routines.html).

Performing data analysis using pandas

The pandas library (http://pandas.pydata.org/) provides support for data structures and data analysis tools. The library is optimized to perform data science tasks especially fast and efficiently. The basic principle behind pandas is to provide data analysis and modeling support for Python that is similar to other languages, such as R.

Implementing machine learning using Scikit-learn

The Scikit-learn library (http://scikit-learn.org/stable/) is one of a number of Scikit libraries that build on the capabilities provided by NumPy and SciPy to allow Python developers to perform domain-specific tasks. In this case, the library focuses on data mining and data analysis. It provides access to the following sorts of functionality:

>> Classification

>> Regression

>> Clustering

>> Dimensionality reduction

>> Model selection

>> Preprocessing

A number of these functions appear as chapter headings in the book. As a result, you can assume that Scikit-learn is the most important library for the book (even though it relies on other libraries to perform its work).

Going for deep learning with Keras and TensorFlow

Keras (https://keras.io/) is an application programming interface (API) that is used to train deep learning models. An *API* often specifies a model for doing something, but it doesn't provide an implementation. Consequently, you need an implementation of Keras to perform useful work, which is where the machine learning platform TensorFlow (https://www.tensorflow.org/) comes into play because Keras runs on top of it.

When working with an API, you're looking for ways to simplify things. Keras makes things easy by offering the following features:

>> **A consistent interface:** The Keras interface is optimized for common use cases with an emphasis on actionable feedback for fixing user errors.

>> **A building-block approach:** Using a black-box approach makes it easy to create models by connecting configurable building blocks together with only a few restrictions on how you can connect them.

>> **Extendability:** You can easily add custom building blocks to express new ideas for research that include new layers, loss functions, and models.

>> **Parallel processing:** To run applications fast today, you need good parallel processing support. Keras runs on both CPUs and GPUs. It will also make use of multiple CPUs, when available.

>> **Direct Python support:** You don't have to do anything special to make the TensorFlow implementation of Keras work with Python, which can be a major stumbling block when working with other sorts of APIs.

Performing analysis efficiently using XGBoost

You use XGBoost (https://xgboost.readthedocs.io/en/stable/), which stands for extreme gradient boosting, to perform data analysis in an efficient, flexible, and portable manner. This library makes it easier to perform analysis using gradient boosting, which is explained in Chapter 20. Chapter 20 also shows how to work with XGBoost to get the most benefit from the analysis process. You can use this library to solve regression, classification, and ranking problems. XGBoost has proven its capabilities by helping individuals and teams win virtually every Kaggle structured-data competition. In addition, XGBoost supports Python, R, Java, Scala, Julia, Perl, and other languages.

Plotting the data using Matplotlib

The Matplotlib library (http://matplotlib.org/) gives you a MATLAB-like interface for creating data presentations of the analysis you perform. The library is currently limited to 2-D output, but it still provides you with the means to express graphically the data patterns you see in the data you analyze. Without this library, you couldn't create output that people outside the data science community could easily understand. Chapter 10 offers a great introduction to Matplotlib.

Creating graphs with NetworkX

To properly study the relationships between complex data in a networked system (such as that used by your GPS setup to discover routes through city streets), you need a library to create, manipulate, and study the structure of network data in various ways. In addition, the library must provide the means to output the resulting analysis in a form that humans understand, such as graphical data. NetworkX (https://networkx.github.io/) enables you to perform this sort of analysis. The advantage of NetworkX is that nodes can be anything (including images) and edges can hold arbitrary data. These features allow you to perform a much broader range of analysis with NetworkX than using custom code would (and such code would be time consuming to create).

Chapter **3**

Setting Up Python for Data Science

Before you can do too much with Python or use it to solve data science problems, you need a workable installation. In addition, you need access to the datasets and code used for this book. Downloading the sample code and installing it on your system is the best way to absorb more understanding from the book. This chapter helps you get your system set up so that you can easily follow the examples in the remainder of the book.

This book relies on Jupyter Notebook version 6.5.2 supplied with the Anaconda 3 environment (version 2023.03) that supports the Python version 3.10.9 to create the coding examples. For the examples to work, you must use Python 3.10.9 and the packages present in Anaconda 3 version 2023.03 (listed as conda version 23.1.0). Older versions of both Python and its packages tend to lack needed features, and newer versions tend to produce breaking changes. If you use some other version of Python, the examples likely won't work as intended. As an alternative to working with Jupyter Notebook on a desktop system, you can also work on Google Colab on your mobile device, as described in Chapter 4.

REMEMBER

Using the downloadable source doesn't prevent you from typing the examples on your own, following them using a debugger, expanding them, or working with the code in all sorts of ways. The downloadable source is there to help you get a good start with your data science and Python learning experience. After you see how the code works when it's correctly typed and configured, you can try to create the examples on your own. If you make a mistake, you can compare what you've typed with the downloadable source and discover precisely where the error exists. You can find the downloadable source for this chapter in the P4DS4D3_03_Sample. ipynb and P4DS4D3_03_Dataset_Load.ipynb files. (The Introduction tells you where to download the source code for this book.)

Working with Anaconda

Anaconda is actually a collection of tools, as described at https://docs. anaconda.com/free/navigator/overview/. Jupyter Notebook is just one of those tools, and it's the one used most often in this book. However, it's also helpful to know about the other tools that Anaconda provides because they can help you create Python applications faster and also work with some other languages. The following sections describe the two Anaconda tools that are used in this book.

Using Jupyter Notebook

Jupyter Notebook is an Integrated Development Environment (IDE) that promotes the concept of literate programming as originally defined by Donald Knuth (https://guides.nyu.edu/datascience/literate-prog). The idea behind literate programming is to make learning as easy as possible as well as provide a means of presenting code that can include graphics and explanatory text. Such an environment works incredibly well in a book because you can both easily experiment and obtain detailed information as you work through the source code.

This chapter doesn't focus much on Jupyter Notebook usage because it's similar to working with Google Colab, which Chapter 4 explains fully. Even though there are slight differences in commands and appearance between the two, the products are essentially the same.

However, you do want to check your versions of Anaconda, Jupyter Notebook, and Python before going too far in the book, and you can use the following code to check them. You also find this code in the P4DS4D3_03_Sample.ipynb file of the downloadable source:

```
import sys
print('Python Version:\n', sys.version)

import os
result = os.popen('conda --version').read()
print('\nAnaconda Version:\n', result)
```

```
result = os.popen('conda list notebook$').read()
print('\nJupyter Notebook Version:\n', result)
```

REMEMBER

This code essentially opens command prompts, executes commands, and returns with the configuration information. Don't worry about how it precisely works for now; the goal is to discover which versions of products you have installed on your system. The outputs show you the versions you have installed. The source code for this book was tested (and mostly written) using these version numbers:

```
Python Version:
 3.10.9 | packaged by Anaconda, Inc. | ...

Anaconda Version:
 conda 23.1.0


Jupyter Notebook Version:
# packages in environment at C:\Users\John\anaconda3:
#
# Name                    Version ...
notebook                  6.5.2   ...
```

Accessing the Anaconda Prompt

You use the Anaconda Prompt to perform many command-line tasks related to working with Jupyter Notebook. For example, you can use it to discover the version numbers of products and libraries you have installed, as in the previous section does. The Anaconda Prompt also provides access to the conda utility, which is used to perform various configuration tasks, such as installing libraries and creating environments so that you can test your code in multiple ways. In short, the Anaconda Prompt provides a gateway to allowing maximum flexibility with your Python programming environment, which is a significant advantage over using Google Colab (where it's a take-it-or-leave-it proposition).

The Anaconda Prompt is available in several places. The easiest way to locate it is in Anaconda Navigator. You can also access it on Windows using the Start⇨ Anaconda Prompt (Anaconda3) command.

REMEMBER

When you open the Anaconda Prompt, you see a window that looks much like any other command window except that the prompt will say something like "(base) C:\Users\John>." The (base) part of the prompt is important because it tells you which environment you're using. The (base) environment is the default and is the one you use most in the book.

Installing Anaconda on Windows

Anaconda comes with a graphical installation application for Windows, so getting a good install means using a wizard, much as you would for any other installation. Of course, you need a copy of the installation file before you begin. The best place to find a particular version of Anaconda is at the Anaconda archive, at `https://repo.anaconda.com/archive/`. The following procedure should work fine on any Windows system, whether you use the 32-bit or the 64-bit version of Anaconda:

1. **Locate the downloaded copy of Anaconda on your system.**

   The name of this file varies, but normally it appears as Anaconda3-2023. 03-1-Windows-x86_64.exe. The download is currently more than 786 MB, so you may not want to try it using the free connection at your favorite coffee shop. The version number is embedded as part of the filename. In this case, the filename refers to version 2023.03, which is the version used for this book. If you use some other version, you may experience problems with the source code and need to make adjustments when working with it.

2. **Double-click the installation file.**

   (You may see an Open File – Security Warning dialog box that asks whether you want to run this file. Click Run if you see this dialog box pop up.) You see an Anaconda 3 Setup dialog box. The exact dialog box you see depends on which version of the Anaconda installation program you download. If you have a 64-bit operating system, it's always best to use the 64-bit version of Anaconda so that you obtain the best possible performance. This first dialog box tells you when you have the 64-bit version of the product.

3. **Click Next.**

   The wizard displays a licensing agreement. Be sure to read through the licensing agreement so that you know the terms of usage.

4. **Click I Agree if you agree to the licensing agreement.**

   You're asked what sort of installation type to perform, as shown in Figure 3-1. In most cases, you want to install the product just for yourself. The exception is if you have multiple people using your system and they all need access to Anaconda.

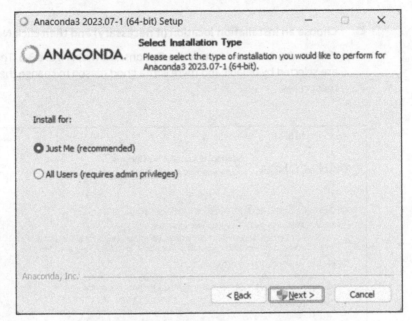

FIGURE 3-1:
Tell the wizard
how to install
Anaconda on
your system.

5. **Choose one of the installation types and then click Next.**

The wizard asks where to install Anaconda on disk, as shown in Figure 3-2.
The book assumes that you use the default location. If you choose some other
location, you may have to modify some procedures later in the book to work
with your setup.

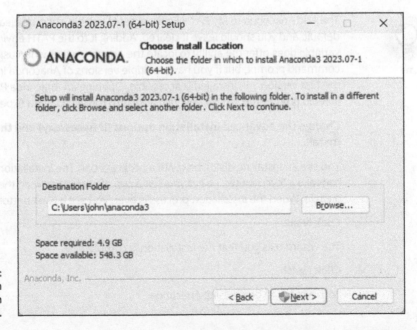

FIGURE 3-2:
Specify an
installation
location.

6. **Choose an installation location (if necessary) and then click Next.**

   You see the Advanced Installation Options, shown in Figure 3-3. These options are selected by default and there isn't a good reason to change them in most cases.

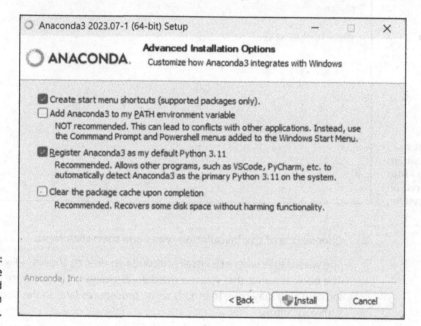

FIGURE 3-3:
Configure the advanced Installation options.

TIP

The Add Anaconda to My PATH Environment Variable option is cleared by default, and you should leave it cleared. Adding it to the PATH environment variable does offer the ability to locate the Anaconda files when using a standard command prompt, but if you have multiple versions of Anaconda installed, only the first version you installed is accessible. Opening an Anaconda Prompt instead is far better so that you gain access to the version you expect.

7. **Change the advanced installation options (if necessary) and then click Install.**

   You see an Installing dialog box with a progress bar. The installation process can take a few minutes, so get yourself a cup of coffee and read the comics for a while. When the installation process is over, you see a Next button enabled.

8. **Click Next.**

   The wizard tells you that the installation is complete.

9. **Click Finish.**

   You're ready to begin using Anaconda.

Installing Anaconda on Linux

You use the command line to install Anaconda on Linux — there is no graphical installation option. Before you can perform the install, you must download a copy of the Linux software from the Anaconda site at `https://repo.anaconda.com/archive/`. On most Linux systems, you can type **curl https://repo.anaconda.com/archive/Anaconda3-2023.03-Linux-x86_64.sh --output Anaconda3-2023.03-Linux-x86_64.sh** and press Enter in the terminal window to get your copy. The following procedure should work fine on any Linux system, whether you use the 32-bit or the 64-bit version of Anaconda.

1. **Open a copy of Terminal.**

   You see the Terminal window appear.

2. **Change directories to the downloaded copy of Anaconda on your system.**

   The name of this file varies, but normally it appears as Anaconda3-2023.03-1-Linux-x86_64.sh. The version number is embedded as part of the filename. In this case, the filename refers to version 2023.03, which is the version used for this book. If you use some other version, you may experience problems with the source code and need to make adjustments when working with it.

3. **Type** bash Anaconda3-2023.03-1-Linux-x86_64.sh **and press Enter.**

   An installation wizard starts that asks you to accept the licensing terms for using Anaconda. Note that this isn't a GUI installation; it's text-based.

4. **Read the licensing agreement and accept the terms using the method required for your version of Linux, which normally consists of typing** yes **and pressing Enter.**

The wizard asks you to provide an installation location for Anaconda. The book assumes that you use the default location of /home/<user name>/anaconda3. If you choose some other location, you may have to modify some procedures later in the book to work with your setup.

5. **Provide an installation location (if necessary) and press Enter (or click Next).**

You see the application extraction process begin. After the extraction is complete, you see a series of installation messages.

6. **Type** yes **and press Enter to initialize Anaconda 3 by running the** conda init **command.**

You see a series of setup messages as conda performs the required initialization tasks.

7. **Close the terminal window and open a new one before you try to work with Anaconda 3.**

When you reopen the terminal, the prompt will change to (base) <username>@<machine name>:~$ unless you specify that you don't want conda starting during the startup process.

TIP

To keep conda from automatically starting each time you log in, type **conda config –set auto_activate_base false** and press Enter at the conda prompt. If you're accessing Jupyter Notebook on a Linux server from a remote browser, follow the instructions at https://docs.anaconda.com/free/anaconda/jupyter-notebooks/remote-jupyter-notebook/.

Installing Anaconda on Mac OS X

The Mac OS X installation comes only in one form: 64-bit. Before you can perform the install, you must download a copy of the Mac OS X software from the Anaconda site at https://repo.anaconda.com/archive/. The following steps help you install Anaconda 64-bit on a Mac system.

1. **Locate the downloaded copy of Anaconda on your system.**

The name of this file varies, but normally it appears as Anaconda3-2023.03-1-MacOSX-x86_64.pkg. The version number is embedded as part of the filename. In this case, the filename refers to version 2023.03, which is the version used for this book. If you use some other version, you may experience problems with the source code and need to make adjustments when working with it.

2. **Double-click the installation file.**

   You see an introduction dialog box.

3. **Click Continue.**

   The wizard asks whether you want to review the Read Me materials. You can read these materials later. For now, you can safely skip the information.

4. **Click Continue.**

   The wizard displays a licensing agreement. Be sure to read through the licensing agreement so that you know the terms of usage.

5. **Click I Agree if you agree to the licensing agreement.**

   The wizard asks you to provide a destination for the installation. The destination controls whether the installation is for an individual user or a group.

WARNING

   You may see an error message stating that you can't install Anaconda on the system. The error message occurs because of a bug in the installer and has nothing to do with your system. To get rid of the error message, choose the Install Only for Me option. You can't install Anaconda for a group of users on a Mac system.

6. **Click Continue.**

   The installer displays a dialog box containing options for changing the installation type. Click Change Install Location if you want to modify where Anaconda is installed on your system (the book assumes that you use the default path of ~/anaconda). Click Customize if you want to modify how the installer works. For example, you can choose not to add Anaconda to your PATH statement. However, the book assumes that you have chosen the default install options and there isn't a good reason to change them unless you have another copy of Python 2.7 installed somewhere else.

7. **Click Install.**

   You see the installation begin. A progress bar tells you how the installation process is progressing. When the installation is complete, you see a completion dialog box.

8. **Click Continue.**

   You're ready to begin using Anaconda.

Downloading the Datasets and Example Code

This book is about using Python to perform data science tasks. Of course, you could spend all your time creating the example code from scratch, debugging it, and only then discovering how it relates to data science, or you can take the easy way and download the prewritten code so that you can get right to work. Likewise, creating datasets large enough for data science purposes would take quite a while. Fortunately, you can access standardized, precreated datasets quite easily using features provided in some of the data science libraries. The following sections help you download and use the example code and datasets so that you can save time and get right to work with data science–specific tasks.

Using Jupyter Notebook

To make working with the relatively complex code in this book easier, you use Jupyter Notebook or Google Colab (see Chapter 4). This interface makes it easy to create Python notebook files that can contain any number of examples, each of which can run individually. The program runs in your browser, so which platform you use for development doesn't matter; as long as it has a browser, you should be OK.

Starting Jupyter Notebook

Most platforms provide an icon to access Jupyter Notebook. All you need to do is open this icon to access Jupyter Notebook. For example, on a Windows system, you choose Start ⇨ Jupyter Notebook (Anaconda 3) (or Start ⇨ Anaconda3 ⇨ Jupyter Notebook on a Windows 10 system). The precise appearance on your system depends on the browser you use and the kind of platform you have installed.

If you have a platform that doesn't offer easy access through an icon, you can normally type **jupyter notebook** and press Enter while in one of the conda environments. To access a conda environment, open an Anaconda Prompt or type **conda activate** and press Enter at the terminal prompt.

Stopping the Jupyter Notebook server

No matter how you start Jupyter Notebook (or just Notebook, as it appears in the remainder of the book), the system generally opens a command prompt or terminal window to host Notebook. This window contains a server that makes the application work. After you close the browser window when a session is complete, select the server window and press Ctrl+C or Ctrl+Break to stop the server. Type **y** and press Enter if asked to do so. To exit the conda environment, type **conda deactivate** and press Enter.

Defining the code repository

The code you create and use in this book will reside in a repository on your hard drive. Think of a *repository* as a kind of filing cabinet where you put your code. Notebook opens a drawer, takes out the folder, and shows the code to you. You can modify it, run individual examples within the folder, add new examples, and simply interact with your code in a natural manner. The following sections get you started with Notebook so that you can see how this whole repository concept works.

Defining a new folder

You use folders to hold your code files for a particular project. The project for this book is P4DS4D3 (which stands for *Python for Data Science For Dummies*, 3rd Edition). The following steps help you create a new folder for this book.

1. **Choose New⇨Folder.**

Notebook creates a new folder for you. The name of the folder can vary, but for Windows users, it's simply listed as Untitled Folder. You may have to scroll down the list of available folders to find the folder in question.

2. **Place a check in the box next to Untitled Folder.**

3. **Click Rename at the top of the page.**

You see the Rename Directory dialog box, shown in Figure 3-4.

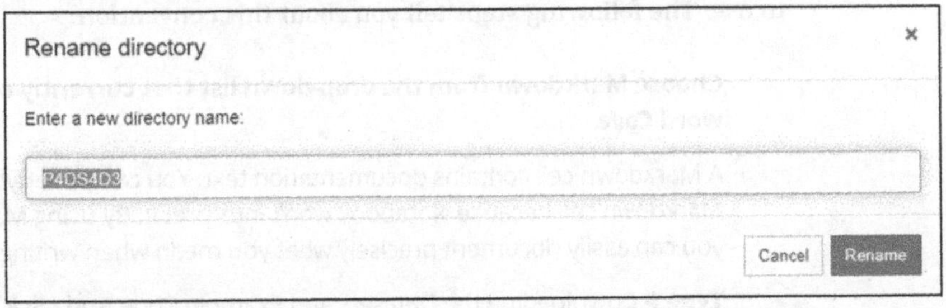

Rename directory   ×

Enter a new directory name:

P4DS4D3

Cancel   Rename

FIGURE 3-4: Create a folder to use to hold the book's code.

4. **Type P4DS4D3 and press Enter.**

Notebook renames the folder for you.

Creating a new notebook

Every new notebook is like a file folder. You can place individual examples within the file folder, just as you would sheets of paper into a physical file folder. Each example appears in a cell. You can put other sorts of things in the file folder, too, but you see how these things work as the book progresses. Use these steps to create a new notebook.

1. **Click the P4DS4D3 entry on the Home page.**

You see the contents of the project folder for this book, which will be blank if you're performing this exercise from scratch.

2. **Choose New ➪ Python 3 (ipykernel).**

You see a new tab open in the browser with the new notebook. Notice that the notebook contains a cell and that Notebook has highlighted the cell so that you can begin typing code in it. The title of the notebook is Untitled right now. That's not a particularly helpful title, so you need to change it.

3. **Click Untitled on the page.**

Notebook asks whether you want to use a new name.

4. **Type P4DS4D3_03_Sample and press Enter.**

The new name tells you that this is a file for *Python for Data Science For Dummies,* 3rd Edition, Chapter 3, Sample.ipynb. Using this naming convention will let you easily differentiate these files from other files in your repository.

Adding notebook content

Of course, the Sample notebook doesn't contain anything just yet. This book follows a convention of putting the source code files together that makes them easy to use. The following steps tell you about this convention:

1. **Choose Markdown from the drop-down list that currently contains the word *Code.***

A Markdown cell contains documentation text. You can put anything in a Markdown cell because Notebook won't interpret it. By using Markdown cells, you can easily document precisely what you mean when writing code.

2. **Type** # Downloading the Datasets and Example Code **and click Run (the button with the right-pointing arrow on the toolbar).**

The hash mark (#) creates a heading. A single # creates a first-level heading. The text that follows contains that actual heading information. Clicking Run turns the formatted text into a heading. Notice that Notebook automatically creates a new cell for you to use.

3. **Choose Markdown, type ## Defining the code repository, and click Run.**

   Notebook creates a second-level heading, which looks smaller than a first-level heading.

4. **Choose Markdown, type ### Adding notebook content, and click Run.**

   Notebook creates a third-level heading. Your headings now match the hierarchy that starts with the first-level heading for this section. Using this approach helps you to easily locate a particular piece of code in the download-able source. As always, Notebook creates a new cell for you, and the cell type automatically changes to Code, so you're ready to type some code for this example.

5. **Type print('Python is really cool!') and click Run.**

   Notice that the code is color coded so that you can tell the difference between a function (`print`) and its associated data (`'Python is really cool!'`). You see the combined output of the various markdown and coding steps in Figure 3-5. The output is part of the same cell as the code. However, Notebook visually separates the output from the code so that you can tell them apart. Notebook automatically creates a new cell for you.

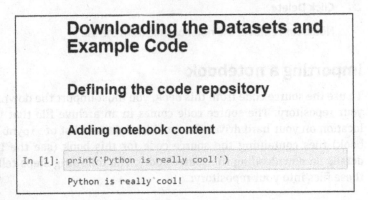

Downloading the Datasets and Example Code

Defining the code repository

Adding notebook content

```
In [1]:  print('Python is really cool!')

         Python is really cool!
```

FIGURE 3-5: Notebook uses cells to store your code.

When you finish working with a notebook, shutting it down is important. To close a notebook, choose File⇨Close and Halt. You return to the P4DS4D3 page, where you can see the notebook you just created added to the list.

Exporting a notebook

It isn't much fun to create notebooks and keep them all to yourself. At some point, you want to share them with other people. To perform this task, you must export your notebook from the repository to a file. You can then send the file to someone else who will import it into their repository.

The previous section shows how to create a notebook named P4DS4D3_03_ Sample. You can open this notebook by clicking its entry in the repository list. The file reopens so that you can see your code again. To export this code, choose File⇨Download As⇨Notebook (.ipynb). What you see next depends on your browser, but you generally see some sort of dialog box for saving the notebook as a file. Use the same method for saving the Notebook file as you use for any other file you save using your browser.

Removing a notebook

Sometimes notebooks get outdated or you simply don't need to work with them any longer. Rather than allow your repository to get clogged with files you don't need, you can remove these unwanted notebooks from the list. Notice the check box next to the P4DS4D3_03_Sample.ipynb entry. Use these steps to remove the file:

1. **Select the check box next to the** P4DS4D3_03_Sample.ipynb **entry.**

2. **Click the Delete (trashcan) icon.**

   You see a Delete notebook warning message.

3. **Click Delete.**

   Notebook removes the notebook file from the list.

Importing a notebook

To use the source code from this book, you must import the downloaded files into your repository. The source code comes in an archive file that you extract to a location on your hard drive. The archive contains a list of .ipynb (IPython Note-book) files containing the source code for this book (see the Introduction for details on downloading the source code). The following steps tell how to import these files into your repository:

1. **Click Upload on the Notebook P4DS4D3 page.**

   What you see depends on your browser. In most cases, you see some type of File Upload dialog box that provides access to the files on your hard drive.

2. **Navigate to the directory containing the files you want to import into Notebook.**

3. **Highlight one or more files to import and click the Open (or other, similar) button to begin the upload process.**

You see the file added to an upload list. The file isn't part of the repository yet — you've simply selected it for upload.

4. **Click Upload.**

Notebook places the file in the repository so that you can begin using it.

Understanding the datasets used in this book

This book uses a number of datasets, all of which appear in the Scikit-learn library. These datasets demonstrate various ways in which you can interact with data, and you use them in the examples to perform a variety of tasks. The following list provides a quick overview of the functions used to import each of the datasets into your Python code:

» `fetch_openml()`: An open repository for machine learning data and experiments. Anyone can upload open datasets to allow access to them.

» `fetch_california_housing()`: Regression analysis with the California housing dataset.

» `https://archive.ics.uci.edu/ml/machine-learning-databases/ statlog/german/`: Analysis with the German Credit dataset described at `https://archive.ics.uci.edu/ml/datasets/statlog+(german+ credit+data)`.

» `https://raw.githubusercontent.com/allisonhorst/palmerpenguins/ main/inst/extdata/penguins.csv`: Analysis with the Palmer Penguins dataset described at `https://allisonhorst.github.io/palmerpenguins/ articles/intro.html`.

» `http://files.grouplens.org/datasets/movielens/ml-1m.zip`: Analysis with the MovieLens dataset described at `https://grouplens.org/ datasets/movielens/`.

The technique for loading each of these datasets is similar across examples (some of them require extra code provided with the book). The following example shows

how to load the California Housing dataset. You can find the code in the
P4DS4D3_03_Dataset_Load.ipynb notebook.

```
from sklearn.datasets import fetch_california_housing
housing = fetch_california_housing()
print(housing.data.shape)
```

To see how the code works, click Run Cell. The output from the print call is
(20640, 8). You can see the output shown in Figure 3-6. (Be patient; the dataset
load can require a few seconds to complete.)

> ## Downloading the Datasets and Example Code
>
> ### Understanding the datasets used in this book
>
> In [1]: `from sklearn.datasets import fetch_california_housing`
>   `housing = fetch_california_housing()`
>   `print(housing.data.shape)`
>
> (20640, 8)

FIGURE 3-6:
The housing
object contains
the loaded
dataset.

Chapter 4

Working with Google Colab

Colaboratory (https://colab.research.google.com/notebooks/welcome.ipynb), or Colab for short, is a free Google cloud-based service that replicates Jupyter Notebook in the cloud. You don't have to install anything on your system to use it. In most respects, you use Colab as you would a desktop installation of Jupyter Notebook (often shortened to Notebook with an uppercase *N* throughout the book). This chapter explores Colab and discusses techniques for working with notebooks using either Jupyter Notebook or Colab.

REMEMBER

Because you may not be using the same versions of products that appear in this book, the book's example source code may or may not work precisely as described in the text when you use Colab. Also when using Colab, you may not see the results as presented in this book because of the differences in hardware between platforms. The introductory sections of this chapter go into more detail about Colab and help you understand what you can expect from it. To use Colab, you must have a free Google account and then access Colab using your account. Otherwise, most of the Colab features won't work.

As with Notebook, you can use Colab to perform specific tasks in a cell-oriented paradigm. The next sections of the chapter go through a range of task-related topics that start with the use of notebooks. If you've used Notebook in previous chapters, you notice a strong resemblance between Notebook and Colab. Of course, you also want to perform other sorts of tasks, such as creating various cell types and using them to create notebooks that look like those you create with Notebook.

Finally, this chapter can't address every aspect of Colab, so the final section of the chapter serves as a handy resource for locating the most reliable information about Colab.

Defining Google Colab

Google Colab is the cloud version of Notebook. In fact, the Welcome page makes this fact apparent. It even uses IPython (the previous name for Jupyter) Notebook (`.ipynb`) files for the site. That's right: You're viewing a Notebook right there in your browser. Even though the two applications are similar and they both use `.ipynb` files, they do have some differences that you need to know about. The following sections help you understand the Colab differences.

Understanding what Google Colab does

You can use Colab to perform many tasks, but for the purpose of this book, you use it to write and run code, create its associated documentation, and display graphics, just as you do with Notebook. The techniques you use are similar, in fact, to using Notebook, but later in the chapter, you find out the small differences between the two. Even so, the downloadable source for this book will run without much effort on your part.

Notebook is a localized application in that you use local resources with it. You could potentially use other sources, but doing so could prove inconvenient or impossible in some cases. For example, according to `https://help.github.com/articles/working-with-jupyter-notebook-files-on-github/`, your Notebook files will appear as static HTML pages when you use a GitHub repository (`https://docs.github.com/en/get-started/quickstart/create-a-repo`). In fact, some features won't work at all. Colab enables you to fully interact with your notebook files using GitHub as a repository. In fact, Colab supports a number of online storage options, so you can regard Colab as your online partner in creating Python code.

The other reason that you really need to know about Colab is that you can use it with your alternative device. During the writing process, some of the example code was tested on an Android-based tablet (an ASUS ZenPad 3S 10). The target tablet has Chrome installed and executes the code well enough to follow the examples. All this said, you likely won't want to try to write code using a tablet of that size — the text was incredibly small, for one thing, and the lack of a keyboard could be a problem, too. The point is that you don't absolutely have to have a

Windows, Linux, or OS X system to try the code, but the alternatives may not provide quite the performance you expect.

REMEMBER

Google Colab generally doesn't work with browsers other than Chrome or Firefox. In most cases, you see an error message and no other display if you try to start Colab in a browser that it doesn't support. Your copy of Firefox may also need some configuration to work properly (see the "Using local runtime support" section, later in this chapter, for details). The amount of configuration that you perform depends on which Colab features you choose to use. Many examples work fine in Firefox without any modification.

Considering the online coding difference

For the most part, you use Colab just as you would Notebook. However, some features work differently. For example, to execute the code within a cell, you select that cell and click the Run button (right-facing arrow) for that cell. The current cell remains selected, which means that you must actually initiate the selection of the next cell as a separate action. A block next to the output lets you clear just that output without affecting any other cell. Hovering the mouse over the block tells you when someone executed the content. On the right side of the cell, you see a vertical ellipsis that you can click to see a menu of options for that cell. The result is the same as when using Notebook, but the process for achieving the result is different.

SOME FIREFOX ODDITIES

Even with online help, you may still find that your copy of Firefox displays a SecurityError: The operation is insecure. error message. The initial error dialog box will point to some unrelated issue, such as cookies, but you see this error message when you click Details. Simply dismissing the dialog box by clicking OK will make Colab appear to be working because it displays your code, but you won't see results from running the code.

As a first step to fixing this problem, make sure that your copy of Firefox is current; older versions won't provide the required support. After you've updated your copy, setting the network.websocket.allowInsecureFromHTTPS preference using About:Config to True should resolve the problem, but sometimes it doesn't. In this case, verify that Firefox actually does allow third-party cookies by selecting Always for the Accept Third Party Cookies and Site Data option and selecting Remember History in the History section on the Privacy & Security tab of the Options dialog box. Restart Firefox after each change and then try Colab again. If none of these fixes works, you must use Chrome to work with Colab on your system.

REMEMBER

The actual process for working with the code also differs from Notebook. Yes, you still type the code as you always have and the resulting code executes without problem in Colab. The difference is in the way you can manage the code. You can upload code from your local drive as desired and then save it to a Google Drive or GitHub. The code becomes accessible from any device at this point by accessing those same sources. All you need to do is load Colab to access it.

If you use Chrome when working with Colab and choose to sync your copy of Chrome among various devices, all your code becomes available on any device you choose to work with. Syncing transfers your choices to all your devices as long as those devices are also set to synchronize their settings. Consequently, you can write code on your desktop, test it on your tablet, and then review it on your smart phone. It's all the same code, all the same repository, and the same Chrome setup, just a different device.

What you may find, however, is that all this flexibility comes at the price of speed and ergonomics. In reviewing the various options, a local copy of Notebook generally executes the code in this book faster than a copy of Colab using any of the available configurations (even when working with a local copy of the .ipynb file). So, you trade speed for flexibility when working with Colab. In addition, viewing the source code on a tablet is hard; viewing it on a smart phone is nearly impossible. If you make the text large enough to see, you can't see enough of the code to make any sort of reasonable editing possible. At best, you could review the code one line at a time to determine how it works.

TIP

Using Notebook has other benefits, too. For example, when working with Colab, you have options to download your source files only as .ipynb or .py files. Colab doesn't include all the other download options, including (but not limited to) HTML, LaTeX, and PDF. Consequently, your options for creating presentations from the online content are also limited to some extent. In short, using Colab and Notebook provides different coding experiences to some degree. They're not mutually exclusive, however, because they share file formats. Theoretically, switching between the two as needed is possible.

One thing to consider when using Notebook and Colab is that the two products use most of the same terminology and many of the same features, but they're not completely the same. The methods used to perform tasks differ, and some of the terminology does as well. For example, a Markdown cell in Notebook is a Text cell in Colab. The "Performing Common Tasks" section of this chapter tells you about other differences you need to consider.

Using local runtime support

The only time you really need local runtime support is when you want to work within a team environment and you need the speed or resource access advantage offered by a local runtime. When using the local runtime support, Colab connects to a local copy of Notebook, so you have to have Notebook installed on your local system. Using a local runtime normally produces better speed than you obtain when relying on the cloud. In addition, a local runtime enables you to access files on your machine. A local runtime also gives you control over the version of Notebook used to execute code. You can read more about local runtime support at https://research.google.com/colaboratory/local-runtimes.html.

WARNING

You need to consider several issues when determining the need for local runtime support. The most obvious is that you need a local runtime, which means that this option won't work with your laptop or tablet unless your laptop has Windows, Linux, or OS X and the appropriate version of Notebook installed. Your laptop or tablet will also need an appropriate browser; Internet Explorer is almost guaranteed to cause problems, assuming that it works at all.

The most important consideration when using a local runtime, however, is that your machine is now open to possible infection from Notebook code. You need to trust the party supplying the code. The local runtime option doesn't open your machine to others that you share code with, however; they must either use their own local runtimes or rely on the cloud to execute code.

TIP

When working with Colab on using local runtime support and Firefox, you must perform some special setups. Make sure to read the Browser Specific Setups section on the Local Runtimes page to ensure that you have Firefox configured correctly. Always verify your setup. Firefox may appear to work correctly with Colab. However, a configuration issue arises when you perform tasks with it, and Colab shows error messages that say the code didn't execute (or something else that isn't particularly helpful).

Working with Notebooks

As with Jupyter Notebook, the notebook forms the basis of interactions with Colab. In fact, Colab is built on notebooks, as previously mentioned. When you place the mouse on certain parts of the Welcome page at https://colab.research.google.com/notebooks/welcome.ipynb, you see opportunities for interacting with the page by adding either code or text entries (which you can use for notes as needed). These entries are active, so you can interact with them. You can also move cells around and copy the resulting material to your Google Drive. Of course, while interacting with the Welcome page is both unexpected and fun, the real purpose of this chapter is to demonstrate how to interact with Colab notebooks. The following sections describe how to perform basic notebook-related tasks with Colab.

Creating a new notebook

To create a new notebook, choose File⇨New Notebook. You see a new Python 3 notebook like the one shown in Figure 4-1. The new notebook looks similar to, but not precisely the same as, those found in Notebook. However, all the same functionality exists.

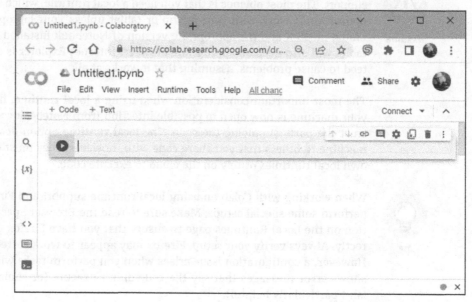

FIGURE 4-1: Create a new Python 3 Notebook using the same techniques as normal.

The notebook shown in Figure 4-1 lets you change the filename by clicking on it, just as you do when working in Notebook. Some features work differently but provide the same results. For example, to run the code in a particular cell, you click the right-pointing arrow on the left side of that cell. In contrast to Notebook, the cell focus doesn't change to the next cell, so you must choose the next cell directly or by clicking the Next Cell or Previous Cell buttons on the toolbar.

Opening existing notebooks

You can open existing notebooks found in local storage, on Google Drive, or on GitHub. You can also open any of the Colab examples or upload files from sources that you can access, such as a network drive on your system. In all cases, you begin by choosing File ⇨ Open Notebook. You see the dialog box shown in Figure 4-2.

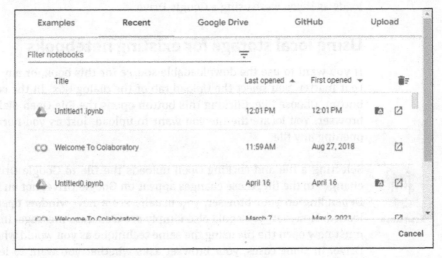

Examples	Recent	Google Drive	GitHub	Upload	
Filter notebooks					
Title		Last opened ▲	First opened ▼		🗑
☁ Untitled1.ipynb		12:01 PM	12:01 PM	🖻	⬀
CO Welcome To Colaboratory		11:59 AM	Aug 27, 2018		⬀
☁ Untitled0.ipynb		April 16	April 16	🖻	⬀
CO Welcome To Colaboratory		March 7	May 2, 2021		⬀
					Cancel

FIGURE 4-2:
Use this dialog
box to open
existing
notebooks.

The default view shows all the files you opened recently, regardless of location. The files appear in alphabetical order. You can filter the number of items displayed by typing a string into the Filter Notebooks field. Across the top are other options for opening notebooks.

TIP Even if you're not logged in, you can still access the Colab example projects. These projects help you understand Colab but won't allow you to do anything with your own projects. Even so, you can still experiment with Colab without logging into Google first. The following sections discuss these options in more detail.

Using Google Drive for existing notebooks

Google Drive is the default location for many operations in Colab, and you can always choose it as a destination. When working with Drive, you see a list of files. To open a particular file, you click its link in the dialog box. The file opens in the current tab of your browser.

Using GitHub for existing notebooks

When working with GitHub, you initially need to provide the location of the source code online. Make sure to select Include Private Repos if you want to work with your private projects in addition to the public ones.

After you make the connection to GitHub, you see two lists: repositories, which are containers for code related to a particular project; and branches, a particular implementation of the code. Selecting a repository and branch displays a list of notebook files that you can load into Colab. Simply click the required link and it loads as if you were using a Google Drive.

Using local storage for existing notebooks

If you want to use the downloadable source for this book, or any local source for that matter, you select the Upload tab of the dialog box. In the center is a single button, Choose File. Clicking this button opens the File Open dialog box for your browser. You locate the file you want to upload, just as you normally would for opening any file.

REMEMBER

Selecting a file and clicking Open uploads the file to Google Drive. If you make changes to the file, those changes appear on Google Drive, not on your local drive. Depending on your browser, you usually see a new window open with the code loaded. However, you could also simply see a success message, in which case you must now open the file using the same technique as you would when using Google Drive. In some cases, your browser asks whether you want to leave the current page. You should tell the browser to do so.

TIP

The File⇨Upload Notebook command also uploads a file to Google Drive. In fact, uploading a notebook works like uploading any other kind of file, and you see the same dialog box. If you want to upload other kinds of files, using the File⇨Upload Notebook command is likely faster.

Saving notebooks

Colab provides a significant number of options for saving your notebook. However, none of these options works with your local drive. After you upload content from your local drive to Google Drive or GitHub, Colab manages the content in the cloud and not on your local drive. To save updates to your local drive, you must download the file using the techniques found in the "Downloading notebooks" section, later in this chapter. The following sections review the cloud-based options for saving notebooks.

Using Drive to save notebooks

The default location for storing your data is Google Drive (https://drive.google.com/). When you choose File⇨Save, the content you create goes to the root directory of your Google Drive. If you want to save the content to a different folder, you need to select that folder in Google Drive.

Colab tracks the versions of your project as you perform saves. However, as these revisions age, Colab removes the older versions. To save a version that won't age, you use the File ⇨ Save and Pin Revision command. To see the revisions for your project, choose File ⇨ Revision History. You see the output shown in Figure 4-3. Notice that the first entry is pinned. You can also pin entries by checking the entry in the History list. The revision history also shows you the modification date, who made the revision, and the size of the resulting file.

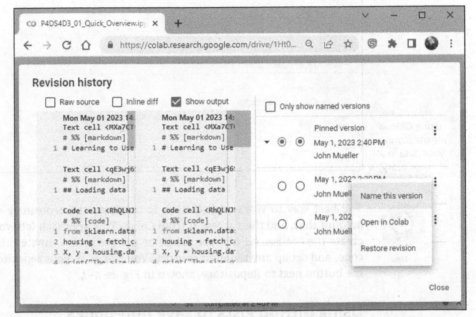

FIGURE 4-3: Colab maintains a history of the revisions for your project.

Click the vertical ellipsis (three dots) next to an entry to see the additional options shown in Figure 4-3. You can name the revision, open it in Colab, or restore the current code to the selected revision. Naming a revision makes it easier to find, and you can use this technique for revisions that have special significance.

You can also save a copy of your project by choosing File ⇨ Save a Copy In Drive. The copy receives the word *Copy* as part of its name. Of course, you can rename it later. Colab stores the copy in the current Google Drive folder.

Using GitHub to save notebooks

GitHub provides an alternative to Google Drive for saving content. It offers an organized method of sharing code for the purpose of discussion, review, and distribution. You can find GitHub at https://github.com/.

To save a file to GitHub, choose File ⇨ Save a Copy in GitHub. If you aren't already signed into GitHub, Colab displays a window that requests your sign-in information. After you sign in, you see a dialog box similar to the one shown in Figure 4-4.

Copy to GitHub

Repository: ↗️
JohnPaulMueller/A4D2E   ⌄

Branch: ↗️
main ⌄

File path
P4DS4D3_01_Quick_Overview.ipynb

Commit message
Created using Colaboratory

☑ Include a link to Colaboratory

Cancel   OK

TIP

The best way to work with GitHub is to create the repository on your GitHub account first, and then access it from Colab. This approach lets you do things like create the Readme.md file, set public or private access, invite others to view the code, and set up any required security. You can go to your repositories by clicking the button next to Repository, shown in Figure 4-4.

Using GitHub gists to save notebooks

You use GitHub gists as a means of sharing single files or other resources with other people. Some people use them for full projects as well, but the idea is that you have a concept that you want to share — something that isn't quite fully formed and doesn't represent a usable application. You can read more about gists at https://help.github.com/articles/about-gists/.

As with GitHub's public and private repositories, gists come in both public and secret (private) form. You can access both public and secret gists from Colab, but Colab automatically keeps your files secret. To save your current project as a gist, you choose File ⇨ Save a Copy as a GitHub Gist. Unlike GitHub, you don't need to create a repository or do anything fancy in this case. The file saves as a gist without any extra effort. The resulting entry always contains an Open in Colab button link, as shown in Figure 4-5.

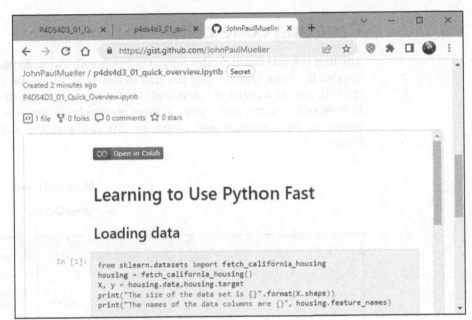

FIGURE 4-5:
Use gists to store individual files or other resources.

Downloading notebooks

Colab supports two methods for downloading notebooks to your local drive: .ipynb files (using File⇨Download .ipynb) and .py files (using File⇨Download .py). In both cases, the file appears in the default download directory for your browser; Colab doesn't offer a method for downloading the file to a specific directory.

Performing Common Tasks

Most tasks in Colab work similar to their Notebook counterparts. For example, you can create code cells just as you do in Notebook. Markdown cells come in three forms: text, heading, and table of contents. They work somewhat differently from the markdown cells found in Notebook, but the idea is the same. You can also edit and move cells, just as you do with Notebook. One important difference is that you can't change a cell type. A cell that you create as a header can't suddenly transform into a code cell. The following sections provide a brief overview of the various features.

Creating code cells

The first cell that Colab creates for you is a code cell. The code you create in Colab uses all the same features that you find in Notebook. However, off to the side of the cell, you see a menu of extras that you can use with Colab that aren't present in Notebook. You can access some of these options by clicking the vertical ellipsis, shown at the rightmost end of the toolbar menu at the side of the cell in Figure 4-6.

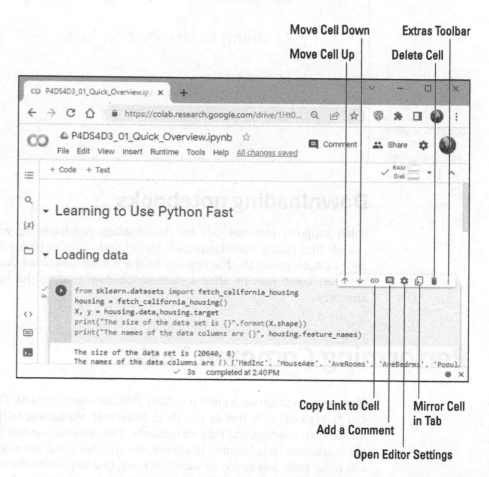

FIGURE 4-6: Colab code cells contain a few extras not found in Notebook.

You use the options shown in Figure 4-6 to augment your Colab code experience. The following list (shown in order of appearance in Figure 4-6) provides a short description of these features:

>> **Move Cell Up:** Moves the selected cell up in the hierarchy of cells by one position.

» **Move Cell Down:** Moves the selected cell down in the hierarchy of cells by one position.

» **Copy Link to Cell:** Places a link to the selected cell on the Clipboard. You can use this link to access a specific cell within the notebook. You can embed this link anywhere on a web page or within a notebook to allow someone to access that specific cell. The person still sees the entire notebook but doesn't have to search for the cell you want to discuss.

» **Add a Comment:** Creates a comment balloon to the right of the cell. This is not the same as a code comment, which exists in line with the code but affects the entire cell. You can edit, delete, or resolve comments. A resolved comment is one that has received attention and is no longer applicable.

» **Open Editor Settings:** Displays the dialog box shown in Figure 4-7 that you can use to modify Colab's behavior.

Settings

Site

Editor

Colab Pro

GitHub

Miscellaneous

Editor key bindings
default

Font size
14 ▾ px

Font family used when rendering code
monospace

Indentation width in spaces
2

Vertical ruler column
80

☑ Automatically trigger code completions
☐ Show line numbers
☐ Show indentation guides
☐ Enable code folding in the editor
☑ Automatically close brackets and quotes in code cells
☑ Enter key accepts suggestions
☐ Font ligatures

Code diagnostics
Syntax checking ▾

Cancel   Save

» **Mirror Cell in Tab:** Creates a mirror view of the selected tab in a side window for more detailed editing.

» **Delete Cell:** Removes the cell from the notebook.

>> **Ellipsis Entries:** Click the vertical ellipsis to see these entries:

- **Select Cell:** Selects all the text in the cell.

- **Copy Cell:** Copies the selected content in the current cell and places it on the Clipboard.

- **Cut Cell:** Removes the selected content from the current cell and places it on the Clipboard.

- **Clear Output:** Removes the output from the cell. You must run the code again to regenerate the output.

- **View Output Fullscreen:** Displays the output (not the entire cell or any other part of the notebook) in full-screen mode on the host device. This option is useful when displaying a significant amount of content or when a detailed view of graphics helps explain a topic. Press Esc to exit full-screen mode.

- **Add a Form:** Inserts a form into the cell to the right of the code. You use forms to provide a graphical input for parameters. Forms don't appear in Notebook, but because of how you create them, they won't prevent you from running the code in Notebook. You can read more about forms at `https://colab.research.google.com/notebooks/forms.ipynb`.

Code cells also tell you about the code and its execution. The little run icon next to the output displays information about the execution when you hover your mouse over it, as shown in Figure 4-8. Clicking the output icon below it clears the output. You must run the code again to regenerate the output.

Creating text cells

Text cells work much like Markup cells in Notebook. However, Figure 4-9 shows that you receive additional help in formatting the text using a graphical interface. The markup is the same, but you have the option of allowing the GUI to help you create the markup. For example, in this case, to create the # sign for a heading, you click the double T icon that appears first in the list. Clicking the double T icon again would increase the header level. To the right, you see how the text will appear in the notebook.

Notice the menu to the right of the text cell. This menu contains many of the same options that a code cell does. For example, you can create a list of links to help people access specific parts of your notebook through an index. Unlike Notebook, you can't execute text cells to resolve the markup they contain.

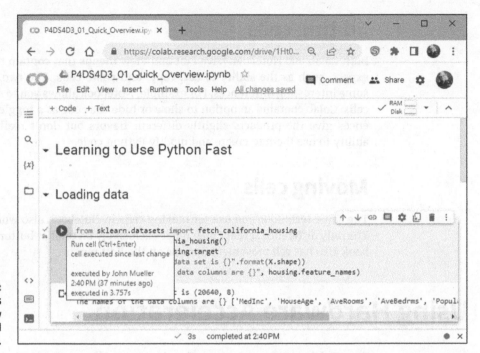

FIGURE 4-8:
Colab code cells contain a few extras not found in Notebook.

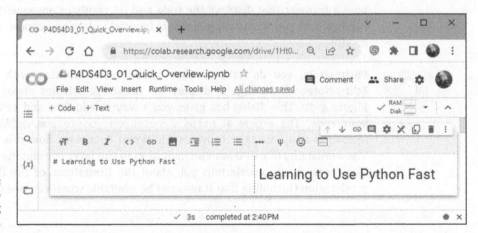

FIGURE 4-9:
Use the GUI to make formatting your text easier.

Creating special cells

The special cells that Colab provides are variations of the text cell. These special cells, which you access using the Insert menu option, make creating the required cells faster. Of these additions, section headers are the most interesting. When you choose Insert ⇨ Section Header Cell, you see a new cell created below the currently selected cell that has the appropriate header level 1 entry in it. You can increase the heading level by clicking the double *T* icon. The GUI looks the same as the one in Figure 4-9, so you have all the standard formatting features for your text.

Editing cells

Both Colab and Notebook have Edit and View menus that contain the options you expect, such as the ability to cut, copy, and paste cells. The two products have some interesting differences. For example, Notebook allows you to split and merge cells. Colab contains an option to show or hide the code as a toggle. These differences give the products slightly different flavors but don't really change your ability to use them to create and modify Python code.

Moving cells

The same technique you use for moving cells in Notebook also works with Colab. The only difference is that Colab relies exclusively on toolbar buttons, while Notebook also has cell movement options on the Edit menu.

Using Hardware Acceleration

Your Colab code executes on a Google server. All your computing device does is host a browser that displays the code and its results. Consequently, any special hardware on your computing device is ignored unless you choose to execute code locally.

TIP

Fortunately, you do have another option when working with Colab. Choose Edit ⇨ Notebook Settings to display the Notebook Settings dialog box shown in Figure 4-10. This dialog box gives you a way to add GPU and TPU execution for your code. The article at `https://research.google.com/colaboratory/faq.html#gpu-availability` provides additional details on how this feature works. The availability of a GPU isn't an invitation to run large computations using Colab. The research site article tells you about the limitations of the Colab hardware acceleration (including that it may not be available when you need it).

Notebook settings

Hardware accelerator

None ⌄ ⓘ

☐ Omit code cell output when saving this notebook

Cancel   Save

FIGURE 4-10: Hardware acceleration speeds code execution.

The Notebook Settings dialog box also lets you choose whether to include cell output when saving the notebook. Given that you store your notebook in the cloud in most cases and that loading large files into your browser can be time consuming, this feature enables you to restart a session more quickly. Of course, the trade-off is that you must now regenerate all the outputs you need.

Executing the Code

For your notebook to be useful, you need to run it at some point. Previous sections have mentioned the right-pointing arrow that appears in the current cell. Clicking it runs just the current cell. Of course, you have other options than clicking the right-pointing arrow, and all these options appear on the Runtime menu. The following list summarizes these options:

>> **Running the current cell:** Besides clicking the right-pointing arrow, you can also choose Runtime ⇨ Run the Focused Cell to execute the code in the current cell.

>> **Running other cells:** Colab provides options on the Runtime menu for executing the code in the next cells, the previous cells, or a selection of cells. Simply choose the option that matches the cell or set of cells you want to execute.

>> **Running all the cells:** In some cases, you want to execute all the code in a notebook. In this case, choose Runtime ⇨ Run All. Execution starts at the top of the notebook, in the first cell containing code, and continues to the last cell that contains code in the notebook. You can stop execution at any time by choosing Runtime ⇨ Interrupt Execution.

TIP

Choosing Runtime ⇨ Manage Sessions displays a dialog box containing a list of all the sessions that are currently executing for your account on Colab. You can use this dialog box to determine when the code in that notebook last executed and how much memory the notebook consumes. Click Terminate to end execution for a particular notebook. Click Close to close the dialog box and return to your current notebook.

Use the Runtime ⇨ Restart Runtime command to restart your runtime after working with the code for a while. Doing so resets everything so that you can verify that your code works as intended after making a lot of changes.

Viewing Your Notebook

A notebook has a Table of Contents icon in its right margin. Clicking this icon displays a pane containing tabs that show various kinds of information about your notebook. You can also choose specific pieces of information to see from the View menu. To close this pane, click the X in the upper-right corner of the pane. The following sections describe each of these pieces of information.

Displaying the table of contents

Choose View⇨Table of Contents to see a table of contents for your notebook, as shown in Figure 4-11. Clicking any of the entries takes you to that section of the notebook.

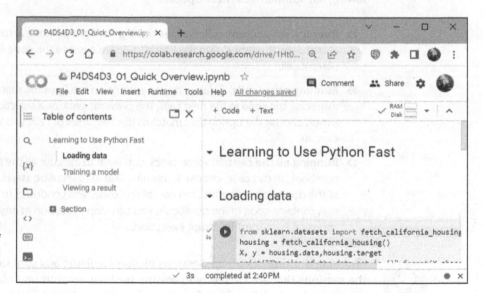

FIGURE 4-11:
Use the table of contents to navigate your notebook.

At the bottom of the pane is a + Section button. Click this button to create a new header cell below the currently selected cell.

Getting notebook information

When you choose View⇨Notebook Info, you see a dialog box open as shown in Figure 4-12. This dialog box contains the notebook size, settings, and owner.

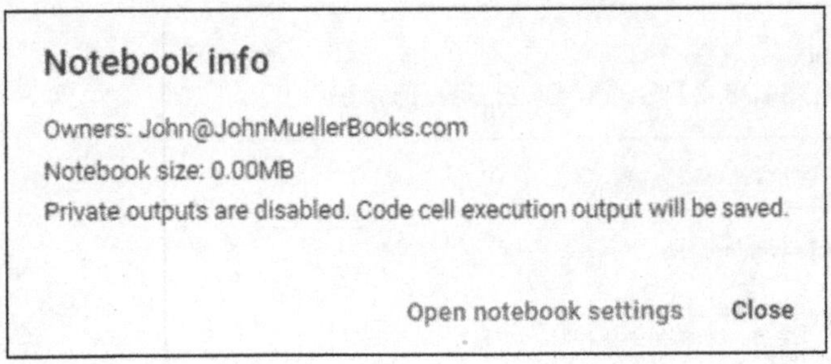

FIGURE 4-12:
The notebook
information
includes both size
and settings.

The Notebook Info tab also includes a link to Open Notebook Settings (see Figure 4-10) in which you can choose whether the notebook relies on hardware acceleration, as described in the "Using Hardware Acceleration" section, earlier in this chapter.

Checking code execution

Colab keeps track of your code as you execute it. Choose View ⇨ Executed Code History to display the Executed Code tab in the pane at the right of the window. Note that the number associated with the entries in the Executed Code tab may not match the numbers associated with the associated cells. In addition, each unique execution of code receives a separate number.

Sharing Your Notebook

You can share your Colab notebooks in a number of ways. For example, you can save them to GitHub or GitHub gists. However, the two most direct methods are the following:

>> Create a share message and send it to the recipient.

>> Obtain a link to the code and send the link to the recipient.

In both cases, you click the Share button in the upper right of the Colab window. The Share dialog box opens (see Figure 4-13).

When you enter one or more names in the People field, an additional field opens in which to add a sharing message. You can type a message and click Send to send the link immediately. If you click Advanced (when available) instead, you see another dialog box, where you can define how to share the notebook.

At the bottom of the Share dialog box, you see the Copy Link button. Clicking Copy Link places the URL on the Clipboard for your device, and you can paste it into messages or other forms of communication with others.

Getting Help

The most obvious place to obtain help with Colab is from the Colab Help menu. This menu contains all the usual entries for accessing frequently asked questions (FAQs) pages. The menu doesn't have a link to general help, but you can find general help at https://colab.research.google.com/notebooks/welcome.ipynb (which requires you to log into the Colab site). The menu also provides options for submitting a bug and sending feedback.

One of the more intriguing Help menu entries is Search Code Snippets. This option opens the pane shown in Figure 4-14, in which you can search for example code that could meet your needs with a little modification. Clicking the Insert button inserts the code at the current cursor location in the cell that has focus. Each of the entries also shows an example of the code.

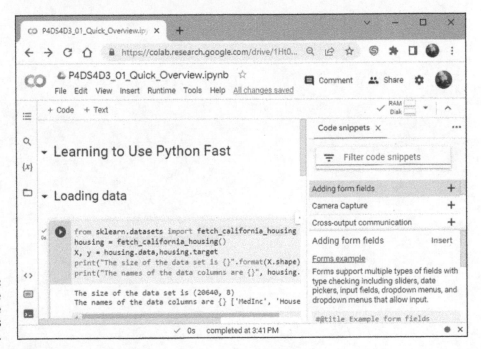

FIGURE 4-14: Use code snippets to write your applications more quickly.

2

Getting Your Hands Dirty with Data

Chapter 5

Working with Jupyter Notebook

U p to this point, the book spends a lot of time working with Python to perform data science tasks without actually engaging the tools provided by Anaconda much. Yes, a good deal of what you do involves typing in code and seeing what happens. However, if you don't actually know how to use your tools well, you miss opportunities to perform tasks easier and faster. Automation is an essential part of performing data science tasks in Python.

This chapter is about working with Jupyter Notebook. Earlier chapters give you some experience with this tool, but those chapters don't explore Jupyter Notebook in any detail, and you need to know it a lot better for upcoming chapters. The skills you develop in this chapter will help you perform tasks in later chapters with greater speed and far less effort.

The chapter also looks at tasks you can perform with your newfound skills. You develop even more skills as the book progresses, but these tasks help put your new skills into perspective and appreciate how you can use them to make working with Python even easier.

REMEMBER

You don't have to manually type the source code for this chapter. In fact, it's a lot easier if you use the downloadable source. The source code for this chapter appears in the P4DS4D3_05_Understanding the Tools.ipynb source code file. (See the Introduction for details on where to locate this file.)

Using Jupyter Notebook

The Jupyter Notebook Integrated Development Environment (IDE) is part of the Anaconda suite of tools. The following sections help you understand some of the interesting things that Jupyter Notebook (simply called Notebook) can help you do.

Working with styles

Here's one of the ways in which Notebook excels over just about any other IDE that you'll ever use: It helps you to create nice-looking output. Rather than have a screen full of a whole bunch of plain-old code, you can use Notebook to create sections and add styles so that the output is nicely formatted. What you can end up with is a good-looking report that just happens to contain executable code. The reason for this improved output is the use of styles.

When you type code into Notebook, you place the code in a cell. Each section of code that you create goes into a separate cell. When you need to create a new cell, you click Insert Cell Below (the button with a plus sign) on the toolbar. Likewise, when you decide that you no longer need a cell, you select it and then click Cut Cell (the button with a scissors) to place the deleted cell on the Clipboard, or choose Edit ⇨ Delete Cells to remove it completely.

The default style for a cell is Code. However, when you click the down arrow next to the Code entry, you see a listing of styles, as shown in Figure 5-1.

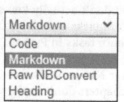

FIGURE 5-1:
Notebook makes adding styles to your work easy.

The various styles shown help you format content in various ways. The Markdown style is most definitely used to separate varies entries. To try it for yourself, choose Markdown from the drop-down list, type the heading for this main chapter section, **# Using Jupyter Notebook**, in the first cell; next, click Run. The content changes to a heading. The single hash (#) tells Notebook that this is a first-level heading. Notice that clicking Run automatically adds a new cell and places the cursor in it. To add a second-level heading, choose Markdown from the drop-down list, type **## Working with styles**, and click Run. Figure 5-2 shows that the two entries are indeed headings and that the second entry is smaller than the first.

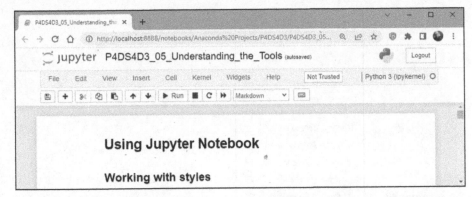

FIGURE 5-2:
Adding headings
makes separating
content in your
notebooks easy.

The Markdown style also lets you add HTML content. This markdown content can contain anything a web page contains with regard to standard HTML tags. Another way to create a first-level heading is to define the cell type as Markdown, type **<h1>Using Jupyter Notebook</h1>**, and then click Run. In general, you use HTML to provide documentation and links to outside material. Relying on HTML tags makes it possible to include things like lists or even pictures. In short, you can actually include an HTML document fragment as part of your notebook, which makes Notebook much more than a simple means of writing down code.

The use of the Raw NBConvert formatting option is outside the scope of this book. However, it provides you with the means for including information that shouldn't be modified by the notebook converter (NBConvert). You can output notebooks in a variety of formats, and NBConvert performs this task for you. You can read about this feature at `https://nbconvert.readthedocs.io/en/latest/`. The goal of the Raw NBConvert style is to allow you to include special content, such as Lamport TeX (LaTeX) content. The LaTeX document system isn't tied to a particular editor — it's simply a means of encoding scientific documents.

Getting Python help

Notebook provides you with the resources to get the commonly required help you need. To obtain help, select one of the entries on the Help menu, shown in Figure 5-3.

As shown in Figure 5-3, you not only get help with Notebook and the markdown used to create entries for a Markdown cell, but you also get a complete Python reference and references to the most common libraries that developers use. When you choose an entry, a new web page opens containing the help information you require.

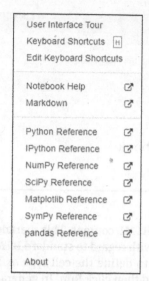

User Interface Tour

Keyboard Shortcuts [H]

Edit Keyboard Shortcuts

Notebook Help ☐

Markdown ☐

Python Reference ☐

IPython Reference ☐

NumPy Reference ☐

SciPy Reference ☐

Matplotlib Reference ☐

SymPy Reference ☐

pandas Reference ☐

About

FIGURE 5-3:
The Help menu contains a selection of common help topics.

TIP

If you need additional help working with the Notepad interface, choose Help ⇨ User Interface Tour. Use the right and left arrows to move between helpful balloons showing the various Notepad features. When you're finished with your review, press Esc to exit the tour.

Using magic functions

Amazingly, you really can get magic on your computer! Jupyter provides a special feature called magic functions. The functions let you perform all sorts of amazing tasks with your Jupyter console. The following sections provide an overview of the magic functions. Some of them are used later in the book as well. However, it pays to spend some time checking out these functions for yourself.

Obtaining the magic functions list

The best way to start working with magic functions is to obtain a list of them by typing **%quickref** and pressing Enter. You see a help (pager) window similar to the one shown in Figure 5-4. The listing can be a little confusing to read, so make sure to take your time with it.

TIP

When you've finished reviewing the material, click the X in the pager window that appears in the lower half of Figure 5-4. To the left of the X is another button that lets you open the pager window in its own tab in the browser for easier reading.

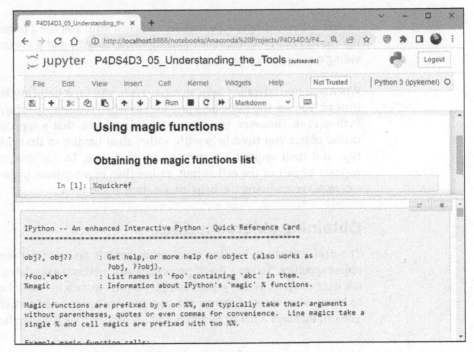

FIGURE 5-4:
Take your time
going through the
magic function
help, which
has a lot of
information.

Working with magic functions

Most magic functions start with either a single percent sign (%) or two percent signs (%%). Those with a single percent sign work at the command-line level, and the ones with two percent signs work at the cell level. You generally use magic functions with a single percent sign.

REMEMBER

Most of the magic functions display status information when you use them by themselves. For example, when you type **%cd** and click Run, you see the current directory. To change directories, you type **%cd** plus the new directory location on your system.

Discovering objects

Python is all about objects. In fact, you can't do anything in Python without working with some sort of object. With this in mind, it's a good idea to know how to discover precisely what object you're working with and what features it provides. The following sections help you discover the Python objects you use as you code.

Getting object help

You can request information about specific objects using the object name and a question mark (?). For example, if you want to know more about a list object named `mylist`, simply type **mylist?** and click Run. You see a pager window showing the `mylist` type, content in string form, length, and a document string providing a quick overview of `mylist`.

When you need detailed help about `mylist`, you type **help(mylist)** and click Run instead. You see the same help provided as when requesting information about the Python `list`. However, you receive the information that's appropriate to the particular object you need help with, rather than having to first discover the object type and then request information for that type. In addition, this information appears as part of the cell output, rather than in a separate pager window, which can make referencing the help information easier later.

Obtaining object specifics

The `dir()` function is often overlooked, but it's an essential way to learn about object specifics. To see a list of properties and methods associated with any object, use `dir(<object name>)`. For example, if you create a list called `mylist` and want to know what sorts of things you can do with it, type **dir(mylist)** and click Run. The cell displays a list of methods and properties that are specific to `mylist`.

Using extended Python object help

Using a single question mark causes Python to clip long content. If you want to obtain the full content for an object, you need to use the double question mark (??). For example, type **mylist??** and click Run to see any clipped details (although there may not be any additional details). Whenever possible, Python provides you with the full source code for the object (assuming that the source code is available).

You can also use magic functions with objects. These functions simplify the help output and provide only the information you need, as shown here:

» %pdoc: Displays the `docstring` for the object

» %pdef: Shows how to call the object (assuming that the object is callable)

» %psource: Displays the source code for the object (assuming that the source is available)

» %pfile: Outputs the name of the file that contains the source code for the object

» %pinfo: Displays detailed information about the object (often more than is provided by help alone)

» %pinfo2: Displays extra detailed information about the object (when available)

Restarting the kernel

Every time you perform a task in your notebook, you create variables, import modules, and perform a wealth of other tasks that modify the environment. At some point, you can't really be sure that something is working as it should. To overcome this problem, you save your document by clicking Save and Checkpoint (the button containing a floppy disk symbol), and then click Restart Kernel (the button with an open circle with an arrow at one end). You can then run your code again to ensure that it does work as you thought it would.

Sometimes an error also causes the kernel to crash. Your document starts acting oddly, updates slowly, or shows other signs of corruption. Again, the answer is to restart the kernel to ensure that you have a clean environment and that the kernel is running as it should.

WARNING

Whenever you click Restart Kernel, you see a warning message. Make sure to pay attention to the warning because you could lose temporary changes during a kernel restart. Always save your document before you restart the kernel.

Restoring a checkpoint

At some point, you may find that you made a mistake. Notebook is notably missing an Undo button: You won't find one anywhere. Instead, you create checkpoints each time you finish a task. Creating checkpoints when your document is stable and working properly helps you recover faster from mistakes.

WARNING

To restore your setup to the condition contained in a checkpoint, choose File ➪ Revert to Checkpoint. You see a listing of available checkpoints. Simply select the one you want to use. When you select the checkpoint, you see a warning message. When you click Revert, any old information is gone and the information found in the checkpoint becomes the current information.

Performing Multimedia and Graphic Integration

Pictures say a lot of things that words can't say (or at least they do it with far less effort). Notebook is both a coding platform and a presentation platform. You may be surprised at just what you can do with it. The following sections provide a brief overview of some of the more interesting features.

Embedding plots and other images

At some point, you might have spotted a notebook with multimedia or graphics embedded into it and wondered why you didn't see the same effects in your own files. In fact, all the graphics examples in the book appear as part of the code. Fortunately, you can perform some more magic by using the %matplotlib magic function. The possible values for this function are: 'gtk', 'gtk3', 'inline', 'nbagg', 'osx', 'qt', 'qt4', 'qt5', 'tk', and 'wx', each of which defines a different plotting backend (the code used to actually render the plot) used to present information onscreen.

When you run %matplotlib inline, any plots you create appear as part of the document. That's how Figure 8-1 (see the section about using NetworkX basics in Chapter 8) shows the plot that it creates immediately below the affected code.

TECHNICAL STUFF

Note that, according to https://stackoverflow.com/questions/65934740/is-matplotlib-inline-still-needed, there are situations in which you no longer need to run %matplotlib inline with newer versions of Python and its associated libraries. However, the documentation at https://pypi.org/project/matplotlib-inline/ still includes this feature and states outright that third-party libraries may continue to need it, so the book will continue to use %matplotlib inline to ensure that the examples work as intended.

Loading examples from online sites

Because some examples you see online can be hard to understand unless you have them loaded on your own system, you should also keep the %load magic function in mind. All you need is the URL of an example you want to see on your system. For example, try %load https://matplotlib.org/_downloads/pyplot_text.py. When you click Run Cell, Notebook loads the example directly in the cell and comments the %load call out. You can then run the example and see the output from it on your own system.

Obtaining online graphics and multimedia

A lot of the functionality required to perform special multimedia and graphics processing appears within Jupyter.display. By importing a required class, you can perform tasks such as embedding images into your notebook. Here's an example of embedding one of the pictures from the author's blog into the notebook for this chapter:

```
from urllib.request import Request, urlopen
from IPython import display
```

```
req = Request('http://blog.johnmuellerbooks.com/' +
    'wp-content/uploads/2015/04/Layer-Hens.jpg',
            headers={'User-Agent': 'XYZ/3.0'})
image = urlopen(req, timeout=10).read()

display.Image(image)
```

The code begins by importing the required resources. It then makes a request for the file from the website. Notice the inclusion of the headers property. If you don't include this property, the call will fail with an error message. The call to urlopen() actually retrieves the image, which is then displayed using display. Image(). The output you see from this example appears in Figure 5-5.

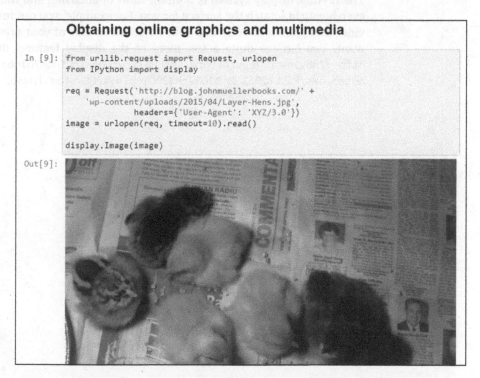

When working with embedded images on a regular basis, you might want to set the form in which the images are embedded. For example, you may prefer to embed them as PDFs. To perform this task, you use code similar to this:

```
from IPython.display import set_matplotlib_formats
set_matplotlib_formats('pdf', 'svg')
```

You have access to a wide number of formats when working with a notebook. The commonly supported formats are `'png'`, `'retina'`, `'jpeg'`, `'svg'`, and `'pdf'`.

Note, you may or may not see a warning message when running certain code in this book. That's because Python relies on a huge number of libraries that are all updated on different schedules, so that if you're using a copy of Python that's one minor version different from the product used in this book, you can see these messages. The blog post at https://blog.johnmuellerbooks.com/2023/05/08/warning-messages-in-jupyter-notebook-example-code/ tells you a lot more about these messages and what to do with them. Warning messages are just that, warnings — they don't keep the downloadable source from running and are generally nothing to worry about.

The IPython display system is nothing short of amazing, and this section hasn't even begun to scratch the surface for you. For example, you can import a YouTube video and place it directly into your notebook as part of your presentation if you want. You can see quite a few more of the display features demonstrated at http://nbviewer.jupyter.org/github/ipython/ipython/blob/1.x/examples/notebooks/Part%205%20-%20Rich%20Display%20System.ipynb.

IN THIS CHAPTER

» **Manipulating data streams**

» **Working with flat and unstructured files**

» **Interacting with relational databases**

» **Using NoSQL as a data source**

» **Interacting with web-based data**

Chapter **6**

Working with Real Data

ata science applications require data by definition. It would be nice if you could simply go to a data store somewhere, purchase the data you need in an easy-open package, and then write an application to access that data. However, data is messy. It appears in all sorts of places, in many different forms, and you can interpret it in many different ways. Every organization has a different method of viewing data and stores it in a different manner as well. Even when the data management system used by one company is the same as the data management system used by another company, the chances are slim that the data will appear in the same format or even use the same data types. In short, before you can do any data science work, you must discover how to access the data in all its myriad forms. Real data requires a lot of work to use, and fortunately, Python is up to the task of manipulating it as needed.

This chapter helps you understand the techniques required to access data in a number of forms and locations. For example, memory streams represent a form of data storage that your computer supports natively; flat files exist on your hard drive; relational databases commonly appear on networks (although smaller relational databases, such as those found in Access, could appear on your hard drive as well); and web-based data usually appears on the internet. You won't visit every form of data storage available (such as that stored on a point-of-sale, or POS, system). An entire book on the topic probably wouldn't suffice to cover the topic of data formats in any detail. However, the techniques in this chapter demonstrate how to access data in the formats you most commonly encounter when working with real-world data.

TIP

The Scikit-learn library includes a number of *toy* datasets (small datasets meant for you to play with). These datasets are complex enough to perform a number of tasks, such as experimenting with Python to perform data science tasks. Because this data is readily available and it's a bad idea to make the examples too complicated to understand, this book relies on toy datasets as input for many of the examples. Still, the demonstrated techniques work equally well on real-world data.

You don't have to type the source code for this chapter, and in fact, using the downloadable source is a lot easier (see the Introduction for download instructions). The source code for this chapter appears in the `P4DS4D3_06_Dataset_Load.ipynb` file.

WARNING

The `Colors.txt`, `Titanic.csv`, `Values.xls`, `Colorblk.jpg`, and `XMLData.xml` files that come with the downloadable source code must appear in the same folder (directory) as your Notebook files. Otherwise, the examples in the following sections fail with an input/output (IO) error. The file location varies according to the platform you're using. For example, on a Windows system, you find the notebooks stored in the `C:\Users\`*Username*`\P4DS4D3` folder, where *Username* is your login name. (The book assumes that you've used the prescribed folder location of P4DS4D3, as described in the "Defining the code repository" section of Chapter 3.) To make the examples work, simply copy the four files from the downloadable source folder into your Notebook folder.

Uploading, Streaming, and Sampling Data

Storing data in local computer memory represents the fastest and most reliable means to access it. The data could reside anywhere. However, you don't actually interact with the data in its storage location. You load the data into memory from the storage location and then interact with it in memory. This is the technique the book uses to access all the toy datasets found in the Scikit-learn library, so you see this technique used relatively often in the book.

REMEMBER

Data scientists call the columns in a database *features* or *variables*. The rows are *cases*. Each row represents a collection of variables that you can analyze.

Uploading small amounts of data into memory

The most convenient method that you can use to work with data is to load it directly into memory. This technique shows up a couple of times earlier in the book but uses the toy dataset from the Scikit-learn library. This section uses the

Colors.txt file, which contains the following color names and numeric equivalents:

Color	Value	Color	Value
Red	1	Orange	2
Yellow	3	Green	4
Blue	5	Purple	6
Black	7	White	8

The example also relies on native Python functionality to get the task done. When you load a file (of any type), the entire dataset is available at all times and the loading process is quite short. Here is an example of how this technique works.

```
with open("Colors.txt", 'r') as open_file:
    print('Colors.txt content:\n' + open_file.read())
```

The example begins by using the open() method to obtain a file object. The open() function accepts the filename and an access mode. In this case, the access mode is read (r). It then uses the read() method of the file object to read all the data in the file. If you were to specify a size argument as part of read(), such as read(15), Python would read only the number of characters that you specify or stop when it reaches the End Of File (EOF). When you run this example, you see the following output:

```
Colors.txt content:
Color    Value
Red      1
Orange   2
Yellow   3
Green    4
Blue     5
Purple   6
Black    7
White    8
```

WARNING

The entire dataset is loaded from the library into free memory. Of course, the loading process will fail if your system lacks sufficient memory to hold the dataset. When this problem occurs, you need to consider other techniques for working with the dataset, such as streaming it or sampling it. In short, before you use this technique, you must ensure that the dataset will actually fit in memory. You won't normally experience any problems when working with the toy datasets in the Scikit-learn library.

Streaming large amounts of data into memory

Some datasets will be so large that you won't be able to fit them entirely in memory at one time. In addition, you may find that some datasets load slowly because they reside on a remote site. Streaming solves both issues by enabling you to work with the data a little at a time. You download individual pieces so that you can work with just part of the data as you receive it, rather than waiting for the entire dataset to download. Here's an example of how you can stream data using Python:

```
with open("Colors.txt", 'r') as open_file:
    for observation in open_file:
        print('Reading Data: ' + observation , end="")
```

This example relies on the Colors.txt file, which contains a header and then a number of records that associate a color name with a value. The open_file file object contains a pointer to the open file.

As the code performs data reads in the for loop, the file pointer moves to the next record. Each record appears one at a time in observation. The code outputs the value in observation using a print statement. You should receive this output:

```
Reading Data: Color    Value
Reading Data: Red       1
Reading Data: Orange    2
Reading Data: Yellow    3
Reading Data: Green     4
Reading Data: Blue      5
Reading Data: Purple    6
Reading Data: Black     7
Reading Data: White     8
```

Python streams each record from the source. This means that you must perform a read for each record you want.

Generating variations on image data

Sometimes you need to import and analyze image data. The source and type of the image does make a difference. A number of examples of working with images appear throughout the book, but a good starting point is to simply read a local image in, obtain statistics about that image, and display the image onscreen, as shown in the following code:

```
import matplotlib.image as img
import matplotlib.pyplot as plt
%matplotlib inline

image = img.imread("Colorblk.jpg")
print(image.shape)
print(image.size)
plt.imshow(image)
plt.show()
```

The example begins by importing two matplotlib libraries, image and pyplot. The image library reads the image into memory, and the pyplot library displays it onscreen.

After the code reads the file, it begins by displaying the image shape property — the number of horizontal pixels, vertical pixels, and pixel depth (the number of bits used to represent colors). Figure 6-1 shows that the image is 100 x 100 x 3 channels (one for each color component: red, green, and blue). The image size property is the combination of these three elements, or 30,000 bytes.

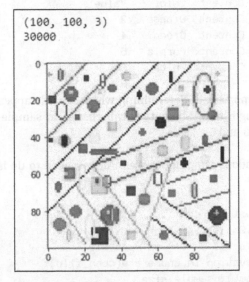

FIGURE 6-1:
The test image is 100 pixels high and 100 pixels long.

The next step is to load the image for plotting by using imshow(). The final call, plt.show(), displays the image onscreen, as shown in Figure 6-1. This technique represents just one of a number of methods for interacting with images using Python so that you can analyze them in some manner.

Sampling data in different ways

Data streaming obtains all the records from a data source. You may find that you don't need all the records. In that case, you can save time and resources by simply sampling the data (retrieving records a set number of records apart, such as every fifth record) or by making random samples. The following code shows how to retrieve every other record in the Colors.txt file:

```
n = 2
with open("Colors.txt", 'r') as open_file:
    for j, observation in enumerate(open_file):
        if j % n==0:
            print('Reading Line: ' + str(j) +
                    ' Content: ' + observation , end="")
```

The basic idea of sampling is the same as streaming. However, in this case, the application uses enumerate() to retrieve a row number. When j % n == 0, the row is one that you want to keep and the application outputs the information. In this case, you see the following output:

```
Reading Line: 0 Content: Color    Value
Reading Line: 2 Content: Orange   2
Reading Line: 4 Content: Green    4
Reading Line: 6 Content: Purple   6
Reading Line: 8 Content: White    8
```

The value of n is important in determining which records appear as part of the dataset. Try changing n to 3. The output will change to sample just the header (Line: 0) and rows 3 and 6.

TIP

You can perform random sampling as well. All you need to do is randomize the selector, like this:

```
from random import random
sample_size = 0.25
with open("Colors.txt", 'r') as open_file:
    for j, observation in enumerate(open_file):
        if random()<=sample_size:
            print('Reading Line: ' + str(j) +
                    ' Content: ' + observation, end="")
```

To make this form of selection work, you must import the random class. The random() method outputs a value between 0 and 1. However, Python randomizes the output so that you don't know what value you receive (assuming you receive any at all). The sample_size variable contains a number between 0 and 1 to determine the sample size. For example, 0.25 selects 25 percent of the items in the file.

The output will still appear in numeric order. For example, you won't see Green come before Orange. However, the items selected are random, and you won't always get precisely the same number of return values. Here is an example of what you may see as output (although your output will likely vary):

```
Reading Line: 1 Content: Red      1
Reading Line: 4 Content: Green    4
Reading Line: 8 Content: White    8
```

Accessing Data in Structured Flat-File Form

In many cases, the data you need to work with won't appear within a library, such as the toy datasets in the Scikit-learn library. Real-world data usually appears in a file of some type, and a flat file presents the easiest kind of file to work with. In a flat file, the data appears as a simple list of entries that you can read one at a time, if desired, into memory. Depending on the requirements for your project, you can read all or part of the file.

A problem with using native Python techniques is that the input isn't intelligent. For example, when a file contains a header, Python simply reads it as yet more data to process, rather than as a header. You can't easily select a particular column of data. The pandas library used in the sections that follow makes it much easier to read and understand flat-file data. Classes and methods in the pandas library interpret (parse) the flat-file data to make it easier to manipulate.

REMEMBER

The least formatted and therefore easiest-to-read flat-file format is the text file. However, a text file also treats all data as strings, so you often have to convert numeric data into other forms. A comma-separated value (CSV) file provides more formatting and more information, but it requires a little more effort to read. At the high end of flat-file formatting are custom data formats, such as an Excel file, which contains extensive formatting and could include multiple datasets in a single file.

The following sections describe these three levels of flat-file dataset and show how to use them. These sections assume that the file structures the data in some way. For example, the CSV file uses commas to separate data fields. A text file might rely on tabs to separate data fields. An Excel file uses a complex method to separate data fields and to provide a wealth of information about each field. You can work with unstructured data as well, but working with structured data is much easier because you know where each field begins and ends.

Reading from a text file

Text files can use a variety of storage formats. However, a common format is to have a header line that documents the purpose of each field, followed by another line for each record in the file. The file separates the fields using tabs. Refer to the "Streaming large amounts of data into memory" section, earlier in this chapter, for an example of the Colors.txt file used for the example in this section.

Native Python provides a wide variety of methods you can use to read such a file. However, it's far easier to let someone else do the work. In this case, you can use the pandas library to perform the task. Within the pandas library, you find a set of *parsers*, or code used to read individual bits of data and determine the purpose of each bit according to the format of the entire file. Using the correct parser is essential if you want to make sense of file content. In this case, you use the read_table() method to accomplish the task, as shown in the following code:

```
import pandas as pd
color_table = pd.io.parsers.read_table("Colors.txt")
print(color_table)
```

The code imports the pandas library, uses the read_table() method to read Colors.txt into a variable named color_table, and then displays the resulting memory data onscreen using the print function. Here's the output you can expect to see from this example.

```
    Color  Value
0   Red      1
1   Orange   2
2   Yellow   3
3   Green    4
4   Blue     5
5   Purple   6
6   Black    7
7   White    8
```

Notice that the parser correctly interprets the first row as consisting of field names. It numbers the records from 0 through 7. Using read_table() method arguments, you can adjust how the parser interprets the input file, but the default settings usually work best. You can read more about the read_table() arguments at https://pandas.pydata.org/docs/reference/api/pandas.read_table.html.

Reading CSV delimited format

A CSV file provides more formatting than a simple text file. In fact, CSV files can become quite complicated. There is a standard that defines the format of CSV files, and you can see it at `https://tools.ietf.org/html/rfc4180`. The CSV file used for this example is quite simple:

>> A header defines each of the fields

>> Fields are separated by commas

>> Records are separated by linefeeds

>> Strings are enclosed in double quotes

>> Integers and real numbers appear without double quotes

Figure 6-2 shows the raw format for the Titanic.csv file used for this example. You can see the raw format using any text editor.

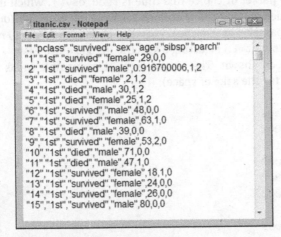

FIGURE 6-2: The raw format of a CSV file is still text and quite readable.

Applications such as Excel can import and format CSV files so that they become easier to read. Figure 6-3 shows the same file in Excel.

Excel actually recognizes the header as a header. If you were to use features such as data sorting, you could select header columns to obtain the desired result. Fortunately, pandas also makes it possible to work with the CSV file as formatted data, as shown in the following example:

```
import pandas as pd
titanic = pd.io.parsers.read_csv("Titanic.csv")
X = titanic[['age']]
print(X)
```

FIGURE 6-3:
Use an
application such
as Excel to create
a formatted CSV
presentation.

Notice that the parser of choice this time is `read_csv()`, which understands CSV files and provides you with new options for working with it. (You can read more about this parser at `https://pandas.pydata.org/docs/reference/api/pandas.read_csv.html`.) Selecting a specific field is quite easy — you just supply the field name as shown. The output from this example looks like this (some values omitted for the sake of space):

```
             age
0        29.0000
1         0.9167
2         2.0000
3        30.0000
4        25.0000
...
1304     14.5000
1305   9999.0000
1306     26.5000
1307     27.0000
1308     29.0000
[1309 rows x 1 columns]
```

Of course, a human-readable output like this one is nice when working through an example, but you may also need the output as a list. To create the output as a list, you simply change the third line of code to read `X = titanic[['age']].values`. Notice the addition of the `values` property. The output changes to something like this (some values omitted for the sake of space):

```
[[29.        ]
 [ 0.91670001]
 [ 2.        ]
 ...
```

```
[26.5       ]
[27.       ]
[29.       ]]
```

Reading Excel and other Microsoft Office files

Excel and other Microsoft Office applications provide highly formatted content. You can specify every aspect of the information these files contain. The `Values.xls` file used for this example provides a listing of sine, cosine, and tangent values for a random list of angles. You can see this file in Figure 6-4.

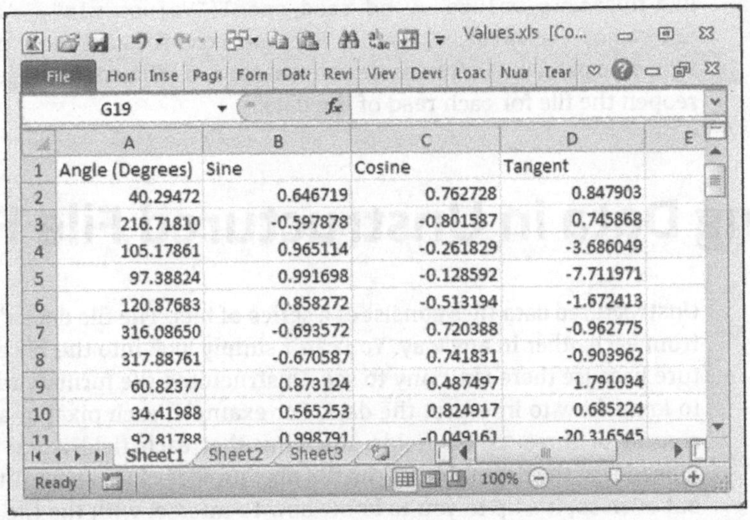

FIGURE 6-4: An Excel file is highly formatted and might contain information of various types.

	A	B	C	D
1	Angle (Degrees)	Sine	Cosine	Tangent
2	40.29472	0.646719	0.762728	0.847903
3	216.71810	-0.597878	-0.801587	0.745868
4	105.17861	0.965114	-0.261829	-3.686049
5	97.38824	0.991698	-0.128592	-7.711971
6	120.87683	0.858272	-0.513194	-1.672413
7	316.08650	-0.693572	0.720388	-0.962775
8	317.88761	-0.670587	0.741831	-0.903962
9	60.82377	0.873124	0.487497	1.791034
10	34.41988	0.565253	0.824917	0.685224
11	92.81788	0.998791	-0.049161	-20.316545

When you work with Excel or other Microsoft Office products, you begin to experience some complexity. For example, an Excel file can contain more than one worksheet, so you need to tell pandas which worksheet to process. In fact, you can choose to process multiple worksheets, if desired. When working with other Office products, you have to be specific about what to process. Just telling pandas to process something isn't good enough. Here's an example of working with the `Values.xls` file.

```
import pandas as pd
xls = pd.ExcelFile("Values.xls")
trig_values = xls.parse('Sheet1', index_col=None,
                        na_values=['NA'])
print(trig_values)
```

TECHNICAL STUFF

Note that you may have to install the `xlrd` library to read the `.xls` file. The downloadable source contains a special line, `!pip install xlrd`, to perform this task.

The code begins by importing the pandas library as normal. It then creates a pointer to the Excel file using the `ExcelFile()` constructor. This pointer, `xls`, lets you access a worksheet, define an index column, and specify how to present empty values. The index column is the one that the worksheet uses to index the records. Using a value of `None` means that pandas should generate an index for you. The `parse()` method obtains the values you request. You can read more about the Excel parser options at `https://pandas.pydata.org/docs/reference/api/pandas.ExcelFile.parse.html`.

TIP

You don't absolutely have to use the two-step process of obtaining a file pointer and then parsing the content. You can also perform the task using a single step like this: `trig_values = pd.read_excel("Values.xls", 'Sheet1', index_col=None, na_values=['NA'])`. Because Excel files are more complex, using the two-step process is often more convenient and efficient because you don't have to reopen the file for each read of the data.

Sending Data in Unstructured File Form

Unstructured data files consist of a series of bits. The file doesn't separate the bits from each other in any way. You can't simply look into the file and see any structure because there isn't any to see. Unstructured file formats rely on the file user to know how to interpret the data. For example, each pixel of a picture file could consist of three 32-bit fields. Knowing that each field is 32-bits is up to you. A header at the beginning of the file may provide clues about interpreting the file, but even so, it's up to you to know how to interact with the file.

The example in this section shows how to work with a picture as an unstructured file. The example image is a public domain offering from `https://commons.wikimedia.org/wiki/Main_Page`. To work with images, you need to access the Scikit-image library (`https://scikit-image.org/`), which is a free-of-charge collection of algorithms used for image processing. You can find a tutorial for this library at `http://scipy-lectures.org/packages/scikit-image/`. The first task is to be able to display the image onscreen using the following code. (This code can require a little time to run. The image is ready when the busy indicator disappears from the Notebook tab.)

```
from skimage.io import imread
from skimage.transform import resize
```

```
from matplotlib import pyplot as plt
import matplotlib.cm as cm

example_file = ("https://upload.wikimedia.org/" +
    "wikipedia/commons/7/7d/Dog_face.png")
image = imread(example_file, as_gray=True)
plt.imshow(image, cmap=cm.gray)
plt.show()
```

The code begins by importing a number of libraries. It then creates a string that points to the example file online and places it in example_file. This string is part of the imread() method call, along with as_gray, which is set to True. The as_gray argument tells Python to turn any color images into gray scale. Any images that are already in gray scale remain that way.

Now that you have an image loaded, it's time to render it (make it ready to display onscreen). The imshow() function performs the rendering and uses a grayscale color map. The show() function actually displays image for you, as shown in Figure 6-5.

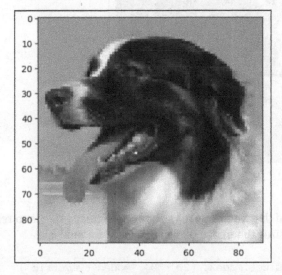

FIGURE 6-5:
The image appears onscreen after you render and show it.

You now have an image in memory, and you may want to find out more about it. When you run the following code, you discover the image type and size:

```
print("data type: %s, shape: %s" %
    (type(image), image.shape))
```

The output from this call tells you that the image type is a `numpy.ndarray` and that the image size is 90 pixels by 90 pixels. The image is actually an array of pixels that you can manipulate in various ways. For example, if you want to crop the image, you can use the following code to manipulate the image array:

```
image2 = image[5:70,0:70]
plt.imshow(image2, cmap=cm.gray)
plt.show()
```

The `numpy.ndarray` in image2 is smaller than the one in `image`. However, you may find that Notebook compensates by making the output appear larger (even though it's actually smaller, as shown by the markings). Figure 6-6 shows typical results. The purpose of cropping the image is to make it a specific size. Both images must be the same size for you to analyze them. Cropping is one way to ensure that the images are the correct size for analysis.

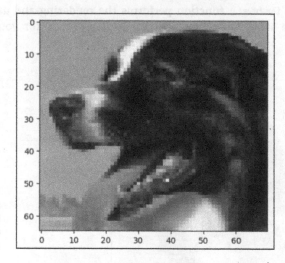

FIGURE 6-6: Cropping the image makes it smaller.

Another method that you can use to change the image size is to resize it. The following code resizes the image to a specific size for analysis:

```
image3 = resize(image2, (30, 30), mode='symmetric')
plt.imshow(image3, cmap=cm.gray)
print("data type: %s, shape: %s" %
      (type(image3), image3.shape))
```

The output from the `print()` function tells you that the image is now 30 pixels by 30 pixels in size. You can compare it to any image with the same dimensions.

After you have all the images the right size, you need to flatten them. A dataset row is always a single dimension, not two dimensions. The image is currently an array of 30 pixels by 30 pixels, so you can't make it part of a dataset. The following code flattens image3 so that it becomes an array of 900 elements that is stored in image_row.

```
image_row = image3.flatten()
print("data type: %s, shape: %s" %
      (type(image_row), image_row.shape))
```

Notice that the type is still a numpy.ndarray. You can add this array to a dataset and then use the dataset for analysis purposes. The size is 900 elements, as anticipated.

Managing Data from Relational Databases

Databases come in all sorts of forms. For example, AskSam (http://asksam. en.softonic.com/) is a kind of free-form textual database. However, the vast majority of data used by organizations rely on relational databases because these databases provide the means for structuring massive amounts of complex data in an organized manner that makes the data easy to manipulate. The goal of a database manager is to make data easy to manipulate. The focus of most data storage is to make data easy to retrieve.

REMEMBER

Relational databases accomplish both the manipulation and data retrieval objectives with relative ease. However, because data storage needs come in all shapes and sizes for a wide range of computing platforms, there are many different relational database products. In fact, for the data scientist, the proliferation of different Database Management Systems (DBMSs) using various data layouts is one of the main problems you encounter with creating a comprehensive dataset for analysis.

The one common denominator between many relational databases is that they all rely on a form of the same language to perform data manipulation, which makes the data scientist's job easier. The Structured Query Language (SQL) (pronounced "sequel") lets you perform all sorts of management tasks in a relational database, retrieve data as needed, and even shape it in a particular way so that performing additional shaping is unnecessary.

Creating a connection to a database can be a complex undertaking. For one thing, you need to know how to connect to that particular database. However, you can divide the process into smaller pieces. The first step is to gain access to the database engine. You use two lines of code similar to the following code (but the code presented here is not meant to execute and perform a task):

```
from sqlalchemy import create_engine
engine = create_engine('sqlite:///:memory:')
```

After you have access to an engine, you can use the engine to perform tasks specific to that DBMS. The output of a read method is always a DataFrame object that contains the requested data. To write data, you must create a DataFrame object or use an existing DataFrame object. You normally use these methods to perform most tasks:

» read_sql_table(): Reads data from a SQL table to a DataFrame object

» read_sql_query(): Reads data from a database using a SQL query to a DataFrame object

» read_sql(): Reads data from either a SQL table or query to a DataFrame object

» DataFrame.to_sql(): Writes the content of a DataFrame object to the specified tables in the database

The sqlalchemy library provides support for a broad range of SQL databases. The following list contains just a few of them:

» SQLite

» MySQL

» PostgreSQL

» SQL Server

» Other relational databases, such as those you can connect to using Open Database Connectivity (ODBC)

You can discover more about working with databases at https://docs. sqlalchemy.org/en/latest/core/engines.html. The techniques that you discover in this book using the toy databases also work with relational databases.

Interacting with Data from NoSQL Databases

In addition to standard relational databases that rely on SQL, you find a wealth of databases of all sorts that don't have to rely on SQL. These Not only SQL (NoSQL) databases are used in large data storage scenarios in which the relational model can become overly complex or can break down in other ways. The databases generally don't use the relational model. Of course, you find fewer of these DBMSes used in the corporate environment because they require special handling and training. Still, some common DBMSes are used because they provide special functionality or meet unique requirements. The process is essentially the same for using NoSQL databases as it is for relational databases:

1. Import required database engine functionality.

2. Create a database engine.

3. Make any required queries using the database engine and the functionality supported by the DBMS.

The details vary quite a bit, and you need to know which library to use with your particular database product. For example, when working with MongoDB (https://www.mongodb.org/), you must obtain a copy of the PyMongo library (https://pypi.org/project/pymongo/) and use the MongoClient class to create the required engine. The MongoDB engine relies heavily on the find() function to locate data. Following is a pseudo-code example of a MongoDB session. (You won't be able to execute this code in Notebook; it's shown only as an example.)

```
import pymongo
import pandas as pd
from pymongo import Connection
connection = Connection()
db = connection.database_name
input_data = db.collection_name
data = pd.DataFrame(list(input_data.find()))
```

Accessing Data from the Web

It would be incredibly difficult (perhaps impossible) to find an organization today that doesn't rely on some sort of web-based data. Most organizations use web services of some type. A *web service* is a kind of web application that provides a means to ask questions and receive answers. Web services usually host a number of input types. In fact, a particular web service may host entire groups of query inputs.

Another type of query system is the microservice. Unlike the web service, *microservices* have a specific focus and provide only one specific query input and output. Using microservices has specific benefits that are outside the scope of this book to address, but essentially they work like tiny web services, so that's how this book addresses them.

One of the most beneficial data access techniques to know when working with web data is accessing XML. All sorts of content types rely on XML, even some web pages. Working with web services and microservices means working with XML (in most cases). With this in mind, the example in this section works with XML data found in the XMLData.xml file, shown in Figure 6-7. In this case, the file is simple and uses only a couple of levels. XML is hierarchical and can become quite a few levels deep.

APIs AND OTHER WEB ENTITIES

A data scientist may have a reason to rely on various web Application Programming Interfaces (APIs) to access and manipulate data. In fact, the focus of an analysis might be the API itself. This book doesn't discuss APIs in any detail because each API is unique, and APIs operate outside the normal scope of what a data scientist might do. For example, you might use a product such as jQuery (https://jquery.com/) to access data and manipulate it in various ways when working with a web application. However, the techniques for doing so are more along the lines of writing an application than employing a data science technique.

It's important to realize that APIs can be data sources and that you may need to use one to achieve some data input or data-shaping goals. In fact, you find many data entities that resemble APIs but don't appear in this book. Windows developers can create Component Object Model (COM) applications that output data onto the web that you could possibly use for analysis purposes. In fact, the number of potential sources is nearly endless. This book focuses on the sources that you use most often and in the most conventional manner. Keeping your eyes open for other possibilities, though, is always a good idea.

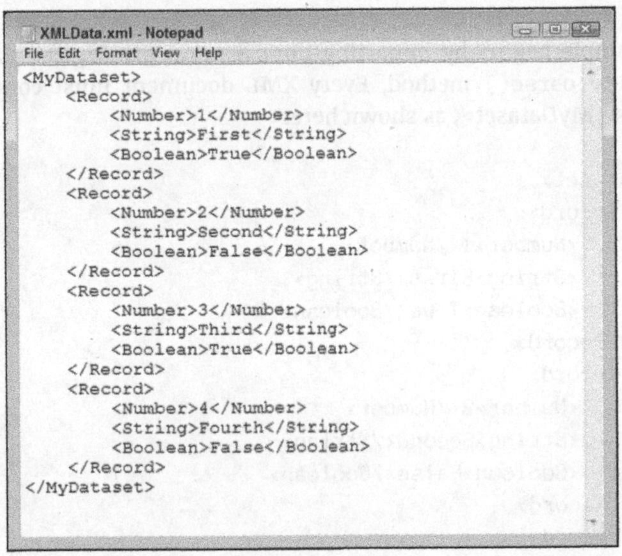

FIGURE 6-7:
XML is a
hierarchical
format that can
become quite
complex.

The technique for working with XML, even simple XML, can be a bit harder than anything else you've worked with so far. Here's the code for this example:

```python
from lxml import objectify
import pandas as pd

xml = objectify.parse(open('XMLData.xml'))
root = xml.getroot()

df = pd.DataFrame(columns=('Number', 'String',
                           'Boolean'))

for i in range(0,4):
    obj = root.getchildren()[i].getchildren()
    row = dict(zip(['Number', 'String', 'Boolean'],
                   [obj[0].text, obj[1].text,
                    obj[2].text]))
    row_s = pd.Series(row)
    row_s.name = i
    row_s = row_s.to_frame().transpose()
    df = pd.concat([df, row_s])

print(df)
```

The example begins by importing libraries and parsing the data file using the `objectify.parse()` method. Every XML document must contain a root node, which is <MyDataset>, as shown here:

```
<MyDataset>
    <Record>
        <Number>1</Number>
        <String>First</String>
        <Boolean>True</Boolean>
    </Record>
    <Record>
        <Number>2</Number>
        <String>Second</String>
        <Boolean>False</Boolean>
    </Record>
    <Record>
        <Number>3</Number>
        <String>Third</String>
        <Boolean>True</Boolean>
    </Record>
    <Record>
        <Number>4</Number>
        <String>Fourth</String>
        <Boolean>False</Boolean>
    </Record>
</MyDataset>
```

The root node encapsulates the rest of the content, and every node under it is a child. To do anything practical with the document, you must obtain access to the root node using the `getroot()` method.

The next step is to create an empty `DataFrame` object that contains the correct column names for each record entry: `Number`, `String`, and `Boolean`. As with all other pandas data handling, XML data handling relies on a `DataFrame`. The `for` loop fills the `DataFrame` with the four records from the XML file (each in a `<Record>` node).

The process looks complex but follows a logical order. The `obj` variable contains all the children for one `<Record>` node. These children are loaded into a dictionary object in which the keys are `Number`, `String`, and `Boolean` to match the `DataFrame` columns.

At this point, row is converted to a Series, row_s. A numeric name value is added to row_s, which is then converted to a DataFrame using the to_frame() function. If you looked at row_s at this point, you'd see that it has the wrong orientation, so a call to transpose() aligns it with DataFrame df.

There is now a DataFrame object that contains the row data. It then concatenates the row to df using the pd.concat() function. To see that everything worked as expected, the code prints the result, which looks like this:

```
   Number  String  Boolean
0       1   First     True
1       2  Second    False
2       3   Third     True
3       4  Fourth    False
```

USING THE JSON ALTERNATIVE

You shouldn't get the idea that all data you work with on the web is in XML format. You may need to consider other popular alternatives as part of your development plans. One of the most popular today is JavaScript Object Notation (JSON) (https://www.json.org/json-en.html). JSON proponents state that JSON takes less space, is faster to use, and is easier to work with than XML (see https://www.w3schools.com/js/js_json_xml.asp for details). Consequently, you may find that your next project relies on JSON data, rather than XML, when dealing with certain web services and microservices.

If your data formatting choices consisted of just XML and JSON, you might feel that interacting with data is quite manageable. However, a lot of other people have ideas of how to format data so that you can parse it quickly and easily. In addition, developers now have a stronger emphasis on understanding the data stream, so some formatting techniques emphasize human readability. You can read about some of these other alternatives at https://slashdot.org/software/p/XML/alternatives. One of the more important of these alternatives is Yet Another Markup Language or YAML Ain't Markup Language (YAML), depending on whom you talk to and which resources you use (https://yaml.org/spec/1.2.2/), but be prepared to do your homework when working through the particulars of any new projects.

Chapter **7**

Processing Your Data

The characteristics, content, type, and other elements that define your data in its entirety forms the data *shape*. The shape of your data determines the kinds of tasks you can perform with it. In order to make your data amenable to certain types of analysis, you must shape it into a different form. Think of the data as clay and you as the potter, because that's the sort of relationship you have with it. Instead of using your hands to shape the data, you rely on functions and algorithms to perform the task. This chapter helps you understand the tools you have available to shape data and the ramifications of shaping it.

TIP

Note that shaping data doesn't mean changing its value. Think more along the lines of rearranging the data so that you can work with it in an easier manner. It's akin to rearranging the contents of a shelf in your home so that you can see the shelf contents more easily.

Also in this chapter, you consider the problems associated with shaping. For example, you need to know what to do when data is missing from a dataset. It's important to shape the data correctly to avoid ending up with an analysis that simply doesn't make sense. Likewise, some data types, such as dates, can present problems. Again, you need to tread carefully to ensure that you get the desired result so that the dataset becomes more useful and amenable to analysis of various sorts.

REMEMBER

The goal of some types of data shaping is to create a larger dataset. In many cases, the data you need to perform an analysis doesn't appear in a single database or in a particular form. You need to shape the data and then combine it so that you have a single dataset in a known format before you can begin the analysis. Combining data successfully can be an art form because data often defies simple analysis or quick fixes.

TIP

You don't have to type the source code for this chapter; using the downloadable source is a lot easier. The source code for this chapter appears in the P4DS4D3_07_ Getting_Your_Data_in_Shape.ipynb file. See the Introduction for the location of this file.

WARNING

Make sure that the XMLData2.xml file that comes with the downloadable source code appears in the same folder (directory) as your Notebook files. Otherwise, the examples in the following sections fail with an input/output (I/O) error. The file location varies according to the platform you're using. For example, on a Windows system, you find the notebooks stored in the C:\Users*Username*\P4DS4D3 folder, where *Username* is your login name. (The book assumes that you've used the prescribed folder location of P4DS4D3, as described in the "Defining the code repository" section of Chapter 3.) To make the examples work, simply copy the file from the downloadable source folder into your Notebook folder. See the Introduction for instructions on downloading the source code.

Juggling between NumPy and pandas

There is no question that you need NumPy at all times. The pandas library is actually built on top of NumPy. However, you do need to make a choice between NumPy and pandas when performing tasks. You need the low-level functionality of NumPy to perform some tasks, but pandas makes things so much easier that you want to use it as often as possible. The following sections describe when to use each library in more detail.

Knowing when to use NumPy

Developers built pandas on top of NumPy. As a result, every task you perform using pandas also goes through NumPy. To obtain the benefits of pandas, you pay a performance penalty in most cases (see https://towardsdatascience.com/speed-testing-pandas-vs-numpy-ffbf80070ee7). Given that computer hardware can make up for a lot of performance differences today, the speed issue may not be a concern at times, but when speed is essential, NumPy is always the better choice.

Knowing when to use pandas

You use pandas to make writing code easier and faster. Because pandas does a lot of the work for you, you could make a case for saying that using pandas also reduces the potential for coding errors. The essential consideration, though, is that the pandas library provides rich time-series functionality, data alignment, NA-friendly statistics, and groupby(), merge(), and join() methods. Normally, you need to code these features when using NumPy, which means you keep reinventing the wheel.

As the book progresses, you discover just how useful pandas can be performing such tasks as *binning* (a data preprocessing technique designed to reduce the effect of observational errors) and working with a *dataframe* (a two-dimensional labeled data structure with columns that can potentially contain different data types) so that you can calculate statistics on it. For example, in Chapter 9, you discover how to perform both discretization and binning. Chapter 13 shows actual binning examples, such as obtaining a frequency for each categorical variable of a dataset. In fact, many of the examples in Chapter 13 don't work without binning. In other words, don't worry too much right now about knowing precisely what binning is or why you need to use it — examples later in the book discuss the topic in detail. All you really need to know is that pandas does make your work considerably easier.

IT'S ALL IN THE PREPARATION

This book may seem to spend a lot of time massaging data and little time in actually analyzing it. However, the majority of a data scientist's time is actually spent preparing data because the data is seldom in any order to actually perform analysis. To prepare data for use, a data scientist must

- Get the data
- Aggregate the data
- Create data subsets
- Clean the data
- Develop a single dataset by merging various datasets together

Fortunately, you don't need to die of boredom while wading your way through these various tasks. Using Python and the various libraries it provides makes the task a lot simpler, faster, and more efficient, which is the point of spending all of the time on seemingly mundane topics in these early chapters. The better you know how to use Python to speed your way through these repetitive tasks, the sooner you begin having fun performing various sorts of analysis on the data.

Validating Your Data

When it comes to data, no one really knows what a large database contains. Yes, everyone has seen bits and pieces of it, but when you consider the size of some databases, viewing it all would be physically impossible. Because you don't know what's in there, you can't be sure that your analysis will actually work as desired and provide valid results. In short, you must validate your data before you use it to ensure that the data is at least close to what you expect it to be. This means performing tasks such as removing duplicate records before you use the data for any sort of analysis (duplicates would unfairly weight the results).

REMEMBER

However, you do need to consider what validation actually does for you. It doesn't tell you that the data is correct or that there won't be values outside the expected range. In fact, later chapters help you understand the techniques for handling these sorts of issues. What validation does is ensure that you can perform an analysis of the data and reasonably expect that analysis to succeed. Later, you need to perform additional massaging of the data to obtain the sort of results that you need in order to perform the task you set out to perform in the first place.

Figuring out what's in your data

Figuring out what your data contains is important because checking data by hand is sometimes simply impossible due to the number of observations and variables. In addition, hand verifying the content is time consuming, error prone, and, most important, really boring. Finding duplicates is important because you end up

>> Spending more computational time to process duplicates, which slows your algorithms down.

>> Obtaining false results because duplicates implicitly overweight the results. Because some entries appear more than once, the algorithm considers these entries more important.

As a data scientist, you want your data to enthrall you, so it's time to get it to talk to you — not literally, of course, but through the wonders of pandas, as shown in the following example:

```
from lxml import objectify
import pandas as pd

xml = objectify.parse(open('XMLData2.xml'))
root = xml.getroot()
df = pd.DataFrame(columns=('Number', 'String', 'Boolean'))
```

```
for i in range(0,4):
    obj = root.getchildren()[i].getchildren()
    row = dict(zip(['Number', 'String', 'Boolean'],
                   [obj[0].text, obj[1].text,
                    obj[2].text]))
    row_s = pd.Series(row)
    row_s.name = i
    row_s = row_s.to_frame().transpose()
    df = pd.concat([df, row_s])

search = pd.DataFrame.duplicated(df)
print(df)
print(f"\n{search[search == True]}")
```

This example shows how to find duplicate rows. It relies on a modified version of the XMLData.xml file, XMLData2.xml, which contains a simple repeated row in it. A real data file contains thousands (or more) of records and possibly hundreds of repeats, but this simple example does the job. The example begins by reading the data file into memory using the same technique you explored in Chapter 6. It then places the data into a DataFrame.

At this point, your data is corrupted because it contains a duplicate row. However, you can get rid of the duplicated row by searching for it. The first task is to create a search object containing a list of duplicated rows by calling pd.DataFrame.duplicated(). The duplicated rows contain a True next to their row number.

Of course, now you have an unordered list of rows that are and aren't duplicated. The easiest way to determine which rows are duplicated is to create an index in which you use search == True as the expression. Following is the output you see from this example. Notice that row 3 is duplicated in the DataFrame output and that row 3 is also called out in the search results:

```
  Number  String Boolean
0      1   First    True
1      2  Second   False
2      3   Third    True
3      3   Third    True

3    True
dtype: bool
```

Removing duplicates

To get a clean dataset, you want to remove the duplicates from it. Fortunately, you don't have to write any weird code to get the job done — pandas does it for you, as shown in the following example:

```python
from lxml import objectify
import pandas as pd

xml = objectify.parse(open('XMLData2.xml'))
root = xml.getroot()
df = pd.DataFrame(columns=('Number', 'String', 'Boolean'))
for i in range(0,4):
    obj = root.getchildren()[i].getchildren()
    row = dict(zip(['Number', 'String', 'Boolean'],
                   [obj[0].text, obj[1].text,
                    obj[2].text]))
    row_s = pd.Series(row)
    row_s.name = i
    row_s = row_s.to_frame().transpose()
    df = pd.concat([df, row_s])

print(df.drop_duplicates())
```

As with the previous example, you begin by creating a DataFrame that contains the duplicate record. To remove the errant record, all you need to do is call drop_duplicates(). Here's the result you get.

```
  Number  String Boolean
0      1   First    True
1      2  Second   False
2      3   Third    True
```

Creating a data map and data plan

You need to know about your dataset — that is, how it looks statistically. A *data map* is an overview of the dataset. You use it to spot potential problems in your data, such as

>> Redundant variables

>> Possible errors

» Missing values

» Variable transformations

Checking for these problems goes into a *data plan*, which is a list of tasks you have to perform to ensure the integrity of your data. The following example shows a data map, A, with two datasets, B and C:

```
import pandas as pd
pd.set_option('display.width', 55)

df = pd.DataFrame({'A': [0,0,0,0,0,1,1],
                   'B': [1,2,3,5,4,2,5],
                   'C': [5,3,4,1,1,2,3]})

a_group_desc = df.groupby('A').describe()
print(a_group_desc)
```

In this case, the data map uses 0s for the first series and 1s for the second series. The groupby() function places the datasets, B and C, into groups. To determine whether the data map is viable, you obtain statistics using describe(). What you end up with is a dataset B with two series 0 and 1 and a dataset C also with two series 0 and 1, as shown in the following output.

```
      B                                                      \
   count mean        std  min   25%  50%   75%  max
A
0    5.0  3.0  1.581139  1.0  2.00  3.0  4.00  5.0
1    2.0  3.5  2.121320  2.0  2.75  3.5  4.25  5.0


      C
   count mean        std  min   25%  50%   75%  max
A
0    5.0  2.8  1.788854  1.0  1.00  3.0  4.00  5.0
1    2.0  2.5  0.707107  2.0  2.25  2.5  2.75  3.0
```

These statistics tell you about the two dataset series. The breakup of the two datasets using specific cases is the *data plan*. As you can see, the statistics tell you that this data plan may not be viable because some statistics are relatively far apart.

The default output from describe() shows the data unstacked (printed horizontally). Unfortunately, the unstacked data can print out with an unfortunate break, making it very hard to read. To keep this from happening, you set the width you want to use for the data by calling pd.set_option('display.width', 55). You can set a number of pandas options this way by using the information found at https://pandas.pydata.org/pandas-docs/stable/reference/api/pandas.set_option.html.

Although the unstacked data is relatively easy to read and compare, you may prefer a more compact presentation. In this case, you can stack the data using the following code:

```
stacked = a_group_desc.stack()
print(stacked)
```

Using stack() creates a new presentation. Here's the output shown in a compact form:

```
                B          C
A
0 count    5.000000   5.000000
  mean     3.000000   2.800000
  std      1.581139   1.788854
  min      1.000000   1.000000
  25%      2.000000   1.000000
  50%      3.000000   3.000000
  75%      4.000000   4.000000
  max      5.000000   5.000000
... Similar values for 1 ...
```

Of course, you may not want all the data that describe() provides. Perhaps you really just want to see the number of items in each series and their mean. Here's how you reduce the size of the information output:

```
print(a_group_desc.loc[:,(slice(None),['count','mean']),])
```

Using loc lets you obtain specific columns. Here's the final output from the example showing just the information you absolutely need to make a decision:

```
        B           C
    count mean count mean
A
0    5.0  3.0   5.0  2.8
1    2.0  3.5   2.0  2.5
```

Manipulating Categorical Variables

In data science, a *categorical variable* is one that has a specific value from a limited selection of values. The number of values is usually fixed. Many developers will know categorical variables by the moniker *enumerations*. Each of the potential values that a categorical variable can assume is a *level*.

To understand how categorical variables work, say that you have a variable expressing the color of an object, such as a car, and that the user can select blue, red, or green. To express the car's color in a way that computers can represent and effectively compute, an application assigns each color a numeric value, so blue is 1, red is 2, and green is 3. Normally when you print each color, you see the value rather than the color.

If you use pandas.DataFrame (https://pandas.pydata.org/pandas-docs/dev/reference/api/pandas.DataFrame.html), you can still see the symbolic value (blue, red, and green), even though the computer stores it as a numeric value. Sometimes you need to rename and combine these named values to create new symbols. Symbolic variables are just a convenient way of representing and storing qualitative data.

CHECKING YOUR VERSION OF PANDAS

The categorical variable examples in this section depend on your having a minimum version of pandas 1.5.0 installed on your system. However, your version of Anaconda may have a previous pandas version installed instead. Use the following code to check your version of pandas:

```
import pandas as pd
print(pd.__version__)
```

You see the version number of pandas you have installed. Another way to check the version is to open the Anaconda Prompt, type **pip show pandas**, and press Enter. If you have an older version, open the Anaconda Prompt, type **pip install pandas --upgrade**, and press Enter. The update process will occur automatically, along with a check of associated packages. When working with Windows, you may need to open the Anaconda Prompt using the Administrator option (right click the Anaconda Prompt entry in the Start menu and choose Run as Administrator from the context menu).

When using categorical variables for machine learning, it's important to consider the algorithm used to manipulate the variables. Some algorithms, such as trees and ensembles of three, can work directly with the numeric variables behind the symbols. Other algorithms, such as linear and logistic regression and SVM, require that you encode the categorical values into binary variables. For example, if you have three levels for a color variable (blue, red, and green), you have to create three binary variables:

>> One for blue (1 when the value is blue, 0 when it is not)

>> One for red (1 when the value is red, 0 when it is not)

>> One for green (1 when the value is green, 0 when it is not)

Creating categorical variables

Categorical variables have a specific number of values, which makes them incredibly valuable in performing a number of data science tasks. For example, imagine trying to find values that are out of range in a huge dataset. In this example, you see one method for creating a categorical variable and then using it to check whether some data falls within the specified limits:

```
import pandas as pd

car_colors = pd.Series(['Blue', 'Red', 'Green'],
                       dtype='category')


car_data = pd.Series(
    pd.Categorical(
        ['Yellow', 'Green', 'Red', 'Blue', 'Purple'],
        categories=car_colors, ordered=False))

find_entries = pd.isnull(car_data)

print(car_colors)
print(f"\n{car_data}")
print(f"\n{find_entries[find_entries == True]}")
```

The example begins by creating a categorical variable, car_colors. The variable contains the values Blue, Red, and Green as colors that are acceptable for a car. Notice that you must specify a dtype property value of category.

The next step is to create another series. This one uses a list of actual car colors, named car_data, as input. Not all the car colors match the predefined acceptable values. When this problem occurs, pandas outputs Not a Number (NaN) instead of the car color.

Of course, you could search the list manually for the nonconforming cars, but the easiest method is to have pandas do the work for you. In this case, you ask pandas which entries are null using `isnull()` and place them in `find_entries`. You can then output just those entries that are actually null. Here's the output you see from the example:

```
0       Blue
1        Red
2      Green
dtype: category
Categories (3, object): ['Blue', 'Green', 'Red']

0        NaN
1      Green
2        Red
3       Blue
4        NaN
dtype: category
Categories (3, object): ['Blue', 'Green', 'Red']

0       True
4       True
dtype: bool
```

Looking at the list of `car_data` outputs, you can see that entries 0 and 4 equal NaN. The output from `find_entries` verifies this fact for you. If this were a large dataset, you could quickly locate and correct errant entries in the dataset before performing an analysis on it.

Renaming levels

There are times when the naming of the categories you use is inconvenient or otherwise wrong for a particular need. Fortunately, you can rename the categories as needed using the technique shown in the following example.

```
import pandas as pd

car_colors = pd.Series(['Blue', 'Red', 'Green'],
                       dtype='category')
car_data = pd.Series(
    pd.Categorical(
```

```
            ['Blue', 'Green', 'Red', 'Blue', 'Red'],
            categories=car_colors, ordered=False))

car_data = car_data.cat.rename_categories(
    ["Purple", "Yellow", "Mauve"])

print(car_data)
```

All you really need to do is set the `cat` property to a new value, as shown. Here is the output from this example:

```
0    Purple
1    Yellow
2     Mauve
3    Purple
4     Mauve
dtype: category
Categories (3, object): ['Purple', 'Yellow', 'Mauve']
```

Combining levels

A particular categorical level may be too small to offer significant data for analysis. Perhaps there are only a few of the values, which may not be enough to create a statistical difference. In this case, combining several small categories may offer better analysis results. The following example shows how to combine categories:

```
import pandas as pd

car_colors = pd.Series(['Blue', 'Red', 'Green'],
    dtype='category')
car_data = pd.Series(
    pd.Categorical(
        ['Blue', 'Green', 'Red', 'Green', 'Red', 'Green'],
        categories=car_colors, ordered=False))

car_data = car_data.cat.set_categories(
    ["Blue", "Red", "Green", "Blue_Red"])
print(car_data.loc[car_data.isin(['Red'])])
car_data.loc[car_data.isin(['Red'])] = 'Blue_Red'
car_data.loc[car_data.isin(['Blue'])] = 'Blue_Red'

car_data = car_data.cat.set_categories(
    ["Green", "Blue_Red"])
print(f"\n{car_data}")
```

What this example shows you is that there is only one Blue item and only two Red items, but there are three Green items, which places Green in the majority. Combining Blue and Red together is a two-step process. First, you add the Blue_Red category to car_data. Then you change the Red and Blue entries to Blue_Red, which creates the combined category. As a final step, you can remove the unneeded categories.

However, before you can change the Red entries to Blue_Red entries, you must find them. This is where a combination of calls to isin(), which locates the Red entries, and loc[], which obtains their index, provides precisely what you need. The first print() statement shows the result of using this combination. Here's the output from this example.

```
2       Red
4       Red
dtype: category
Categories (4, object): ['Blue', 'Red', 'Green', 'Blue_Red']

0       Blue_Red
1          Green
2       Blue_Red
3          Green
4       Blue_Red
5          Green
dtype: category
Categories (2, object): ['Green', 'Blue_Red']
```

Notice that there are now three Blue_Red entries and three Green entries. The Blue and Red categories are no longer in use. The result is that the levels are now combined as expected.

Dealing with Dates in Your Data

Dates can present problems in data. For one thing, dates are stored as numeric values. However, the precise value of the number depends on the representation for the particular platform and could even depend on the users' preferences. For example, Excel users can choose to start dates in 1900 or 1904 (https://support.microsoft.com/en-us/help/214330/differences-between-the-1900-and-the-1904-date-system-in-excel). The numeric encoding for each is different, so the same date can have two numeric values depending on the starting date.

In addition to problems of representation, you also need to consider how to work with time values. Creating a time value format that represents a value the user can understand is hard. For example, you may need to use Greenwich Mean Time (GMT) in some situations but a local time zone in others. Transforming between various times is also problematic. With this in mind, the following sections provide you with details on dealing with time issues.

Formatting date and time values

Obtaining the correct date and time representation can make performing analysis a lot easier. For example, you often have to change the representation to obtain a correct sorting of values. Python provides two common methods of formatting date and time. The first technique is to call str(), which simply turns a datetime value into a string without any formatting. The strftime() function requires more work because you must define how you want the datetime value to appear after conversion. When using strftime(), you must provide a string containing special directives that define the formatting. You can find a listing of these directives at https://strftime.org/.

Now that you have some idea of how time and date conversions work, it's time to see an example. The following example creates a datetime object and then converts it into a string using two different approaches:

```
import datetime as dt

now = dt.datetime.now()

print(str(now))
print(now.strftime('%a, %d %B %Y'))
```

In this case, you can see that using str() is the easiest approach. However, as shown by the following output, it may not provide the output you need. Using strftime() is infinitely more flexible, even though the output from str() is storable.

```
2023-05-20 10:29:47.290505
Sat, 20 May 2023
```

Using the right time transformation

Time zones and differences in local time can cause all sorts of problems when performing analysis. For that matter, some types of calculations simply require a time shift in order to get the right results. No matter what the reason, you may need to transform one time into another time at some point. The following examples show some techniques you can employ to perform the task:

```
import datetime as dt

now = dt.datetime.now()
timevalue = now + dt.timedelta(hours=2)

print(now.strftime('%H:%M:%S'))
print(timevalue.strftime('%H:%M:%S'))
print(timevalue - now)
```

The timedelta() function makes the time transformation straightforward. You can use any of these parameter names with timedelta() to change a time and date value: days, seconds, microseconds, milliseconds, minutes, hours, and weeks.

You can also manipulate time by performing addition or subtraction on time values. You can even subtract two time values to determine the difference between them. Here's the output from this example (note that the output shows the effect of Daylight Saving Time, or DST):

```
10:34:40
12:34:40
2:00:00
```

Note that now is the local time, timevalue is two time zones different from this one, and there is a two-hour difference between the two times. You can perform all sorts of transformations using these techniques to ensure that your analysis always shows precisely the time-oriented values you need.

Dealing with Missing Data

Sometimes the data you receive is missing information in specific fields. For example, a customer record may be missing an age. If enough records are missing entries, any analysis you perform will be skewed and the results of the analysis weighted in an unpredictable manner. Having a strategy for dealing with missing data is important. The following sections give you some ideas on how to work through these issues and produce better results.

Finding the missing data

Finding missing data in your dataset is essential to avoid getting incorrect results from your analysis. The following code shows how you can obtain a listing of missing values without too much effort:

```
import pandas as pd
import numpy as np

s = pd.Series([1, 2, 3, np.NaN, 5, 6, None])

print(s.isnull())
print(f"\n{s[s.isnull()]}")
```

A dataset can represent missing data in several ways. In this example, you see missing data represented as np.NaN (NumPy Not a Number) and the Python None value.

Use the isnull() method to detect the missing values. The output shows True when the value is missing. By adding an index into the dataset, you obtain just the entries that are missing. The example shows the following output:

```
0    False
1    False
2    False
3     True
4    False
5    False
6     True
dtype: bool

3    NaN
6    NaN
dtype: float64
```

Encoding missingness

After you figure out that your dataset is missing information, you need to consider what to do about it. The three possibilities are to ignore the issue, fill in the missing items, or remove (drop) the missing entries from the dataset. Ignoring the problem could lead to all sorts of problems for your analysis, so it's the option you use least often. The following example shows one technique for filling in missing data or dropping the errant entries from the dataset:

```
import pandas as pd
import numpy as np

s = pd.Series([1, 2, 3, np.NaN, 5, 6, None])

print(s.fillna(int(s.mean())))
print(f"\n{s.dropna()}")
```

The two methods of interest are `fillna()`, which fills in the missing entries, and `dropna()`, which drops the missing entries. When using `fillna()`, you must provide a value to use for the missing data. This example uses the mean of all the values, but you could choose a number of other approaches. Here's the output from this example:

```
0    1.0
1    2.0
2    3.0
3    3.0
4    5.0
5    6.0
6    3.0
dtype: float64

0    1.0
1    2.0
2    3.0
4    5.0
5    6.0
dtype: float64
```

TECHNICAL STUFF

Working with a series is straightforward because the dataset is so simple. When working with a `DataFrame`, however, the problem becomes significantly more complicated. You still have the option of dropping the entire row. When a column is sparsely populated, you may drop the column instead. Filling in the data also becomes more complex because you must consider the dataset as a whole, in addition to the needs of the individual feature.

Imputing missing data

The previous section hints at the process of imputing missing data (ascribing characteristics based on how the data is used). The technique you use depends on the sort of data you're working with. For example, when working with a tree ensemble (you can find discussions of trees in the "Performing Hierarchical Clustering" section of Chapter 15 and the "Starting with a Plain Decision Tree" section of Chapter 20), you may simply replace missing values with a –1 and rely on the imputer (a transformer algorithm used to complete missing values) to define the best possible value for the missing data. The following example shows a technique you can use to impute missing data values:

```
import pandas as pd
import numpy as np
from sklearn.impute import SimpleImputer

s = pd.DataFrame([1, 2, 3, np.nan, 5, 6, np.nan])

imp = SimpleImputer(missing_values=np.nan,
                    add_indicator=True,
                    strategy='mean')

imp.fit(s)
x = imp.transform(s)
print(x)
```

In this example, s is missing some values. The code creates an Imputer to replace these missing values. The missing_values parameter defines what to look for, which is np.nan. The add_indicator parameter creates a new binary feature that will mark the imputed values, which is incredibly useful for many machine learning models to show both the original values and the manipulated ones. Finally, the strategy parameter defines how to replace the missing values. (You can discover more about the Imputer parameters at https://scikit-learn.org/stable/modules/generated/sklearn.impute.SimpleImputer.html.)

>> mean: Replaces the values by using the mean

>> median: Replaces the values by using the median

>> most_frequent: Replaces the values by using the most frequent value

Before you can impute anything, you must provide statistics for the Imputer to use by calling fit(). The code then calls transform() on s to fill in the missing values. Here's the result of the process with the missing values filled in and the additional binary indicator:

```
[[1.  0. ]
 [2.  0. ]
 [3.  0. ]
 [3.4 1. ]
 [5.  0. ]
 [6.  0. ]
 [3.4 1. ]]
```

Slicing and Dicing: Filtering and Selecting Data

You may not need to work with all the data in a dataset. In fact, looking at just one particular column may be beneficial, such as age, or a set of rows with a significant amount of information. You perform two steps to obtain just the data you need to perform a particular task:

1. Filter rows to create a subset of the data that meets the criterion you select (such as all the people between the ages of 5 and 10).

2. Select data columns that contain the data you need to analyze. For example, you probably don't need the individuals' names unless you want to perform some analysis based on name.

The act of slicing and dicing data, gives you a subset of the data suitable for analysis. The following sections describe various ways to obtain specific pieces of data to meet particular needs.

Slicing rows

Slicing can occur in multiple ways when working with data, but the technique of interest in this section is to slice data from a row of 2-D or 3-D data. A 2-D array may contain temperatures (x axis) over a specific time frame (y axis). Slicing a row would mean seeing the temperatures at a specific time. In some cases, you may associate rows with cases in a dataset.

A 3-D array may include an axis for place (x axis), product (y axis), and time (z axis) so that you can see sales for items over time. Perhaps you want to track whether sales of an item are increasing, and specifically where they are increasing. Slicing a row would mean seeing all the sales for one specific product for all locations at any time. The following example demonstrates how to perform this task:

```
x = np.array([[[1, 2, 3], [4, 5, 6], [7, 8, 9],],
              [[11,12,13], [14,15,16], [17,18,19],],
              [[21,22,23], [24,25,26], [27,28,29]]])
x[1]
```

In this case, the example builds a 3-D array. It then slices row 1 of that array to produce the following output:

```
array([[11, 12, 13],
       [14, 15, 16],
       [17, 18, 19]])
```

Slicing columns

Using the examples from the previous section, slicing columns would obtain data at a 90-degree angle from rows. In other words, when working with the 2-D array, you would want to see the times at which specific temperatures occurred. Likewise, you may want to see the sales of all products for a specific location at any time when working with the 3-D array. In some cases, you may associate columns with features in a dataset. The following example demonstrates how to perform this task using the same array as in the previous section:

```
x = np.array([[[1, 2, 3], [4, 5, 6], [7, 8, 9],],
              [[11,12,13], [14,15,16], [17,18,19],],
              [[21,22,23], [24,25,26], [27,28,29]]])
x[:,1]
```

Note that the indexing now occurs at two levels. The first index refers to the row. Using the colon (:) for the row means to use all the rows. The second index refers to a column. In this case, the output will contain column 1. Here's the output you see:

```
array([[ 4,  5,  6],
       [14, 15, 16],
       [24, 25, 26]])
```

REMEMBER

This is a 3-D array. Therefore, each of the columns contains all the z axis elements. What you see is every row — 0 through 2 for column 1 with every z axis element 0 through 2 for that column.

Dicing

The act of dicing a dataset means to perform both row and column slicing such that you end up with a data wedge. For example, when working with the 3-D array, you may want to see the sales of a specific product in a specific location at any time. The following example demonstrates how to perform this task using the same array as in the previous two sections:

```
x = np.array([[[1, 2, 3], [4, 5, 6], [7, 8, 9],],
              [[11,12,13], [14,15,16], [17,18,19],],
              [[21,22,23], [24,25,26], [27,28,29]]])
print(x[1,1])
print(x[:,1,1])
print(x[1,:,1])
print(f"\n{x[1:2, 1:2]}")
```

This example dices the array in four different ways. First, you get row 1, column 1. Of course, what you may actually want is column 1, z axis 1. If that's not quite right, you could always request row 1, z axis 1 instead. Then again, you may want rows 1 and 2 of columns 1 and 2. Here's the output of all four requests:

```
[14 15 16]
[ 5 15 25]
[12 15 18]

[[[14 15 16]]]
```

Concatenating and Transforming

Data used for data science purposes seldom comes in a neat package. You may need to work with multiple databases in various locations — each of which has its own data format. It's impossible to perform analysis on such disparate sources of information with any accuracy. To make the data useful, you must create a single dataset (by *concatenating*, or combining, the data from various sources).

Part of the process is to ensure that each field you create for the combined dataset has the same characteristics. For example, an age field in one database may appear as a string, but another database could use an integer for the same field. For the fields to work together, they must appear as the same type of information.

The following sections help you understand the process involved in concatenating and transforming data from various sources to create a single dataset. After you have a single dataset from these sources, you can begin to perform tasks such as analysis on the data. Of course, the trick is to create a single dataset that truly represents the data in all those disparate datasets.

Adding new cases and variables

You often find a need to combine datasets in various ways or even to add new information for the sake of analysis purposes. The result is a combined dataset that includes either new cases or variables. The following example shows techniques for performing both tasks:

```python
import pandas as pd

df = pd.DataFrame({'A': [2,3,1],
                   'B': [1,2,3],
                   'C': [5,3,4]})

df1 = pd.DataFrame({'A': [4],
                    'B': [4],
                    'C': [4]})

df = pd.concat([df, df1])
df = df.reset_index(drop=True)
print(df)

df.loc[df.last_valid_index() + 1] = [5, 5, 5]
print(f"\n{df}")

df2 = pd.DataFrame({'D': [1, 2, 3, 4, 5]})

df = pd.DataFrame.join(df, df2)
print(f"\n{df}")
```

The easiest way to add more data to an existing DataFrame is to rely on the concat() method. In this case, the three cases found in df are added to the single case found in df1. To ensure that the data is appended as anticipated, the columns in df and df1 must match. When you append two DataFrame objects in this manner, the new DataFrame contains the old index values. Use the reset_index() method to create a new index to make accessing cases easier.

You can also add another case to an existing DataFrame by creating the new case directly. Any time you add a new entry at a position that is one greater than the last_valid_index(), you get a new case as a result.

Sometimes you need to add a new variable (column) to the DataFrame. In this case, you rely on join() to perform the task. The resulting DataFrame will match cases with the same index value, so indexing is important. In addition, unless you want blank values, the number of cases in both DataFrame objects must match. Here's the output from this example:

```
    A  B  C
0   2  1  5
1   3  2  3
2   1  3  4
3   4  4  4

    A  B  C
0   2  1  5
1   3  2  3
2   1  3  4
3   4  4  4
4   5  5  5

    A  B  C  D
0   2  1  5  1
1   3  2  3  2
2   1  3  4  3
3   4  4  4  4
4   5  5  5  5
```

Removing data

At some point, you may need to remove cases or variables from a dataset because they aren't required for your analysis. In both cases, you rely on the drop() method to perform the task. The difference in removing cases or variables is in how you describe what to remove, as shown in the following example:

```
import pandas as pd

df = pd.DataFrame({'A': [2,3,1],
                   'B': [1,2,3],
                   'C': [5,3,4]})

df = df.drop(df.index[[1]])
print(df)

df = df.drop(columns=['B'])
print(f"\n{df}")
```

The example begins by removing a case from df. Notice how the code relies on an index to describe what to remove. You can remove just one case (as shown), ranges of cases, or individual cases separated by commas. The main concern is to ensure that you have the correct index numbers for the cases you want to remove.

Removing a column is different. This example shows how to remove a column using a column name. Here's the output from this example:

```
   A  B  C
0  2  1  5
2  1  3  4

   A  C
0  2  5
2  1  4
```

Sorting and shuffling

Sorting and shuffling are two ends of the same goal — to manage data order. In the first case, you put the data into order, while in the second, you remove any systematic patterning from the order. In general, you don't sort datasets for the purpose of analysis because doing so can cause you to get incorrect results. However, you may want to sort data for presentation purposes. The following example shows both sorting and shuffling:

```python
import pandas as pd
import numpy as np

df = pd.DataFrame({'A': [2,1,2,3,3,5,4],
                   'B': [1,2,3,5,4,2,5],
                   'C': [5,3,4,1,1,2,3]})

df = df.sort_values(by=['A', 'B'], ascending=[True, True])
df = df.reset_index(drop=True)
print(df)

index = df.index.tolist()
np.random.shuffle(index)
df = df.loc[df.index[index]]
df = df.reset_index(drop=True)
print(f"\n{df}")
```

It turns out that sorting the data is a bit easier than shuffling it. To sort the data, you use the sort_values() method and define which columns to use for indexing purposes. You can also determine whether the sort order is in ascending or descending order. Make sure to always call reset_index() when you're done so that the index appears in order for analysis or other purposes.

To shuffle the data, you first acquire the current index using df.index.tolist() and place it in index. A call to random.shuffle() creates a new order for the index. You then apply the new order to df using loc[]. As always, you call reset_index() to finalize the new order. Here's the output from this example (but note that the second output may not match your output because it has been shuffled):

```
   A  B  C
0  1  2  3
1  2  1  5
2  2  3  4
3  3  4  1
4  3  5  1
5  4  5  3
6  5  2  2

   A  B  C
0  4  5  3
1  1  2  3
2  3  5  1
3  2  3  4
4  5  2  2
5  3  4  1
6  2  1  5
```

Aggregating Data at Any Level

Aggregation is the process of combining or grouping data together into a set, bag, or list. The data may or may not be alike. However, in most cases, an aggregation function combines several rows together statistically using algorithms such as average, count, maximum, median, minimum, mode, or sum. There are several reasons to aggregate data:

>> Make it easier to analyze

>> Reduce the ability of anyone to deduce the data of an individual from the dataset for privacy or other reasons

>> Create a combined data element from one data source that matches a combined data element in another source

The most important use of data aggregation is to promote anonymity in order to meet legal or other concerns. Sometimes even data that should be anonymous turns out to provide identification of an individual using the proper analysis techniques. Here's an example that shows how to perform aggregation tasks:

```
import pandas as pd

df = pd.DataFrame({'Map': [0,0,0,1,1,2,2],
                   'Values': [1,2,3,5,4,2,5]})

df['S'] = df.groupby('Map')['Values'].transform(np.sum)
df['M'] = df.groupby('Map')['Values'].transform(np.mean)
df['V'] = df.groupby('Map')['Values'].transform(np.var)

print(df)
```

In this case, you have two initial features for this DataFrame. The values in Map define which elements in Values belong together. For example, when calculating a sum for Map index 0, you use the Values 1, 2, and 3.

To perform the aggregation, you must first call groupby() to group the Map values. You then index into Values and rely on transform() to create the aggregated data using one of several algorithms found in NumPy, such as np.sum. Here are the results of this calculation:

```
   Map  Values  S    M    V
0   0        1  6  2.0  1.0
1   0        2  6  2.0  1.0
2   0        3  6  2.0  1.0
3   1        5  9  4.5  0.5
4   1        4  9  4.5  0.5
5   2        2  7  3.5  4.5
6   2        5  7  3.5  4.5
```

Chapter **8**

Reshaping Data

T he previous chapter, Chapter 7, demonstrates techniques for working with data as an entity — as something you work with in Python. But data doesn't exist in a vacuum. It doesn't just suddenly appear within Python for absolutely no reason at all. As demonstrated in Chapter 6, you load the data; however, loading may not be enough — you may have to reshape the data as part of loading it. That's the purpose of this chapter. You discover how to work with a variety of container types in a way that enables you to load data from a number of complex container types.

REMEMBER

As you progress through the book, you discover that data takes all kinds of forms and shapes. As far as the computer is concerned, data consists of 0s and 1s. Humans give the data meaning by formatting, storing, and interpreting it in a certain way. The same group of 0s and 1s could be a number, date, or text, depending on the interpretation. The data container provides clues as to how to interpret the data, which is why this chapter is so important to you as a data scientist using Python to discover data patterns. You find that you can discover patterns in places where you may have thought patterns couldn't exist.

REMEMBER

You don't have to type the source code for this chapter manually; using the downloadable source is a lot easier (see the Introduction for download instructions). The source code for this chapter appears in the `P4DS4D3_08_Shaping_Data.ipynb` file.

Using the Bag of Words Model to Tokenize Data

The goal of most data imports is to perform some type of analysis. Before you can perform analysis on textual data, you must tokenize (break into linguistic pieces) every word within the dataset. The act of tokenizing the words creates a *bag of words*. You can then use the bag of words to train *classifiers*, a special kind of algorithm used to break words down into categories. The following sections provide additional insights into the bag of words model and show you how to work with it. You also discover how to perform various kinds of data-shaping tasks after you have a bag of words to use.

Understanding the bag of words model

As mentioned in the introduction, in order to perform textual analysis of various sorts, you need to first tokenize the words and create a bag of words from them. The bag of words uses numbers to represent words, word frequencies, and word locations that you can manipulate mathematically to see patterns in the way that the words are structured and used. The bag of words model ignores grammar and even word order, instead focusing on simplifying the text so that you can easily analyze it.

GETTING THE 20 NEWSGROUPS DATASET

The examples in the sections that follow rely on the 20 Newsgroups dataset (http://qwone.com/~jason/20Newsgroups/) that's part of the Scikit-learn installation. The host site provides some additional information about the dataset, but essentially it's a good dataset to use to demonstrate various kinds of text analysis.

You don't have to do anything special to work with the dataset because Scikit-learn already knows about it. However, when you run the first example, you see the message "WARNING:sklearn.datasets.twenty_newsgroups: Downloading dataset from http://people.csail.mit.edu/jrennie/20Newsgroups/20news-bydate.tar.gz (14MB)." All this message tells you is that you need to wait for the data download to complete. There is nothing wrong with your system. Look at the left side of the code cell in IPython Notebook and you see the familiar In [*]: entry. When this entry changes to show a number, the download is complete. The message doesn't go away until the next time you run the cell.

The creation of a bag of words revolves around Natural Language Processing (NLP) and Information Retrieval (IR). Before you perform this sort of processing, you normally remove any special characters (such as HTML formatting from a web source), remove the *stop words* (nonmeaningful words, such as "to"), and possibly perform *stemming* (reduce words to their root form) as well. For the purpose of this example, you use the 20 Newsgroups dataset directly. Here's an example of how you can obtain textual input and create a bag of words from it:

```
from sklearn.datasets import fetch_20newsgroups
from sklearn.feature_extraction.text import *

categories = ['comp.graphics', 'misc.forsale',
              'rec.autos', 'sci.space']
twenty_train = fetch_20newsgroups(subset='train',
                                  categories=categories,
                                  shuffle=True,
                                  random_state=42)

count_vect = CountVectorizer()
X_train_counts = count_vect.fit_transform(
    twenty_train.data)

print("BOW shape:", X_train_counts.shape)
caltech_idx = count_vect.vocabulary_['caltech']
print('"Caltech": %i' % X_train_counts[0, caltech_idx])
```

REMEMBER

A number of the examples you see online are unclear as to where the list of categories they use come from. Helpfully, the host site at http://qwone.com/~jason/20Newsgroups/ lists the categories you can use. The category list doesn't come from a magic hat somewhere, but many examples online simply don't bother to document some information sources. Always refer to the host site when you have questions about issues such as dataset categories.

The call to fetch_20newsgroups() loads the dataset into memory. You see the resulting training object, twenty_train, described as a *bunch*. At this point, you have an object that contains a listing of categories and associated data, but the application hasn't tokenized the data, and the algorithm used to work with the data isn't trained.

Now that you have a bunch of data to use, you can begin creating a bag of words with it. The first step is to create a matrix of token counts using the Count Vectorizer() object, count_vect. The bag of words process begins by assigning an integer value (an index of a sort) to each unique word in the training set. In addition, each document receives an integer value. The next step is to count every occurrence of these words in each document and create a list of document and count pairs so that you know which words appear and how often in each document.

Naturally, some words from the master list aren't used in some documents, thereby creating a *high-dimensional sparse dataset*. The `scipy.sparse` matrix is a data structure that lets you store only the nonzero elements of the list in order to save memory. When the code makes the call to `count_vect.fit_transform()`, it places the resulting bag of words into `X_train_counts`. You can see the resulting number of entries by accessing the `shape` property and the counts for the word "Caltech" in the first document:

```
BOW shape: (2356, 34750)
"Caltech": 3
```

Sequencing text items with n-grams

An *n-gram* is a continuous sequence of items in the text you want to analyze. The items are phonemes, syllables, letters, words, or base pairs. The *n* in n-gram refers to a size. An n-gram that has a size of one, for example, is a unigram. The example in this section uses a size of three, making a trigram. You use n-grams in a probabilistic manner to perform tasks such as predicting the next sequence in a series, which wouldn't seem very useful until you start thinking about applications such as search engines that try to predict the word you want to type based on the previous letters you've supplied. However, the technique has all sorts of applications, such as in DNA sequencing and data compression. The following example shows how to create n-grams from the 20 Newsgroups dataset:

```
from sklearn.datasets import fetch_20newsgroups
from sklearn.feature_extraction.text import *

categories = ['sci.space']

twenty_train = fetch_20newsgroups(subset='train',
                                  categories=categories,
                                  remove=('headers',
                                          'footers',
                                          'quotes'),
                                  shuffle=True,
                                  random_state=42)

count_chars = CountVectorizer(analyzer='char_wb',
                              ngram_range=(3,3),
                              max_features=10)
```

```
count_chars.fit(twenty_train['data'])

count_words = CountVectorizer(analyzer='word',
                              ngram_range=(2,2),
                              max_features=10,
                              stop_words='english')

count_words.fit(twenty_train['data'])

X = count_chars.transform(twenty_train.data)

print(count_chars.get_feature_names_out())
print(X[1].todense())
print(count_words.get_feature_names_out())
```

The beginning code is the same as in the previous section, "Understanding the bag of words model." You still begin by fetching the dataset and placing it into a bunch. However, in this case, the vectorization process takes on new meaning. The arguments process the data in a special way.

In this case, the first parameter, `analyzer`, determines how the application creates the n-grams. You can choose words (`word`), characters (`char`), or characters within word boundaries (`char_wb`). The second parameter, `ngram_range`, requires two inputs in the form of a tuple (the storing of multiple data items in a single variable): The first argument determines the minimum n-gram size, and the second determines the maximum n-gram size. The third parameter, `max_features`, determines how many features the vectorizer returns. In the second vectorizer call, the `stop_words` argument removes the terms contained in the English *pickle*, which is a method of serializing an object in Python so that you can store it on disk, as explained at `https://docs.python.org/3/library/pickle.html`). At this point, the application fits the data to the transformation algorithm.

The example provides three outputs. The first shows the top ten trigrams for characters from the document. The second is the n-gram for the first document. It shows the frequency of the top ten trigrams. The third is the top ten trigrams for words. Here's the output from this example:

```
[' an', ' in', ' of', ' th', ' to', 'he ', 'ing', 'ion',
 'nd ', 'the']
[[0 0 2 5 1 4 2 2 0 5]]
['anonymous ftp', 'commercial space', 'gamma ray',
 'nasa gov', 'national space', 'remote sensing',
 'sci space', 'space shuttle', 'space station',
 'washington dc']
```

Implementing TF-IDF transformations

The *Term Frequency times Inverse Document Frequency (TF-IDF)* transformation is a technique used to help compensate for words found relatively often in different documents, which makes it hard to distinguish between the documents because the words are too common (stop words are a good example). What this transformation is really telling you is the importance of a particular word to the uniqueness of a document. The greater the frequency of a word in a document, the more important it is to that document. However, the measurement is offset by the document size — the total number of words the document contains — and by how often the word appears in other documents.

Even if a word appears many times inside a document, that frequency doesn't imply that the word is important for understanding the document itself; in many documents, you find stop words with the same frequency as the words that relate to the document's general topics. For example, if you analyze documents with science fiction–related discussions (such as in the 20 Newsgroups dataset), you may find that many of them deal with UFOs; therefore, the acronym *UFO* can't represent a distinction between different documents. Moreover, longer documents contain more words than shorter ones, and repeated words are easily found when the text is abundant.

REMEMBER

In fact, a word found a few times in a single document (or possibly a few others) could prove quite distinctive and helpful in determining the document type. If you're working with documents discussing sci fi and automobile sales, the acronym *UFO* can be distinctive because it easily separates the two topic types in your documents.

Search engines often need to weight words in a document in a way that helps determine when the word is important in the text. You use words with the higher weight to index the document so that when you search for those words, the search engine will retrieve that document. This is the reason that the TD-IDF transformation is used quite often in search engine applications.

Getting into more details, the TF part of the TF-IDF equation determines how frequently the term appears in the document, and the IDF part of the equation determines the term's importance because it represents the inverse of the frequency of that word among all the documents. A large IDF implies a seldom-found word and that the TF-IDF weight will also be larger. A small IDF means that the word is common, and that will result in a small TF-IDF weight. You can see some actual calculations of this particular measure at `https://tfidf.com/`. Here's an example of how to calculate TF-IDF using Python:

```
from sklearn.datasets import fetch_20newsgroups
from sklearn.feature_extraction.text import *
```

```
categories = ['comp.graphics', 'misc.forsale',
              'rec.autos', 'sci.space']
twenty_train = fetch_20newsgroups(subset='train',
                                  categories=categories,
                                  shuffle=True,
                                  random_state=42)

count_vect = CountVectorizer()
X_train_counts = count_vect.fit_transform(
    twenty_train.data)

tfidf = TfidfTransformer().fit(X_train_counts)
X_train_tfidf = tfidf.transform(X_train_counts)

caltech_idx = count_vect.vocabulary_['caltech']
print('"Caltech" scored in a BOW:')
print('count: %0.3f' % X_train_counts[0, caltech_idx])
print('TF-IDF: %0.3f' % X_train_tfidf[0, caltech_idx])
```

This example begins much the same as the other examples in this section have, by fetching the 20 Newsgroups dataset. It then creates a word bag, much like the example in the "Understanding the bag of words model" section, earlier in this chapter. However, now you see something you can do with the word bag.

In this case, the code calls upon `TfidfTransformer()` to convert the raw news-group documents into a matrix of TF-IDF features. The `use_idf` controls the use of inverse-document-frequency reweighting, which it turned on in this case. The vectorized data is fitted to the transformation algorithm. The next step, calling `tfidf.transform()`, performs the actual transformation process. Here's the result you get from this example:

```
"Caltech" scored in a BOW:
count: 3.000
TF-IDF: 0.123
```

Notice how the word *Caltech* now has a lower value in the first document compared to the example in the previous paragraph, where the counting of occurrences for the same word in the same document scored a value of 3. To understand how counting occurrences relates to TF-IDF, compute the average word count and average TF-IDF:

```
import numpy as np
count = np.mean(X_train_counts[X_train_counts>0])
tfif = np.mean(X_train_tfidf[X_train_tfidf>0])
```

```
print('mean count: %0.3f' % np.mean(count))
print('mean TF-IDF: %0.3f' % np.mean(tfif))
```

The results demonstrate that no matter how you count occurrences of *Caltech* in the first document or use its TF-IDF, the value is always double the average word, revealing that it is a keyword for modeling the text:

```
mean count: 1.698
mean TF-IDF: 0.064
```

REMEMBER

TF-IDF helps you to locate the most important word or n-grams and exclude the least important one or ones. It is also very helpful as an input for linear models, because they work better with TF-IDF scores than word counts. At this point, you normally train a classifier and perform various sorts of analysis. Don't worry about this next part of the process just yet. Starting with Chapters 12 and 15, you get introduced to classifiers. In Chapter 17, you begin working with classifiers in earnest.

Working with Graph Data

Imagine data points that are connected to other data points, such as how one web page is connected to another web page through hyperlinks. Each of these data points is a *node*. The nodes connect to each other using *links* (also called *edges*). Not every node links to every other node, so the node connections become important. By analyzing the nodes and their links, you can perform all sorts of interesting tasks in data science, such as defining the best way to get from work to your home using streets and highways. The following sections describe how graphs work and how to perform basic tasks with them.

Understanding the adjacency matrix

An *adjacency matrix* represents the connections between nodes of a graph. When a connection exists between one node and another, the matrix indicates it as a value greater than 0. The precise representation of connections in the matrix depends on whether the graph is directed (where the direction of the connection matters) or undirected.

A problem with many online examples is that the authors keep them simple for explanation purposes. However, real-world graphs are often immense and defy easy analysis simply through visualization. Just think about the number of nodes that even a small city would have when considering street intersections (with the links being the streets themselves). Many other graphs are far larger, and simply looking at them will never reveal any interesting patterns. Data scientists call the problem in presenting any complex graph using an adjacency matrix a *hairball*.

One key to analyzing adjacency matrices is to sort them in specific ways. For example, you may choose to sort the data according to properties other than the actual connections. A graph of street connections may include the date the street was last paved with the data, enabling you to look for patterns that direct someone based on the streets that are in the best repair. In short, making the graph data useful becomes a matter of manipulating the organization of that data in specific ways.

Using NetworkX basics

Working with graphs could become difficult if you had to write all the code from scratch. Fortunately, the NetworkX package for Python makes it easy to create, manipulate, and study the structure, dynamics, and functions of complex networks (or graphs). Even though this book covers only graphs, you can use the package to work with digraphs and multigraphs as well.

The main emphasis of NetworkX is to avoid the whole issue of hairballs (explained in the previous section, "Understanding the adjacency matrix"). The use of simple calls hides much of the complexity of working with graphs and adjacency matrices from view. The following example shows how to create a basic adjacency matrix from one of the NetworkX-supplied graphs:

```
import networkx as nx
G = nx.cycle_graph(10)
A = nx.adjacency_matrix(G)
print(A.todense())
```

Note that you may see a FutureWarning when running this code (see the blog post at https://blog.johnmuellerbooks.com/2023/05/08/warning-messages-in-jupyter-notebook-example-code/ for details). The example begins by importing the required package. It then creates a graph using the cycle_graph() template. The graph contains ten nodes. Calling adjacency_matrix() creates the adjacency matrix from the graph. The final step is to print the output as a matrix, as shown here:

```
[[0 1 0 0 0 0 0 0 0 1]
 [1 0 1 0 0 0 0 0 0 0]
 [0 1 0 1 0 0 0 0 0 0]
 [0 0 1 0 1 0 0 0 0 0]
 [0 0 0 1 0 1 0 0 0 0]
 [0 0 0 0 1 0 1 0 0 0]
 [0 0 0 0 0 1 0 1 0 0]
 [0 0 0 0 0 0 1 0 1 0]
 [0 0 0 0 0 0 0 1 0 1]
 [1 0 0 0 0 0 0 0 1 0]]
```

TIP

You don't have to build your own graph from scratch for testing purposes. The NetworkX site documents a number of standard graph types that you can use, all of which are available within IPython. The list appears at https://networkx.github.io/documentation/latest/reference/generators.html.

It's interesting to see how the graph looks after you generate it. The following code displays the graph for you. Figure 8-1 shows the result of the plot.

```
import matplotlib.pyplot as plt
%matplotlib inline
nx.draw_networkx(G)
plt.show()
```

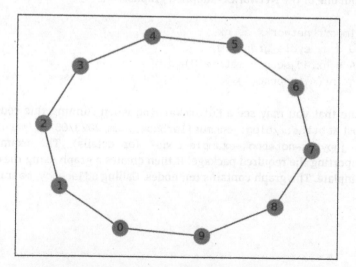

FIGURE 8-1:
Plotting the
original graph.

The plot shows that you can add an edge between nodes 1 and 5. Here's the code needed to perform this task using the add_edge() function. Figure 8-2 shows the result. (The plot you see will likely vary in appearance from the one in Figure 8-2, but the connections and nodes will be the same.)

```
G.add_edge(1,5)
nx.draw_networkx(G)
plt.show()
```

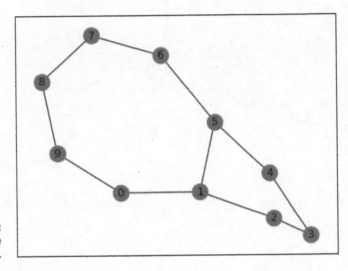

FIGURE 8-2:
Plotting the
graph addition.

Chapter 9

Putting What You Know into Action

Previous chapters have all been preparatory in nature. You have discovered how to perform essential data science tasks using Python. In addition, you spent time working with the various tools that Python provides to make data science tasks easier. All this information is essential, but it doesn't help you see the big picture — where all the pieces go. This chapter shows you how to employ the techniques you discovered in previous chapters to solve real data science problems.

REMEMBER

This chapter isn't the end of the journey — it's the beginning. Think of previous chapters in the same way as you think about packing your bags, making reservations, and creating an itinerary before you go on a trip. This chapter is the trip to the airport, during which you start to see everything come together.

The chapter begins by looking at the aspects you normally have to consider when trying to solve a data science problem. You can't just jump in and start performing an analysis; you must understand the problem first, as well as consider the resources (in the form of data, algorithms, computational resources) to solve it. Putting the problem into a context, a setting of a sort, helps you understand the problem and define how the data relates to that problem. The context is essential because, like language, context alters the meaning of both the problem and its associated data. For example, when you say, "I have a red rose" to your significant other, the meaning behind the sentence has one connotation. If you say the same sentence to a fellow gardener, the connotation is different. The red rose is a sort of data, and the person you're speaking to is the context. There is no meaning to saying, "I have a red rose" unless you know the context in which the statement is made. Likewise, data has no meaning; it doesn't answer any question until you know the context in which the data is used. Saying "I have data" expresses the question, "What does the data mean?"

In the end, you'll need one or more datasets. Two-dimensional datatables (datasets) consist of *cases* (the rows) and *features* (the columns). You can also refer to features as *variables* when using a statistical terminology. The features you decide to use for any given dataset determine the kinds of analysis you can perform, the ways in which you can manipulate the data, and ultimately the sorts of results you obtain. Determining what sorts of features you can create from source data and how you must transform the data to ensure that it works for the analysis you want to perform is an essential part of developing a data science solution.

After you get a picture of what your problem is, the resources you have to solve it, and the inputs you need to work with to solve it, you're ready to perform some actual work. The last section of this chapter shows you how to perform simple tasks efficiently. You can usually perform tasks using more than one methodology, but when working with big data, the fastest routes are better. By working with arrays and matrices to perform specific tasks, you'll notice that certain operations can take a long time unless you leverage some computational tricks. Using computational tricks is one of the most basic forms of manipulation you perform, but knowing about them from the beginning is essential. Applying these techniques paves the road to later chapters when you start to look at the magic that data science can truly accomplish in helping you see more in the data you have than is nominally apparent.

REMEMBER

You don't have to type the source code for this chapter manually; using the downloadable source is a lot easier (see the Introduction for download instructions). The source code for this chapter appears in the P4DS4D3_09_Operations_On_ Arrays_and_Matrices.ipynb file.

Contextualizing Problems and Data

Putting your problem in the correct context is an essential part of developing a data science solution for any given problem and associated data. Data science is definitively applied science, and abstract manual approaches may not work all that well on your specific situation. Running a Hadoop cluster or building a deep neural network may sound cool in front of fellow colleagues, and make you feel as though you're doing great data science projects, but they may not provide what you need to solve your problem. Putting the problem in the correct context isn't just a matter of deliberating on whether to use a certain algorithm or transform the data in a certain way — it's the art of critically examining the problem and available resources and creating an environment in which to solve the problem and obtain a desired solution.

REMEMBER

The key point here is the *desired* solution, in that you could come up with solutions that aren't desirable because they don't tell you what you need to know — or, when they do tell you what you need to know, they waste too much time and resources. The following sections provide an overview of the process you follow to contextualize both problems and data.

Evaluating a data science problem

When working through a data science problem, you need to start by considering your goal and the resources you have available for achieving that goal. The resources are data, computational resources such as available memory, CPUs, and disk space. In the real world, no one will hand you ready-made data and tell you to perform a particular analysis on it. Most of the time, you have to face completely new problems, and you have to build your solution from scratch. During your first evaluation of a data science problem, you need to consider the following:

>> **The data available in terms of accessibility, quantity, and quality.** You must also consider the data in terms of possible biases that could influence or even distort its characteristics and content. Data never contains absolute truths, only relative truths that offer you a more or less useful view of a problem (see the "Considering the five mistruths in data" sidebar for details). Always be aware of the truthfulness of data and apply critical reasoning as part of your analysis of it.

>> **The methods you can feasibly use to analyze the dataset.** Consider whether the methods are simple or complex. You must also decide how well you know a particular methodology. Start by using simple approaches, and never fall in love with any particular technique. There are neither free lunches nor Holy Grails in data science.

>> **The questions you want to answer by performing your analysis and how you can quantitatively measure whether you achieved a satisfactory answer to them.** "If you can' not measure it, you can not improve it," as Lord Kelvin stated (see https://zapatopi.net/kelvin/quotes/). If you can measure performance, you can determine the impact of your work and even make a monetary estimation. Stakeholders will be delighted to know that you've figured out what to do and what benefits your data science project will bring about.

CONSIDERING THE FIVE MISTRUTHS IN DATA

Humans are used to seeing data for what it is in many cases: an opinion. In fact, in some cases, people skew data to the point where it becomes useless, a *mistruth*. A computer can't tell the difference between truthful and untruthful data; all it sees is data. Consequently, as you perform analysis with data, you must consider the truth value of that data as part of your analysis. The best you can hope to achieve is to see the errant data as outliers and then filter it out, but that technique doesn't necessarily solve the problem because a human would still use the data and attempt to determine a truth based on the mistruths it contains. Here are the five mistruths you commonly find in data (using a car accident reporting process as an illustration):

- **Commission:** Mistruths of commission are those that reflect an outright attempt to substitute truthful information for untruthful information. For example, when filling out an accident report, someone could state that the sun momentarily blinded them, making it impossible to see someone they hit. In reality, perhaps the person was distracted by something else or wasn't actually thinking about driving (possibly considering a nice dinner). If no one can disprove this theory, the person might get by with a lesser charge. However, the point is that the data would also be contaminated.

- **Omission:** Mistruths of omission occur when a person tells the truth in every stated fact but leaves out an important fact that would change the perception of an incident as a whole. Thinking again about the accident report, say that someone strikes a deer, causing significant damage to their car. The driver truthfully says that the road was wet; it was near twilight so the light wasn't as good as it could be; was a little late in pressing on the brake; and the deer simply ran out from a thicket at the side of the road. The conclusion would be that the incident is simply an accident. However, the person has left out an important fact. The driver was texting at the time. If law enforcement knew about the texting, it would change the reason for the accident to inattentive driving. The driver might be fined and the insurance adjuster would use a different reason when entering the incident into the database.

- **Perspective:** Mistruths of perspective occur when multiple parties view an incident from multiple vantage points. For example, in considering an accident involving a struck pedestrian, the person driving the car, the person getting hit by the car, and a bystander who witnessed the event would all have different perspectives. An officer taking reports from each person would understandably get different facts from each one, even assuming that each person tells the truth as each knows it. In fact, experience shows that this is almost always the case, and what the officer submits as a report is the middle ground of what each of those involved state, augmented by personal experience. In other words, the report will be close to the truth, but not completely true. When dealing with perspective, it's important to consider vantage point. The driver of the car can see the dashboard and knows the car's condition at the time of the accident. This is information that the other two parties lack. Likewise, the person getting hit by the car has the best vantage point for seeing the driver's facial expression (intent). The bystander might be in the best position to see whether the driver made an attempt to stop, and assess issues such as whether the driver tried to swerve. Each party will have to make a report based on seen data without the benefit of hidden data.

- **Bias:** Mistruths of bias occur when someone is able to see the truth, but personal concerns or beliefs distort or obscure that vision. For example, when thinking about an accident, a driver might focus attention so completely on the middle of the road that the deer at the edge of the road becomes virtually invisible. Consequently, the driver has no time to react when the deer suddenly decides to bolt out into the middle of the road in an effort to cross. A problem with bias is that it can be incredibly hard to categorize. For example, a driver who fails to see the deer can have a genuine accident, meaning that the deer was hidden from view by shrubbery. However, the driver might also be guilty of inattentive driving because of incorrect focus. The driver might also experience a momentary distraction. In short, the fact that the driver didn't see the deer isn't the question; instead, it's a matter of why the driver didn't see the deer. In many cases, confirming the source of bias becomes important when creating an algorithm designed to avoid a bias source.

- **Frame of reference:** Of the five mistruths, frame of reference need not actually be the result of any sort of error, but one of understanding. A frame-of-reference mistruth occurs when one party describes something, such as an event like an accident, and the second party's lack of experience with the event makes the details muddled or completely misunderstood. Comedy routines abound that rely on frame-of-reference errors. One famous example is from Abbott and Costello, *Who's On First?*, as shown at https://www.youtube.com/watch?v=kTcRRaXV-fg. Getting one person to understand what a second person is saying can be impossible when the first person lacks experiential knowledge — the frame of reference.

Researching solutions

Data science is a complex system of knowledge at the intersection of computer science, math, statistics, and business. Very few people can know everything about it, and, if someone has already faced the same problem or dilemmas as you face, reinventing the wheel makes little sense. Now that you have contextualized your project, you know what you're looking for and you can search for it in different ways.

>> **Check the Python documentation.** You might be able to find examples that suggest a possible solution. NumPy (https://docs.scipy.org/doc/numpy/user/), SciPy (https://docs.scipy.org/doc/), pandas (http://pandas.pydata.org/pandas-docs/version/2.0.2/), and especially Scikit-learn (https://scikit-learn.org/stable/user_guide.html) have detailed in-line and online documentation with plenty of data science–related examples.

>> **Seek out online articles and blogs that hint at how other practitioners solved similar problems.** Q&A websites such as Quora (https://www.quora.com/), Stack Overflow (https://stackoverflow.com/), and Cross Validated (https://stats.stackexchange.com/) can provide you with plenty of answers to similar problems.

>> **Consult academic papers.** For example, you can query your problem on Google Scholar at https://scholar.google.it/ or Microsoft Academic at https://www.microsoft.com/en-us/research/project/academic/. You can find a series of scientific papers that can tell you about preparing the data, or they can detail the kind of algorithms that work better for a particular problem.

REMEMBER

It may seem trivial, but the solutions you create have to reflect the problem you're trying to solve. As you research solutions, you may find that some of them seem promising at first, but then you can't successfully apply them to your case because something in their context is different. For instance, your dataset may be incomplete or may not provide enough input to solve the problem. In addition, the analysis model you select may not actually provide the answer you need or the answer might prove inaccurate. As you work through the problem, don't be afraid to perform your research multiple times as you discover, test, and evaluate possible solutions that you could apply given the resources available and your actual constraints.

Formulating a hypothesis

At some point, you have everything you think you need to solve the problem. Of course, it's a mistake to assume now that the solutions you create can actually solve the problem. You have a hypothesis, rather than a solution, because you have to demonstrate the efficacy of the potential solution in a scientific way. In order to form and test a hypothesis, you must train a model using a training dataset and then test it using an entirely different dataset. Later chapters in the book spend a great deal of time helping you through the process of training and testing the algorithms used to perform analysis, so don't worry too much if you don't understand this aspect of the process right now.

Preparing your data

After you have some idea of the problem and its solution, you know the inputs required to make the algorithm work. Unfortunately, your data probably appears in multiple forms, you get it from multiple sources, and some data is missing entirely. Moreover, the developers of the features that existing data sources provide may have devised them for different purposes (such as accounting or marketing) than yours and you have to transform them so that you can use your algorithm at its fullest power. To make the algorithm work, you must prepare the data. This means checking for missing data, creating new features as needed, and possibly manipulating the dataset to get it into a form that your algorithm can actually use to make a prediction.

Considering the Art of Feature Creation

Features have to do with the columns in your dataset. Of course, you need to determine what those columns should contain. They might not end up looking precisely like the data in the original data source. The original data source may present the data in a form that leads to inaccurate analysis or even prevent you from getting a desired outcome because it's not completely suited to your algorithm or your objectives. For example, the data may contain too much information redundancy inside multiple variables, which is a problem called *multivariate correlation*. The task of making the columns work in the best manner for data analysis purposes is *feature creation* (also called feature engineering). The following sections help you understand feature creation and why it's important. (Future chapters provide all sorts of examples of how you actually employ feature creation to perform analysis.)

Defining feature creation

Feature creation may seem a bit like magic or weird science to some people, but it really does have a firm basis in math. The task is to take existing data and transform it into something that you can work with to perform an analysis. For example, numeric data could appear as strings in the original data source. To perform an analysis, you must convert the string data to numeric values in many cases. The immediate goal of feature creation is to achieve better performance from the algorithms used to accomplish the analysis than you can when using the original data.

In many cases, the transformation is less than straightforward. You may have to combine values in some way or perform math operations on them. The information you can access may appear in all sorts of forms, and the transformation process lets you work with the data in new ways so that you can see patterns in it. For example, consider this popular Kaggle competition: `https://www.kaggle.com/competitions/predict-student-performance-from-game-play`. The goal is to use all sorts of statistics to predict student performance during game-based learning in real-time. Imagine trying to derive disparate measures from various game sources that interact with students in different ways, and you can begin to grasp the need to create features in a dataset.

REMEMBER

As you might imagine, feature creation truly is an art form, and everyone has an opinion on precisely how to perform it. This book provides you with some good basic information on feature creation as well as a number of examples, but it leaves advanced techniques to experimentation and trial. As Pedro Domingos, professor at the University of Washington, Seattle, stated in his data science paper, "A Few Useful Things to Know about Machine Learning" (see `https://homes.cs.washington.edu/~pedrod/papers/cacm12.pdf`), feature engineering is "easily the most important factor" in determining the success or failure of a machine-learning project, and nothing can really replace the "smarts you put into feature engineering."

Combining variables

Data often comes in a form that doesn't work at all for an algorithm. Consider a simple real-life situation in which you need to determine whether one person can lift a board at a lumber yard. You receive two datatables. The first contains the height, width, thickness, and wood types of boards. The second contains a list of wood types and the amount they weigh per board foot (a piece of wood 12" x 12" x 1"). Not every wood type comes in every size, and some shipments come unmarked, so you don't actually know what type of wood you're working with. The goal is to create a prediction so that the company knows how many people to send to work with the shipments.

In this case, you create a two-dimensional dataset by combining variables. The resulting dataset contains only two features. The first feature contains just the length of the boards. It's reasonable to expect a single person to carry a board that is up to ten feet long, but you want two people carrying a board ten feet or longer. The second feature is the weight of the board. A board that is 10 feet long, 12 inches wide, and 2 inches thick contains 20 board feet. If the board is made of ponderosa pine (with a board foot rating, BFR, of 2.67), the overall weight of the board is 53.4 pounds, and one person could probably lift it. However, when the board is made of hickory (with a BFR of 4.25), the overall weight is now 85 pounds. Unless you have the Hulk working for you, you really do need two people lifting that board, even though the board is short enough for one person to lift.

Getting the first feature for your dataset is easy. All you need is the lengths of each of the boards that you stock. However, the second feature requires that you combine variables from both tables:

```
Length (feet) * Width (feet) * Thickness (inches) * BFR
```

The resulting dataset will contain the weight for each length of each kind of wood you stock. Having this information means that you can create a model that predicts whether a particular task will require one, two, or even three people to perform.

Understanding binning and discretization

To perform some types of analysis, you need to break numeric values into classes. For example, you might have a dataset that includes entries for people from ages 0 to 80. To derive statistics that work in this case (such as running the Naïve Bayes algorithm), you might want to view the variable as a series of levels in ten-year increments. The process of dividing the dataset into these ten-year increments is *binning*. Each bin is a numeric category that you can use.

Binning may improve the accuracy of predictive models by reducing noise or by helping model nonlinearity. In addition, it allows easy identification of *outliers* (values outside the expected range) and invalid or missing values of numerical variables.

Binning works exclusively with single numeric features. *Discretization* is a more complex process, in which you place combinations of values from different features in a bucket — limiting the number of states in any given bucket. In contrast to binning, discretization works with both numeric and string values. It's a more generalized method of creating categories. For example, you can obtain a discretization as a byproduct of cluster analysis.

Using indicator variables

Indicator variables are features that can take on a value of 0 or 1. Another name for indicator variables is dummy variables. No matter what you call them, these variables serve an important purpose in making data easier to work with. For example, if you want to create a dataset in which individuals under 25 are treated one way and individuals 25 and over are treated another, you could replace the age feature with an indicator variable that contains a 0 when the individual is under 25 or a 1 when the individual is 25 and older.

TIP

Using an indicator variable lets you perform analysis faster and categorize cases with greater accuracy than you can without this variable. The indicator variable removes shades of gray from the dataset. Someone is either under 25 or 25 and older — there is no middle ground. Because the data is simplified, the algorithm can perform its task faster, and you have less ambiguity to contend with.

TECHNICAL STUFF

The practice of using indicator variables can also assist in meeting data-cleaning requirements now enforced by many countries. Saying that someone is 25 years old is personally identifiable; saying that they're in group 1 is less so. So, using indicator variables can help you meet legal requirements as well.

Transforming distributions

A *distribution* is an arrangement of the values of a variable that shows the frequency at which various values occur. After you know how the values are distributed, you can begin to understand the data better. All sorts of distributions exist (see a gallery of distributions at https://www.itl.nist.gov/div898/handbook/eda/section3/eda366.htm), and most algorithms can easily deal with them. However, you must match the algorithm to the distribution.

WARNING

Pay particular attention to uniform and skewed distributions. They are quite difficult to deal with for different reasons. The bell-shaped curve, the normal distribution, is always your friend. When you see a distribution shaped differently from a bell distribution, you should think about performing a transformation.

When working with distributions, you might find that the distribution of values is skewed in some way and that, because of the skewed values, any algorithm applied to the set of values produces output that simply won't match your expectations. Transforming a distribution means to apply some sort of function to the values in order to achieve specific objectives, such as fixing the data skew, so that the output of your algorithm is closer to what you expected. In addition, transformation helps make the distribution friendlier, such as when you transform a dataset to appear as a normal distribution. Transformations that you should always try on your numeric features are

>> Logarithm np.log(x) and exponential np.exp(x)

>> Inverse 1/x, square root np.sqrt(x), and cube root x**(1.0/3.0)

>> Polynomial transformations such as x**2, x**3, and so on

Performing Operations on Arrays

A basic form of data manipulation is to place the data in an array or matrix and then use standard math-based techniques to modify its form. Using this approach puts the data in a convenient form to perform other operations done at the level of every single observation, such as in iterations, because they can leverage your computer architecture and some highly optimized numerical linear algebra routines present in CPUs. These routines are callable from every operating system. The larger the data and the computations, the more time you can save. In addition, using these techniques also spares you from writing long and complex Python code. The following sections describe how to work with arrays for data science purposes.

Using vectorization

Your computer provides you with powerful routine calculations, and you can use them when your data is in the right format. NumPy's ndarray is a multidimensional data-storage structure that you can use as a dimensional datatable. In fact, you can use it as a cube or even a hypercube when there are more than three dimensions.

Using ndarray makes computations easy and fast. The following example creates a dataset of three observations with seven features for each observation. In this case, the example obtains the maximum value for each observation and subtracts it from the minimum value to obtain the range of values for each observation.

```
import numpy as np
dataset = np.array([[2, 4, 6, 8, 3, 2, 5],
                    [7, 5, 3, 1, 6, 8, 0],
                    [1, 3, 2, 1, 0, 0, 8]])
print(np.max(dataset, axis=1) - np.min(dataset, axis=1))
```

The print statement obtains the maximum value from each observation using np.max() and then subtracts it from the minimum value using np.min(). The maximum values for the observations are [8 8 8]. The minimum values for the observations are [2 0 0]. As a result, you get the following output:

```
[6 8 8]
```

Performing simple arithmetic on vectors and matrices

Most operations and functions from NumPy that you apply to arrays leverage vectorization, so they're fast and efficient — much more efficient than any other solution or handmade code. Even the simplest operations such as additions or divisions can take advantage of vectorization.

For instance, many times, the form of the data in your dataset won't quite match the form you need. A list of numbers could represent percentages as whole numbers when you really need them as fractional values. In this case, you can usually perform some type of simple math to solve the problem, as shown here:

```
import numpy as np
a = np.array([15.0, 20.0, 22.0, 75.0, 40.0, 35.0])
a = a*.01
print(a)
```

The example creates an array, fills it with whole number percentages, and then uses 0.01 as a multiplier to create fractional percentages. You can then multiply these fractional values against other numbers to determine how the percentage affects that number. The output from this example is

```
[0.15 0.2 0.22 0.75 0.4 0.35]
```

Performing matrix vector multiplication

The most efficient vectorization operations are matrix manipulations in which you add and multiply multiple values against other multiple values. NumPy makes performing multiplication of a vector by a matrix easy, which is handy if you have to estimate a value for each observation as a weighted summation of the features. Here's an example of this technique:

```
import numpy as np
a = np.array([2, 4, 6, 8])
b = np.array([[1, 2, 3, 4],
              [2, 3, 4, 5],
              [3, 4, 5, 6],
              [4, 5, 6, 7]])
c = np.dot(a, b)
print(c)
```

Notice that the array formatted as a vector must appear before the array formatted as a matrix in the multiplication or you get an error. The example outputs these values:

```
[60 80 100 120]
```

To obtain the values shown, you multiply every value in the array against the matching column in the matrix; that is, you multiply the first value in the array against the first column, first row of the matrix. For example, the first value in the output is 2 * 1 + 4 * 2 + 6 * 3 + 8 * 4, which equals 60.

Performing matrix multiplication

You can also multiply one matrix against another. In this case, the output is the result of multiplying rows in the first matrix against columns in the second matrix. Here is an example of how you multiply one NumPy matrix against another:

```
import numpy as np
a = np.array([[2, 4, 6, 8],
              [1, 3, 5, 7]])
b = np.array ([[1, 2],
               [2, 3],
               [3, 4],
               [4, 5]])
c = np.dot(a, b)
print(c)
```

In this case, you end up with a 2-x-2 matrix as output. Here are the values you should see when you run the application:

```
[[60 80]
 [50 66]]
```

Each row in the first matrix is multiplied by each column of the second matrix. For example, to get the value 50 shown in row 2, column 1 of the output, you match up the values in row two of matrix a with column 1 of matrix b, like this: 1 * 1 + 3 * 2 + 5 * 3 + 7 * 4.

3
Visualizing Information

IN THIS CHAPTER

» Creating a basic graph

» Adding measurement lines to your graph

» Dressing your graph up with styles and color

» Documenting your graph with labels, annotations, and legends

Chapter **10**

Getting a Crash Course in Matplotlib

Most people visualize information better when they see it in graphic, versus textual, format. Graphics help people see relationships and make comparisons with greater ease. Even if you can deal with the abstraction of textual data with ease, performing data analysis is all about communication. Unless you can communicate your ideas to other people, the act of obtaining, shaping, and analyzing the data has little value beyond your own personal needs. Fortunately, Python makes the task of converting your textual data into graphics relatively easy using Matplotlib, which is actually a simulation of the MATLAB application. You can see a comparison of the two at https://pyzo.org/python_vs_matlab.html. (If you don't know how to use MATLAB, see *MATLAB For Dummies*, by John Paul Mueller [Wiley]), if you'd like to learn.)

TIP

If you already know how to use MATLAB, moving over to Matplotlib is relatively easy because they both use the same sort of state machine to perform tasks, and they have a similar method of defining graphic elements. A number of people feel that Matplotlib is superior to MATLAB because you can do things like perform tasks using less code when working with Matplotlib than when using MATLAB (see https://phillipmfeldman.org/Python/Advantages_of_Python_Over_Matlab.html). Others have noted that the transition from MATLAB to Matplotlib is relatively straightforward (see https://realpython.com/matlab-vs-python/). However, what matters most is what you think. You may find that you like to experiment with data using MATLAB and then create applications based on your findings using Python with Matplotlib. It's a matter of personal taste rather than a question of which one is correct.

This chapter focuses on getting you up to speed quickly with Matplotlib. You do use Matplotlib quite a few times later in the book, so this short overview of how it works is important, even if you already know how to work with MATLAB. That said, the MATLAB experience will be incredibly helpful as you progress through the chapter, and you may find that you can simply skim through some sections. Make sure to keep this chapter in mind as you start working with Matplotlib in more detail later in the book.

REMEMBER

You don't have to type the source code for this chapter manually; in fact, using the downloadable source code is a lot easier. The source code for this chapter appears in the P4DS4D3_10_Getting_a_Crash_Course_in_MatPlotLib.ipynb file (see the Introduction for where to find this code).

Starting with a Graph

A graph or chart is simply a visual representation of numeric data. Matplotlib makes a large number of graph and chart types available to you. Of course, you can choose any of the common graph and graph types such as bar charts, line graphs, or pie charts. As with MATLAB, you can also access a huge number of statistical plot types, such as boxplots, error bar charts, and histograms. You can see a gallery of the various graph types that Matplotlib supports at https://matplotlib.org/gallery.html. Remember, though, that you can combine graphic elements in an almost infinite number of ways to create your own presentation of data no matter how complex that data may be. The following sections describe how to create a basic graph, but you have access to a lot more functionality than these sections tell you about.

Defining the plot

Plots show graphically what you've defined numerically. To define a plot, you need some values, the matplotlib.pyplot module, and an idea of what you want to display, as shown in the following code:

```
import matplotlib.pyplot as plt
%matplotlib inline

values = [1, 5, 8, 9, 2, 0, 3, 10, 4, 7]
plt.plot(range(1,11), values)
plt.show()
```

In this case, the code tells the plt.plot() function to create a plot using x-axis values between 1 and 11 and y-axis values as they appear in the values variable. Calling plot.show() displays the plot in a separate dialog box, as shown in Figure 10-1. Notice that the output is a line graph. Chapter 11 shows you how to create other chart and graph types.

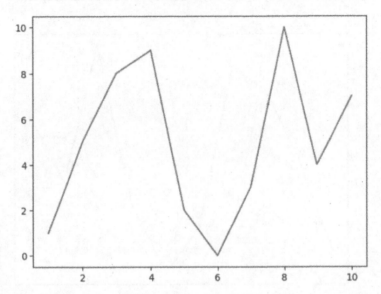

FIGURE 10-1:
Creating a basic plot that shows just one line.

TECHNICAL STUFF

The %matplotlib inline magic function (see the "Embedding plots and other images" section of Chapter 5) has become optional in newer versions of Python. However, including it is still a good idea, especially if you share your code with other people.

Drawing multiple lines and plots

You encounter many situations in which you must use multiple plot lines, such as when comparing two sets of values. To create such plots using Matplotlib, you simply call plt.plot() multiple times — once for each plot line, as shown in the following example:

```
import matplotlib.pyplot as plt
%matplotlib inline

values = [1, 5, 8, 9, 2, 0, 3, 10, 4, 7]
values2 = [3, 8, 9, 2, 1, 2, 4, 7, 6, 6]
plt.plot(range(1,11), values)
```

```
plt.plot(range(1,11), values2)
plt.show()
```

When you run this example, you see two plot lines, as shown in Figure 10-2. Even though you can't see it in the printed book, the line graphs are different colors (chosen for you by the library) so that you can tell them apart.

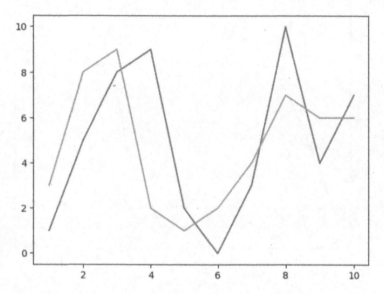

FIGURE 10-2:
Defining a plot
that contains
multiple lines.

Saving your work to disk

Jupyter Notebook makes it easy to include your graphs within the notebooks you create, enabling you to define reports that everyone can easily understand. When you need to save a copy of your work to disk for later reference or to use it as part of a larger report, you save the graphic programmatically using the plt.savefig() function, as shown in the following code:

```
import matplotlib.pyplot as plt
%matplotlib auto

values = [1, 5, 8, 9, 2, 0, 3, 10, 4, 7]
plt.plot(range(1,11), values)
plt.ioff()
plt.savefig('MySamplePlot.png', format='png')
```

In this case, you must provide a minimum of two inputs. The first input is the filename. You may optionally include a path for saving the file. The second input is the file format. In this case, the example saves the file in Portable Network Graphic

(PNG) format, but you have other options: Portable Document Format (PDF), Post-script (PS), Encapsulated Postscript (EPS), and Scalable Vector Graphics (SVG).

REMEMBER

Note the presence of the `%matplotlib auto` magic in this case. Using this call removes the inline display of the graph. You do have options for other Matplotlib backends, depending on which version of Python and Matplotlib you use. For example, some developers prefer the `notebook` backend to the `inline` backend because it provides additional functionality. However, to use the `notebook` back-end, you must also restart the kernel, and you may not always see what you expect. To see the backend list, use the `%matplotlib -l` magic. In addition, calling `plt.ioff()` turns plot interaction off.

Setting the Axis, Ticks, and Grids

It's hard to know what the data actually means unless you provide a unit of mea-sure or at least some means of performing comparisons. The use of axes, ticks, and grids makes it possible to illustrate graphically the relative size of data ele-ments so that the viewer gains an appreciation of comparative measure. You won't use these features with every graphic, and you may employ the features differ-ently based on viewer needs, but it's important to know that these features exist and how you can use them to help document your data within the graphic environment.

TECHNICAL STUFF

The following examples use the `%matplotlib notebook` magic so that you can see the difference between it and the `%matplotlib inline` magic. The two inline displays rely on a different graphic engine. Consequently, you must choose Kernel⇨Restart to restart the kernel before you run any of the examples in the sections that follow.

Getting the axes

The axes define the x and y plane of the graphic. The x axis runs horizontally, and the y axis runs vertically. In many cases, you can allow Matplotlib to perform any required formatting for you. However, sometimes you need to obtain access to the axes and format them manually. The following code shows how to obtain access to the axes for a plot:

```
import matplotlib.pyplot as plt
%matplotlib notebook

values = [0, 5, 8, 9, 2, 0, 3, 10, 4, 7]
ax = plt.axes()
```

```
plt.plot(range(1,11), values)
plt.show()
```

The reason you place the axes in a variable, ax, instead of manipulating them directly is to make writing the code simpler and more efficient. In this case, you simply turn on the default axes by calling plt.axes(); then you place a handle to the axes in ax. A *handle* is a sort of pointer to the axes. Think of it as you would a frying pan. You wouldn't lift the frying pan directly but would instead use its handle when picking it up.

Formatting the axes

Simply displaying the axes won't be enough in many cases. Instead, you may want to change the way Matplotlib displays them. For example, you may not want the highest value to reach to the top of the graph. The following example shows just a small number of tasks you can perform after you have access to the axes:

```
import matplotlib.pyplot as plt
%matplotlib notebook
plt.figure()

values = [0, 5, 8, 9, 2, 0, 3, 10, 4, 7]
ax = plt.axes()
ax.set_xlim([0, 11])
ax.set_ylim([-1, 11])
ax.set_xticks([1, 2, 3, 4, 5, 6, 7, 8, 9, 10])
ax.set_yticks([0, 1, 2, 3, 4, 5, 6, 7, 8, 9, 10])
plt.plot(range(1,11), values)
plt.show()
```

In this case, the set_xlim() and set_ylim() calls change the axes limits — the minimum and maximum coordinate values of each axis. The set_xticks() and set_yticks() calls change the ticks used to display data. The ways in which you can change a graph using these calls can become quite detailed. For example, you can choose to change individual tick labels if you want.

REMEMBER

Notice also the call to plt.figure(). If you don't make this call, the code will modify the first plot (figure) from the previous section (Figure 10-2), rather than create a new figure. In fact, what it will actually do is add to that previous figure, so what you end up with is a mess that no one can figure out! Figure 10-3 shows the output from this example. Notice how the changes affect how the line graph displays.

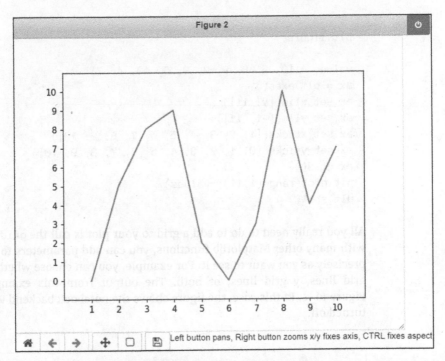

Figure 2

FIGURE 10-3:
Specifying how the axes should appear to the viewer.

Left button pans, Right button zooms x/y fixes axis, CTRL fixes aspect

TECHNICAL STUFF

As you can see by viewing the differences between Figures 10-1, 10-2, and 10-3, the %matplotlib notebook magic produces a significantly different display. The controls at the bottom of the display let you pan and zoom the display, move between views you've created, and download the figure to disk when working with Jupyter Notebook (they may not work at all in Google Colab). The button to the right of the Figure 2 heading in Figure 10-3 lets you stop interacting with the graph after you've finished working with it. Any changes you've made to the presentation of the graph remain afterward so that anyone looking at your notebook will see the graph in the manner you intended for them to see it. The ability to interact with the graph ends when you display another graph.

Adding grids

Grid lines enable you to see the precise value of each element of a graph. You can more quickly determine both the x and y coordinates, which allow you to perform comparisons of individual points with greater ease. Of course, grids also add noise (added information) and make seeing the actual flow of data harder. The point is that you can use grids to good effect to create particular effects. The following code shows how to add a grid to the graph in the previous section:

```
import matplotlib.pyplot as plt
%matplotlib notebook
```

```
plt.figure()

values = [0, 5, 8, 9, 2, 0, 3, 10, 4, 7]
ax = plt.axes()
ax.set_xlim([0, 11])
ax.set_ylim([-1, 11])
ax.set_xticks([1, 2, 3, 4, 5, 6, 7, 8, 9, 10])
ax.set_yticks([0, 1, 2, 3, 4, 5, 6, 7, 8, 9, 10])
ax.grid()
plt.plot(range(1,11), values)
plt.show()
```

All you really need to do to add a grid to your plot is call the grid() function. As with many other Matplotlib functions, you can add parameters to create the grid precisely as you want to see it. For example, you can choose whether to add the x grid lines, y grid lines, or both. The output from this example appears in Figure 10-4. In this case, the figure shows the notebook backend with interaction turned off.

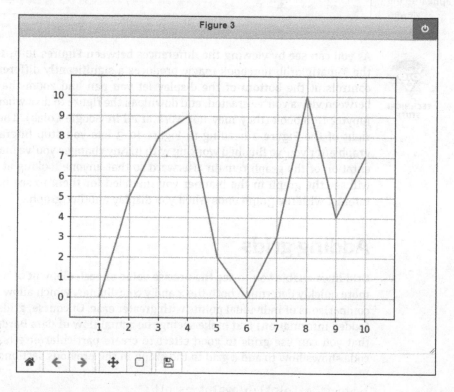

FIGURE 10-4:
Adding grids makes the values easier to read.

Defining the Line Appearance

Just drawing lines on a page won't do much for you if you need to help the viewer understand the importance of your data. In most cases, you need to use different line styles to ensure that the viewer can tell one data grouping from another. However, to emphasize the importance or value of a particular data grouping, you need to employ color. The use of color communicates all sorts of ideas to the viewer. For example, green often denotes that something is safe, and red communicates danger. The following sections help you understand how to work with line style and color to communicate ideas and concepts to the viewer without using any text.

Working with line styles

Line styles help differentiate graphs by drawing the lines in various ways. Using a unique presentation for each line helps you distinguish each line so that you can call it out (even when the printout is in shades of gray). You could also call out a particular line graph by using a different line style for it (and using the same style for the other lines). Table 10-1 shows the various Matplotlib line styles.

The line style appears as a third argument to the plot() function call. You simply provide the desired string for the line type, as shown in the following example.

```
import matplotlib.pyplot as plt
%matplotlib inline

values = [1, 5, 8, 9, 2, 0, 3, 10, 4, 7]
values2 = [3, 8, 9, 2, 1, 2, 4, 7, 6, 6]
plt.plot(range(1,11), values, '--')
plt.plot(range(1,11), values2, ':')
plt.show()
```

MAKING GRAPHICS ACCESSIBLE

Avoiding assumptions about someone's ability to see your graphic presentation is essential. For example, someone who is color blind may not be able to tell that one line is green and the other red. Likewise, someone with low vision may not be able to distinguish between a dashed line and one that combines dashes and dots. Using multiple methods to distinguish each line helps ensure that everyone can see your data in a manner that is comfortable to each person.

TABLE 10-1

Matplotlib Line Styles

Character	Line Style
'-'	Solid line
'--'	Dashed line
'-.'	Dash-dot line
':'	Dotted line

In this case, the first line graph uses a dashed line style, while the second line graph uses a dotted line style. (Note that you must restart the kernel again to switch from the %matplotlib notebook to the %matplotlib inline style.) You can see the results of the changes in Figure 10-5.

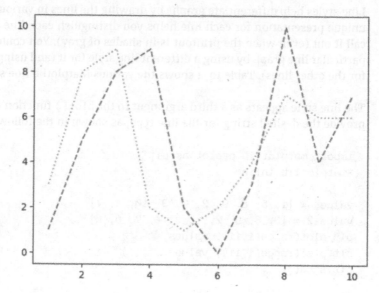

FIGURE 10-5:
Line styles help differentiate between plots.

Using colors

Color is another way in which to differentiate line graphs. Of course, this method has certain problems. The most significant problem occurs when someone makes a black-and-white copy of your colored graph — hiding the color differences as shades of gray. Another problem is that someone with color blindness may not be able to tell one line from the other. All this said, color does make for a brighter, eye-grabbing presentation. Table 10-2 shows the colors that Matplotlib supports.

TABLE 10-2

Matplotlib Colors

Character	Color
'b'	Blue
'g'	Green
'r'	Red
'c'	Cyan
'm'	Magenta
'y'	Yellow
'k'	Black
'w'	White

As with line styles, the color appears in a string as the third argument to the `plot()` function call. In this case, the viewer sees two lines — one in red and the other in magenta. The data points are the same as those used for Figure 10-2, just with different colors. If you're reading the printed version of the book, Figure 10-2 appears in shades of gray instead of color, as does this new presentation.

```
import matplotlib.pyplot as plt
%matplotlib inline

values = [1, 5, 8, 9, 2, 0, 3, 10, 4, 7]
values2 = [3, 8, 9, 2, 1, 2, 4, 7, 6, 6]
plt.plot(range(1,11), values, 'r')
plt.plot(range(1,11), values2, 'm')
plt.show()
```

Adding markers

Markers add a special symbol to each data point in a line graph. Unlike line style and color, markers tend to be a little less susceptible to accessibility and printing issues. Even when the specific marker isn't clear, people can usually differentiate one marker from the other. Table 10-3 shows the list of markers that Matplotlib provides.

TABLE 10-3

Matplotlib Markers

Character	Marker Type
'.'	Point
','	Pixel
'o'	Circle
'v'	Triangle 1 down
'^'	Triangle 1 up
'<'	Triangle 1 left
'>'	Triangle 1 right
'1'	Triangle 2 down
'2'	Triangle 2 up
'3'	Triangle 2 left
'4'	Triangle 2 right
's'	Square
'p'	Pentagon
'*'	Star
'h'	Hexagon style 1
'H'	Hexagon style 2
'+'	Plus
'x'	X
'D'	Diamond
'd'	Thin diamond
'|'	Vertical line
'_'	Horizontal line

As with line style and color, you add markers as the third argument to a `plot()` call. In the following example, you see the effects of combining line style with a marker to provide a unique line-graph presentation.

```
import matplotlib.pyplot as plt
%matplotlib inline
```

```
values = [1, 5, 8, 9, 2, 0, 3, 10, 4, 7]
values2 = [3, 8, 9, 2, 1, 2, 4, 7, 6, 6]
plt.plot(range(1,11), values, 'o--')
plt.plot(range(1,11), values2, 'v:')
plt.show()
```

Notice how the combination of line style and marker makes each line stand out in Figure 10-6. Even when printed in black and white, you can easily differentiate one line from the other, which is why you usually want to combine presentation techniques.

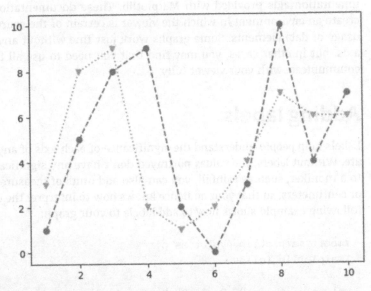

FIGURE 10-6:
Markers help to emphasize individual values.

Using Labels, Annotations, and Legends

To fully document your graph, you usually have to resort to labels, annotations, and legends. Each of these elements has a different purpose, as follows:

>> **Label:** Provides positive identification of a particular data element or grouping. The purpose is to make it easy for the viewer to know the name or kind of data illustrated.

>> **Annotation:** Augments the information the viewer can immediately see about the data with notes, sources, or other useful information. In contrast to a label, the purpose of annotation is to help extend the viewer's knowledge of the data rather than simply identify it.

>> **Legend:** Presents a listing of the data groups within the graph and often provides cues (such as line type or color) to make identification of the data group easier. For example, all the red points may belong to group A, and all the blue points may belong to group B.

The following sections help you understand the purpose and usage of various documentation aids provided with Matplotlib. These documentation aids help you create an environment in which the viewer is certain of the source, purpose, and usage of data elements. Some graphs work just fine without any documentation aids, but in other cases, you may find that you need to use all three in order to communicate with your viewer fully.

Adding labels

Labels help people understand the significance of each axis of any graph you create. Without labels, the values portrayed don't have any significance. In addition to a moniker, such as rainfall, you can also add units of measure, such as inches or centimeters, so that your audience knows how to interpret the data shown. The following example shows how to add labels to your graph:

```
import matplotlib.pyplot as plt
%matplotlib inline

values = [1, 5, 8, 9, 2, 0, 3, 10, 4, 7]
plt.xlabel('Entries')
plt.ylabel('Values')
plt.plot(range(1,11), values)
plt.show()
```

The call to xlabel() documents the x axis of your graph, while the call the ylabel() documents the y axis of your graph. Figure 10-7 shows the output of this example.

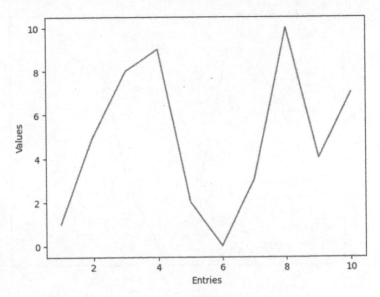

FIGURE 10-7:
Use labels to
identify the axes.

Annotating the chart

You use annotation to draw special attention to points of interest on a graph. For example, you may want to point out that a specific data point is outside the usual range expected for a particular dataset. The following example shows how to add annotation to a graph:

```
import matplotlib.pyplot as plt
%matplotlib inline

values = [1, 5, 8, 9, 2, 0, 3, 10, 4, 7]
plt.annotate(xy=[1,1], text='First Entry')
plt.plot(range(1,11), values)
plt.show()
```

The call to annotate() provides the labeling you need. You must provide a location for the annotation by using the xy parameter, as well as provide text to place at the location by using the text parameter. The annotate() function also provides other parameters that you can use to create special formatting or placement onscreen. Figure 10-8 shows the output from this example.

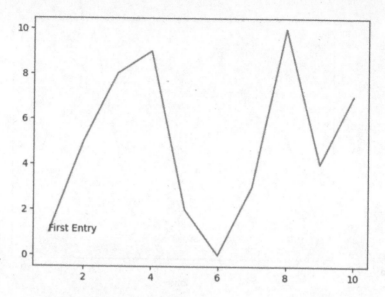

FIGURE 10-8:
Annotation can
identify points of
interest.

Creating a legend

A legend documents the individual elements of a plot. Each line is presented in a table that contains a label for it so that people can differentiate between each line. For example, one line may represent sales for one year and another line may represent sales during the next year, so you include an entry in the legend for each line that is labeled with the years. The following example shows how to add a legend to your plot.

```
import matplotlib.pyplot as plt
%matplotlib inline

values = [1, 5, 8, 9, 2, 0, 3, 10, 4, 7]
values2 = [3, 8, 9, 2, 1, 2, 4, 7, 6, 6]
line1 = plt.plot(range(1,11), values)
line2 = plt.plot(range(1,11), values2)
plt.legend(['First', 'Second'], loc=4)
plt.show()
```

The call to legend() occurs after you create the plots, not before, as with some of the other functions described in this chapter. The call contains a list of the labels you want to use in the order of the plots you generate. So, 'First' is associated with line1, and 'Second' is associated with line2.

The default location for the legend is the upper-right corner of the plot, which proved inconvenient for this particular example. Adding the `loc` parameter lets you place the legend in a different location. See the `legend()` function documentation at `https://matplotlib.org/2.0.2/api/pyplot_api.html#matplotlib.pyplot.figlegend` for additional legend locations. Figure 10-9 shows the output from this example.

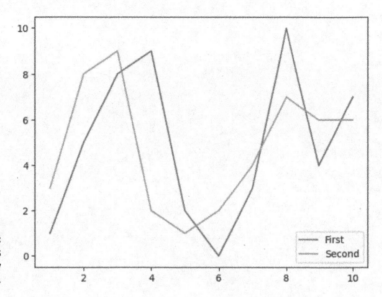

FIGURE 10-9:
Use legends to identify individual lines.

Chapter **11**

Visualizing the Data

Chapter 10 helps you understand the mechanics of working with Matplotlib, which is an important first step toward using it. This chapter takes the next step in helping you use Matplotlib to perform useful work. The main goal of this chapter is to help you visualize your data in various ways. Creating a graphic presentation of your data is essential if you want to help other people understand what you're trying to say. Even though you can see what the numbers mean in your mind, other people will likely need graphics to see what point you're trying to make by manipulating data in various ways.

The chapter starts by looking at some basic graph types that Matplotlib supports. You don't find the full list of graphs and plots listed in this chapter — it could take an entire book to explore them all in detail. However, you do find the most common types.

In the remainder of the chapter, you begin exploring specific sorts of plotting as it relates to data science. Of course, no book on data science would be complete without exploring scatterplots, which are used to help people see patterns in seemingly unrelated data points. Because much of the data that you work with today is time related or geographic in nature, the chapter devotes two special sections to these topics. You also get to work with both directed and undirected graphs, which is fine for social media analysis.

REMEMBER

You don't have to type the source code for this chapter; in fact, using the downloadable source is a lot easier. The source code for this chapter appears in the P4DS4D3_11_Visualizing_the_Data.ipynb (see the Introduction for details on how to find that source file).

Choosing the Right Graph

The kind of graph you choose determines how people view the associated data, so choosing the right graph from the outset is important. For example, when you want people to form opinions on how data elements compare through the use of precise counts, you use a bar chart. The idea is to choose a graph that naturally leads people to draw the conclusion that you need them to draw about the data that you've carefully massaged from various data sources. (You also have the option of using line graphs — a technique demonstrated in Chapter 10.) The following sections describe the various graph types and provide you with basic examples of how to use them.

Creating comparisons with bar charts

Bar charts make comparing values easy. The wide bars and segregated measurements emphasize the differences between values, rather than the flow of one value to another as a line graph would do. Fortunately, you have all sorts of methods at your disposal for emphasizing specific values and performing other tricks. The following example shows just some of the things you can do with a vertical bar chart:

```
import matplotlib.pyplot as plt
%matplotlib inline

values = [5, 8, 9, 10, 4, 7]
widths = [0.7, 0.8, 0.7, 0.7, 0.7, 0.7]
colors = ['b', 'r', 'b', 'b', 'b', 'b']
plt.bar(range(0, 6), values, width=widths,
        color=colors, align='center')

plt.show()
```

To create even a basic bar chart, you must provide a series of x coordinates and the heights of the bars. The example uses the range() function to create the x coordinates, and values contains the heights.

Of course, you may want more than a basic bar chart, and Matplotlib provides a number of ways to get the job done. In this case, the example uses the width parameter to control the width of each bar, emphasizing the second bar by making it slightly larger. The larger width would show up even in a black-and-white printout. It also uses the color parameter to change the color of the target bar to red (the rest are blue).

As with other chart types, the bar chart provides some special features that you can use to make your presentation stand out. The example uses the align parameter to center the data on the x coordinate (the standard position is to the left). You can also use other parameters, such as hatch, to enhance the visual appearance of your bar chart. Figure 11-1 shows the output of this example.

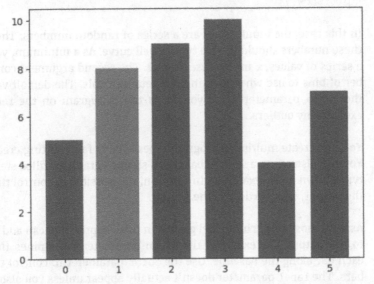

FIGURE 11-1:
Bar charts make it easier to perform comparisons.

This chapter helps you get started using Matplotlib to create a variety of chart and graph types. Of course, more examples are better, so you can also find some more advanced examples on the Matplotlib site at https://matplotlib.org/stable/gallery/index.html. Some of the examples, such as those that demonstrate animation techniques, become quite advanced, but with practice you can use any of them to improve your own charts and graphs.

Showing distributions using histograms

Histograms categorize data by breaking it into *bins*, where each bin contains a subset of the data range. A histogram then displays the number of items in each bin so that you can see the distribution of data and the progression of data from bin to bin. In most cases, you see a curve of some type, such as a bell curve. The following example shows how to create a histogram with randomized data:

```
import numpy as np
import matplotlib.pyplot as plt
%matplotlib inline
```

```
x = 20 * np.random.randn(10000)

plt.hist(x, 25, range=(-50, 50), histtype='stepfilled',
         align='mid', color='g', label='Test Data')
plt.legend()
plt.title('Step Filled Histogram')
plt.show()
```

In this case, the input values are a series of random numbers. The distribution of these numbers should show a type of bell curve. As a minimum, you must provide a series of values, x in this case, to plot. The second argument contains the number of bins to use when creating the data intervals. The default value is 10. Using the range parameter helps you focus the histogram on the relevant data and exclude any outliers.

You can create multiple histogram types. The default setting creates a bar chart. You can also create a stacked bar chart, stepped graph, or filled stepped graph (the type shown in the example). In addition, it's possible to control the orientation of the output, with vertical as the default.

As with most other charts and graphs in this chapter, you can add special features to the output. For example, the align parameter determines the alignment of each bar along the baseline. Use the color parameter to control the colors of the bars. The label parameter doesn't actually appear unless you also create a legend (as shown in this example). Figure 11-2 shows typical output from this example.

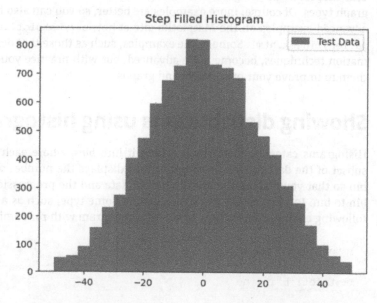

FIGURE 11-2: Histograms let you see distributions of numbers.

REMEMBER

Random data varies call by call. Every time you run the example, you see slightly different results because the random-generation process differs.

Depicting groups using boxplots

Boxplots provide a means of depicting groups of numbers through their *quartiles* (three points dividing a group into four equal parts). A boxplot may also have lines, called *whiskers*, indicating data outside the upper and lower quartiles. The spacing shown within a boxplot helps indicate the skew and dispersion of the data. The following example shows how to create a boxplot with randomized data:

```
import numpy as np
import matplotlib.pyplot as plt
%matplotlib inline

spread = 100 * np.random.rand(100)
center = np.ones(50) * 50
flier_high = 100 * np.random.rand(10) + 100
flier_low = -100 * np.random.rand(10)
data = np.concatenate((spread, center,
                       flier_high, flier_low))

plt.boxplot(data, sym='gx', widths=.75, notch=True)
plt.show()
```

To create a usable dataset, you need to combine several different number-generation techniques, as shown at the beginning of the example. Here's how these techniques work:

>> spread: Contains a set of random numbers between 0 and 100

>> center: Provides 50 values directly in the center of the range of 50

>> flier_high: Simulates outliers between 100 and 200

>> flier_low: Simulates outliers between 0 and –100

The code combines all these values into a single dataset using concatenate(). Being randomly generated with specific characteristics (such as a large number of points in the middle), the output will show specific characteristics but will work fine for the example.

The call to boxplot() requires only data as input. All other parameters have default settings. In this case, the code sets the presentation of outliers to green Xs by setting the sym parameter. You use widths to modify the size of the box (made extra-large in this case to make the box easier to see). Finally, you can create a square box or a box with a notch using the notch parameter (which normally defaults to False). Figure 11-3 shows typical output from this example.

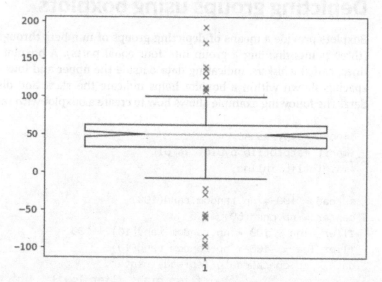

The box shows the three data points as the box, with the red line in the middle being the median. The two black horizontal lines connected to the box by whiskers show the upper and lower limits (for four quartiles). The outliers appear above and below the upper and lower limit lines as green Xs.

Seeing data patterns using scatterplots

Scatterplots show clusters of data rather than trends (as with line graphs) or discrete values (as with bar charts). The purpose of a scatterplot is to help you see multidimensional data patterns. The following example shows how to create a scatterplot using randomized data:

```
import numpy as np
import matplotlib.pyplot as plt
%matplotlib inline


x1 = 5 * np.random.rand(40)
x2 = 5 * np.random.rand(40) + 25
x3 = 25 * np.random.rand(20)
x = np.concatenate((x1, x2, x3))
```

```
y1 = 5 * np.random.rand(40)
y2 = 5 * np.random.rand(40) + 25
y3 = 25 * np.random.rand(20)
y = np.concatenate((y1, y2, y3))

plt.scatter(x, y, s=[100], marker='^', c='m')
plt.show()
```

The example begins by generating random x and y coordinates. For each x coordinate, you must have a corresponding y coordinate. It's possible to create a scatterplot using just the x and y coordinates.

You can dress up a scatterplot in a number of ways. In this case, the s parameter determines the size of each data point. The marker parameter determines the data point shape. You use the c parameter to define the colors for all the data points, or you can define a separate color for individual data points. Figure 11-4 shows the output from this example.

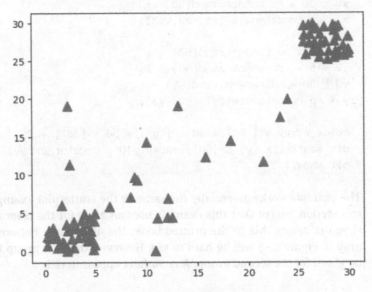

FIGURE 11-4:
Use scatterplots to show groups of data points and their associated patterns.

Creating Advanced Scatterplots

Scatterplots are especially important for data science because they can show data patterns that aren't obvious when viewed in other ways. You can see data groupings with relative ease and help the viewer understand when data belongs to a particular group. You can also show overlaps between groups and even demonstrate when certain data is outside the expected range. Showing these various kinds of relationships in the data is an advanced technique that you need to know in order to make the best use of Matplotlib. The following sections demonstrate how to perform these advanced techniques on the scatterplot you created earlier in the chapter.

Depicting groups

Color is the third axis when working with a scatterplot. Using color lets you highlight groups so that others can see them with greater ease. The following example shows how you can use color to show groups within a scatterplot:

```
import numpy as np
import matplotlib.pyplot as plt
%matplotlib inline

x1 = 5 * np.random.rand(50)
x2 = 5 * np.random.rand(50) + 25
x3 = 30 * np.random.rand(25)
x = np.concatenate((x1, x2, x3))

y1 = 5 * np.random.rand(50)
y2 = 5 * np.random.rand(50) + 25
y3 = 30 * np.random.rand(25)
y = np.concatenate((y1, y2, y3))

color_array = ['b'] * 50 + ['g'] * 50 + ['r'] * 25
plt.scatter(x, y, s=[50], marker='D', c=color_array)
plt.show()
```

The example works essentially the same as the scatterplot example in the previous section, except that this example uses an array for the colors. Unfortunately, if you're seeing this in the printed book, the differences between the shades of gray in Figure 11-5 will be hard to see. However, the first group is blue, followed by green for the second group. Any outliers appear in red.

Showing correlations

In some cases, you need to know the general direction that your data is taking when looking at a scatterplot. Even if you create a clear depiction of the groups, the actual direction that the data is taking as a whole may not be clear. In this case, you add a trendline to the output. Here's an example of adding a trendline to a scatterplot that includes groups whose data points aren't as clearly separated as in the scatterplot shown previously in Figure 11-5:

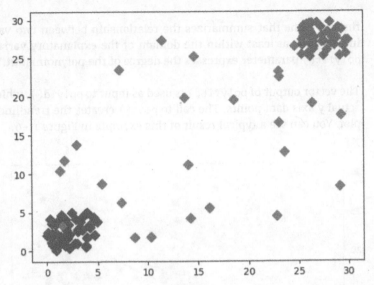

FIGURE 11-5:
Color arrays can
make the
scatterplot
groups stand
out better.

```
import numpy as np
import matplotlib.pyplot as plt
import matplotlib.pylab as plb
%matplotlib inline

x1 = 15 * np.random.rand(50)
x2 = 15 * np.random.rand(50) + 15
x3 = 30 * np.random.rand(25)
x = np.concatenate((x1, x2, x3))

y1 = 15 * np.random.rand(50)
y2 = 15 * np.random.rand(50) + 15
y3 = 30 * np.random.rand(25)
y = np.concatenate((y1, y2, y3))

color_array = ['b'] * 50 + ['g'] * 50 + ['r'] * 25
plt.scatter(x, y, s=[90], marker='*', c=color_array)
z = np.polyfit(x, y, 1)
p = np.poly1d(z)
plb.plot(x, p(x), 'm-')
plt.show()
```

The code for creating the scatterplot is essentially the same as in the example in
the "Depicting groups" section, earlier in the chapter, but the plot doesn't
define the groups as clearly. Adding a trendline means calling the NumPy
polyfit() function with the data, which returns a vector of coefficients, p, that
minimizes the least-squares error. (Least-square regression is a method for

finding a line that summarizes the relationship between two variables, x and y in this case, at least within the domain of the explanatory variable x. The third `polyfit()` parameter expresses the degree of the polynomial fit.)

The vector output of `polyfit()` is used as input to `poly1d()`, which calculates the actual y axis data points. The call to `plot()` creates the trendline on the scatterplot. You can see a typical result of this example in Figure 11-6.

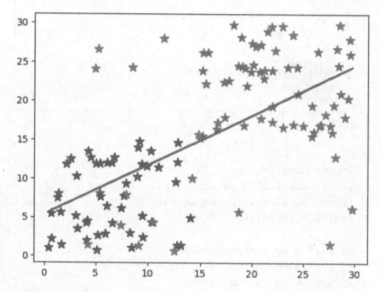

FIGURE 11-6:
Scatterplot trendlines can show you the general data direction.

Plotting Time Series

Nothing is truly static. When you view most data, you see an instant of time — a snapshot of how the data appeared at one particular moment. Of course, such views are both common and useful. However, sometimes you need to view data as it moves through time — to see it as it changes. Only by viewing the data as it changes can you expect to understand the underlying forces that shape it. The following sections describe how to work with data on a time-related basis.

Representing time on axes

Many times, you need to present data over time. The data could come in many forms, but generally you have some type of time tick (one unit of time), followed by one or more features that describe what happens during that particular tick. The following example shows a simple set of days and sales on those days for a particular item in whole (integer) amounts.

```
import pandas as pd
import matplotlib.pyplot as plt
import datetime as dt
%matplotlib inline

start_date = dt.datetime(2023, 7, 29)
end_date = dt.datetime(2023, 8, 7)
daterange = pd.date_range(start_date, end_date)
sales = (np.random.rand(
    len(daterange)) * 50).astype(int)
df = pd.DataFrame(sales, index=daterange,
                  columns=['Sales'])
print(df)
```

The example begins by specifying the start_date and end_date, then using them to create daterange, the range of dates used for the output. It then creates a series of random values to use as data points and places them in sales. The number of values must match the length for daterange and normally you'd rely on actual data. The next step is to create a DataFrame to hold the information using daterange as an index and the values in sales as the data. So, what you end up with is a table of dates and associated values similar to this (the data values you see will vary):

```
            Sales
2023-07-29    14
2023-07-30    47
2023-07-31    17
2023-08-01     4
2023-08-02    38
2023-08-03    18
2023-08-04     0
2023-08-05    25
2023-08-06     9
2023-08-07     2
```

Now that you have some properly formatted data to use, it's time to create a plot. The following code shows a typical method of plotting data in the DataFrame format shown previously:

```
df.loc['Jul 30 2023':'Aug 05 2023'].plot()
plt.ylim(0, 50)
plt.xlabel('Sales Date')
plt.ylabel('Sale Value')
plt.title('Plotting Time')
plt.show()
```

Using df.loc accesses rows and columns in a DataFrame using labels, which are dates in string format in this case. So, the resulting plot won't show all of the data in df, it will instead show just the data from 'Jul 30 2023' to 'Aug 05 2023'. The call to plot() creates a line graph containing the requested data. The rest of the code provides various formatting and labeling features for the plot, which is then displayed using plt.show(). Figure 11-7 shows the result.

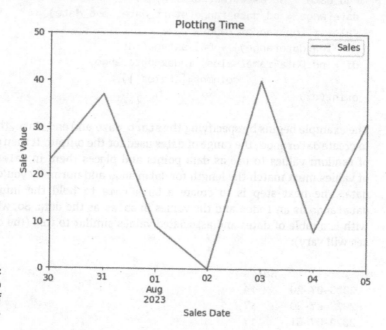

FIGURE 11-7: Use line graphs to show the flow of data over time.

Plotting trends over time

As with any other data presentation, sometimes you really can't see what direction the data is headed in without help. The following example starts with the plot from the previous section and adds a trendline to it:

```
import numpy as np
import pandas as pd
import matplotlib.pyplot as plt
import datetime as dt
%matplotlib inline

start_date = dt.datetime(2023, 7, 29)
end_date = dt.datetime(2023, 8, 7)
daterange = pd.date_range(start_date, end_date)
sales = (np.random.rand(
```

```
    len(daterange)) * 50).astype(int)
df = pd.DataFrame(sales, index=daterange,
                columns=['Sales'])

lr_coef = np.polyfit(range(0, len(df)), df['Sales'], 1)
lr_func = np.poly1d(lr_coef)
trend = lr_func(range(0, len(df)))
df['trend'] = trend
df.loc['Jul 30 2023':'Aug 05 2023'].plot()

plt.xlabel('Sales Date')
plt.ylabel('Sale Value')
plt.title('Plotting Time')
plt.legend(['Sales', 'Trend'])
plt.show()
```

REMEMBER

The "Showing correlations" section, earlier in this chapter, shows how most people add a trendline to their graph. In fact, this is the approach that you often see used online. You'll also notice that a lot of people have trouble using this approach in some situations. This example takes a slightly different approach by adding the trendline directly to the DataFrame. If you print df after the call to df['trend'] = trend, you see trendline data similar to the values shown here:

```
              Sales        trend
2023-07-29       41    28.181818
2023-07-30        6    26.896970
2023-07-31       14    25.612121
2023-08-01       29    24.327273
2023-08-02       46    23.042424
2023-08-03       14    21.757576
2023-08-04       33    20.472727
2023-08-05        6    19.187879
2023-08-06       28    17.903030
2023-08-07        7    16.618182
```

Using this approach makes it ultimately easier to plot the data. You call plot() only once and avoid relying on the matplotlib.pylab function shown in the example in the "Showing correlations" section.

When you plot the initial data, the call to plot() automatically generates a legend for you. Matplotlib doesn't automatically add the trendline, so you must also create a new legend for the plot. Figure 11-8 shows typical output from this example using randomly generated data.

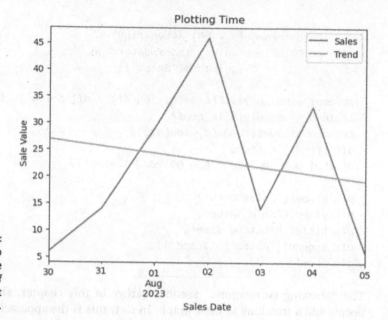

Plotting Time

FIGURE 11-8:
Add a trendline to
show the average
direction of
change in a chart
or graph.

Plotting Geographical Data

Knowing where data comes from or how it applies to a specific place can be important. For example, if you want to know where food shortages have occurred and
plan how to deal with them, you need to match the data you have to geographical
locations. The same holds true for predicting where future sales will occur. You
may find that you need to use existing data to determine where to put new stores.
Otherwise, you could put a store in a location that won't receive much in the way
of sales, and the effort will lose money rather than make it. The following sections
describe how to work with Cartopy (https://pypi.org/project/Cartopy/) to
interact with geographical data.

WARNING

You must shut the Notebook environment down before you make any changes to
it or else conda will complain that some files are in use. To shut the Notebook
environment down, close and halt the kernel for any Notebook files you have open
and then click Quit in the Jupyter page or press Ctrl+C in the Notebook terminal
window. Wait a few seconds to give the files time to close properly before you
attempt to do anything.

**TECHNICAL
STUFF**

If you're working with Google Colab, you can skip the process of creating an environment described in the "Using an environment in Notebook" section that follows. All you need to do is add a cell at the beginning of the downloadable source
that contains a single line: !pip install Cartopy and run it every time you want
to use Cartopy. Although this means having to reinstall Cartopy before every use,
it does simplify the initial setup somewhat.

Using an environment in Notebook

Some of the packages you install have a tendency to also change your Notebook environment by installing other packages that may not work well with your baseline setup. Consequently, you see problems with code that functioned earlier. Normally, these problems consist mostly of warning messages, such as deprecation warnings as discussed in the "Avoiding outdated libraries: The Basemap Toolkit" section, later in this chapter. The "Warning Messages in Jupyter Notebook Example Code" blog post at `http://blog.johnmuellerbooks.com/2023/05/08/warning-messages-in-jupyter-notebook-example-code/` also provides helpful information about the potential for warning messages in Jupyter Notebooks.

In some cases, however, the changed packages can also tweak the output you obtain from code. Perhaps a newer package uses an updated algorithm or interacts with the code differently. When you have a package, such as Cartopy, that makes changes to the overall baseline configuration and you want to maintain your current configuration, you need to set up an environment for it. An environment keeps your baseline configuration intact but also allows the new package to create the environment it needs to execute properly. The following steps help you create the Cartopy environment used for this chapter:

1. **Open an Anaconda Prompt.**

   Notice that the prompt shows the location of your folder on your system, but that it's preceded by (base). The (base) indicator tells you that you're in your baseline environment — the one you want to preserve.

2. **Type** conda create -n Cartopy python=3.10 anaconda=2023.03 **and press Enter.**

   This action creates a new Cartopy environment. This new environment will use Python 3.10 and Anaconda 2023.03-1. You get precisely the same baseline as you've been using so far.

3. **Type** y **and press Enter when asked if you want to proceed.**

   The installation process begins. This process can take a while to complete, especially when the software needs to download packages from online, so you need to be patient.

4. **Type** conda activate Cartopy **and press Enter.**

   You have now changed over to the Cartopy environment. Notice that the prompt no longer says (base); it says (Cartopy) instead.

5. **Type** conda install -c conda-forge cartopy **and press Enter to install your copy of Cartopy.**

6. **Type** y **and press Enter when asked if you want to proceed.**

   The installation process begins.

7. **(Optional) After the installation, make sure you're in your Notebooks directory using a command such as** cd \Users\John\Anaconda Projects **(for Windows developers).**

8. **Type** Jupyter Notebook **and press Enter.**

You see Notebook start, but it uses the Cartopy environment, rather than the (base) environment. This copy of Notebook works precisely the same as any other copy of Notebook that you've used. The only difference is the environment in which it operates.

REMEMBER

This same technique works for any special package that you want to install. You should reserve it for packages that you don't intend to use every day. For example, this book uses Cartopy for just one example, so creating an environment for it is appropriate.

After you have finished using the Cartopy environment, press Ctrl+C to stop the server, type **conda deactivate** at the prompt, and press Enter. You see the prompt change back to (base).

Using Cartopy to plot geographic data

Now that you have a good installation of Cartopy, you can do something with it. To start with, you need to import all the required packages:

```
import numpy as np
import matplotlib.pyplot as plt
import matplotlib.ticker as mticker
import cartopy.crs as ccrs
import cartopy
from cartopy.mpl.gridliner import \
    LONGITUDE_FORMATTER, LATITUDE_FORMATTER
%matplotlib inline
```

These various packages let you download the map, format it, and add points of interest to it. The following example shows how to draw a map and place pointers to specific locations on it:

```
austin = (-97.75, 30.25)
hawaii = (-157.8, 21.3)
washington = (-77.01, 38.90)
chicago = (-87.68, 41.83)
losangeles = (-118.25, 34.05)

ax = plt.axes(projection=ccrs.Mercator(
    central_longitude=-110))
```

```
ax.coastlines()
ax.set_extent([-60, -160, 50, 10],
              crs=ccrs.PlateCarree())

ax.add_feature(cartopy.feature.OCEAN, zorder=0,
               facecolor='aqua')
ax.add_feature(cartopy.feature.LAND, zorder=0,
               edgecolor='black', facecolor='lightgray')
ax.add_feature(cartopy.feature.LAKES, zorder=0,
               edgecolor='black', facecolor='lightblue')
ax.add_feature(cartopy.feature.BORDERS, zorder=0,
               edgecolor='gray')

x, y = list(zip(*[austin, hawaii, washington,
                  chicago, losangeles]))

gl = ax.gridlines(
    crs=ccrs.PlateCarree(), draw_labels=True,
    linewidth=2, color='gray', alpha=0.5,
    linestyle='--')
gl.xlabels_top = False
gl.left_labels = False
gl.xlocator = mticker.FixedLocator(list(x))
gl.ylocator = mticker.FixedLocator(list(y))
gl.xformatter = LONGITUDE_FORMATTER
gl.yformatter = LATITUDE_FORMATTER

ax.plot(x, y, 'ro', markersize=6,
        transform=ccrs.Geodetic())

plt.title("Mercator Projection")
plt.show()
```

The example begins by defining the longitude and latitude for various cities. It then creates the basic map. The `projection` parameter defines the basic map appearance. You can find a listing of projection types at https://scitools. org.uk/cartopy/docs/v0.15/crs/projections.html. The `central_longitude` parameter defines where the map is centered. To see the coastlines of the various countries, you use the `coastlines()` method. This example doesn't look at the whole world, so it uses the `set_extent()` method to crop the map to size.

The example uses the `add_feature()` to add features to the basic map. You can color the features in various ways to provide a distinctive look for your map. The features are documented more fully at https://scitools.org.uk/cartopy/docs/v0.14/matplotlib/feature_interface.html.

In this case, the example creates x and y coordinates using the previously stored longitude and latitude values. As part of displaying the coordinates, the map also creates gridlines to show their longitude and latitude with the gridlines() method. The resulting object, gl, allows you to modify the grid characteristics. The documentation at https://scitools.org.uk/cartopy/docs/v0.13/matplotlib/gridliner.html tells you more about working with gridlines.

The code then plots these locations on the map in a contrasting color so that you can easily see them. The final step is to display the map, as shown in Figure 11-9.

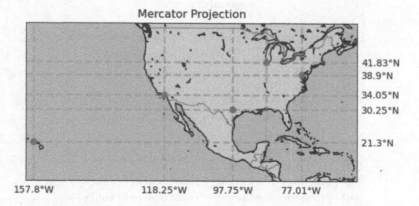

FIGURE 11-9:
Maps can illustrate data in ways other graphics can't.

Avoiding outdated libraries: The Basemap Toolkit

The previous edition of this book used Basemap to provide geographic presentation support because it was one of the better products available at the time. However, in reading the message thread at https://github.com/matplotlib/basemap/issues/267, you find that Basemap isn't going to be maintained for a number of reasons, so this edition of the book has moved to Cartopy, a decision based partly on the suggestion of the Basemap creator. Unfortunately, this situation happens way too often with Python developers, and it can present problems if you're working in a production environment under significant deadlines. It isn't that Basemap or any of these other packages are ill-conceived or that the code owners simply don't care; it's the fact that maintaining any package is a lot of work. With these realities in mind, here are some useful tips for avoiding outdated libraries:

» Wait until the package has been around for a while before you use it in a production environment.

» Ensure that the package has broad community support.

>> Look for packages that are created by groups rather than just a few individuals.

>> Try to verify that the package creator will stay around to support the package in the long run.

>> Monitor new releases and updates to determine the sorts of features and bug fixes that the code owner is providing.

>> Check to see whether the code owner is responsive to user queries about upgrades, product features, bugs, and usage requirements.

Visualizing Graphs

A *graph* (in the network sense of the word) is a depiction of data showing the connections between data points (called *nodes*) using lines (called *edges*). The purpose is to show that some data points relate to other data points, but not all the data points that appear on the graph. Think about a map of a subway system. Each of the stations connects to other stations, but no single station connects to all the stations in the subway system. Graphs are a popular data science topic because of their use in social media analysis. When performing social media analysis, you depict and analyze networks of relationships, such as friends or business connections, from social hubs such as Facebook, Google+, Twitter, or LinkedIn.

REMEMBER

The two common depictions of graphs are *undirected*, where the graph simply shows lines between data elements, and *directed*, where arrows added to the line show that data flows in a particular direction. For example, consider a depiction of a water system. The water would flow in just one direction in most cases, so you could use a directed graph to depict not only the connections between sources and targets for the water but also to show water direction by using arrows. The following sections help you understand the two types of graphs better and show you how to create them.

Developing undirected graphs

As previously stated, an undirected graph simply shows connections between nodes. The output doesn't provide a direction from one node to the next. For example, when establishing connectivity between web pages, no direction is implied. The following example shows how to create an undirected graph:

```
import networkx as nx
import matplotlib.pyplot as plt
%matplotlib inline
```

```
G = nx.Graph()
H = nx.Graph()
G.add_node(1)
G.add_nodes_from([2, 3])
G.add_nodes_from(range(4, 7))
H.add_node(7)
G.add_nodes_from(H)

G.add_edge(1, 2)
G.add_edge(1, 1)
G.add_edges_from([(2,3), (3,6), (4,6), (5,6)])
H.add_edges_from([(4,7), (5,7), (6,7)])
G.add_edges_from(H.edges())

nx.draw_networkx(G, node_color='yellow')
plt.show()
```

In contrast to the canned example found in the "Using NetworkX basics" section of Chapter 8, this example builds the graph using a number of different techniques. It begins by importing the Networkx package you use in Chapter 8. To create a new undirected graph, the code calls the Graph() constructor, which can take a number of input arguments to use as attributes. However, you can build a perfectly usable graph without using attributes, which is what this example does.

The easiest way to add a node is to call add_node() with a node number. You can also add a list, dictionary, or range() of nodes using add_nodes_from(). In fact, you can import nodes from other graphs if you want.

REMEMBER

Even though the nodes used in the example rely on numbers, you don't have to use numbers for your nodes. A node can use a single letter, a string, or even a date. Nodes do have some restrictions. For example, you can't create a node using a Boolean value.

Nodes don't have any connectivity at the outset. You must define connections (edges) between them. To add a single edge, you call add_edge() with the numbers of the nodes that you want to add. As with nodes, you can use add_edges_from() to create more than one edge using a list, dictionary, or another graph as input. Figure 11-10 shows the output from this example. (Your output may differ slightly but should have the same connections.)

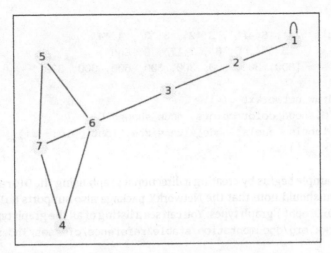

FIGURE 11-10:
Undirected
graphs connect
nodes to form
patterns.

Developing directed graphs

You use directed graphs when you need to show a direction, say from a start point to an end point. When you get a map that shows you how to get from one specific point to another, the starting node and ending node are marked as such, and the lines between these nodes (and all the intermediate nodes) show direction.

TIP

Your graphs need not be boring. You can dress them up in all sorts of ways so that the viewer gains additional information in different ways. For example, you can create custom labels, use specific colors for certain nodes, or rely on color to help people see the meaning behind your graphs. You can also change edge line weight and use other techniques to mark a specific path between nodes as the better one to choose. The following example shows many (but not nearly all) the ways in which you can dress up a directed graph and make it more interesting:

```
import networkx as nx
import matplotlib.pyplot as plt
%matplotlib inline

G = nx.DiGraph()

G.add_node(1)
G.add_nodes_from([2, 3])
G.add_nodes_from(range(4, 9))

G.add_edge(1, 2)
G.add_edges_from([(1,4), (4,5), (2,3), (3,6),
                  (5,6), (6,7), (7,8)])

colors = ['r', 'g', 'g', 'g', 'g', 'm', 'm', 'r']
```

```
labels = {1:'Start', 2:'2', 3:'3', 4:'4',
          5:'5', 6:'6', 7:'7', 8:'End'}
sizes = [800, 300, 300, 300, 300, 600, 300, 800]

nx.draw_networkx(
    G, node_color=colors, node_shape='D',
    labels=labels, node_size=sizes, font_color='w')
plt.show()
```

The example begins by creating a directional graph using the DiGraph() construc-tor. You should note that the NetworkX package also supports MultiGraph() and MultiDiGraph() graph types. You can see a listing of all the graph types at https://networkx.org/documentation/stable/reference/classes/index.html.

Adding nodes is much like working with an undirected graph. You can add single nodes using add_node() and multiple nodes using add_nodes_from(). The order of nodes in the call is important. The flow from one node to another is from left to right in the list supplied to the call.

REMEMBER

Adding edges is much the same as working with an undirected graph, too. You can use add_edge() to add a single edge or add_edges_from() to add multiple edges at one time. However, the order of the node numbers is important. The flow goes from the left node to the right node in each pair.

This example adds special node colors, labels, shape (only one shape is used), and sizes to the output. You still call on draw_networkx() to perform the task. However, adding the parameters shown changes the appearance of the graph. Figure 11-11 shows the output from this example.

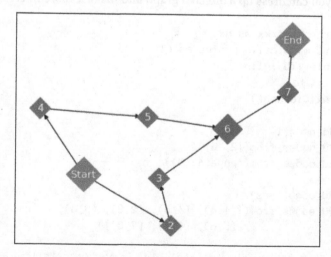

FIGURE 11-11: Use directed graphs to show direction between nodes.

4

Wrangling Data

Chapter **12**

Stretching Python's Capabilities

I f you've gone through the previous chapters, by this point you've dealt with all the basic data loading and manipulation methods offered by Python. Now it's time to begin utilizing some more advanced instruments for data transformation and pipelining in machine learning. The final step of most data science projects is to build a data tool able to automatically transform, predict, and recommend directly from your data.

Before taking that final step, you still have to process your data by enforcing transformations that are even more radical. That's the *data wrangling* or *data munging* part, where sophisticated transformations are followed by visual and statistical explorations, and then, eventually, by further transformations, if your explorations have pointed out something interesting to pursue.

From here onward, you use the Scikit-learn package more (which means knowing more about it — the full documentation appears at https://scikit-learn.org/ stable/documentation.html). The Scikit-learn package offers a single repository containing almost all the tools that you need to be a data scientist and for your data science project to be successful. In this chapter, you discover important characteristics of Scikit-learn, how it is structured in modules, classes, and functions, and some advanced Python time savers for improving performance with highly time-consuming data and computational operations.

REMEMBER

You don't have to type the source code for this chapter in by hand; in fact, using the downloadable source is a lot easier (see the Introduction for download instructions). The source code for this chapter appears in the P4DS4D3_12_Stretching_Pythons_Capabilities.ipynb file.

Playing with Scikit-learn

Sometimes the best way to discover how to use something is to spend time playing with it. The more complex a tool, the more important play becomes. Given the complex math tasks you perform using Scikit-learn, playing becomes especially important. The following sections use the idea of playing with Scikit-learn to help you discover important concepts in using Scikit-learn to perform amazing feats of data science work.

Understanding classes in Scikit-learn

Understanding how classes work is an important prerequisite for being able to use the Scikit-learn package appropriately. Scikit-learn is the package for machine learning and data science experimentation favored by most data scientists. It contains a wide range of well-established learning algorithms, error functions, and testing procedures.

At its core, Scikit-learn features some base classes on which all the algorithms are built. Apart from BaseEstimator, the class from which all other classes inherit, there are four class types covering all the basic machine-learning functionalities:

» Classifying (ClassifierMixin)

» Regressing (RegressorMixin)

» Grouping by clusters (ClusterMixin)

» Transforming data (TransformerMixin)

Even though each base class has specific methods and attributes, the core functionalities for data processing and machine learning are guaranteed by one or more series of methods and attributes called interfaces. The interfaces provide a uniform Application Programming Interface (API) to enforce similarity of methods and attributes between all the different algorithms present in the package. There are four Scikit-learn object-based interfaces:

>> estimator: For fitting parameters by learning them from data according to the algorithm

>> predictor: For generating predictions from the fitted parameters

>> transformer: For transforming data, implementing the fitted parameters

>> model: For reporting goodness of fit or other score measures

The package groups the algorithms built on base classes and one or more object interfaces into modules, each module displaying a specialization in a particular type of machine-learning solution. For example, the linear_model module is for linear modeling, and metrics is for score and loss measure.

To find a specific algorithm in Scikit-learn, you must first find the module containing the same kind of algorithm that interests you, and then select it from the list of contents of the module. The algorithm is typically a class whose methods and attributes are already known because they're common to other algorithms in Scikit-learn.

TIP

Getting accustomed to the Scikit-learn class approach may take some time. However, the API is the same for all the tools available in the package, so learning one class necessarily tells you about all the other classes. The best approach is to learn one class completely and then apply what you know to other classes.

Defining applications for data science

Figuring out ways to use data science to obtain constructive results is important. For example, you can apply the estimator interface to a

>> **Classification problem:** Guessing that a new observation is from a certain group

>> **Regression problem:** Guessing the value of a new observation

It works with the method fit(X, y) where X is the bidimensional array of predictors (the set of observations to learn) and y is the target outcome (another array, unidimensional).

When you apply fit() to the data, the information in X is related to y, so that when you have some new information with the same characteristics of X, it's possible to guess y correctly. In the process, some parameters are estimated internally by the fit() method. These are the model weights, which the model learned from data. In addition, hyperparameters are other parameters that affect how the model learns its weights. They aren't directly derived from data but are decided by you, using trial and error, when you instantiate the learner.

Instantiation involves assigning a Scikit-learn class to a Python variable. In addition to hyperparameters, you can also fix other working parameters, such as requiring normalization or setting a seed (which is normally a random value) to reproduce the same results for each call, given the same input data.

Here is an example with linear regression, a very basic and common machine learning algorithm. You upload some data to use this example from the examples that Scikit-learn provides. The California dataset, for instance, contains predictor variables that the example code can match against house prices, which helps build a predictor that can calculate the value of a house in an area, given its characteristics and location in the state of California:

```
import numpy as np
import pandas as pd
from sklearn.datasets import fetch_california_housing

def load_california_housing_data():
    dataset = fetch_california_housing()
    X = pd.DataFrame(data=dataset.data,
                     columns=dataset.feature_names)
    y = pd.Series(data=dataset.target, name="target")
    return X, y

X, y = load_california_housing_data()
print(f"X:{X.shape} y:{y.shape}")
```

The returned dimensions for the X and y variables are

```
X:(20640, 8) y:(20640,)
```

The output specifies that both arrays have the same number of rows and that X has 8 features. The shape() method performs array analysis and reports the arrays' dimensions.

TIP

The number of X rows must equal those in y. You also ensure that X and y correspond, because learning from data happens when the algorithm matches the rows of X with the corresponding element of y. If you randomize the two arrays, no learning is possible.

REMEMBER

The characteristics of X, expressed as X's columns, are called *variables* (a more statistical term) or *features* (a term more related to machine learning).

The transform class in Scikit-learn applies transformations derived from the fitting phase to other data arrays. All preprocessing algorithms do have a transformation method. For example, StandardScaler(), from the Scikit-learn preprocessing module, can transform values using the statistical normalization, that is, subtracting the mean and dividing by the standard deviation, after learning the transformation parameters from an example array using the fit() method:

```
from sklearn.preprocessing import StandardScaler

scaler = StandardScaler()
scaler.fit(X)
scaled_X = scaler.transform(X)
```

After importing the LinearRegression class, you can instantiate a variable called linear_regression and fit it to the scaled X array and to the y target. After fitting, you inspect the internal weights, known as coefficients, to ensure that the model has learned from the data:

```
from sklearn.linear_model import LinearRegression

linear_regression = LinearRegression()
linear_regression.fit(scaled_X, y)
print(linear_regression.coef_.round(5))
```

After executing fit(), the code prints the coefficients of the linear regression model:

```
[ 0.82962  0.11875 -0.26553  0.3057  -0.0045  -0.03933
 -0.89989 -0.87054]
```

After fitting, the linear_regression model holds the learned parameters, and you visualize them using the coef_() method, which is typical of all the linear models (where the model output is a summation of variables weighted by coefficients). You can also call this fitting activity training (as in, *training a machine learning algorithm*).

REMEMBER

A *hypothesis* is a way to describe a learning algorithm trained with data. The hypothesis defines a possible representation of y given X that you test for validity. Therefore, it's a hypothesis in both scientific and machine learning language.

Apart from the estimator class, the predictor and the model object classes are also important. The predictor class, which predicts the probability of a certain result, obtains the result of new observations using the predict() and predict_proba() methods, as in this script:

```
values = [[1.21315, 32., 3.31767135, 1.07731985, 898.,
           2.1424809, 37.82, -122.27]]
obs = pd.DataFrame(values, columns=X.columns)

scaled_obs = scaler.transform(obs)

pred = linear_regression.predict(scaled_obs)
value = pred[0] * 100_000
print(f"Estimated median house value: {value:.2f} USD")
```

The single observation is thus converted into a prediction:

```
Estimated median house value: 141088.56 USD
```

TIP

Make sure that new observations have the same feature number and in the same order as in the training X; otherwise, the prediction will be incorrect.

Each class from Scikit-learn has some specific methods and some common ones, such as fit(), transform(), and predict(). Even if the method is a common one, however, it may have extra parameters. In order to know what methods are available and the parameters they require, please consult the online documentation of each algorithm or ask for help on the Python console:

```
help(LinearRegression)
```

For instance, LinearRegression has the score() method that provides information about the quality of the regression, as shown here:

```
linear_regression.score(scaled_X, y)
```

The quality is expressed as a float number:

```
0.606232685199805
```

In this case, score() returns the coefficient of determination R^2 of the prediction. R^2 is a measure ranging from 0 to 1, comparing our predictor to a simple mean. Higher values show that the predictor is working well. Different learning algorithms may use different scoring functions.

Using Transformative Functions

In Scikit-learn, transformative functions are a kind of data processing step that you use to manipulate and transform data. You typically use these functions as part of a machine learning pipeline to apply specific operations on the data before feeding it into a machine learning model for training or prediction. All these functions are mentioned in the reference page https://scikit-learn.org/stable/modules/preprocessing.html. Here are some of the most important transformers or types of transformers to remember:

>> StandardScaler() (https://scikit-learn.org/stable/modules/generated/sklearn.preprocessing.StandardScaler.html): Used for standardizing numerical features by scaling them to have zero mean and unit variance, which can be important for many machine learning algorithms.

>> MinMaxScaler() (https://scikit-learn.org/stable/modules/generated/sklearn.preprocessing.MinMaxScaler.html): Scales numerical features to a specific range (usually between 0 and1), making them suitable for algorithms that are sensitive to the scale of the input features.

>> OneHotEncoder() (https://scikit-learn.org/stable/modules/generated/sklearn.preprocessing.OneHotEncoder.html): Used for encoding categorical features into a binary vector representation, making them suitable for algorithms that cannot handle categorical data directly.

>> OrdinalEncoder() (https://scikit-learn.org/stable/modules/generated/sklearn.preprocessing.OrdinalEncoder.html): Used for encoding categorical features with integer labels, which can be useful for algorithms that can handle integer-encoded categorical data.

>> SimpleImputer() (https://scikit-learn.org/stable/modules/generated/sklearn.impute.SimpleImputer.html): Used for handling missing values in the data by filling them with appropriate values, such as mean, median, or most frequent values.

>> PolynomialFeatures() (https://scikit-learn.org/stable/modules/generated/sklearn.preprocessing.PolynomialFeatures.html): Used for generating polynomial features from the original features, which can be helpful for capturing nonlinear relationships in the data.

>> **Feature selection:** Scikit-learn provides various techniques for feature selection, explained in detail in Chapter 18, which can be used to select the most important features from the original feature set.

>> **Text processing tools:** Scikit-learn provides various tools for text processing, such as CountVectorizer() and TfidfVectorizer(), which can be used for converting text data into numerical representations suitable for machine learning.

Because all data problems present differences in features and data characteristics, you need a customized approach when you process them — that is, particular combinations of the Scikit-learn transformative functions applied to different portions of your data. The following sections explore additional Scikit-learn classes that can help you effectively combine and apply these transformative functions for optimal outcomes.

Chaining estimators

You can use transformative functions as stand-alone functions, but they necessarily function in sequence and in association with machine learning algorithms. For this reason, it's extremely useful to chain together different transformative functions and predictive models into a `Pipeline()`. A *pipeline* is a useful tool in Scikit-learn for chaining multiple data processing steps together, such as feature selection, normalization, and classification, into one sequence. A pipeline offers several benefits:

>> **Fitting and predicting on your data with just one call,** making it easy to apply a series of processing steps in a single line of code.

>> **Performing optimizations of all the estimators in the pipeline simultaneously,** simplifying the hyperparameter tuning process.

>> **Preventing statistics leaking from your test data into your trained model** during cross-validation. This leaking is prevented because the same samples are used to train both the transformers and predictors, ensuring consistency in data processing.

It's important to note that all estimators in a pipeline, except the last one, must be transformers, meaning they must have a transform method. The last estimator can be of any type, such as a transformer, classifier, or other model.

Creating a Scikit-learn pipeline requires first defining the steps and then plugging them into the pipeline. Defining each single step requires you to create a tuple or a list containing the step's name and the Scikit-learn class you want executed. Providing the step's name is important because it helps you later when you want to access each single step and its parameters. After you have plugged all the steps into the pipeline, you use the pipeline as you would any other Scikit-learn class:

>> Fit it on training data and then use it to perform a transformation if there is no predictor inside.

>> Perform a prediction if it closes with a machine learning model.

You can find all the details of the command at https://scikit-learn.org/stable/modules/generated/sklearn.pipeline.Pipeline.html.

Transforming targets

Transformation sometimes includes the target in addition to the features. Because the distribution of target values can present multiple modes or become skewed to the right or to the left, you may find that first transforming the target, and then fitting the model, and finally inverse-transforming its predictions bring better predictive results. The purpose of transformations is to increase the symmetry and normality of the target distribution, which is not a requirement or recommendation for machine learning models, but rather a factual observation because those models have been known to perform better with transformations.

In Scikit-learn, a *transformative function* is a kind of data processing step that you use to manipulate and transform data. Transformative functions are usually logarithmic. A transformative function relies on the exponential function as its inverse, particularly for skewed targets. It uses the square root transformation (and its inverse, squaring) when the target variable is moderately skewed, has a positive skewness, and you want to reduce the influence of outliers.

Before fitting a regression model, the TransformedTargetRegressor() method modifies the targets (y). Afterward, the predictions are restored to their original space using an inverse transform. To perform this transformation, the function that wraps Scikit-learn's regressor models into a single entity requires two arguments: the regressor utilized for prediction, and the transformer that is applied to the target variable.

Composing features

A Scikit-learn pipeline operates on all the data, piping it into sequential transformations, but not all transformations are suitable for all the features of your dataset. For this reason, you use ColumnTransformer(), which is a pipeline that operates only on a selection of the features, and FeatureUnion(), which combines the work of multiple ColumnTransformer objects into a single dataset.

The ColumnTransformer() has three main input parameters:

>> Transformers: Accepts a list of tuples, where each tuple consists of a name for the transformer, the corresponding preprocessing transformer (such as StandardScaler or SimpleImputer), and the list of columns to which the transformer should be applied.

>> Remainder: Specifies how to handle the columns that were not selected for transformation. The default value is "drop", which means that these columns will be ignored.

» FeatureUnion: Takes a list of transformers as input and concatenates the output of each transformer horizontally. Each transformer extracts a set of features from the input data and returns them as a NumPy array. The output of all the transformers is concatenated horizontally to form a single NumPy array that represents the full set of features for each input sample.

Handling heterogeneous data

The section on transformative functions in Scikit-learn concludes with an example showing you how to approach heterogeneous data, which is typical of real-world data, using the previously illustrated tools. The example starts by loading the California Housing dataset, which contains features such as median house value, median income, housing age, and various other factors that can be used to predict housing prices in different regions of California.

```
from sklearn.compose \
    import ColumnTransformer, make_column_selector
from sklearn.pipeline import FeatureUnion, Pipeline
from sklearn.preprocessing \
    import StandardScaler, KBinsDiscretizer
from sklearn.linear_model import LinearRegression

X, y = load_california_housing_data()
```

By distinguishing the different types of features present in the dataset, the code can proceed to process them separately. In particular, it distinguishes between numeric features, which are standardized, and latitude and longitude geographical coordinates, which are discretized from continuous values into discrete bins. By discretizing the geographical coordinates, it's possible to enable a series of analyses to identify regions with similar geographic characteristics, such as areas with similar climate, terrain, or land-use patterns.

REMEMBER

Discretization refers to the process of converting continuous data into discrete or categorical data. In the context of data analysis, discretization involves dividing a continuous variable, which has a range of possible values, into a set of discrete intervals or bins.

You can achieve distinct transformations on the numeric features and the geographical coordinates by means of two different ColumnTransformer() operations:

```
num_cols = ['MedInc', 'HouseAge', 'AveRooms',
            'AveBedrms', 'Population', 'AveOccup']
```

```
cords = ['Latitude', 'Longitude']

num_transformer = ColumnTransformer([
    ("scaler", StandardScaler(), num_cols)],
     remainder="drop")

cords_transformer = ColumnTransformer([
    ("discretizer",
    KBinsDiscretizer(n_bins=20, encode="onehot-dense"),
    cords)])
```

At this point, you combine the two feature transformation steps into a single transformer:

```
preprocessor = FeatureUnion(
    transformer_list=[("num_transformer",
                        num_transformer),
                      ("cords_transformer",
                        cords_transformer)])
```

You can test how it works by fitting and transforming the data and checking its resulting shape:

```
preprocessor.fit_transform(X).shape
```

You should see an output of:

```
(20640, 46)
```

After checking that everything works properly as expected, you enclose the data transformer in a predictive pipeline using a linear regression model in this case:

```
predictive_pipeline = Pipeline([
    ("preprocessor", preprocessor),
    ("model", LinearRegression())])
```

You're finally ready to use the set-up predictive pipeline to train on data and check how it fitted the data in terms of score:

```
predictive_pipeline.fit(X, y)
predictive_pipeline.score(X, y)
```

You get the score of the R^2 measure after training. The obtained R^2 score indicates how much better the model is in predictive performance when compared to a baseline such as the statistical mean, on a scale from 0 to 1. This score allows you to assess the effectiveness of your model and provides valuable insights for further analysis and optimization:

```
0.6667462444130221
```

You can apply the same approach to handle various data types in your datasets. Begin by categorizing the data into different types, such as numerical, categorical, and text data. Next, create a `ColumnTransformer` object for each type, which allows you to apply specific transformations to each type of data separately. Finally, bring all the transformed data together using a `FeatureUnion` class, which merges the outputs from multiple transformers into a single feature space.

By following this methodology, you can easily handle diverse data types in your datasets. This approach provides flexibility and scalability, allowing you to apply different preprocessing techniques to different types of data. For instance, you can apply scaling or normalization to numerical data, one-hot encoding or label encoding to categorical data, and conversion of text data into a bag of words. You can also include additional transformers or custom functions as needed to suit your specific data preprocessing requirements.

Considering Timing and Performance

As the book introduces more and more complex themes, you may start to wonder how all this processing influences application speed. The increased processing requirements affect both running time and available memory.

Managing the best use of machine resources is indeed an art, the art of optimization, and it requires time to master. However, you can start immediately becoming proficient in it by doing some accurate speed measurement and realizing what your problems really are if your code seems to run too slowly. Profiling the time that performing a data transformation on your data requires, or measuring how much memory adding more data takes, can help you to spot the bottlenecks in your code and start looking for alternative solutions.

As described in Chapter 5, Jupyter Notebook or Google Colab are the perfect environments for experimenting, tweaking, and improving your code. Working on blocks of code, recording the results and outputs, and writing additional notes and comments will help your data science solutions take shape in a controlled and reproducible way.

Benchmarking with timeit

In Chapter 8, you find out to work with `CountVectorizer()` to convert text into a bag of words that can be used as input to various machine learning algorithms for text classification, clustering, or other natural language processing tasks. This text processing class transforms text into a matrix of token counts. It performs the following operations under the hood:

>> **Tokenization:** Breaks the text into individual tokens (words, characters, or n-grams)

>> **Lowercase and accent stripping:** Converts all the tokens into lowercase and removes accents for text standardization

>> **Stopwords removal:** Filters out common words, such as "the," "and," "a," and "an," which don't add much value to the analysis

>> **Count Vectorization:** Converts the text into a matrix of token counts, where each row represents a document and each column represents a token, with the values being the number of times the token appears in that document

Each of these operations takes time and memory to run and you may be concerned with application performance when the number of texts to process is large. It's important to measure performance before creating a machine learning solution. Jupyter offers an easy, out-of-the-box solution, to measure speed using these line magics:

>> `%timeit`: Calculates the best performance time for an instruction

>> `%%timeit`: Calculates the best time performance for all the instructions in a cell, apart from the one placed on the same cell line as the cell magic (which could therefore be an initialization instruction)

Both magic commands report the best performance in r trials repeated for n loops. When you add the -r and -n parameters, the notebook chooses the number automatically in order to provide a fast answer. Here is an example of determining the time required to assign a list 10**6 ordinal values by using list comprehension:

```
%timeit l = [k for k in range(10**6)]
```

The reported timing will look like this (the actual times will vary according to your system's capabilities):

```
76 ms ± 798 µ per loop
(mean ± std. dev. of 7 runs, 10 loops each)
```

The result for the list comprehension can be tested by incrementing both the sample performance and repetitions of the test:

```
%timeit -n 20 -r 5 l = [k for k in range(10**6)]
```

After a while, the timing similar to this one is reported:

```
76 ms ± 1.06 ms per loop
(mean ± std. dev. of 5 runs, 20 loops each)
```

As a comparison, you can check the time required to assign the values in a for loop. Because the for loop requires an entire cell, the example uses the cell magic, %%timeit, call. Notice that the first line that assigns the value of 10**6 to a variable is not considered in the performance.

```
%%timeit
l = list()
for k in range(10**6):
    l.append(k)
```

The resulting timing will look like this:

```
123 ms ± 279 µs per loop
(mean ± std. dev. of 7 runs, 10 loops each)
```

The results show that list comprehension is about 40 percent faster than using a for loop. You can then perform a similar test using the text encoding CountVectorizer():

```
import sklearn.feature_extraction.text as txt
count_vectorizer = txt.CountVectorizer(
    binary=True, max_features=20)

texts = ["Python for data science",
         "Python for machine learning",
         "Artificial intelligence in Python"]

count_vectorizer.fit(texts)
vectorized = count_vectorizer.transform(texts)
```

After performing initial loading of the class and instantiating it, you can test the solution:

```
%timeit count_vectorizer.fit(texts)
```

Here is the timing for fitting the word encoder based on the `CountVectorizer()`:

```
314 µs ± 9.15 µs per loop
(mean ± std. dev. of 7 runs, 1000 loops each)
```

You now run the test on the transformation phase:

```
%timeit vectorized = count_vectorizer.transform(texts)
```

You obtain the following much better timing (µs [microseconds] are smaller than ms [milliseconds]):

```
93 µs ± 1.05 µs per loop
(mean ± std. dev. of 7 runs, 10000 loops each)
```

The transformation operation is faster than the fit operation because, in the fit phase, the function has to scan through the text, recording and counting the word occurrences in the internal data structures. In the transformation phase, the operations to be done are simpler because the text is just split, and each word is recognized and transformed into a binary feature.

Jupyter Notebook is always the best environment to benchmark the speed of your data science solution code. However, if you'd like to track performance on the command line or in a script running from an IDE, you can import the `timeit` class and use the `timeit()` function for tracking performance of the command by providing the input parameter as a string. The `timeit()` function returns a `float` number that represents the total number of seconds it took to execute an operation. If you are running multiple operations, divide the returned total seconds by the number of operations to obtain the time it took for a single operation.

The input that `timeit()` expects is a string that contains the command to be executed. If your command needs variables, classes, or functions that aren't available in the base Python (such as the Scikit-learn classes), you can provide them as a second input parameter by using the `setup` parameter. You formulate a string in which Python imports all the necessary objects from the main environment, as shown in the following example:

```
import timeit

cumulative_time = timeit.timeit(
    "vectorized = count_vectorizer.transform(texts)",
    setup="from __main__ import count_vectorizer, texts",
    number=10000)
print(cumulative_time / 10000.0)
```

The output from this example will look like this and tell you the time for each loop:

```
0.00010361055000003035
```

USING THE PREFERRED INSTALLER PROGRAM (PIP)

Python provides a huge number of packages that you can install. Many of these packages come as separate, downloadable modules. Some of them have an executable suitable for a platform such as Windows, which means you can easily install the package. However, many other packages rely on **pip**, the preferred installer program, which is a feature that you can access directly from the command line.

To use pip, you open the command line prompt. If you need to install a package from scratch, such as NumPy, you type **pip install numpy**, and the software will download the package as well as all the related packages that it needs to work, and will install everything. You can even install a specific version by typing, for example, **pip install -U numpy==1.24.2**, or simply update the package to its most recent version if is already installed: **pip install -U numpy**.

If you installed Anaconda, you can use conda instead of pip, which is even more efficient when installing because it sets all the other packages to the right version for your newly installed Python package (which implies that it can install, upgrade or even downgrade existing packages on your system). Using conda for installing a new package is achieved from the Anaconda Prompt, as well, by entering **conda install numpy**. The software analyzes your system, reports the changes, and then asks whether it should proceed. Press y if you want to proceed with the installation. You also use conda to update existing packages (enter **conda update numpy**) or the entire system (enter **conda update --all**).

This book uses Jupyter Notebook and Google Colab, actually based on the Jupyter Notebook open source, as its environment. Installing and upgrading while using Jupyter Notebook is a bit more complicated. Jake VanderPlas from the University of Washington wrote a very informative post about this issue, which you can find at `https://jakevdp.github.io/blog/2017/12/05/installing-python-packages-from-jupyter/`. The article proposes a few ways to handle package installation and upgrading while using the Jupyter Notebook interface. At the beginning, until you gain confidence and experience, the best option is to install and update your system first and then run Jupyter Notebook, making the installation much easier and smoother.

Working with the memory profiler

As you've seen when testing your application code for performance (speed) characteristics, you can obtain analogous information about memory usage. Keeping track of memory consumption could tell you about possible problems in the way data is processed or transmitted to the learning algorithms. The `memory_profiler` package implements the required functionality. This package is not provided as a default Python package and it requires installation. Use the following command to install the package directly from a cell within Jupyter Notebook, as explained by Jake VanderPlas's post described in the "Using the preferred installer program (pip)" sidebar:

```
import sys
!{sys.executable} -m pip install memory_profiler
```

Use the following command for each Jupyter Notebook session you want to monitor:

```
%load_ext memory_profiler
```

After performing these tasks, you can easily track how much memory a command consumes:

```
vectorized = count_vectorizer.transform(texts)
%memit dense_hashing = vectorized.toarray()
```

The output is in mebibyte (MiB), a International Electrotechnical Commission (IEC) unit of measure specifically for memory (see `https://digilent.com/blog/mib-vs-mb-whats-the-difference/` for details). The reported peak memory and increment tell you about memory usage (the numbers you see may vary due to system differences):

```
peak memory: 268.60 MiB, increment: 0.01 MiB
```

Obtaining a complete overview of memory consumption is possible by saving a notebook cell to disk and then profiling it using the line magic %mprun on an externally imported function. (The line magic works only by operating with external Python scripts.) Profiling produces a detailed report, command by command, as shown in the following example:

```
%%writefile example_code.py

import sklearn.feature_extraction.text as txt

def comparison_test(text):
    count_vectorizer = txt.CountVectorizer(
        binary=True, max_features=20)
    count_vectorizer.fit(text)
    vectorized = count_vectorizer.transform(text)
    return vectorized.toarray()
```

The previous code writes a python script on your work directory where your test is wrapped into a Python function. As a next step, you import the function from the script and evaluate its memory usage using the %mprun line magic:

```
from example_code import comparison_test

texts = ["Python for data science",
         "Python for machine learning",
         "Artificial intelligence in Python"]

%mprun -f comparison_test comparison_test(texts)
```

You will get an output similar to that shown in Figure 12-1 (the output appears in a separate window at the bottom of the notebook display by default):

FIGURE 12-1:
The output from
the memory test
shows memory
usage for each
line of code.

```
Filename: C:\Users\John\Anaconda Projects\P4DS4D3\example_code.py

Line #    Mem usage    Increment   Occurrences   Line Contents
================================================================
     4    157.3 MiB    157.3 MiB           1     def comparison_test(text):
     5    157.3 MiB      0.0 MiB           2         count_vectorizer = txt.CountVectorizer(
     6    157.3 MiB      0.0 MiB           1             binary=True, max_features=20)
     7    157.3 MiB      0.0 MiB           1         count_vectorizer.fit(text)
     8    157.3 MiB      0.0 MiB           1         vectorized = count_vectorizer.transform(text)
     9    157.3 MiB      0.0 MiB           1         return vectorized.toarray()
```

FIGURE 12-1:
The output from
the memory test
shows memory
usage for each
line of code.

The resulting report details the memory usage from every line in the function, pointing out the major increments in memory usage.

REDUCING MEMORY USAGE AND COMPUTING FAST

You use NumPy arrays or pandas DataFrames when working with data. However, even if they appear as different data structures: one focuses on storing data as a matrix and the other on handling complex datasets stored in different ways — DataFrames rely on NumPy arrays. Understanding how arrays work and are used by pandas allows you to reduce memory usage and achieve faster computations.

NumPy arrays are a tool for handling data by using contiguous memory blocks to store the values. Because the data appears in the same area of computer memory, Python can retrieve the data faster and slice it more easily. It's the same principle as disk fragmentation: If your data is scattered on disk, it occupies more space and requires more handling time.

Depending on your needs, you can order array data by rows (the default choice of both NumPy and the C/C++ programming language) or columns. Computer memory stores cells one after the other in a line. Consequently, you can record your array row after row, allowing fast processing by rows, or column by column, allowing faster processing by columns. All these details, though hidden from your eyes, are crucial because they render working with NumPy arrays fast and efficient for data science (which uses numeric matrices and often computes information by rows). This is why all Scikit-learn algorithms expect a NumPy array as an input, and why NumPy arrays have a fixed data type (they can be only of the same type as the data sequence; they can't vary).

pandas DataFrames are just well-arranged collections of NumPy arrays. Your variables in DataFrame, depending on the type, are compacted in an array. For instance, all your integer variables are together in an *IntBlock*, all your float data in a *FloatBlock*, and the rest in an *ObjectBlock*. This means that when you want to operate on a single variable, you are actually operating on all the variables. Consequently, if you have an operation to apply, it's better to apply it to all variables of the same type simultaneously. In addition, this also means that working with string variables is incredibly expensive in terms of memory and computations. Even if you store something as simple as a short series of color names in a variable, it will require the use of a complete string (at least 50 bytes) and handling it will be quite cumbersome using the NumPy engine. As suggested in Chapter 7, you can transform your string data in categorical variables; by doing so, behind the scenes, strings are transformed into numbers. In this way, you greatly reduce the memory usage and increase the speed you experience when manipulating the data.

Running in Parallel on Multiple Cores

Most computers today are multicore (bearing two or more processors in a single package), with some having multiple physical CPUs. One of the most important limitations of Python is that it uses a single core by default (it was created in a time when single cores were the norm).

Data science projects require quite a lot of computations. In particular, a part of the scientific aspect of data science relies on repeated tests and experiments on different data matrices. Don't forget that working with huge data quantities means that most time-consuming transformations repeat observation after observation (for example, identical and not related operations on different parts of a matrix).

Using more CPU cores accelerates a computation by a factor that almost matches the number of cores. For example, having four cores would mean working at best four times faster. You don't receive a full fourfold increase because there is overhead when starting a parallel process — new running Python instances have to be set up with the right in-memory information and launched; consequently, the improvement will be less than potentially achievable but still significant. Knowing how to use more than one CPU is therefore an advanced but incredibly useful skill for increasing the number of analyses completed and for speeding up your operations both when setting up and when using your data products.

REMEMBER

Multiprocessing works by replicating the same code and memory content in various new Python instances (the workers), calculating the result for each of them, and returning the pooled results to the main original console. If your original instance already occupies much of the available RAM memory, it won't be possible to create new instances, and your machine may run out of memory.

Performing multicore parallelism

To perform multicore parallelism with Python, you integrate the Scikit-learn package with the joblib package for time-consuming operations, such as replicating models for validating results or for looking for the best hyperparameters. In particular, Scikit-learn allows multiprocessing when

» **Cross-validating:** Testing the results of a machine-learning hypothesis using different training and testing data (discussed in Chapter 18)

» **Grid-searching:** Systematically changing the hyperparameters of a machine-learning hypothesis and testing the consequent results (also discussed in Chapter 18)

» **Multilabel prediction:** Running an algorithm multiple times against multiple targets when there are many different target outcomes to predict at the same time (discussed in Chapter 17 in various sections, including "Considering the case when there are more classes")

>> **Ensemble machine-learning methods:** Modeling a large host of classifiers, each one independent from the other, such as when using RandomForest-based modeling (discussed in Chapter 20)

You don't have to do anything special to take advantage of parallel computations — you can activate parallelism by setting the n_jobs parameter to a number of cores more than 1 or by setting the value to −1, which means you want to use all the available CPU instances.

WARNING

If you aren't running your code from the console or from a notebook in Jupyter Notebook, it is extremely important that you separate code that will execute in parallel from any package import or global variable assignment in your script by using the if __name__=='__main__': command at the beginning of any code that executes multicore parallelism. The if statement checks whether the program is directly run or is called by an already-running Python console, avoiding any confusion or error by the multiparallel process (such as recursively calling the parallelism).

Demonstrating multiprocessing

It's a good idea to use a notebook when you run a demonstration of how multiprocessing can really save you time during data science projects. Using Jupyter Notebook offers the advantage of using the %timeit magic command for timing execution. You start by loading a multiclass dataset, a complex machine learning algorithm (the Support Vector Classifier, or SVC, a topic explained in all the details in Chapter 19), and a cross-validation procedure for estimating reliable resulting scores from all the procedures. You find details about all these tools later in the book. The most important thing to know is that the procedures become quite large because the SVC is required to produce 7 models, which it repeats 20 times each using cross-validation, for a total of 140 generated models.

```
from sklearn.datasets import load_digits
digits = load_digits()

X, y = digits.data, digits.target
from sklearn.svm import SVC
from sklearn.model_selection import cross_val_score
```

After loading the digits data, representing images of handwritten digits from 0 to 9, test the timing of a cross-validation on 20 folds using a single core. Here is the code (even though the command may appear on several lines in the book, you use a single line in your code):

```
%timeit single_core = cross_val_score( \
    SVC(), X, y, cv=20, n_jobs=1)
```

As a result, you get the recorded average running time for a single core similar to this:

```
1.56 s ± 11.7 ms per loop
(mean ± std. dev. of 7 runs, 1 loop each)
```

After this test, you need to activate the multicore parallelism and time the results using the following command (even though the command may appear on several lines in the book, you use a single line in your code):

```
%timeit multi_core = cross_val_score( \
    SVC(),X, y, cv=20, n_jobs=-1)
```

Running on multiple cores allows for a much better average time:

```
692 ms ± 28.5 ms per loop
(mean ± std. dev. of 7 runs, 1 loop each)
```

Running on all the available cores may render your computer unusable for any other task. In Scikit-learn, setting n_jobs to -2 refers to using all available CPUs except one to parallelize the execution of a particular task. Leaving one CPU reserved for system processes avoids overloading the CPU, leading to slower processing times and preventing you from using your computer for other, non-intensive tasks.

```
%timeit multi_core = cross_val_score( \
    SVC(), X, y, cv=20, n_jobs=-2)
```

As expected, because you are leaving one CPU out of the game, the average time worsens a little bit, but in exchange you have a usable computer, especially if the training or testing takes a long time:

```
744 ms ± 8.4 ms per loop
(mean ± std. dev. of 7 runs, 1 loop each)
```

The example machine demonstrates a positive advantage using multicore processing, despite using a small dataset where Python spends most of the time starting consoles and running a part of the code in each one. This overhead, a few seconds, is still significant given that the total execution extends for a handful of seconds. Just imagine what would happen if you worked with larger sets of data — your execution time could be easily cut by two or three times.

Chapter **13**

Exploring Data Analysis

D ata science relies on complex algorithms for building predictions and spotting important signals in data, and each algorithm presents different strong and weak points. In short, you select a range of algorithms, you have them run on the data, you optimize their parameters as much as you can, and finally you decide which one will best help you build your data product or generate insight into your problem. However, even if some of these tools seem like black or even magic boxes, no matter how powerful the machine learning algorithms you use are, you won't obtain good results if your data has something wrong in it. It is all a matter of GIGO. GIGO stands for "Garbage In/Garbage Out." It has been a well-known adage in statistics (and computer science) for a long time.

In this chapter, you discover the philosophy of Exploratory Data Analysis (EDA), which means finding out how to

» Describe your variables

» Estimate correlations and associations

» Visualize value distributions, relationships between variables, and groups

The goal of EDA is to clean and transform data for optimal learning by machine learning algorithms. EDA is a general approach to exploring datasets by means of

simple summary statistics and graphic visualizations to gain a deeper understanding of data. EDA helps you become more effective in the subsequent data
analysis and modeling. In this chapter, you discover all the necessary and indispensable basic descriptions of the data and see how those descriptions can help
you decide how to proceed using the most appropriate data transformation and
solutions.

REMEMBER

You don't have to type the source code for this chapter manually; using the downloadable source is a lot easier. The source code for this chapter appears in the
P4DS4D3_13_Exploring_Data_Analysis.ipynb file. (See the Introduction for
details on where to locate this file.)

The EDA Approach

EDA was developed at Bell Labs by John Tukey, a mathematician and statistician
who wanted to promote more questions and actions on data based on the data
itself (the exploratory motif) in contrast to the dominant confirmatory approach
of the time. A *confirmatory approach* relies on the use of a theory or procedure —
the data is just there for testing and application. EDA emerged at the end of the
70s, long before the big data flood appeared. Tukey could already see that certain
activities, such as testing and modeling, were easy to make automatic. In one of
his famous writings, Tukey said:

*"The only way humans can do BETTER than computers is to take a chance of
doing WORSE than them."*

The statement emphasizes that there are areas where human intuition, creativity,
and contextual understanding can provide an edge over computers, a statement
truly ahead of its time that remains relevant in today's era of AI. The statement
also explains why, as a data scientist, your role and tools aren't limited to automatic learning algorithms but also to manual and creative exploratory tasks. Computers are unbeatable at optimizing, but humans are strong at discovery by taking
unexpected routes and trying unlikely but in the end very effective solutions.

If you've been through the examples in the previous chapters, you have already
worked on quite a bit of data, but using EDA is a bit different because it checks
beyond the basic assumptions about data workability, which actually comprises
the Initial Data Analysis (IDA). Up to now, the book has shown how to

>> Complete observations or mark missing cases by appropriate features

>> Transform text or categorical variables

>> Create new features based on domain knowledge of the data problem

>> Have at hand a numeric dataset where rows are observations and columns are variables

EDA goes further than IDA. It's moved by a different attitude: going beyond basic assumptions. With EDA, you

>> Describe of your data

>> Closely explore data distributions

>> Understand the relations between variables

>> Notice unusual or unexpected situations

>> Place the data into groups

>> Notice unexpected patterns within groups

>> Take note of group differences

REMEMBER

You will read a lot in the following pages about how EDA can help you learn about variable distribution in your dataset. *Variable distribution* is the list of values you find in that variable compared to their *frequency*, that is, how often they occur. Being able to determine variable distribution tells you a lot about how a variable could behave when fed into a machine learning algorithm and, thus, help you take appropriate steps to have it perform well in your project.

Defining Descriptive Statistics for Numeric Data

The first actions that you can take with the data are to produce some synthetic measures to determine what is going on with it. You acquire knowledge of measures such as maximum and minimum values, and you define which intervals are the best places to start.

During your exploration, you use a simple but useful dataset, the Palmer Penguins dataset. This dataset was collected in the Palmer Archipelago, Antarctica, by Dr. Kristen Gorman and the Palmer Station Long-Term Ecological Research (LTER) program. It contains detailed information about three different species of penguins: Adélie, Gentoo, and Chinstrap. It includes various measurements such as the penguins' bill length, bill depth, body mass, flipper length, and several other attributes. You can load it by using the following code, which will select a few variables:

```python
import numpy as np
import pandas as pd

def load_palmer_penguins(no_missing=True):
    url = "https://raw.githubusercontent.com/"
    url += "allisonhorst/palmerpenguins/main/"
    url += "inst/extdata/penguins.csv"
    numeric_features = [
        "bill_length_mm", "bill_depth_mm",
        "flipper_length_mm", "body_mass_g"]
    target = ["species"]
    data = pd.read_csv(url)
    if no_missing:
        data = data.dropna()
    return data[numeric_features + target]

penguins = load_palmer_penguins(no_missing=True)
```

Having loaded the Palmer Penguins dataset into a pandas DataFrame, as a last preparatory activity before starting data exploration, you can check your pandas and NumPy versions:

```python
print(f"Your pandas version is: {pd.__version__}")
print(f"Your NumPy version is {np.__version__}")
```

REMEMBER

NumPy, Scikit-learn, and especially pandas are packages under constant development, so before you start working with EDA, it's a good idea to check the product version numbers. Using an older or newer version could cause your output to differ from that shown in the book, or cause some commands to fail. For this edition of the book, use pandas version 1.3.5 and NumPy version 1.21.6 (see Chapter 3 for an explanation of how to set up your desktop system for use with Anaconda).

TIP

This chapter presents a series of pandas and NumPy commands that help you explore the structure of data. Even though applying single explorative commands grants you more freedom in your analysis, it's nice to know that you can obtain most of these statistics using the describe() method applied to your pandas DataFrame: such as, print(penguins.describe()), when you're in a hurry in your data science project.

Measuring central tendency

Mean and median are the first measures to calculate for numeric variables when starting EDA. They can provide you with an estimate when the variables are centered and somehow symmetric.

Using pandas, you can quickly compute both means and medians. Here is the command for getting the mean from the penguins DataFrame:

```
print(penguins.mean(numeric_only=True))
```

```
Here is the resulting output for the mean statistic:
bill_length_mm          43.992793
bill_depth_mm           17.164865
flipper_length_mm      200.966967
body_mass_g           4207.057057
dtype: float64
```

Similarly, here is the command that will output the median:

```
print(penguins.median(numeric_only=True))
```

You then obtain the median estimates for all the variables:

```
bill_length_mm          44.5
bill_depth_mm           17.3
flipper_length_mm      197.0
body_mass_g           4050.0
dtype: float64
```

The median provides the central position in the series of values. When creating a variable, it is a measure less influenced by anomalous cases or by an asymmetric distribution of values around the mean. What you should notice here is that the means are not centered (no variable is zero mean) and that the median of body mass is different from the mean, requiring further inspection.

When checking for central tendency measures, you should:

>> Verify whether means are zero

>> Check whether they are different from each other

>> Notice whether the median is different from the mean

Measuring variance and range

As a next step, you should check the variance by using its square root, the standard deviation. The standard deviation is as informative as the variance, but comparing to the mean is easier because it's expressed in the same unit of measure. The standard deviation is a good indicator of whether a mean is a suitable indicator of the variable distribution because it tells you how the values of a variable distribute around the mean. The higher the standard deviation, the farther you can expect some values to appear from the mean.

```
print(penguins.std(numeric_only=True))
```

The printed output for each variable:

```
bill_length_mm          5.468668
bill_depth_mm           1.969235
flipper_length_mm      14.015765
body_mass_g           805.215802
dtype: float64
```

In addition, you also check the range, which is the difference between the maximum and minimum value for each quantitative variable, and it is quite informative about the difference in scale among variables:

```
print(penguins.max(numeric_only=True)
      - penguins.min(numeric_only=True))
```

Here you can find the output of the preceding command:

```
bill_length_mm         27.5
bill_depth_mm           8.4
flipper_length_mm      59.0
body_mass_g          3600.0
dtype: float64
```

Note the standard deviation and the range in relation to the mean and median. A standard deviation or range that's too high with respect to the measures of centrality (mean and median) may point to a possible problem, with extremely unusual values affecting the calculation or an unexpected distribution of values around the mean.

Working with percentiles

Because the median is the value in the central position of your distribution of values, you may need to consider other notable positions. Apart from the minimum and maximum, the position at 25 percent of your values (the lower quartile) and the position at 75 percent (the upper quartile) are useful for determining the data distribution, and they are the basis of an illustrative graph called a *boxplot*, which is one of the topics discussed in this chapter.

```
print(penguins.select_dtypes(np.number).
      quantile([0,.25,.50,.75,1]))
```

You can see the output as a matrix — a comparison that uses quartiles for rows and the different dataset variables as columns. So, the 25-percent quartile for bill_length_mm is 32.1, which means that 25 percent of the dataset values for this measure are less than 32.1.

	bill_length_mm	bill_depth_mm	flipper_length_mm...
0.00	32.1	13.1	172.0...
0.25	39.5	15.6	190.0...
0.50	44.5	17.3	197.0...
0.75	48.6	18.7	213.0...
1.00	59.6	21.5	231.0...

REMEMBER

The difference between the first quartile (25th percentile) and the third quartile (75th percentile) constitutes the interquartile range (IQR), which is a measure of the spread in the central portion of the variable. You don't need to calculate it, but you will find it in the boxplot because it helps to determine the plausible limits of the core of your distribution. What lies after the "whiskers" of the boxplot, which are typically located at 1.5 times the IQR beyond the first and third quartiles, are considered cases that can potentially affect the results of your analysis in a negative way. Such cases are called outliers — and they're the topic of Chapter 16.

Defining measures of normality

The last indicative measures of how the numeric variables used for these examples are structured are skewness and kurtosis:

>> *Skewness* defines the asymmetry of data with respect to the mean. If the skew is negative, the left tail is too long and the mass of the observations are on the right side of the distribution. If it is positive, it is exactly the opposite.

>> *Kurtosis* shows whether the data distribution, especially the peak and the tails, are of the right shape. If the kurtosis is above zero, the distribution has a marked peak. If it is below zero, the distribution is too flat instead.

Although reading the numbers can help you determine the shape of the data, taking notice of such measures presents a formal test to select the variables that may need some adjustment or transformation in order to become more similar to the Gaussian distribution. Remember that you also visualize the data later, so this is a first step in a longer process.

REMEMBER

The normal, or Gaussian, distribution is the most useful distribution in statistics thanks to its frequent recurrence and particular mathematical properties. It's essentially the foundation of many statistical tests and models, with some of them, such as the linear regression, widely used in data science. In a Gaussian distribution, mean and median have the same values, the values are symmetrically distributed around the mean (it has the shape of a bell), and its standard deviation points out the distance from the mean where the distribution curve changes from being concave to convex (it is called the inflection point). All these characteristics make the Gaussian distribution a special distribution, and they can be leveraged for statistical computations.

TIP

You seldom encounter a Gaussian distribution in your data. Even if the Gaussian distribution is important for its statistical properties, in reality you'll have to handle completely different distributions, hence the need for EDA and measures such as skewness and kurtosis.

As an example, a previous example in this chapter shows that the `bill_length_mm` feature presents differences between the mean and the median (see "Measuring variance and range," earlier in this chapter). In this section, you test the same example for skewness and kurtosis to determine whether the variable requires intervention.

When performing the skewness and kurtosis tests, you determine whether the p-value is less than or equal 0.05. If so, you have to reject normality (your variable distributed as a Gaussian distribution), which implies that you could obtain better results if you try to transform the variable into a normal one. The following code shows how to perform the required test:

```
from scipy.stats import skew, skewtest
variable = penguins["body_mass_g"]
s = skew(variable)
zscore, pvalue = skewtest(variable)
print(f"Skewness {s:.3f} z-score " \
      f"{zscore:.3f} p-value {pvalue:.3f}")
```

Here are the skewness scores you get:

```
Skewness 0.470 z-score 3.414 p-value 0.001
```

You can perform another test for kurtosis, as shown in the following code:

```
from scipy.stats import kurtosis, kurtosistest
variable = penguins["body_mass_g"]
k = kurtosis(variable)
zscore, pvalue = kurtosistest(variable)
print(f"Kurtosis {k:.3f} z-score {zscore:.3f} " \
      f"p-value {pvalue:.3f}")
```

Here are the kurtosis scores you obtain:

```
Kurtosis -0.740 z-score -4.337 p-value 0.000
```

The test results tell you that the data is kind of flat and that it has a longer tail to the right, but not enough to make it unusable (see "The Complete Guide to Skewness and Kurtosis" at https://www.simplilearn.com/tutorials/statistics-tutorial/skewness-and-kurtosis if you aren't familiar with how this all works). The real problem is that the curve is not bell shaped, so you should investigate the matter further.

TIP

It's a good practice to test all variables for skewness and kurtosis automatically. You should then proceed to inspect those whose values are the highest visually. Non-normality of a distribution may also conceal different issues, such as outliers to groups that you can perceive only by a graphical visualization.

Counting for Categorical Data

The Palmer Penguin dataset is made of four metric variables and a qualitative target outcome. Just as you use means and variance as descriptive measures for metric variables, so do frequencies strictly relate to qualitative ones.

Because the dataset is made up of metric measurements (depth and lengths in millimeters; mass in grams), you must render it qualitative by dividing it into bins according to specific intervals. The pandas package features two useful functions, cut() and qcut(), that can transform a metric variable into a qualitative one:

>> cut() expects a series of edge values used to cut the measurements or an integer number of groups used to cut the variables into equal-width bins

>> qcut() expects a series of percentiles used to cut the variable

You can obtain a new categorical DataFrame using the following command, which concatenates a binning (see the "Understanding binning and discretization" section of Chapter 9 for details) for each variable:

```
pcts = [0, .25, .5, .75, 1]
penguins_binned = pd.concat(
    [pd.qcut(penguins.iloc[:,0], pcts, precision=1),
     pd.qcut(penguins.iloc[:,1], pcts, precision=1),
     pd.qcut(penguins.iloc[:,2], pcts, precision=1),
     pd.qcut(penguins.iloc[:,3], pcts, precision=1)],
    join='outer', axis = 1)
```

TIP

This example relies on binning (as explained in the "Understanding binning and discretization" section of Chapter 9). However, it could also help to explore when the variable is above or below a singular hurdle value, usually the mean or the median. In this case, you set pd.qcut to the 0.5 percentile or pd.cut to the mean value of the variable.

REMEMBER

Binning transforms numerical variables into categorical ones. This transformation can improve your understanding of data and the machine learning phase that follows by reducing the noise (outliers) or nonlinearity of the transformed variable.

Understanding frequencies

You can obtain a frequency for each categorical variable of the dataset, both for the predictive variable and for the outcome, by using the following code:

```
print(penguins["species"].value_counts())
```

The resulting frequencies show that each group is of a similar size:

```
Adelie       146
Gentoo       119
Chinstrap     68
```

You can try also computing frequencies for the binned body_mass_g that you obtained from the previous paragraph:

```
print(penguins_binned['body_mass_g'].value_counts())
```

In this case, binning produces different groups:

```
(2699.9, 3550.0]    86
(3550.0, 4050.0]    86
```

```
(4775.0, 6300.0]    83
(4050.0, 4775.0]    78
```

The value_counts() provide the range of each bin for 'body_mass_g' in this case and the frequencies, such as 86 for the top range of (2699.9, 3550.0], for each bin. The following example provides you with some basic frequency information, such as the number of unique values in each variable and the mode of the frequency (top and freq rows in the output). The next section of the chapter gives you additional details about where these value come from using a crosstab presentation.

```
print(penguins_binned.describe())
```

Here is the binning description:

```
        bill_length_mm bill_depth_mm flipper_length_mm...
count              333           333               333...
unique               4             4                 4...
top       (32.0, 39.5]  (13.0, 15.6]    (171.9, 190.0]...
freq                86            85                95...
```

Frequencies can signal a number of interesting characteristics of qualitative features:

>> The mode of the frequency distribution that is the most frequent category

>> The other most frequent categories, especially when they are comparable with the mode (bimodal distribution) or if there is a large difference between them

>> The distribution of frequencies among categories, if rapidly decreasing or equally distributed

>> Rare categories

Creating contingency tables

By matching different categorical frequency distributions, you can display the relationship between qualitative variables. The pandas.crosstab() function can match variables or groups of variables, helping to locate possible data structures or relationships.

In the following example, you check how the outcome variable is related to body mass and observe how certain species and body classes seldom appear together.

Figure 13-1 shows the various penguin types along the left side of the output, followed by the output as related to body mass.

```
print(pd.crosstab(penguins["species"],
                  penguins_binned['body_mass_g']))
```

body_mass_g species	(2699.9, 3550.0]	(3550.0, 4050.0]	(4050.0, 4775.0]	(4775.0, 6300.0]
Adelie	64	50	32	0
Chinstrap	22	35	10	1
Gentoo	0	1	36	82

FIGURE 13-1:
A contingency table based on groups and binning.

Creating Applied Visualization for EDA

Up to now, the chapter has explored variables by looking at each one separately. Technically, if you've followed along with the examples, you have created a *univariate* (that is, you've paid attention to stand-alone variations of the data only) description of the data. The data is rich in information because it offers a perspective that goes beyond the single variable, presenting more variables with their reciprocal variations. The way to use more of the data is to create a *bivariate* (seeing how couples of variables relate to each other) exploration. This is also the basis for complex data analysis based on a *multivariate* (simultaneously considering all the existent relations between variables) approach.

If the univariate approach inspected a limited number of descriptive statistics, then matching different variables or groups of variables increases the number of possibilities. Such exploration overloads the data scientist with different tests and bivariate analysis. Using visualization is a rapid way to limit test and analysis to only interesting traces and hints. Visualizations, using a few informative graphics, can convey the variety of statistical characteristics of the variables and their reciprocal relationships with greater ease.

Inspecting boxplots

Boxplots provide a way to represent distributions and their extreme ranges, signaling whether some observations are too far from the core of the data — a problematic situation for some learning algorithms. The following code shows how to create a basic boxplot using the Palmer Penguins dataset after having selected only the numeric variables, thanks to the select_dtypes() method, and having standardized them with the StandardScaler from Scikit-learn (https://scikit-learn.org/stable/modules/generated/sklearn.preprocessing.Standard Scaler.html) in order to have comparable units between variables:

```
from sklearn.preprocessing import StandardScaler

scaler = StandardScaler()
numeric_features = penguins.select_dtypes(
    include=['number'])
penguins_std = pd.DataFrame(
    scaler.fit_transform(numeric_features),
    columns=numeric_features.columns)

boxplots = penguins_std.boxplot(fontsize=9)
```

In Figure 13-2, you see the structure of each variable's distribution at its core, represented by the 25° and 75° percentile (the sides of the box) and the median (at the center of the box). The lines, the so-called whiskers, represent 1.5 times the IQR from the box sides (or by the distance to the most extreme value, if within 1.5 times the IQR). The boxplot marks every observation outside the whisker (deemed an unusual value) by a sign.

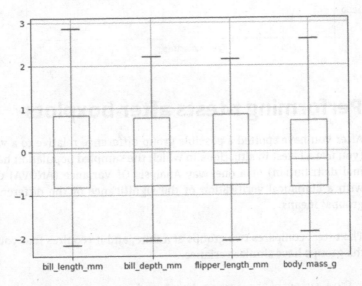

FIGURE 13-2: A boxplot comparing all the standardized variables.

Boxplots are also extremely useful for visually checking group differences. Note in Figure 13-3 how a boxplot can hint that the Gentoo penguin group have on average different body mass, with only partially overlapping values at the fringes of the other two penguin groups.

```
%matplotlib inline
import matplotlib.pyplot as plt
boxplots = penguins.boxplot(column='body_mass_g',
                               by="species", fontsize=10)
plt.show()
```

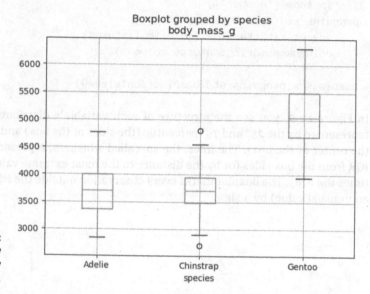

FIGURE 13-3:
A boxplot of body mass arranged by penguin groups.

Performing t-tests after boxplots

After you have spotted a possible group difference relative to a variable, a t-test (you use a t-test in situations in which the sampled population has an exact normal distribution) or a one-way Analysis Of Variance (ANOVA) can provide you with a statistical verification of the significance of the difference between the groups' means.

The t-test compares two groups at a time, and it requires that you check whether the groups have similar variance.

```
from scipy.stats import ttest_ind

group0 = penguins['species'] == 'Adelie'
group1 = penguins['species'] == 'Chinstrap'
```

```
group2 = penguins['species'] == 'Gentoo'
variable = penguins['body_mass_g']

print(f"var1 {variable[group0].var():.3f} " \
      f"var2 {variable[group1].var():03f}")
```

If you compare the variances in body mass of the Adélie group to the Chinstrap group, they appear quite different:

```
var1 210332.428 var2 147713.454785
```

In this case, you set the equal_var parameter to False because their variances are not the same:

```
variable = penguins['body_mass_g']
t, pvalue = ttest_ind(variable[group0], variable[group1],
                      axis=0, equal_var=False)
print(f"t statistic {t:.3f} p-value {pvalue:.3f}")
```

The resulting t statistic and its p-values are

```
t statistic -0.448 p-value 0.655
```

You interpret the pvalue as the probability that the calculated t statistic difference is just due to chance. Usually, when it is below 0.05, you can confirm that the groups' means are significantly different. In our example, with a pvalue of 0.655, which is greater than the typical significance level of 0.05, we do not have sufficient evidence to conclude that the observed difference is statistically significant.

You can simultaneously check more than two groups using the one-way ANOVA test. In this case, the pvalue has an interpretation similar to the t-test:

```
from scipy.stats import f_oneway

variable = penguins['body_mass_g']
f, pvalue = f_oneway(variable[group0],
                     variable[group1],
                     variable[group2])
print(f"One-way ANOVA F-value {f:.3f} p-value "
      f"{pvalue:.3f}")
```

The result from the ANOVA test implies that at least one group is different from the others:

```
One-way ANOVA F-value 341.895 p-value 0.000
```

Observing parallel coordinates

Parallel coordinates can help spot which groups in the outcome variable you could easily separate from the other. It is a truly multivariate plot, because at a glance it represents all your data at the same time. The following example shows how to use parallel coordinates:

```
from pandas.plotting import parallel_coordinates

penguins_std["species"] = penguins["species"].values
pll = parallel_coordinates(penguins_std, "species")
```

As shown in Figure 13-4, on the abscissa axis you find all the quantitative variables aligned. On the ordinate, you find all the observations, carefully represented as parallel lines, each one of a different color given its ownership to a different group.

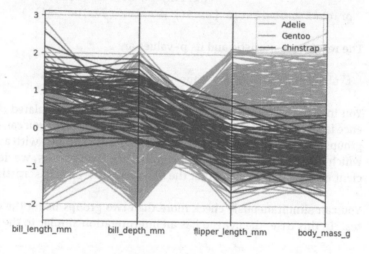

FIGURE 13-4:
Parallel coordinates anticipate whether groups are easily separable.

If the parallel lines of each group stream together along the visualization in a separate part of the graph far from other groups, the group is easily separable. The visualization also provides the means to assert the capability of certain features to separate the groups.

Graphing distributions

You usually render the information that boxplot and descriptive statistics provide into a curve or a histogram, which shows an overview of the complete distribution of values. The output shown in Figure 13-5 represents all the distributions in the dataset. Different variable scales and shapes are immediately visible, such as the fact that penguins' flipper-length feature displays two peaks.

```
densityplot = (penguins["flipper_length_mm"]
                .plot(kind="density"))
```

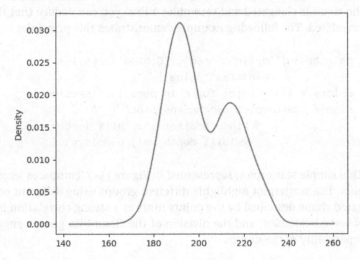

Histograms present another, more detailed, view over distributions:

```
single_distribution = (penguins["flipper_length_mm"]
                        .plot(kind="hist", bins=30))
```

Figure 13-6 shows the histogram of flipper length. It reveals a gap in the distribution that could be a promising discovery if you can relate it to a certain group. (Hint: Look at the Gentoo group.)

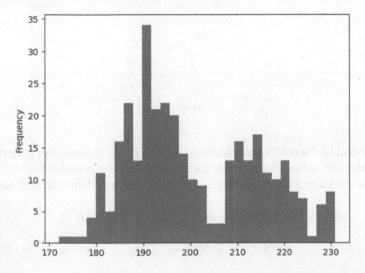

Plotting scatterplots

In scatterplots, the two compared variables provide the coordinates for plotting the observations as points on a plane. The result is usually a cloud of points. When the cloud is elongated and resembles a line, you can deduce that the variables are correlated. The following example demonstrates this principle:

```
palette = {'Adelie': 'red', 'Gentoo': 'yellow',
           'Chinstrap':'blue'}
colors = [palette[c] for c in penguins['species']]
simple_scatterplot = penguins.plot(
                kind='scatter', x='bill_length_mm',
                y='bill_depth_mm', c=colors)
```

This simple scatterplot, represented in Figure 13-7, compares length and depth of bills. The scatterplot highlights different groups using different colors. The elongated shape described by the points hints at a strong correlation between the two observed variables, and the division of the cloud into groups suggests a possible separability of the groups.

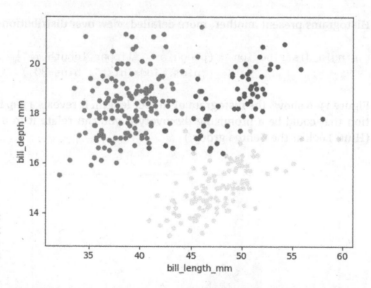

FIGURE 13-7:
A scatterplot reveals how two variables relate to each other.

Because the number of variables isn't too large, you can also generate all the scatterplots automatically from the combination of the variables. This representation is a matrix of scatterplots. The following example demonstrates how to create one:

```
from pandas.plotting import scatter_matrix

palette = palette = {'Adelie': 'red', 'Gentoo': 'yellow',
```

```
                   'Chinstrap':'blue'}
colors = [palette[c] for c in penguins['species']]
matrix_of_scatterplots = scatter_matrix(
    penguins, figsize=(6, 6),
    color=colors, diagonal='kde')
```

In Figure 13-8, you can see the resulting visualization for the Palmer Penguins dataset. The diagonal representing the density estimation can be replaced by a histogram using the parameter `diagonal='hist'`.

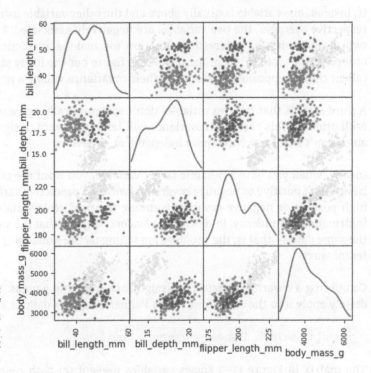

FIGURE 13-8:
A matrix of
scatterplots
displays more
information at
one time.

Understanding Correlation

Just as the relationship between variables is graphically representable, it is also measurable by a statistical estimate. When working with numeric variables, the estimate is a correlation, and the Pearson's correlation is the most famous. The Pearson's correlation is the foundation for complex linear estimation models. When you work with categorical variables, the estimate is an association, and the chi-square statistic is the most frequently used tool for measuring association between features.

Using covariance and correlation

Covariance is the first measure of the relationship of two variables. It determines whether both variables have a coincident behavior with respect to their mean. If the single values of two variables are usually above or below their respective averages, the two variables have a positive association. It means that they tend to agree, and you can figure out the behavior of one of the two by looking at the other. In such a case, their covariance will be a positive number, and the higher the number, the higher the agreement.

If, instead, one variable is usually above and the other variable usually below their respective averages, the two variables are negatively associated. Even though the two disagree, it's an interesting situation for making predictions, because by observing the state of one of them, you can figure out the likely state of the other (albeit they're opposite). In this case, their covariance will be a negative number.

A third state is that the two variables don't systematically agree or disagree with each other. In this case, the covariance will tend to be zero, a sign that the variables don't share much and have independent behaviors.

Ideally, when you have a numeric target variable, you want the target variable to have a high positive or negative covariance with the predictive variables. Having a high positive or negative covariance among the predictive variables is a sign of information redundancy. *Information redundancy* signals that the variables point to the same data — that is, the variables are telling us the same thing in slightly different ways.

Computing a covariance matrix is straightforward using pandas. You can immediately apply it to the DataFrame of the Palmer Penguins dataset as shown here:

```
penguins.select_dtypes(np.number).cov()
```

The matrix in Figure 13-9 shows variables present on both rows and columns. By observing different row and column combinations, you can determine the value of covariance between the variables chosen. After observing these results, you can immediately understand that little relationship exists between bill length and bill depth, meaning that they're different informative values. However, there could be a special relationship between body mass and flipper length, but the example doesn't tell what this relationship is because the measure is not easily interpretable.

	bill_length_mm	bill_depth_mm	flipper_length_mm	body_mass_g
bill_length_mm	29.906333	-2.462091	50.058195	2595.623304
bill_depth_mm	-2.462091	3.877888	-15.947248	-748.456122
flipper_length_mm	50.058195	-15.947248	196.441677	9852.191649
body_mass_g	2595.623304	-748.456122	9852.191649	648372.487699

FIGURE 13-9:
A covariance matrix of the Palmer Penguins dataset.

The scale of the variables you observe influences covariance, so you should use a different, but standard, measure. The solution is to use correlation, which is the covariance estimation after having standardized the variables. Here is an example of obtaining a correlation using a simple pandas method:

```
penguins.select_dtypes(np.number).corr()
```

You can examine the resulting correlation matrix in Figure 13-10:

	bill_length_mm	bill_depth_mm	flipper_length_mm	body_mass_g
bill_length_mm	1.000000	-0.228626	0.653096	0.589451
bill_depth_mm	-0.228626	1.000000	-0.577792	-0.472016
flipper_length_mm	0.653096	-0.577792	1.000000	0.872979
body_mass_g	0.589451	-0.472016	0.872979	1.000000

FIGURE 13-10:
A correlation matrix of the Palmer Penguins dataset.

Now that's even more interesting, because correlation values are bound between values of −1 and +1, so the relationship between body mass and flipper length is positive and, with a 0.87, it is very near to the maximum possible.

You can compute covariance and correlation matrices also by means of NumPy commands, as shown here:

```
import numpy as np

covariance_matrix = np.cov(penguins.iloc[:,:4], rowvar=0)
correlation_matrix = np.corrcoef(penguins.iloc[:,:4],
                                 rowvar=0)
```

REMEMBER

In statistics, this kind of correlation is a *Pearson correlation*, and its coefficient is a *Pearson's r*.

TIP

Another nice trick is to square the correlation. By squaring it, you lose the sign of the relationship. The new number tells you the percentage of the information shared by two variables. In this example, a correlation of 0.76 implies that 76 percent of the information is shared between the two variables. You can obtain a squared correlation matrix using this command: `penguins.select_dtypes(np.number).corr()**2`.

TECHNICAL STUFF

Something important to remember is that covariance and correlation are based on means, so they tend to represent relationships that you can express using linear formulations. Variables in real-life datasets usually don't have nice linear formulations. Instead they are highly nonlinear, with curves and bends. You can rely on mathematical transformations to make the relationships linear between variables anyway. A good rule to remember is to use correlations only to assert relationships between variables, not to exclude them.

Using nonparametric correlation

Correlations can work fine when your variables are numeric and their relationship is strictly linear. Sometimes, your feature could be ordinal (a numeric variable but with orderings) or you may suspect some nonlinearity due to non-normal distributions in your data. A possible solution is to test the doubtful correlations with a nonparametric correlation, such as a Spearman rank-order correlation (which means that it has fewer requirements in terms of distribution of considered variables). A *Spearman correlation* transforms your numeric values into rankings and then correlates the rankings, thus minimizing the influence of any nonlinear relationship between the two variables under scrutiny. The resulting correlation, commonly denoted as *rho*, is to be interpreted in the same way as a Pearson's correlation.

As an example, you verify the relationship between bill length and bill depth whose Pearson correlation was quite weak:

```
from scipy.stats import spearmanr
from scipy.stats import pearsonr

a = penguins['bill_length_mm']
b = penguins['bill_depth_mm']
rho_coef, rho_p = spearmanr(a, b)
r_coef, r_p = pearsonr(a, b)
print(f"Pearson r {r_coef:.3f} | "
      f"Spearman rho {rho_coef:.3f}")
```

Here is the resulting comparison:

```
Pearson r -0.229 | Spearman rho -0.214
```

In this case, the code confirms the weak association between the two variables using the nonparametric test because the outputs are fairly close to 0 (see "Conduct and Interpret a Spearman Rank Correlation" at `https://www.statistics solutions.com/free-resources/directory-of-statistical-analyses/ spearman-rank-correlation/` for a more detailed discussion of this topic).

Considering chi-square for tables

You can apply another nonparametric test for relationship when working with cross-tables. This test is applicable to both categorical and numeric data (after it has been discretized into bins). The chi-square statistic tells you when the table distribution of two variables is statistically comparable to a table in which the two variables are hypothesized as not related to each other (the so-called independence hypothesis). Here is an example of how you use this technique to figure out whether the bill length associates with the penguin species:

```
from scipy.stats import chi2_contingency

table = pd.crosstab(penguins["species"],
                    penguins_binned["bill_length_mm"])
chi2, p, dof, expected = chi2_contingency(table.values)
print(f"Chi-square {chi2:.2f} p-value {p:.3f}")
```

The resulting chi-square statistic is

```
Chi-square 264.02 p-value 0.000
```

As seen before, the p-value is the chance that the chi-square difference is just by chance. The high chi-square value and the significant p-value are signaling that the `bill_length_mm` variable can be effectively used for distinguishing between penguins groups.

REMEMBER

The larger the chi-square value, the greater the probability that two variables are related, yet, the chi-square measure value depends on how many cells the table has. Do not use the chi-square measure to compare different chi-square tests unless you know that the tables in comparison are of the same shape.

TIP

The chi-square is particularly interesting for assessing the relationships between binned numeric variables, even in the presence of strong nonlinearity that can fool Person's r. Contrary to correlation measures, it can inform you of a possible association, but it won't provide clear details of its direction or absolute magnitude.

Working with Cramér's V

Testing whether an association exists between categorical features and between numeric and categoricals can provide useful information, but it would be more actionable if you could quantify such an association, as you can between numeric features with Pearson correlation and nonparametric rank-order measures. A solution is to use *Cramér's V*, a measure that translates chi-square statistics into a measure of association ranging from −1 to 1, just like the Pearson correlation.

To calculate Cramér's V, you first need to calculate the chi-square statistic between the two categorical variables, which you can do by using the SciPy function `chi2_contingency()`, as shown in the "Considering chi-square for tables" section of the chapter. After you have the chi-square statistic, you can calculate Cramér's V using the following formula:

```
V = sqrt(chi_square / (n * min(k-1, r-1)))
```

where n is the total number of observations, k is the number of rows in the contingency table, and r is the number of columns. The `min()` function ensures that the calculation does not exceed the maximum possible value of V, which is 1. Here you can find everything translated into code:

```
n = len(penguins)
k, r = table.shape
V = np.sqrt(chi2 / (n * min(k-1, r-1)))
print(f"Cramer's V {V:.2f}")
```

Here is the estimated association between species and the bill length:

```
Cramer's V 0.63
```

Modifying Data Distributions

As a by-product of data exploration, in an EDA phase you can do the following:

>> Obtain new feature creation from the combination of different but related variables

>> Spot hidden groups or strange values lurking in your data

>> Try some useful modifications of your data distributions by binning (or other discretizations such as binary variables)

When performing EDA, you need to consider the importance of data transformation in preparation for the learning phase, which also means using certain mathematical formulas. Most machine learning algorithms work best when the Pearson's correlation is maximized between the variables you have to predict and the variable you use to predict them. The following sections present an overview of the most common procedures used during EDA in order to enhance the relationship between variables. The data transformation you choose depends on the actual distribution of your data, therefore it's not something you decide beforehand; rather, you discover it by EDA and multiple testing. In addition, these sections highlight the need to match the transformation process to the mathematical formula you use.

Using different statistical distributions

During data science practice, you'll meet with a wide range of different distributions — with some of them named by probabilistic theory, others not. For some distributions, the assumption that they should behave as a normal distribution may hold, but for others, it may not, and that could be a problem depending on what algorithms you use for the learning process. As a general rule, if your model is a linear regression or part of the linear model family because it boils down to a summation of coefficients, then both variable standardization and distribution transformation should be considered.

REMEMBER

Apart from the linear models, many other machine learning algorithms are actually indifferent to the distribution of the variables you use. However, transforming the variables in your dataset to render their distribution more Gaussian-like could result in positive effects.

Creating a Z-score standardization

In your EDA process, you may have realized that your variables have different scales and are heterogeneous in their distributions. As a consequence of your analysis, you need to transform the variables in a way that makes them easily comparable:

```
from sklearn.preprocessing import StandardScaler

scaler = StandardScaler()
bill_depth_mm = scaler.fit_transform(
    penguins[['bill_depth_mm']])
```

REMEMBER

Some algorithms will work in unexpected ways if you don't rescale your variables using standardization. As a rule of thumb, pay attention to any linear models, cluster analysis, and any algorithm that claims to be based on statistical measures.

Transforming other notable distributions

When you check variables with high skewness and kurtosis for their correlation, the results may disappoint you. As you find out in the "Defining measures of normality" section, earlier in this chapter, using a nonparametric measure of correlation, such as Spearman's, may tell you more about two variables than Pearson's r may tell you. In this case, you should transform your insight into a new, transformed feature. Scikit-learn offers the QuantileTransformer that can convert any distribution into a uniform or a normal distribution. Here's how it works on bill depth, a variable with a non-normal distribution:

```
from sklearn.preprocessing import QuantileTransformer

uniform = QuantileTransformer(
    n_quantiles=30, output_distribution="uniform")
bill_depth_mm = uniform.fit_transform(
    penguins[['bill_depth_mm']])
plt.hist(bill_depth_mm, bins=30);
```

In Figure 13-11 you can see how the QuantileTransformer has distributed the values in a shape that resembles a uniform distribution. (Although the result is not perfect, it is still impressive.) It's possible to use it to transform the same variable into a normally distributed one as well:

```
normal = QuantileTransformer(
    n_quantiles=30, output_distribution="normal")
bill_depth_mm = normal.fit_transform(
    penguins[['bill_depth_mm']])
plt.hist(bill_depth_mm, bins=30);
```

In Figure 13-12 you can see the results. It's important to keep in mind that such transformations are useful if they increase their association with the target of your machine learning model and if, by transforming the distribution, you don't harm how the variable interacts with the others.

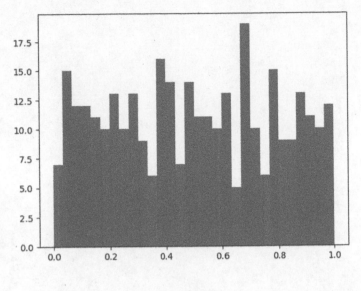

FIGURE 13-11:
The distribution
of bill depth
transformed into
a uniform
distribution.

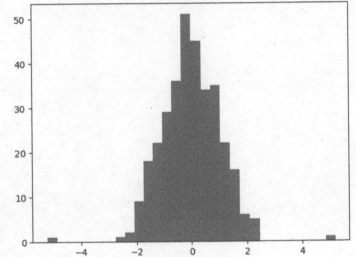

FIGURE 13-12:
The distribution
of bill depth
transformed into
a normal
distribution.

Chapter **14**

Reducing Dimensionality

Big data is defined as an extensive collection of data that is so massive that traditional processing techniques struggle to handle it effectively. The manipulation of big data differentiates statistical problems, which are based on small samples, from data science problems. You typically use traditional statistical techniques on small problems and data science techniques on big problems.

Data may be viewed as big because it consists of many examples, and this is the first kind of big that spontaneously comes to mind. Analyzing a database of millions of customers and interacting with them all simultaneously is really challenging, but that isn't the only possible perspective of big data. Another view of big data is data dimensionality, which refers to how many aspects of the cases an application tracks. Data with high dimensionality may offer many features (variables) — often hundreds or thousands of them. And that may turn into a real problem. Even if you're observing only a few cases for a short time, dealing with too many features can make most analysis intractable.

The complexity of working with so many dimensions drives the necessity for various data techniques to filter the information — keeping the data that seems to solve the problem better. The filter reduces dimensionality by removing redundant information in high-dimension datasets. The focus in this chapter is on reducing data dimensions when the data has too many repetitions of the same information. You can view this reduction as a kind of information compression, which is similar to compressing files on a hard disk in order to save space.

REMEMBER

You don't have to type the source code for this chapter manually; using the downloadable source is a lot easier (see the Introduction for download instructions). The source code for this chapter appears in the P4DS4D3_14_Reducing_Dimensionality.ipynb file.

Understanding SVD

The core of data reduction magic lies in an operation of linear algebra called Singular Value Decomposition (SVD). *SVD* is a mathematical method that takes data as input in the form of a single matrix and gives back three resulting matrices that, multiplied together, return the original input matrix. (You can find a short introduction to SVD at https://machinelearningmastery.com/singular-value-decomposition-for-machine-learning/.) The formula of SVD is

$$M = U * s * Vh$$

Here is a short explanation of the letters used in the equation:

>> **U:** Contains all the information about the rows (observations)
>> **Vh:** Contains all the information about the columns (features)
>> **s:** Records the SVD process (a type of log record)

Creating three matrices out of one seems counterproductive when the goal is to reduce data dimensions. When using SVD, you seem to be generating more data, not reducing it. However, SVD conceals the magic in the process, because as it builds these new matrices, it separates the information regarding the rows from the columns of the original matrix. As a result, it compresses all the valuable information into the first columns of the new matrices.

The resulting matrix s shows how the compression happened. The sum of all the values in s tells you how much information was previously stored in your original matrix, and each value in s reports how much data has accumulated in each respective column of U and Vh.

To understand how this all works, you need to look at individual values. For instance, if the sum of s is 100 and the first value of s is 99, that means that 99 percent of the information is now stored in the first column of U. Therefore, you can happily discard all the remaining columns after the first column without losing any important information for your data science knowledge-discovery process.

Looking for dimensionality reduction

It's time to see how Python can help you reduce data complexity. The following example demonstrates a method for reducing your big data. You can use this technique in many other interesting applications, too.

```
import numpy as np
A = np.array([[1, 3, 4], [2, 3, 5], [1, 2, 3], [5, 4, 6]])
print(A)
```

The code prints matrix A, which appears in the following examples:

```
[[1 3 4]
 [2 3 5]
 [1 2 3]
 [5 4 6]]
```

Matrix, A contains the data you want to reduce. A is made of four observations containing three features each. Using the module linalg from NumPy, you can access the svd function that exactly splits your original matrix into three variables: U, s, and Vh.

```
U, s, Vh = np.linalg.svd(A, full_matrices=False)
print(np.shape(U), np.shape(s), np.shape(Vh))
print(s)
```

The output enumerates the shapes of U, s, and Vh, respectively, and prints the content of the s variable:

```
(4, 3) (3,) (3, 3)
[12.26362747 2.11085464 0.38436189]
```

Matrix U, representing the rows, has four row values. Matrix Vh is a square matrix, and its three rows represent the original columns. Matrix s is a diagonal matrix. A diagonal matrix contains zeros in every element but its diagonal. The length of its diagonal is exactly that of the three original columns. Inside s, you find that most of the values are in the first elements, indicating that the first column is what holds the most information (about 83 percent), the second has some values (about 14 percent), and the third contains the residual values. To obtain these percentages, you add the three values together to obtain 14.758844 and then use that number to divide the individual columns. For example, 12.26362747 / 14.758844 is 0.8309341483655495 or about 83 percent.

You can check whether the SVD keeps its promises by viewing the example output. The example reconstructs the original matrix using the dot NumPy function to multiply U, s (diagonal), and Vh. The dot function performs matrix multiplication, which is a multiplication procedure slightly different from the arithmetic one. Here is an example of a full matrix reconstruction:

```
print(np.dot(np.dot(U, np.diag(s)), Vh))
```

The code prints the reconstructed original matrix A:

```
[[ 1.  3.  4.]
 [ 2.  3.  5.]
 [ 1.  2.  3.]
 [ 5.  4.  6.]]
```

The reconstruction is perfect, but clearly you need to keep the same number of components in the resulting matrix U as variables as appeared in the original dataset. No dimensionality reduction really happened, you just restructured data in a way that makes the new variables uncorrelated (and this is useful for clustering algorithms, as you discover in Chapter 15).

TIP

When working with SVD, you usually care about the resulting matrix U, the matrix representing the rows, because it's a replacement of your initial dataset.

Now it's time to play with the results a little and obtain some real reduction. For example, you might want to see what happens when you exclude the third column from matrix U, the less important of the three. The following example shows what happens when you cut the last column from all three matrices.

```
print(np.round(np.dot(np.dot(U[:,:2], np.diag(s[:2])),
                      Vh[:2,:]),1))
```

The code prints the reconstruction of the original matrix using the first two components:

```
[[ 1.  2.8 4.1]
 [ 2.  3.2 4.8]
 [ 1.  2.  3. ]
 [ 5.  3.9 6. ]]
```

The output is almost perfect. It means that you could drop the last component and use U as a reasonable substitute for the original dataset. There are a few decimal points of difference. To take the example further, the following code removes both the second and third columns from matrix U:

```
print(np.round(np.dot(np.dot(U[:,:1], np.diag(s[:1])),
                 Vh[:1,:]),1))
```

Here is the reconstruction of the original matrix using a single component:

```
[[ 2.1 2.5 3.7]
 [ 2.6 3.1 4.6]
 [ 1.6 1.8 2.8]
 [ 3.7 4.3 6.5]]
```

Now there are more errors. Some elements of the matrix are missing more than a few decimal points. However, you can see that most of the numeric information is intact, and you could safely use matrix U in place of your initial data. Just imagine the potential of using such a technique on a larger matrix, one with hundreds of columns that you can first transform into a U matrix and then safely drop most of the columns.

TIP

One of the difficult issues to consider is determining how many columns to keep. Creating a cumulated sum of the diagonal matrix s (using the NumPy cumsum function is perfect for this task) is useful for keeping track of how information is expressed, and by how many columns. As a general rule, you should consider solutions maintaining from 70 to 99 percent of the original information; however, that's not a strict rule — it really depends on how important it is for you to be able to reconstruct the original dataset.

Using SVD to measure the invisible

A property of SVD is to compress the original data at such a level and in such a smart way that, in certain situations, the technique can really create new meaningful and useful features, not just compressed variables. Therefore, you could have used the three columns of the U matrix in the previous example as new features.

If your data contains hints and clues about a hidden cause or motif, an SVD can put them together and offer you proper answers and insights. That is especially true when your data is made up of interesting pieces of information like the ones in the following list:

>> **Text in documents hint at ideas and meaningful categories.** Just as you can make up your mind about treated themes by reading blogs and newsgroups, so also can SVD help you deduce a meaningful classification of groups of documents or the specific topics being written about in each of them.

>> **Reviews of specific movies or books hint at your personal preferences and at larger product categories.** So if you say that you loved the original *Star Trek* series collection on a rating site, it becomes easy to determine what you like in terms of other films, consumer products, or even personality types.

An example of a method based on SVD is *Latent Semantic Indexing* (LSI), which has been successfully used to associate documents and words on the basis of the idea that words, though different, tend to have the same meaning when placed in similar contexts. This type of analysis suggests not only synonymous words but also higher grouping concepts. For example, an LSI analysis on some sample sports news may group together baseball teams of the Major League Baseball (MLB) teams based solely on the co-occurrence of team names in similar articles, without any previous knowledge of what a baseball team or the MLB are.

Performing Factor Analysis and PCA

SVD operates directly on the numeric values in data, but you can also express data as a relationship between variables. Each feature has a certain variation. You can calculate the variability as the variance measure around the mean. The more the variance, the more the information contained inside the variable. In addition, if you place the variable into a set, you can compare the variance of two variables to determine whether they correlate, which is a measure of how strongly they have similar values.

Checking all the possible correlations of a variable with the others in the set, you can discover that you may have two types of variance:

>> **Unique variance:** Some variance is unique to the variable under examination. It cannot be associated to what happens to any other variable.

>> **Shared variance:** Some variance is shared with one or more other variables, creating redundancy in the data. Redundancy implies that you can find the same information, with slightly different values, in various features and across many observations.

Of course, the next step is to determine the reason for shared variance. Trying to answer such a question, as well as determining how to deal with unique and shared variances, led to the creation of factor analysis and principal component analysis (commonly referred to as PCA).

Considering the psychometric model

Long before many machine learning algorithms were thought up, *psychometrics*, the discipline in psychology that is concerned with psychological measurement, tried to find a statistical solution to effectively measure dimensions in personality. Our personality, as with other aspects of ourselves, is not directly measurable. For example, it isn't possible to measure precisely how much a person is introverted or intelligent. Questionnaires and psychological tests only hint at these values.

Psychologists knew of SVD and tried to apply it to the problem. Shared variance attracted their attention: If some variables are almost the same, they should have the same root cause, they thought. Psychologists created *factor analysis* to perform this task and instead of applying SVD directly to data, they applied it to a newly created matrix tracking the common variance, in the hope of condensing all the information and recovering new useful features called *factors*.

Looking for hidden factors

A good way to show how to use factor analysis is to start with the Palmer Penguins dataset used in Chapter 13:

```python
import pandas as pd
from sklearn.preprocessing import StandardScaler

def load_palmer_penguins():
    url = "https://raw.githubusercontent.com/allisonhorst/" \
          "palmerpenguins/main/inst/extdata/penguins.csv"
    numeric_features = ["bill_length_mm", "bill_depth_mm",
                        "flipper_length_mm", "body_mass_g"]
    data = pd.read_csv(url).dropna()
    target = data.species.replace({'Adelie':1, 'Gentoo':2,
                                   'Chinstrap':3})
    data[numeric_features] = StandardScaler().\
        .fit_transform(data[numeric_features])
    return data[numeric_features], target

X, y = load_palmer_penguins()
```

After the code uploads the data, it can proceed with the process of recombining it into factors:

```python
from sklearn.decomposition import FactorAnalysis
factor = FactorAnalysis(n_components=4).fit(X)
```

In the above code snippet, the FactorAnalysis class is initialized with a request to look for four factors. The data is then fitted. You can explore the results by observing the components_ attribute, which returns an array containing measures of the relationship between the newly created factors, placed in rows, and the original features, placed in columns:

```
print(pd.DataFrame(factor.components_, columns=X.columns).T)
```

In the output, you find how the factors produced by the code, indicated in the columns, relate to the original variables depicted on the rows. You can interpret the numbers as being correlations:

	0	1	2	3
bill_length_mm	0.665834	0.179744	-0.0	0.0
bill_depth_mm	-0.561658	0.236985	0.0	-0.0
flipper_length_mm	0.874881	-0.009841	0.0	-0.0
body_mass_g	0.840450	0.010157	0.0	0.0

At the intersection of each factor and feature, a positive number indicates that a positive correlation exists between the two; a negative number points out that they diverge and that one is contrary to the other. In the test on the Palmer Penguins dataset, for example, the resulting factors should be a maximum of 2, not 4, because only two factors have significant connections with the original features. You can use these two factors as new variables in your project because they reflect an unseen but important feature that the previously available data only hinted at.

TIP

You have to test different values of n_components because you can't know how many factors exist in the data. If the algorithm is required for more factors than exist, it will generate factors with low or zero values in the components_ array.

Using components, not factors

If an SVD could be successfully applied to the common variance, you might wonder why you can't apply it to all the variances. Using a slightly modified starting matrix, all the relationships in the data could be reduced and compressed in a similar way to how SVD does it. The results of this process, which are quite similar to SVD, are called *principal components analysis* (PCA). The newly created features are named *components*. In contrast to factors, components aren't described as the root cause of the data structure but are just restructured data, so you can view them as a big, smart summation of selected variables.

For data science applications, PCA and SVD are quite similar. However, PCA isn't affected by the scale of the original features (because it works on correlation measures that are all bound between −1 and +1 values) and PCA focuses on rebuilding the relationship between the variables, thus offering different results from SVD.

Achieving dimensionality reduction

The procedure to obtain a PCA is quite similar to the factor analysis. The difference is that you don't specify the number of components to extract. When you declare n_components as "mle", you are using the maximum likelihood estimation (MLE) method to guess the right number of dimensions. MLE figures out a plausible guess by using statistics and probability. It looks at the data or information you have and tries to find the values that are most likely to have produced that data. The following example shows how to perform this task:

```
from sklearn.decomposition import PCA
pca = PCA(n_components="mle").fit(X)
print('Explained variance by each component:',
      pca.explained_variance_ratio_.round(5),"\n")
print(pd.DataFrame(pca.components_, columns=X.columns).T)
```

In the output, you can observe how the initial variance of the dataset distributes across the components (for instance, here the first component accounts for 68.6 percent of the variance initially present in the dataset) and the resulting PCA matrix of components, where each component (displayed in the rows) relates to each original variable (placed on the columns):

```
Explained variance by each component: [0.68634 0.19453 0.09216]

                          0         1         2
bill_length_mm      0.453753  0.600195  0.642495
bill_depth_mm      -0.399047  0.796170 -0.425800
flipper_length_mm   0.576825  0.005788 -0.236095
body_mass_g         0.549675  0.076464 -0.591737
```

In this decomposition of the Palmer Penguins dataset, the vector array provided by explained_variance_ratio_ indicates that most of the information is concentrated into the first component (68.6 percent). You saw this same sort of result after the factor analysis. In this case it's possible to reduce the entire dataset to three components, providing a reduction of noise and redundant information from the original dataset.

Squeezing information with t-SNE

Because SVD and PCA reduce data complexity, you can use the reduced dimensions for visualization. However, often PCA scatter plots aren't helpful for visualization because you need more plots to see how examples relate to each other. Therefore, scientists created algorithms for *nonlinear dimensionality reduction* (also called *manifold learning*), such as t-SNE, to visualize relations in complex datasets of hundreds of variables using simple bidimensional scatter plots.

The t-SNE algorithm starts by randomly projecting the data into the indicated number of dimensions (usually two for a bidimensional representation) as points. Then, in a series of iterations, the algorithm tries to push points that refer to similar examples in the dataset (similarity is calculated using probability) together and push points that are too different from each other apart. After a few iterations, similar points should arrange themselves in clusters separated from the other points. This arrangement helps represent data as a plot, and you inspect it to gain insight about the data and its meaning.

This example uses the handwritten number dataset in Scikit-learn. The dataset contains the grayscale images of handwritten numbers represented as an 8-x-8 matrix of values ranging from zero to one. (They are shades, where zero is pure black, and one is white.)

```
from sklearn.datasets import load_digits
digits = load_digits()
X = digits.data
y = digits.target
```

After loading the dataset, you run the t-SNE algorithm to squeeze the data:

```
from sklearn.manifold import TSNE
tsne = TSNE(n_components=2,
            learning_rate="auto",
            init="random",
            random_state=0,
            perplexity=50,
            early_exaggeration=25,
            n_iter=300)

Tx = tsne.fit_transform(X)
```

This example sets the initial `perplexity`, `early_exaggeration` and `n_iter` parameters, which contribute to the quality of the ending representation. You can try different values of these parameters and obtain slightly different solutions. When the dataset is reduced, you can plot it and place the original number label to the area of the plot where most of the similar examples are, as follows:

```
%matplotlib inline
import numpy as np
import matplotlib.pyplot as plt
plt.xticks([], [])
plt.yticks([], [])
for target in np.unique(y):
```

```
selection = y==target
X1, X2 = Tx[selection, 0], Tx[selection, 1]
c1, c2 = np.median(X1), np.median(X2)
plt.plot(X1, X2, 'o', ms=5)
plt.text(c1, c2, target, fontsize=18)
```

In Figure 14-1 you see the resulting plot, which reveals how some handwritten numbers such as zero, six, or four are easily distinguishable from others, whereas numbers such as three and nine (or five and eight) could be more easily misinterpreted.

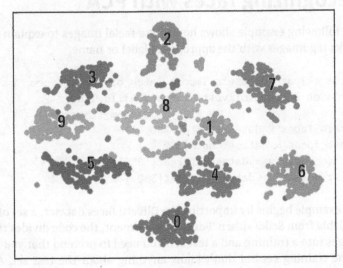

FIGURE 14-1:
The resulting projection of the handwritten data by the t-SNE algorithm.

According to the article "How to t-SNE Effectively" (source: https://distill.pub/2016/misread-tsne/), it is crucial to use the t-SNE technique appropriately. This is because it's easy to mistakenly perceive clusters and patterns in data where they may not actually exist. However, despite these potential pitfalls, our experience suggests that, when you're trying to figure how your data works, t-SNE can provide more insightful results compared to other methods like PCA or SVD.

Understanding Some Applications

Understanding the algorithms that compose the family of SVD-derived data decomposition techniques is complex because of their mathematical complexity and numerous variants (such as Factor, PCA, and SVD). A few examples will help you understand the best ways to employ these powerful data science tools. In the following paragraphs, you work with algorithms you likely seen in action when

>> Performing a search of images on a search engine or publishing an image on a social network

>> Automatically labeling blog posts or questions to Q&A websites

>> Receiving purchase recommendations on e-commerce websites

Recognizing faces with PCA

The following example shows how to use facial images to explain how social networks tag images with the appropriate label or name.

```
from sklearn.datasets import fetch_olivetti_faces
dataset = fetch_olivetti_faces(shuffle=True,
                               random_state=101)
train_faces = dataset.data[:350,:]
test_faces = dataset.data[350:,:]
train_answers = dataset.target[:350]
test_answers = dataset.target[350:]
```

The example begins by importing the Olivetti faces dataset, a set of images readily available from Scikit-learn. For this experiment, the code divides the set of labeled images into a training and a test set. You need to pretend that you know the labels of the training set but don't know anything about the test set. As a result, you want to associate images from the test set to the most similar image from the training set.

The Olivetti dataset consists of 400 photos taken of 40 people (so there are 10 photos of each person). Even though the photos represent the same person, each photo is taken at different times during the day, with different light and facial expressions or details (for example, with glasses and without). The images are 64 x 64 pixels, so unfolding the pixels into features creates a dataset made of 400 cases and 4,096 variables. You can obtain additional dataset information using: print(dataset.DESCR), as shown in the downloadable source code. For additional information about the dataset, refer to AT&T Laboratories Cambridge web pages: https://cam-orl.co.uk/facedatabase.html. The following code snippet transforms and reduces the images using a PCA algorithm from Scikit-learn:

```
from sklearn.decomposition import PCA
n_components = 25
```

```
Rpca = PCA(svd_solver='randomized',
           n_components=n_components,
           whiten=True)
Rpca.fit(train_faces)
print(f"Explained variance by {n_components}")
print(f"components: ",
       f"{np.sum(Rpca.explained_variance_ratio_):0.3f}")
compressed_train_faces = Rpca.transform(train_faces)
compressed_test_faces  = Rpca.transform(test_faces)
```

When executed, the run outputs the proportion of variance retained by the first 25 components of the resulting PCA:

```
Explained variance by 25 components: 0.794.
```

The `svd_solver='randomized'` setting indicates that a randomized algorithm is used to perform the calculations in PCA. This works better when the dataset is large (many rows and variables). The decomposition creates 25 new variables (`n_components` parameter) and whitening (`whiten=True`), thus removing some constant noise (created by textual and photo granularity) from images. The resulting decomposition uses 25 components, which is about 80 percent of information held in 4,096 features.

```
%matplotlib inline
import matplotlib.pyplot as plt

photo = 17
print(f"The represented person is subject "
      f"{test_answers[photo]}")
plt.subplot(1, 2, 1)
plt.axis('off')
plt.title(f"Unknown photo {photo} in test set")
plt.imshow(test_faces[photo].reshape(64, 64),
           cmap=plt.cm.gray, interpolation="nearest")
plt.show()
```

Figure 14-2 represents subject number 34, whose photo number 17 has been chosen as the test set.

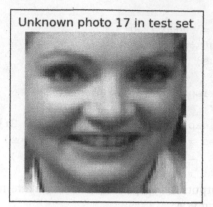

FIGURE 14-2:
The example
application would
like to find
similar photos.

After test set decomposition, the example takes the data relative only to photo 17 and subtracts it from the decomposition of the training set. Now the training set is made of differences with respect to the example photo. The code squares them (to remove negative values) and sums them by row, which results in a series of summed errors. The most similar photos are the ones with the least-squared errors, the ones whose differences are the least.

```python
mask = compressed_test_faces[photo,]
squared_errors = np.sum((compressed_train_faces
                         - mask)**2, axis=1)
minimum_error_face = np.argmin(squared_errors)
most_resembling = list(np.where(squared_errors < 20)[0])
print(f"Best resembling subject in training set: "
      f"{train_answers[minimum_error_face]}")
```

The preceding code returns the code number of the best resembling person in the dataset, which effectively corresponds with the code of the subject chosen from the test set:

```
Best resembling subject in training set: 34
```

You check the work done by the code by displaying photo 17 from the test set next to the top three images from the training set that best resemble it (as shown in Figure 14-3):

```python
%matplotlib inline
import matplotlib.pyplot as plt
plt.subplot(2, 2, 1)
plt.axis('off')
plt.title(f'Unknown face {photo} in test set')
plt.imshow(test_faces[photo].reshape(64, 64),
```

```
            cmap=plt.cm.gray,
            interpolation='nearest')
for k,m in enumerate(most_resembling[:3]):
    plt.subplot(2, 2, 2+k)
    plt.title(f'Match in train set no. {m}')
    plt.axis('off')
    plt.imshow(train_faces[m].reshape(64, 64),
            cmap=plt.cm.gray,
            interpolation='nearest')
plt.show()
```

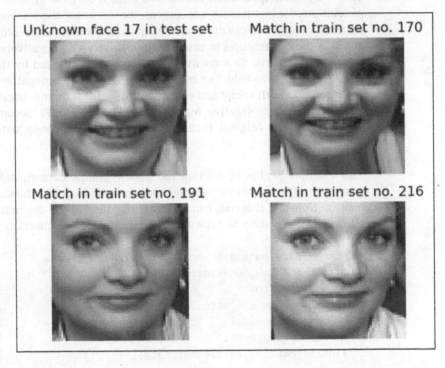

FIGURE 14-3: The output shows the results that resemble the test image.

Even though the most similar photo from the training data it is just a differently scaled version of the one in the test set, the other two photos are displaying a different pose of the same person present in the test photo 17. This example using PCA, starting from an example image, accurately finds other photos of the very same person from a set of images.

Extracting topics with NMF

Textual data is another field of application for the family of data reduction algorithms. The idea that prompted such application is that if a group of people talks or writes about something, they tend to use words from a limited set because they refer or relate to the same topic; they share some meaning or are part of the same group. Consequently, if you have a collection of texts and don't know what topics the text references, you can reverse the previous reasoning — you can simply look for groups of words that tend to associate, so the group newly formed by dimensionality reduction hints at the topics you'd like to know about.

This is a perfect application for the SVD family, because by reducing the number of columns, the features (in a document, the words are the features) will gather in dimensions, and you can discover the topics by checking high-scoring words. SVD and PCA provide features to relate both positively and negatively with the newly created dimensions. So a resulting topic may be expressed by the presence of a word (high positive value) or by the absence of it (high negative value), making interpretation both tricky and counterintuitive for humans. Luckily, Scikit-learn includes the Non-Negative Matrix Factorization (NMF) decomposition class, which allows an original feature to relate only positively with the resulting dimensions.

This example begins by loading the 20newsgroups dataset, selecting only the posts regarding objects for sale and automatically removing headers, footers, and quotes. (Note that this code can require a long time to run depending on the capabilities of your system and the speed of your network connection.)

```
from sklearn.datasets import fetch_20newsgroups
dataset = fetch_20newsgroups(
    shuffle=True,
    categories = ['misc.forsale'],
    remove=('headers', 'footers', 'quotes'),
    random_state=101)
print(f'Posts: {len(dataset.data)}')
```

The code loads the dataset and prints the number of posts it contains:

```
Posts: 585
```

The TfidVectorizer class is imported and set up to remove stop words (common words such as "the" or "and") and keep only distinctive words, producing a matrix whose columns point to distinct words.

```
from sklearn.feature_extraction.text import \
    TfidfVectorizer
from sklearn.decomposition import NMF

vectorizer = TfidfVectorizer(max_df=0.95, min_df=2,
                             stop_words='english')
tfidf = vectorizer.fit_transform(dataset.data)

n_topics = 5
nmf = NMF(n_components=n_topics,
          init="nndsvda",
          random_state=101).fit(tfidf)
```

REMEMBER

Term frequency–inverse document frequency (Tf–idf) is a simple calculation based on the frequency of a word in document. It's weighted by word rarity in the available documents. Weighting words is an effective way to rule out words that can't help you to classify or to identify the document when processing text. For example, you can eliminate common parts of speech or other common words.

As with other algorithms from the `sklearn.decomposition` module, the `n_components` parameter indicates the number of desired components. If you'd like to look for more topics, you use a higher number. As the required number of topics increases, the `reconstruction_err_` method reports lower error rates. It's up to you to decide when to stop given the trade-off between more time spent on computations and more topics.

The last part of the script outputs the resulting five topics. By reading the printed words, you can decide on the meaning of the extracted topics, thanks to product characteristics (for instance, the words *drive*, *hard*, *card*, and *floppy* refer to computers) or the exact product (for instance, *comics*, *car*, *stereo*, *games*).

```
feature_names = vectorizer.get_feature_names_out()
n_top_words = 15
for topic_idx, topic in enumerate(nmf.components_):
    print(f'Topic #{topic_idx+1}:', end="\t")
    topics = topic.argsort()[:-n_top_words - 1:-1]
    print(' '.join([feature_names[i] for i in topics]))
```

The topics appear in order, accompanied by their most representative keywords. You can explore the resulting model by looking into the attribute `components_` from the trained NMF model. It consists of a NumPy ndarray holding positive values for words connected to the topic. By using the `argsort` method, you can get the indexes of the top associations, whose high values indicate that they are the most representative words. This code extracts the indexes of the top representative words for the topic 1:

```
print(nmf.components_[0,:].argsort()[:-n_top_words-1:-1])
```

The output is a list of indexes, each one corresponding to a word:

```
[1075 1459  632 2463  740  888 2476 2415 2987   10 2305
    1 3349  923 2680]
```

Decoding the words' indexes creates readable strings by calling them from the array derived from the get_feature_names method applied to the Tfidf Vectorizer that was previously fitted. In the following snippet, you see how to extract the word related to the 2463 index, the top explicative word of the topic 1:

```
word_index = 2463
print(vectorizer.get_feature_names_out()[word_index])
```

Here's the word related to the 2463 index:

```
Offer
```

Recommending movies

Other interesting applications for data reduction are systems that generate recommendations for things you may like to buy or know more about. You likely see recommenders in action on most e-commerce websites after logging-in and visiting some product pages. As you browse, you rate items or put them in your electronic basket. Based on these actions and those of other customers, you see other buying opportunities (this method is *collaborative filtering*).

You can implement collaborative recommendations based on simple means or frequencies calculated on other customers' set of purchased items or on ratings using SVD. This approach helps you reliably generate recommendations even in the case of products the vendor seldom sells or that are quite new to users. For this example, you use a well-known database created by the MovieLens website, collected from its users' ratings of a movie they liked or disliked. The following code snippet will download all the necessary data for you directly from the MovieLens database:

```
import urllib.request
import zipfile

def get_movielens():
    url = ("http://files.grouplens.org/datasets"
            "/movielens/ml-1m.zip")
    filename = 'ml-1m.zip'
    urllib.request.urlretrieve(url, filename)
    params = {"sep":"::", "engine":"python",
                "encoding":"latin-1"}

    with zipfile.ZipFile('ml-1m.zip', 'r') as zip_file:
        with zip_file.open('ml-1m/users.dat') as file:
            users = pd.read_csv(
                file,
                names=['user_id', 'gender', 'age',
                        'occupation', 'zip'],
                **params)
        with zip_file.open('ml-1m/ratings.dat') as file:
            ratings = pd.read_csv(
                file,
                names=['user_id', 'movie_id', 'rating',
                        'timestamp'],
                **params)
        with zip_file.open('ml-1m/movies.dat') as file:
            movies = pd.read_csv(
                file,
                names=['movie_id', 'title', 'genres'],
                **params)
    return pd.merge(pd.merge(ratings, users), movies)

movielens = get_movielens()
```

Using pandas will help create a datatable containing information in rows about users and in columns about movie titles. A movie index will keep track of what movie each column represents:

```
ratings_mtx_df = movielens.pivot_table(values='rating',
        index='user_id', columns='title', fill_value=0)
movie_index = ratings_mtx_df.columns
```

The following code reduces the dimensionality of the ratings datatable using TruncatedSVD with fifteen components and stores the transformed data in a new matrix, R:

```
from sklearn.decomposition import TruncatedSVD
recom = TruncatedSVD(n_components=15, random_state=101)
R = recom.fit_transform(ratings_mtx_df.values.T)
```

The TruncatedSVD class easily reduces the datatable to fifteen components. This class offers a more scalable algorithm than SciPy's linalg.svd used in earlier examples. TruncatedSVD computes result matrices of exactly the shape you decide by the n_components parameter (the full resulting matrices are not calculated), resulting in a faster output and less memory usage.

By calculating the Vh matrix, you can reduce the ratings of different but similar users (each user's scores are expressed by row) into compressed dimensions that reconstruct general tastes and preferences. Also, because you're interested in the Vh matrix (the columns/movies reduction) but the algorithm provides you with only the U matrix (the decomposition based on rows), you need to input the transposition of the datatable (using transposition means that the columns become rows and you obtain TruncatedSVD output, which is the Vh matrix). You now look for a specific movie:

```
movie = 'Star Wars: Episode V \
- The Empire Strikes Back (1980)'
movie_idx = list(movie_index).index(movie)
print(f"movie index: {movie_idx}")
print(R[movie_idx])
```

The output points out the index of a *Star Wars* episode and its SVD coordinates:

```
movie index: 3154
[184.72254552 -17.77612872  47.33450866  51.4664494
  47.92058216
  17.65033116  14.3574635  -12.82219207  17.51347857
   5.46888807
   7.5430805   -0.57117869 -30.74032355   2.4088565
 -22.50368497]
```

Using the movie label, you can find out what column the movie is in (column index 3154 in this case) and print the values of the ten components. This sequence provides the movie profile. You now try getting all the movies with scores similar to the target movie and highly correlated with it. A good strategy is to calculate a correlation matrix of all movies, get the slice related to your movie, and find out

inside it what are the most related (characterized by high positive correlation —
say at least 0.98) movie titles using indexing as shown in the following code:

```
import numpy as np
correlation_matrix = np.corrcoef(R)
P = correlation_matrix[movie_idx]
print(list(movie_index[(P > 0.95) & (P < 1.0)]))
```

The code will return names of films most similar to your movie; they are intended
as suggestions based on a preference for that film.

```
['Raiders of the Lost Ark (1981)',
 'Star Wars: Episode IV - A New Hope (1977)',
 'Star Wars: Episode VI - Return of the Jedi (1983)',
 'Terminator, The (1984)']
```

Star Wars fans would like quite a few titles, such as *Star Wars Episodes IV* and *VI* (of
course). In addition, fans might like *Raiders of the Lost Ark*, because of the actor
Harrison Ford, the main character in all these films.

REMEMBER

SVD will always find the best way to relate a row or column in your data, discovering complex interactions or relations you didn't imagine before. You don't need to
imagine anything in advance; it's fully a data-driven approach.

Inside, what are the most related (characterized by their pairwise correlation, say at least 0.95) movie titles using indexing as shown in the following codes:

The code will return names of films most similar to your movie; they are intended as suggestions based on a preference for that film.

Star Wars fans would likely quite a few titles, such as Star Wars Episode IV and VI (of course). In addition, fans might like Raiders of the Lost Ark because of the actor Harrison Ford, the main character in all the editing.

SVD will always find the best way to relate a row or column in your data, discover the complex interactions or relations you didn't imagine before. You don't need to imagine anything in advance, it's fully a data-driven approach.

Chapter **15**

Clustering

One of the basic abilities that humans have exercised since primitive times is to divide the known world into separate classes, with individual objects sharing common features deemed important by the classifier. Starting with primitive cave dwellers classifying the natural world they lived in, distinguishing plants and animals useful or dangerous for their survival, in modern times, marketing departments classify consumers into target segments and then act with proper marketing plans.

Dealing with big data streams today requires the same classificatory ability of our ancestors, but on a different scale. To leverage the information in data requires specialized algorithms capable of performing two tasks: learning to assign examples to predefined classes (the *supervised* approach) and identifying new and interesting classes that we weren't aware of (*unsupervised* learning).

A data-driven approach to classification based on unsupervised learning, called *clustering,* is presented in the first part of this chapter, and it will prove to be of great help in achieving success for your data project when you need to provide new insights from scratch and lack labeled data or want to create new labels for it. The second part of the chapter presents specific algorithms for clustering, such as K-means, agglomerative clustering, and DBScan.

Even though your main routine as a data scientist will be to put into practice your predictive skills, you'll also have to provide useful insight into possible novel information present in your data. For example, you'll often need to locate new features in order to strengthen the predictive power of your models, find an easy way to make complex comparisons inside the data, and discover communities in social networks.

Clustering techniques, as a set of *unsupervised classification* methods, can create meaningful classes by directly processing your data, without any previous knowledge or hypothesis about the groups that may be present. If all supervised algorithms need labeled examples (class labels), unsupervised ones can figure out by themselves what the most appropriate labels could be.

REMEMBER

You don't have to type the source code for this chapter manually; in fact, using the downloadable source is a lot easier (see the Introduction for download instructions). The source code for this chapter appears in the P4DS4D3_15_Clustering. ipynb file.

Clustering with K-means

There are a few kinds of clustering techniques, and you can distinguish between them by using the following guidelines:

>> Assigning every example to a unique group (*partitioning*) or to multiple ones (*fuzzy clustering*)

>> Determining the heuristic — that is, the rule of thumb — that they use to figure out whether an example is part of a group

>> Specifying how they quantify the difference between observations, that is, the so-called distance measure

TIP

Clustering can help you to summarize huge quantities of data. It's an effective technique for presenting data to a nontechnical audience and for feeding a supervised algorithm with group variables, thus providing the algorithm with concentrated, significant information.

Most of the time you use *partition-clustering techniques* (a data point can be part of only one group, so the groups don't overlap; their membership is distinct) and among partitioning methods, you use K-means the most. In addition, this chapter mentions other useful methods that are based on agglomerative methods and data density.

Agglomerative methods set data into clusters based on a distance measure. *Data density approaches* take advantage of the idea that groups are very dense and continuous, so if you notice a decrease in density when exploring a part of a group of points, it could mean that you arrived at one of its borders.

TIP

Because you normally don't know what you're looking for, different methods can provide you with different solutions and points of view on the data. The secret of a successful clustering is to try as many of the recipes as possible, compare the results, and try to find a reason to consider certain observations as part of one group rather than another.

The first clustering technique described in this chapter is *K-means*, which is an iterative algorithm that has become very popular in machine learning because of its simplicity, speed, and scalability to a large number of data points. The K-means algorithm relies on the idea that there are a specific number of data groups, called *clusters*. Each data group is scattered around a central point with which they share some key characteristics.

You can actually imagine the central point of a cluster, called a *centroid*, as a sun. The data points distribute around the centroid like planets. As star systems are separated by the void of space, clusters are also expected to clearly separate from each other, so as groups of points, they are both internally homogeneous and different from each other.

REMEMBER

The K-means algorithm expects to find clusters in your data. Therefore, it will find them even when none exist. It's important to check inside the groups to determine whether the group is a true gold nugget.

Given such assumptions, all you have to do is to specify the number of groups you expect (you can use a guess or try a number of possible desirable solutions), and the K-means algorithm will look for them, using a heuristic to discover the position of the central points.

The cluster centroids should be evident by their different characteristics and positions from each other. Even if you start by randomly guessing where they could be, in the end, after a few corrections, you always find them by using the many data points that gravitate around them.

Understanding centroid-based algorithms

The procedure for finding the centroids using an algorithm is straightforward. During this time, the algorithm does the following:

1. Sets a K number of clusters as an objective.

2. Picks K centroids from the data points or chooses them so that they are placed in the data in very distant positions from each other.

3. Forms the initial clusters: assigns all the points to their nearest centroid based on the Euclidean distance.

4. Recomputes new centroids based on the points assigned to their cluster.

5. Reassigns the points to the centroids and reiterate computing the centroids until you notice that your solution doesn't change anymore.

6. Recalculates the centroids as an average of all the points present in the group. All the data points are reassigned to the groups based on the distance from the new centroids.

The iterative process of assigning cases to the most plausible centroid and then averaging the assigned ones to find a new centroid will slowly shift the centroid position toward the areas where most data points gravitate. The result is that you end up with the true centroid position.

The procedure has only two weak points that you need to consider. First, you choose the initial centroids randomly, which means that you could start from a bad starting point. As a result, the iterative process will stop at some unlikely solution — for example, having a centroid in the middle of two groups. To ensure that your solution is the most probable, you have to try the algorithm a few times and track the results. The more often you try, the more likely you are to confirm the right solution. The Python Scikit-learn implementation of K-means will do that for you, so you just have to decide how many times you intend to try. (The trade-off is that more iterations produce better results, but each iteration consumes valuable time.)

The second weak point is due to the distance that K-means uses, the *Euclidean distance*, which is the distance between two points in Euclidean space (a concept that you likely studied at school using a two-dimensional plane). In a K-means application, each data point is a vector of features, so when comparing the distance of two points, you do the following:

1. Create a list containing the differences of the elements in the two prints.

2. Square all the elements of the difference vector.

3. Calculate the square root of the summed elements.

You can try a simple example in Python. Pretend that you have two points, A and B, and they have three numeric features. If A and B are the data representation of two persons, their distinguishing features could be measured in height (cm), weight (kg), and age (years), as shown in the following code:

```
import numpy as np
A = np.array([165, 55, 70])
B = np.array([185, 60, 30])
```

The following example shows how to calculate the differences between the three elements, square all the resulting elements, and determine the square root of the summed squared values:

```
D = (A - B)
D = D**2
D = np.sqrt(np.sum(D))
print(D)
```

You will get the value 45 as a result, which is the Euclidean distance between A and B.

In the end, the Euclidean distance is really just the square root of a big sum. When the variables making up the difference vector are significantly different in scale from each other (in this example, the height could have been expressed in meters and the weight in milligrams), you end up with a distance dominated by the elements with the largest scale. It is very important to rescale the variables so that they use a similar scale before applying the K-means algorithm. You can use a fixed range or a statistical normalization with zero mean and unit variance to achieve this goal.

Another problem that may arise is due to correlation between variables, causing redundancy of information. If two variables are highly correlated, that means that a part of their information content is repeated. Replication implies counting the same information more than once in the summation used to calculate the distance. If you're not aware of the correlation issue, some variables will dominate your distance measure calculation — a situation that may lead to not finding the useful clusters that you want. The solution is to remove the correlation thanks to a dimensionality reduction algorithm such as Principal Component Analysis (PCA), as described in Chapter 14. It's up to you to remember to evaluate scale and correlation before employing K-means and other clustering techniques using the Euclidean distance measure.

Creating an example with image data

An example with image data demonstrates how to apply the tool and how to get insight from clusters. An ideal example is clustering the handwritten digits dataset provided by the Scikit-learn package. Hand-written numbers are naturally different from each other — they possess variability in that there are several ways to write certain numbers. Of course, we all have different writing styles, so each person's numbers naturally differ slightly. The following code shows how to import the image data.

```
from sklearn.datasets import load_digits
from sklearn.preprocessing import StandardScaler

digits = load_digits()
scaler = StandardScaler()
X = scaler.fit_transform(digits.data)
ground_truth = digits.target
```

The example begins by importing the digits dataset from Scikit-learn and assigning the data to a variable. It then stores the labels in another variable for later verification. The original 64 variables are pixel values, which are comparable in terms of value range. In this example, you actually don't need to apply any PCA, but the example transforms the values using the StandardScaler, which subtracts the mean and divides by the standard deviation. Using this transformation emphasizes the importance of the relative variations in pixel intensity, rather than their absolute values. In this way, common patterns across the same handwritten numbers should be more evident.

After importing the KMeans class, the code defines its main parameters:

» n_clusters is the K number of centroids to find.

» n_init is the number of times to try the K-means with different starting centroids. The code needs to test the procedure a sufficient number of times, such as 10, as shown here:

```
from sklearn.cluster import KMeans
clustering = KMeans(n_clusters=10,
                    n_init=10, random_state=1)
clustering.fit(X)
```

After creating the parameters, the clustering class is ready for use. You can apply the fit() method to the X dataset, which computes the clusters from the dataset.

Looking for optimal solutions

As mentioned in the previous section, the example is clustering ten different numbers. It's time to start checking the solution with K = 10 first. The following code compares the previous clustering result to the *ground truth* — the true labels — to determine whether there is any correspondence:

```
import numpy as np
import pandas as pd
ms = np.column_stack((ground_truth,clustering.labels_))
df = pd.DataFrame(ms,
                  columns = ['Ground truth','Clusters'])
pd.crosstab(df['Ground truth'], df['Clusters'],
            margins=True)
```

Converting the solution, given by the labels variable internal to the clustering class, into a pandas DataFrame allows it to apply a cross-tabulation and compare the original labels with the labels derived from clustering. You can observe the results in Figure 15-1. Because rows represent ground truth, you can look for numbers whose majority of observations are split among different clusters. These observations are the handwritten examples that are more difficult to figure out by K-means.

Clusters Ground truth	0	1	2	3	4	5	6	7	8	9	All
0	1	0	0	0	0	0	0	0	176	1	178
1	0	59	0	27	0	1	0	95	0	0	182
2	0	5	100	46	4	1	0	21	0	0	177
3	0	0	13	1	154	1	0	14	0	0	183
4	158	6	0	0	0	2	8	7	0	0	181
5	1	0	16	0	30	131	0	2	0	2	182
6	0	1	0	0	0	0	0	1	1	178	181
7	1	2	6	0	0	1	18	151	0	0	179
8	0	14	7	0	55	6	0	88	0	4	174
9	0	19	0	0	144	5	3	9	0	0	180
All	161	106	142	74	387	148	29	388	177	185	1797

FIGURE 15-1: Cross-tabulation of ground truth and K-means clusters.

Notice how numbers such as six or zero are concentrated into a single major cluster, whereas others, such as one and eight, tend to be misunderstood by the algorithm and assigned to different clusters. From such a discovery, you can deduce that certain handwritten numbers are easy to guess, while others aren't.

TIP

Cross-tabulation has been particularly useful in this example because you can compare the clustering result to the ground truth. However, in many clustering applications, you won't have any ground truth to compare with. In such cases, representing the variables' values using the cluster centroids you found is particularly useful. You can use descriptive statistics to perform this task by applying the mean or the median, as described in Chapter 13, on each cluster and comparing the different descriptive stats between clusters.

Another observation you can make is that even though there are just ten numbers in this example, there are more types of handwritten forms of each, hence the necessity of finding more clusters. Of course, the problem is to determine just how many clusters you need.

You use inertia to measure the viability of a cluster. *Inertia* is the sum of all the differences between every cluster member and its centroid. If the examples in the group are similar to the centroid, the difference is small and so is the inertia. Inertia as an individual measure reveals little. Moreover, when comparing inertia from different clusters in general, you notice that the more groups you have, the less the inertia. You want to compare the inertia of a cluster solution with the previous cluster solution. This comparison provides you with the rate of change, a more interpretable measure. To obtain the inertia rate of change in Python, you will have to create a loop. Try progressive cluster solutions inside the loop, recording their values. Here is a script for the handwritten digit example:

```
import numpy as np
inertia = list()
for k in range(1,21):
    clustering = KMeans(n_clusters=k,
                        n_init=10, random_state=1)
    clustering.fit(X)
    inertia.append(clustering.inertia_)
delta_inertia = np.diff(inertia) * -1
```

You use the `inertia` variable inside the clustering class after fitting the clustering. The inertia variable is a list containing the rate of change of inertia between a solution and the previous one. Here is some code that prints a line graph of the rate of change, as depicted by Figure 15-2.

```
%matplotlib inline
import matplotlib.pyplot as plt

plt.figure()
x_range = [k for k in range(2, 21)]
plt.xticks(x_range)
plt.plot(x_range, delta_inertia, 'ko-')
plt.xlabel('Number of clusters')
plt.ylabel('Rate of change of inertia')
plt.show()
```

When examining `inertia`'s rate of change, look for jumps in the rate itself. If the rate jumps up, it means that adding a cluster to the previous solution brings much more benefit than expected; if it jumps down instead, you're likely forcing a cluster more than necessary. The cluster solution before a jump down may be a good candidate, according to the principle of parsimony (the jump signals a sophistication in our analysis, but the right solution is usually the simplest one). In the example, there are jumps at k=10 and k=17, but k=17 seems to be the most promising jump down because the previous solution k=16 has a spike up signaling a cluster solution that fits the data better than expected.

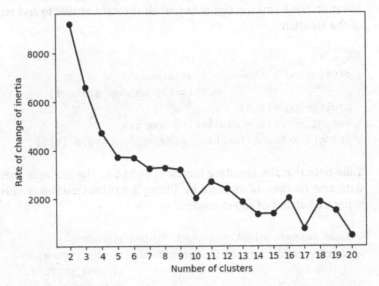

FIGURE 15-2:
Rate of change of inertia for solutions up to k=20.

REMEMBER

The rate of change in inertia will provide you with just a few tips where there could be good cluster solutions. It is up to you to decide which to pick if you need to get some extra insight on data. If, instead, clustering is just a step in a complex data science project, you don't need to spend much effort in looking for an optimal number of clusters; you just pass a solution featuring enough clusters to the next machine learning algorithm and let it decide which is best.

Clustering big data

K-means is a way to reduce the complexity of your data by summarizing the many examples in your dataset. To perform this task, you load the data into your computer's memory, and that won't always be feasible, especially if you are working with big data. Scikit-learn offers an alternative way to apply K-means; the MiniBatchKMeans is a variant that can progressively cluster separated chunks of data. In fact, a batch learning procedure usually processes the data part by part. There are only two differences between the standard K-means function and MiniBatchKMeans:

>> You cannot automatically test different starting centroids unless you try running the analysis again.

>> The analysis will start when there is a batch made of at least a minimum number of cases. This value is usually set to 100 (but the more cases there are, the better the result) by the batch_size parameter.

A simple demonstration on the previous handwritten dataset shows how effective and easy it is to use the MiniBatchKMeans clustering class. First, the example runs a test on the K-means algorithm on all the data available and records the inertia of the solution:

```
k = 10
clustering = KMeans(n_clusters=k,
                    n_init=10, random_state=1)
clustering.fit(X)
kmeans_inertia = clustering.inertia_
print(f"K-means inertia: {kmeans_inertia:0.1f}")
```

Take note that the resulting inertia is 69944.5. The example then tests the same data and number of clusters by fitting a MiniBatchKMeans clustering by small separate batches of 100 examples:

```
from sklearn.cluster import MiniBatchKMeans
batch_clustering = MiniBatchKMeans(n_clusters=k,
                                   random_state=1,
                                   n_init=3)
batch = 100
for row in range(0, len(X), batch):
    if row+batch < len(X):
        feed = X[row:row+batch,:]
    else:
        feed = X[row:,:]
    batch_clustering.partial_fit(feed)
batch_inertia = batch_clustering.score(X) * -1

print(f"MiniBatchKmeans inertia: {batch_inertia:.1f}")
```

This script iterates through the indexes of the handwritten dataset, creating batches of 100 observations each. Using the partial_fit method, it fits a K-means clustering on each batch, using the centroids found by the previous call. The algorithm stops when it runs out of data. Using the score method on all the data available, it then reports its inertia for a ten-clusters solution. Now the reported inertia is 76426.4. Note that MiniBatchKmeans results in a higher inertia than the standard algorithm. Though the difference is small, the fitted solution is inferior, thus you should reserve this approach for those times when you really cannot work with in-memory datasets.

Windows users of this example may see a warning about a potential memory leak. You can safely ignore this warning for this example but will want to take the warning's advice when working through data of your own.

Performing Hierarchical Clustering

If the K-means algorithm is concerned with centroids, hierarchical (also known as agglomerative) clustering tries to link each data point, by a distance measure, to its nearest neighbor, creating a cluster. Reiterating the algorithm using different linkage methods, the algorithm gathers all the available points into a rapidly diminishing number of clusters, until all the points reunite into a single group in the end.

The results, if visualized, will closely resemble the biological classifications of living beings that you may have studied in school or seen on posters at the local natural history museum: an upside-down tree whose branches are all converging into a trunk. Such a figurative tree is a *dendrogram*, and you see it used in medical and biological research. Scikit-learn implementation of agglomerative clustering does not offer the possibility of depicting a dendrogram from your data because such a visualization technique works fine with only a few cases, whereas you can expect to work on many examples.

Compared to K-means, agglomerative algorithms are more cumbersome and do not scale well to large datasets. Agglomerative algorithms are more suitable for statistical studies (they can be easily found in natural sciences, archeology, and sometimes psychology and economics). These algorithms do offer the advantage of creating a complete range of nested cluster solutions, so you just need to pick the right one for your purpose.

To use agglomerative clustering effectively, you have to know about the different linkage methods (the heuristics for clustering) and the distance metrics. There are three linkage methods:

>> **Ward:** Tends to look for spherical clusters, very cohesive inside and extremely differentiated from other groups. Another nice characteristic is that the method tends to find clusters of similar size. It works only with the Euclidean distance.

>> **Complete:** Links clusters using their furthest observations, that is, their most dissimilar data points. Consequently, clusters created using this method tend to be composed of highly similar observations, making the resulting groups quite compact.

>> **Average:** Links clusters using their centroids and ignoring their boundaries. The method creates larger groups than the complete method. In addition, the clusters can be of different sizes and shapes, contrary to the Ward method's solutions. Consequently, this approach sees successful use in the field of biological sciences, easily catching natural diversity.

There are also three distance metrics:

>> **Euclidean (euclidean or l2):** As seen in K-means.

>> **Manhattan (manhattan or l1):** Similar to Euclidean, but the distance is calculated by summing the absolute value of the difference between the dimensions. In a map, if the Euclidean distance is the shortest route between two points, the Manhattan distance implies moving straight, first along one axis and then along the other — as a car in the city would, reaching a destination by driving along city blocks (the distance is also known as city-block distance, rectilinear distance, and taxicab distance).

>> **Cosine (cosine):** A good choice when there are too many variables and you worry that some variable may not be significant (being just noise). Cosine distance reduces noise by taking the shape of the variables, more than their values, into account. It tends to associate observations that have the same maximum and minimum variables, regardless of their effective value.

Using a hierarchical cluster solution

If your dataset doesn't contain too many observations, it's worth trying agglomerative clustering with all the combinations of linkage and distance and then comparing the results carefully. In clustering, you rarely already know the right answers, and agglomerative clustering can provide you with another useful potential solution. For example, you can recreate the previous analysis with K-means and handwritten digits, using the ward linkage and the Euclidean distance as follows (the output appears in Figure 15-3):

```
from sklearn.cluster import AgglomerativeClustering

hclustering = AgglomerativeClustering(
    n_clusters=10, metric='euclidean',
    linkage='ward')
hclustering.fit(X)
```

```
ms = np.column_stack((ground_truth,hclustering.labels_))
df = pd.DataFrame(ms,
                    columns = ['Ground truth','Clusters'])
pd.crosstab(df['Ground truth'],
            df['Clusters'], margins=True)
```

Clusters Ground truth	0	1	2	3	4	5	6	7	8	9	All
0	0	0	0	0	0	178	0	0	0	0	178
1	1	150	0	27	0	0	0	0	4	0	182
2	0	15	1	160	1	0	0	0	0	0	177
3	0	11	0	4	168	0	0	0	0	0	183
4	1	4	1	0	0	0	0	12	163	0	181
5	168	0	0	1	12	0	1	0	0	0	182
6	0	1	0	0	0	180	0	0	0	0	181
7	1	1	0	0	1	0	0	25	0	151	179
8	1	168	0	3	2	0	0	0	0	0	174
9	3	38	0	0	135	0	1	3	0	0	180
All	175	388	2	195	319	178	182	40	167	151	1797

FIGURE 15-3:
Cross-tabulation of ground truth and Ward method's agglomerative clusters.

The results, in this case, are certainly better than K-means, although, you may have noticed that completing the analysis using this approach may take longer than using K-means. When working with a large number of observations, the computations for a hierarchical cluster solution may take hours to complete, making this solution less feasible.

Visualizing aggregative clustering solutions

When you don't have many examples in your dataset, you can also find agglomerative clustering feasible for visualizations. This example uses a small sample of the handwritten data:

```
ground_truth[10:20]
```

Each example within the range of 10 to 19 corresponds to a distinct number, and you can visualize them using a plot from the Matplotlib package:

```
%matplotlib inline
import matplotlib.pyplot as plt

for k, img in enumerate(range(10)):
    plt.subplot(2, 5, k+1)
    plt.imshow(digits.images[10+img],
               cmap='binary',
               interpolation='none')
plt.show()
```

The idea is to cluster them and check how each number aggregates with the others to determine which numbers are more similar in handwriting. The following code performs the agglomerative clustering:

```
hclustering = AgglomerativeClustering(
    n_clusters=10, metric='euclidean',
    linkage='ward')
hclustering.fit(X[10:20, :])
```

After the data is fitted, you can visualize the hierarchical structure of the clusters, called a *dendrogram* (explained at the start of "Performing Hierarchical Clustering") using a few functions from SciPy as shown in the following code (the results appear in Figure 15-4):

```
from scipy.cluster.hierarchy import dendrogram, linkage

linkage_matrix = linkage(hclustering.children_, 'ward')
dendrogram(linkage_matrix)
plt.title('Hierarchical Clustering Dendrogram')
plt.show()
```

From the plot in Figure 15-4, you can see how numbers like 6 and 8 or 2 and 3 can be easily misunderstood one for the other and how. Interestingly the clustering doesn't catch the similarity between 1 and 7, but that's probably because they were dissimilar in the samples used for the demonstration (in this case the 7 had its distinctive dash).

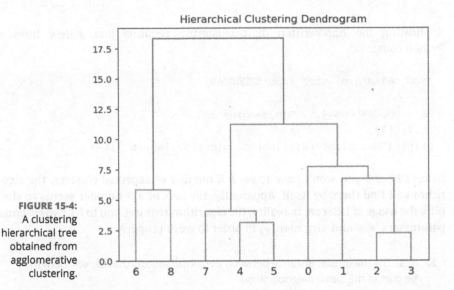

Hierarchical Clustering Dendrogram

FIGURE 15-4:
A clustering
hierarchical tree
obtained from
agglomerative
clustering.

Discovering New Groups with DBScan

Both K-means and agglomerative clustering, especially if you are using the Ward method's linkage criteria, will produce cohesive groups, similar to bubbles, equally spread in all directions. Reality can sometimes produce complex and unsettling results — groups may have strange forms far from the canonical bubble. The Scikit-learn's datasets module (see https://scikit-learn.org/stable/modules/clustering.html for an overview) offers a wide range of mind-teasing shapes that you can't successfully crunch using either K-means or agglomerative clustering: large circles containing smaller ones, interleaved small circles, and spiraling Swiss roll datasets (named after the sponge cake roll because of how the data points are arranged).

DBScan is another clustering algorithm based on a smart intuition that can solve even the most difficult problems. DBScan relies on the idea that clusters are dense, so to start by exploring the data space in every direction and marking a cluster boundary when the density decreases should be sufficient. Areas of the data space with insufficient density of points are just considered empty, and all the points there are noise or *outliers*, that is, points characterized by unusual or strange values.

DBScan is more complex and requires more running time than K-means (but it is faster than agglomerative clustering). It automatically guesses the number of clusters and points out strange data that doesn't easily fit into any class. This difference in classification approach makes DBScan different from the previous algorithms that try to force every observation into a class.

Replicating the handwritten digit clustering requires just a few lines of Python code:

```python
from sklearn.cluster import DBSCAN

db = DBSCAN(eps=4.5, min_samples=20)
db.fit(X)
print(f"No. clusters: {len(np.unique(db.labels_))}")
```

Using DBScan, you won't have to set a K number of expected clusters; the algorithm will find them by itself. Apparently, the lack of a K number seems to simplify the usage of DBScan; in reality, the algorithm requires you to fix two essential parameters, eps and min_sample, in order to work properly:

>> eps: The maximum distance between two observations that allows them to be part of the same neighborhood

>> min_sample: The minimum number of observations in a neighborhood that transform them into a core point

The algorithm works by walking around the data and building clusters by linking observations arranged into neighborhoods. A *neighborhood* is a small cluster of data points all within a distance value of eps. If the number of points in the neighborhood is less than the number min_sample, then DBScan doesn't form the neighborhood.

No matter what the shape of the cluster, DBScan links all the neighborhoods if they are near enough (under the distance value of eps). When no more neighborhoods are within reach, DBScan tries to aggregate even single data points to a group, if they are within eps distance. The data points that aren't associated with any group are treated as noisy points (being too peculiar to be part of a group).

TIP

Try many values of eps and min_sample. The resulting clusters may also change drastically with respect to the values set into these two parameters. Start with a low number of min_samples. Using a lower number allows many neighborhoods to cluster together. The default number 5 is fine. Then try different numbers for eps, starting from 0.1 upward. Don't be disappointed if you can't get a viable result initially — keep trying different combinations.

Getting back to the example from earlier in this section, after this brief explanation of DBScan details, some data exploration can allow you to observe the results under the right point of view. First, count the clusters:

```python
from collections import Counter
print(f"No. clusters: {len(np.unique(db.labels_))}")
```

```
print(Counter(db.labels_))

ms = np.column_stack((ground_truth, db.labels_))
df = pd.DataFrame(ms,
                  columns = ['Ground truth', 'Clusters'])

pd.crosstab(df['Ground truth'],
            df['Clusters'], margins=True)
```

More than half the observations are assigned to the cluster labeled –1, which represents the noise (noise is defined as examples that are too unusual to group). Given the number of dimensions (64 variables representing single pixels) in the data and its high variability (they are handwritten samples), many cases do not naturally fall together into the same group. Figure 15-5 shows the output from this example.

```
No. clusters: 10
Counter({-1: 1032, 0: 172, 1: 157, 4: 111, 3: 95, 5: 90, 7: 64,
   6: 35, 2: 21, 8: 20})
```

Clusters / Ground truth	-1	0	1	2	3	4	5	6	7	8	All
0	6	172	0	0	0	0	0	0	0	0	178
1	73	0	0	20	0	89	0	0	0	0	182
2	175	0	0	0	0	2	0	0	0	0	177
3	94	0	0	0	0	0	89	0	0	0	183
4	126	0	0	0	0	0	0	35	0	20	181
5	179	0	1	0	0	0	0	0	2	0	182
6	25	0	156	0	0	0	0	0	0	0	181
7	84	0	0	0	95	0	0	0	0	0	179
8	154	0	0	0	0	20	0	0	0	0	174
9	116	0	0	1	0	0	1	0	62	0	180
All	1032	172	157	21	95	111	90	35	64	20	1797

FIGURE 15-5:
Cross-tabulation of ground truth and DBScan.

REMEMBER

The strength of DBScan is to provide reliable, consistent clusters. DBScan isn't forced, as are K-means and agglomerative clustering, to reach a solution with a certain number of clusters, even when such a solution does not exist.

Chapter **16**

Detecting Outliers in Data

E rrors happen when you least expect, and that's also true in regard to your data. In addition, data errors are difficult to spot, especially when your dataset contains many variables of different types and scale. Data errors can take a number of forms. For example, the values may be systematically missing on certain variables, erroneous numbers could appear here and there, and the data could include outliers.

In this chapter, you not only will learn what is an outlier and why it differs from a novelty value, but you will find techniques to detect and replace those examples that deviate from the data distribution you want to be represented by your machine learning models.

REMEMBER

You don't have to type the source code for this chapter manually; using the downloadable source is a lot easier (see the Introduction for download instructions). The source code for this chapter appears in the P4DS4D3_16_Detecting_Outliers.ipynb file.

Considering Outlier Detection

As a general definition, *outliers* are data that differ significantly (they're distant) from other data in a sample. The reason they're distant is that one or more values are significantly higher or lower compared to the majority of the values. They could be deemed outliers because they display an almost unique combination of values. For instance, if you are analyzing records of students enlisted in a university, students who are too young or too old may catch your attention. Students studying unusual mixes of different subjects would also require scrutiny.

Outliers skew your data distributions and affect all your basic central tendency statistics. Means are pushed upward or downward, influencing all other descriptive measures. You see outliers generated in all sorts of ways, as a result of everything from sensor and user-input errors to outright fraud. An outlier will always inflate variance and modify correlations, so you may obtain incorrect assumptions about your data and the relationships between variables.

This simple example can display the effect (on a small scale) of a single outlier with respect to more than one thousand regular observations:

```
import numpy as np

np.random.seed(1)
normal = np.random.normal(loc=0.0, scale=1.0, size=1000)
mean = np.mean(normal)
median = np.median(normal)
variance = np.var(normal)
print(f"Mean: {mean:.3f} Median: {median:.3f} ",
      f"Variance: {variance:.3f}")
```

Using the NumPy random generator, `np.random.normal`, the example creates the variable named `normal`, which contains 1000 observations with most values between -2 and +2 derived from a standard normal distribution. Basic descriptive statistics (mean, median, variance) do not show anything unexpected:

```
Mean: 0.039 Median: 0.041 Variance: 0.962
```

Now the code changes a single value by inserting an outlying value:

```
from scipy.stats import pearsonr

outlying = normal.copy()
outlying[0] = 50.0
mean = np.mean(outlying)
```

```
median = np.median(outlying)
variance = np.var(outlying)
print(f"Mean: {mean:.3f} Median: {median:.3f} ",
      f"Variance: {variance:.3f}")
corr_coef, p_value = pearsonr(normal, outlying)
print(f"Pearson's correlation: {corr_coef:.3f} ",
      f"p-value: {p_value:.3f}")
```

You can call this new variable outlying and put an outlier into it (at index 0, you have a positive value of 50.0). Now you obtain much different descriptive statistics:

```
Mean: 0.087 Median: 0.041 Variance: 3.454
Pearsons correlation coefficient: 0.570 p-value: 0.000
```

The statistics show that the mean and variance are much higher than before. Only the median, which relies on position (it tells you the value occupying the middle position when all the observations are arranged in order) is not affected by the change.

More significant, the correlation of the original variable and the outlying variable is quite far from being +1.0 (the correlation value of a variable in respect of itself), indicating that the measure of linear relationship between the two variables has been seriously damaged. In a real-world scenario, you might perform this calculation using one variable that contains expected or statistically average data and a second variable containing new data.

Finding more things that can go wrong

Outliers do not simply shift key measures in your explorative statistics — they also change the structure of the relationships between variables in your data. Outliers can affect machine learning algorithms in two ways:

» Algorithms based on coefficients may take the wrong coefficient in order to minimize their inability to understand the outlying cases. Linear models are a clear example (they are sums of coefficients), but they are not the only ones. Outliers can also influence tree-based learners such as Adaboost or Gradient Boosting Machines.

» Because algorithms learn from data samples, outliers may induce the algorithm to overweight the likelihood of extremely low or high values given a certain variable configuration.

Both situations limit the capacity of a learning algorithm to generalize well to new data. In other words, they make your learning process overfit to the present dataset.

There are a few remedies for outliers — some of them require that you modify your present data and others that you choose a suitable error function for your machine learning algorithm. (Some algorithms offer you the possibility of choosing a different error function as a parameter when setting up the learning procedure.)

REMEMBER

Most machine learning algorithms can accept different error functions. The error function is important because it helps the algorithm to learn by understanding errors and enforcing adjustments in the learning process, but some error functions are extremely sensitive to outliers, while others are quite resistant to them. For instance, a squared error measure tends to emphasize outliers because errors deriving from examples with large values are squared, thus becoming even more prominent.

Understanding anomalies and novel data

Because outliers occur as mistakes or in extremely rare cases, detecting an outlier is never an easy job; it is, however, an important one for obtaining effective results from your data science project. In certain fields, detecting anomalies is itself the purpose of data science: fraud detection in insurance and banking, fault detection in manufacturing, system monitoring in health and other critical applications, and event detection in security systems and for early warning.

An important distinction is when you look for existing outliers in data, or when you check for any new data containing anomalies with respect to existing cases. Maybe you spent a lot of time cleaning your data or you developed a machine learning application based on available data, so it would be critical to figure out whether the new data is similar to the old data and whether the algorithms will continue working well in classification or prediction.

In such cases, data scientists instead talk of novelty detection, because they need to know how well the new data resembles the old. Being exceptionally new is considered an anomaly: Novelty may conceal a significant event or may risk preventing an algorithm from working properly because machine learning heavily relies on learning from past examples and it may not generalize to completely novel cases. When working with new data, you should retrain the algorithm.

Experience teaches that the world is rarely stable. Sometimes novelties do naturally appear because the world is so mutable. Consequently, your data changes over time in unexpected ways, in both target and predictor variables. This phenomenon is called *concept drift*. The term *concept* refers to your target and *drift* to the source data used to perform a prediction that moves in a slow but uncontrollable way, like a boat drifting because of strong tides. When considering a data science model, you distinguish between different concept drift and novelties situations:

» **Physical:** Face or voice recognition systems, or even climate models, never really change. Don't expect novelties, but check for outliers that result from data problems, such as erroneous measurements.

» **Political and economic:** These models sometimes change, especially in the long run. You have to keep an eye out for long-term effects that start slowly and then propagate and consolidate, rendering your models ineffective.

» **Social behavior:** Social networks and the language you use every day change over time. Expect novelties to appear and take precautionary steps; otherwise, your model will suddenly deteriorate and turn unusable.

» **Search engine data, banking, and e-commerce fraud schemes:** These models change quite often. You need to exercise extra care in checking for the appearance of novelties, telling you to train a new model to maintain accuracy.

» **Cyber security threats and advertising trends:** These models change continuously. Spotting novelties is the norm, and reusing the same models over a long time is a hazard.

REMEMBER

The world changes, and so does the data that represents it. The presence of novelty, or the occurrence of new and previously unseen patterns or instances in the data, often indicates the presence of concept drift, and you need to retrain your model using the new data.

Examining a Simple Univariate Method

When looking for outliers, a good way to start, no matter how many variables you have in your data, is to look at every single variable by itself, using both graphical and statistical inspection. This is the univariate approach, which allows you to spot an outlier given an incongruous value on a variable. The pandas package can make spotting outliers quite easy thanks to

» A straightforward describe method that informs you on mean, variance, quartiles, and extremes of your numeric values for each variable

» A system of automatic boxplot visualizations

Using both techniques in tandem makes it easy to know when you have outliers and where to look for them. The diabetes dataset, from the Scikit-learn datasets module, is a good example to start with.

```python
import pandas as pd
from sklearn.datasets import load_diabetes

def load_diabetes_data():
    diabetes = load_diabetes()
    X = pd.DataFrame(diabetes.data,
                     columns=diabetes.feature_names)
    y = pd.DataFrame(diabetes.target, columns=['target'])
    return X, y

X, y = load_diabetes_data()
```

After these commands, all the data is contained in the X variable, a NumPy ndarray. The example then transforms it into a pandas DataFrame and asks for some descriptive statistics (see the output in Figure 16-1):

```python
pd.options.display.float_format = '{:.2f}'.format
X.describe()
```

	age	sex	bmi	bp	s1	s2	s3	s4	s5	s6
count	442.00	442.00	442.00	442.00	442.00	442.00	442.00	442.00	442.00	442.00
mean	-0.00	0.00	-0.00	0.00	-0.00	0.00	-0.00	0.00	-0.00	-0.00
std	0.05	0.05	0.05	0.05	0.05	0.05	0.05	0.05	0.05	0.05
min	-0.11	-0.04	-0.09	-0.11	-0.13	-0.12	-0.10	-0.08	-0.13	-0.14
25%	-0.04	-0.04	-0.03	-0.04	-0.03	-0.03	-0.04	-0.04	-0.03	-0.03
50%	0.01	-0.04	-0.01	-0.01	-0.00	-0.00	-0.01	-0.00	-0.00	-0.00
75%	0.04	0.05	0.03	0.04	0.03	0.03	0.03	0.03	0.03	0.03
max	0.11	0.05	0.17	0.13	0.15	0.20	0.18	0.19	0.13	0.14

FIGURE 16-1:
Descriptive statistics for the Diabetes DataFrame from Scikit-learn.

You can spot the problematic variables by looking at the extremities of the distribution (the maximum value of a variable). For example, you must consider whether the minimum and maximum values lie respectively far from the 25th and 75th percentile. As shown in the output, many variables have suspiciously large maximum values. A boxplot analysis will clarify the situation. The following command creates the boxplot of all variables shown in Figure 16-2.

```
%matplotlib inline
import matplotlib.pyplot as plt
plt.style.use("seaborn-v0_8-whitegrid")

fig, axes = plt.subplots(nrows=1, ncols=1,
                         figsize=(10, 5))
features = ["bmi", "bp", "s1", "s2", "s3", "s4", "s5" ,"s6"]
X[features].boxplot(ax=axes);
```

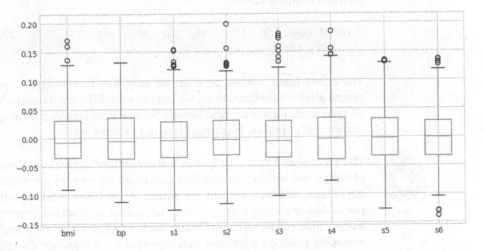

FIGURE 16-2:
Boxplots.

Boxplots generated from pandas DataFrame will have whiskers set to plus or minus 1.5 IQR (*interquartile range* or the distance between the lower and upper quartile) with respect to the upper and lower side of the box (the upper and lower quartiles). This boxplot style is called the Tukey boxplot (from the name of statistician John Tukey, who created and promoted it among statisticians together with other explanatory data techniques) and it allows a visualization of the presence of cases outside the whiskers. (All points outside these whiskers are deemed outliers.)

Leveraging on the Gaussian distribution

Another effective check for outliers in your data is accomplished by leveraging the normal distribution. Even if your data isn't normally distributed, standardizing it will allow you to assume certain probabilities of finding anomalous values. For instance, 99.7% of values found in a standardized normal distribution should be inside the range of +3 and −3 standard deviations from the mean, as shown in the following code.

```
from sklearn.preprocessing import StandardScaler

Xs = StandardScaler().fit_transform(X[features])
X[features][(np.abs(Xs)>3).any(1)].index
```

As a result, you get the indexes indicating the rows in the dataset featuring some possibly outlying values:

```
Int64Index([58, 123, 216, 230, 256, 260, 261, 269, 322, 336,
    367, 441], dtype='int64')
```

The Scikit-learn module provides an easy way to standardize your data and to record all the transformations for later use on different datasets. This means that all your data, no matter whether it's for machine learning training or for performance test purposes, is standardized in the same way.

TIP

The 68-95-99.7 rule says that in a standardized normal distribution, 68 percent of values are within one standard deviation, 95 percent are within two standard deviations, and 99.7 percent are within three. When working with skewed data, the 68-95-99.7 rule may not hold true, and in such an occurrence, you may need some more conservative estimate, such as Chebyshev's inequality. *Chebyshev's inequality* relies on a formula that says that for k standard deviations around the mean, no more cases than a percentage of $1/k^2$ should be over the mean. Therefore, at seven standard deviations around the mean, your probability of finding a legitimate value is at most two percent, no matter what the distribution is (two percent is a low probability; your case could be deemed almost certainly an outlier).

TIP

Chebyshev's inequality is conservative. A high probability of being an outlier corresponds to seven or more standard deviations away from the mean. Use it when it may be costly to deem a value an outlier when it isn't. For all other applications, the 68-95-99.7 rule will suffice.

Remediating outliers

Having found some possible univariate outliers, you now have to decide how to deal with them. If you completely distrust the outlying cases, under the assumption that they were unfortunate errors or mistakes, you could just delete them. (In Python, you can just deselect them using fancy indexing.) Here is the code for performing *listwise deletion* of examples in the data where the feature values deviate by three standard deviations from the mean. After execution, a print statement will indicate that there are now 430 examples remaining, down from the initial 442.

```
mean = X[features].mean()
std = X[features].std()
all_valid_mask = (np.abs(X[features] - mean) <=
                  (3 * std)).all(axis=1)
listwise_del = X[all_valid_mask]
print(listwise_del.shape)
```

TIP

Modifying the values in your data or deciding to exclude certain values is a decision to make after you understand why there are some outliers in your data. You can rule out unusual values or cases for which you presume that some error in measurement has occurred, in recording or previous handling of the data. If instead you realize that the outlying case is a legitimate, though rare one, the best approach would be to underweight it (if your learning algorithms use weighting for the observations) or to increase the size of your data sample.

In this case, deciding to keep the data and having standardized it, you could just cap the outlying values. In doing so, you can use a slightly more sophisticated approach called winsorizing. When using *winsorizing*, the values deemed outliers are clipped to the value of specific percentiles that act as value limits (usually the 5th percentile for the lower bound, the 95th for the upper):

```
from scipy.stats.mstats import winsorize

winsorized = X.copy()
winsorized[features] = winsorized [features].apply(
    lambda x: winsorize(x, limits=(0.05, 0.05)))
```

In this way, you create a different *hurdle* value (a range of acceptable values that the value must jump to pass) for larger and smaller values — taking into account any asymmetry in the data distribution. Whatever you decide for capping (by standard deviation or by winsorizing), your data is now ready for further processing and analysis.

Finally, an alternative, automatic solution is to let Scikit-learn automatically transform your data and clip outliers by using the RobustScaler, a scaler based on the IQR (as in the boxplot previously discussed in this chapter):

```
from sklearn.preprocessing import RobustScaler

robust_rescale = RobustScaler().fit_transform(
    X[features])
```

Developing a Multivariate Approach

Working on single variables allows you to spot a large number of outlying observations. However, outliers do not necessarily display values too far from the norm. Sometimes outliers are made of unusual combinations of values in more variables. They are rare, but influential, combinations that can especially trick machine learning algorithms.

In such cases, the precise inspection of every single variable won't suffice to rule out anomalous cases from your dataset. Only a few selected techniques, taking in consideration more variables at a time, will manage to reveal problems in your data.

The presented techniques approach the problem from different points of view:

» Dimensionality reduction

» Density clustering

» Nonlinear distribution modeling

Using these techniques allows you to compare their results, taking notice of the recurring signals on particular cases — sometimes already located by the univariate exploration, sometimes as yet unknown.

Using principal component analysis

Principal component analysis (PCA) can completely restructure the data, removing redundancies and ordering newly obtained components according to the amount of the original variance that they express. This type of analysis offers a synthetic and complete view over data distribution, making multivariate outliers particularly evident.

The first two components, being the most informative in term of variance, can depict the general distribution of the data if visualized. The output provides a good hint at possible evident outliers.

The last two components, being the most residual, depict all the information that could not be otherwise fitted by the PCA() method. They can also provide a suggestion about possible but less evident outliers.

```
%matplotlib inline
from sklearn.decomposition import PCA
from sklearn.preprocessing import scale
```

```
from pandas.plotting import scatter_matrix
import pandas as pd
import matplotlib.pyplot as plt

pca = PCA()
pca_mat = pca.fit_transform(scale(X))
first_comps = sum(pca.explained_variance_ratio_[:2] * 100)
last_comps = sum(pca.explained_variance_ratio_[-2:] * 100)
print(f"variance by the first two components: "
      f"{first_comps:.1f}%")
print(f"variance by the last two components: "
      f"{last_comps:.1f}%")
df_pca = pd.DataFrame(
    pca_mat, columns=[f"comp_{j}" for j in range(10)])
fig, axes = plt.subplots(nrows=1, ncols=2, figsize=(15, 5))
first_two = df_pca.plot.scatter(
    x="comp_0", y="comp_1", s=50, grid=True,
    c="Azure", edgecolors="DarkBlue", ax=axes[0])
last_two = df_pca.plot.scatter(
    x="comp_8", y="comp_9", s=50, grid=True,
    c="Azure", edgecolors="DarkBlue", ax=axes[1])
plt.show()
```

Figure 16-3 shows two scatterplots of the first and last components. The output also reports the variance explained by the first two components (half of the informative content of the dataset) of the PCA and by the last two ones:@

```
variance by the first two components : 55.2%
variance by the last two components: 0.9%
```

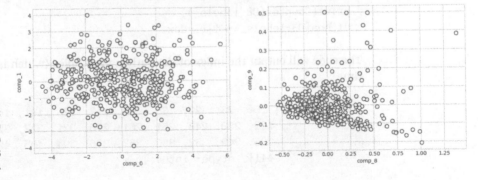

FIGURE 16-3: The first two and last two components from the PCA.

Pay particular attention to the data points along the axis (where the x axis defines the independent variable and the y axis defines the dependent variable). You can see a possible threshold to use for separating regular data from suspect data.

Using the two last components, you can locate a few points to investigate using the threshold of −0.3 for the tenth component and of −1.0 for the ninth. All cases below these values are possible outliers.

```
outlying = (pca_mat[:,-1] > 0.3) | (pca_mat[:,-2] > 1.0)
df_pca[outlying].index
```

The selection will point out the index of the outlying examples:

```
Int64Index([23, 58, 110, 169, 254, 322, 323, 353, 371, 394],
    dtype='int64')
```

Using cluster analysis for spotting outliers

Outliers are isolated points in the space of variables, and DBScan is a clustering algorithm that links dense data parts together and marks the too-sparse parts. DBScan is therefore an ideal tool for an automated exploration of your data for possible outliers to verify.

Here is an example of how you can use DBScan for outlier detection:

```
from sklearn.cluster import DBSCAN
DB = DBSCAN(eps=2.5, min_samples=25)
DB.fit(pca_mat)

from collections import Counter
print(Counter(DB.labels_))
df_pca[DB.labels_==-1].index
```

The code will output the index of the outlying examples (which is quite long this time):

```
Int64Index([ 15,   23,   29,   35,   78, 117, 123, 141, 161,
           169, 230, 248, 251, 261, 276, 321, 322, 323,
           336, 349, 352, 353, 367, 376, 394, 405, 422,
           441], dtype='int64')
```

DBSCAN requires two parameters, eps and min_samples. Finding the optimal values for these parameters often involves multiple iterations, which can make parameter selection a bit challenging and tricky.

As hinted in the previous chapter, start with a low value of `min_samples` and try growing the values of `eps` from 0.1 upward. After every trial with modified parameters, check the situation by counting the number of observations in the class −1 inside the attribute `labels`, and stop when the number of outliers seems reasonable for a visual inspection.

TIP

There will always be points on the fringe of the dense parts' distribution, so it's hard to provide you with a threshold for the number of cases that might be classified in the −1 class. Normally, outliers should not be more than 5 percent of cases, so use this indication as a generic rule of thumb.

The output from the previous example will report to you how many examples are in the −1 group, which the algorithm considers not part of the main cluster, and the list of the cases that are part of it.

TIP

It is less automated, but you can also use the K-means clustering algorithm for outlier detection. You first run a cluster analysis with a reasonable enough number of clusters. (You can try different solutions if you're not sure.) Then you look for clusters featuring just a few examples (or maybe a single one); they are probably outliers because they appear as small, distinct clusters that are separate from the large clusters that contain the majority of examples.

Automating detection with Isolation Forests

Random Forests and Extremely Randomized Trees are powerful machine learning techniques. They work by dividing your dataset into smaller sets based on certain variable values to make it easier to predict the classification or regression on each smaller subset (a *divide et impera*, or divide and conquer, solution).

`IsolationForest` is an algorithm that takes advantage of the fact that an outlier is easier to separate from majority cases based on differences between its values or combination of values. The algorithm keeps track of how long it takes to separate a case from the others and get it into its own subset. The less effort it takes to separate it, the more likely the case is an outlier. As a measure of such effort, `IsolationForest` produces a distance measurement (the shorter the distance, the more likely the case that it's an outlier).

TIP

When your machine learning algorithms are in production, a trained `Isolation Forest` can act as a sanity check because many machine learning algorithms cannot cope with outlying and novel examples.

To set IsolationForest to catch outliers, all you have to decide is the level of contamination, which is the percentage of cases considered outliers based on the distance measurement. You decide such a percentage based on your experience and expectation of data quality. Executing the following script creates a working IsolationForest:

```
from sklearn.ensemble import IsolationForest

auto_detection = IsolationForest(max_samples=50,
                                 contamination=0.05,
                                 random_state=0)
auto_detection.fit(pca_mat)
iforest = auto_detection.predict(pca_mat)
df_pca[iforest==-1].index
```

The output reports the index list of the cases suspected of being outliers:

```
Int64Index([ 10,  11,  15,  23,  32,  58, 110, 123, 141,
            202, 230, 260, 261, 269, 286, 321, 322, 323,
            352, 353, 382, 394, 441], dtype='int64')
```

In addition, the algorithm is trained to recognize what normal examples in the dataset should look like. When you provide new cases to the dataset and you evaluate them using the trained IsolationForest, you can immediately spot whether something is wrong with your new data.

REMEMBER

IsolationForest is a computationally intensive algorithm. Performing an analysis on a large dataset takes a long time and a lot of memory.

5

Learning from Data

Chapter 17

Exploring Four Simple and Effective Algorithms

I n this new part of the book, you start to explore algorithms and tools necessary for learning from data, meaning a training a model, and being capable of predicting a numeric estimate (such as house pricing in some areas of California) or a class (such as the species of penguins that can be found in the Palmer Archipelago in Antarctica) given any new example that you didn't have before. In this chapter, you start with the simplest algorithms and work toward those that are more complex. The four algorithms in this chapter represent a good starting point for any data scientist.

REMEMBER You don't have to type the source code for this chapter manually; using the downloadable source is a lot easier (see the Introduction for download instructions). The source code for this chapter appears in the P4DS4D3_17_ Exploring_Four_ Simple_and_Effective_Algorithms.ipynb file.

Guessing the Number: Linear Regression

Regression has a long history in statistics, from building simple but effective linear models of economic, psychological, social, or political data, to hypothesis testing for understanding group differences, to modeling more complex problems with ordinal values, binary and multiple classes, count data, and hierarchical relationships. Regression is also a common tool in data science; it's a Swiss Army knife of machine learning that you can use for every problem. Stripped of most of its statistical assumptions, linear regression is perceived by data science practitioners as an easily explainable, yet effective, algorithm for numeric estimations, and, in its logistic regression version, for classification as well.

Defining the family of linear models

Linear regression is a statistical model that defines the relationship between a target variable and a set of predictive features. It does so by using a formula of the following type:

$$y = bx + a$$

You can translate this formula into something readable and useful for a wide range of real-world problems. For instance, if you're trying to guess your sales based on historical results and available data about advertising expenditures, the preceding formula becomes

$$sales = b * (advertising\ expenditure) + a$$

CONSIDERING SIMPLE AND COMPLEX FORMULATIONS

The concepts of *simple* and *complex* in machine learning refer to the mathematical formulation underlying the algorithm's operations. Some algorithms are simple summations, while others require complex calculations and data manipulations (and Python deals with both the simple and complex algorithms for you). Although complex algorithms generally demonstrate higher predictive accuracy, it's not an absolute rule. As a good practice, test multiple models, starting from the basic ones. You may discover that a simple solution performs better in many cases. For example, you may want to keep things simple and use a linear model, which is based on simple summations of data, instead of a more sophisticated approach. This type of situation is in essence what is implied by the "no free lunch" theorem: No one approach suits all problems, and even the most simple solution may hold the key to solving an important problem.

The "no free lunch" theorem by David Wolpert and William Macready states that "any two optimization algorithms are equivalent when their performance is averaged across all possible problems." If the algorithms are equivalent in the abstract, no one algorithm is superior to the other unless proved in a specific, practical problem. See the discussion at http://www.no-free-lunch.org/ for more details about no-free-lunch theorems; two of them are actually used for machine learning.

TIP

Memories from your high school algebra and geometry tell you that the formulation $y = bx + a$ is a line in a coordinate plane made of an x axis (the abscissa) and a y axis (the ordinate). Most machine learning mathematics is actually at the high school level, making them easily understandable and applicable to real-world problems.

You can demystify the formula by explaining its components: a is the value of the intercept (the value of y when x is zero) and b is a coefficient that expresses the slope of the line (the relationship between x and y). If b is positive, y increases and decreases as x increases and decreases. When b is negative, y behaves in the opposite manner. You can understand b as the unit change in y given a unit change in x. When the value of b is near zero, the effect of x on y is slight, but if the value of b is high, either positive or negative, the effect of changes in x on y are great.

Linear regression, therefore, can find the best $y = bx + a$ and represent the relationship between your target variable, y, with respect to your predictive feature, x. The values of both a (alpha or intercept) and b (beta coefficient) are determined based on the data, and they are found using the linear regression algorithm so that the difference between all the real y target values and all the y values derived from the linear regression formula are the minimum possible.

You can express this relationship graphically as the sum of the square of all the vertical distances between all the data points and the regression line. Such a sum is always the minimum possible when you calculate the regression line correctly using an estimation called *ordinary least squares,* which is derived from statistics or the equivalent machine learning method, named *gradient descent.* The differences between the real y values and the regression line (the predicted y values) are defined as *residuals* (because they are what are left after a regression: the errors).

Using more variables

When employing a single variable to predict y, the linear regression is considered simple, whereas when working with multiple variables, it becomes a multiple linear regression. When you have many variables, their scale isn't important in producing accurate predictions. But a good habit is to statistically standardize your variables (a procedure discussed in Chapter 13) because their scale can ease the computations of certain types of regression (as discussed later), and comparing coefficients in terms of their impact on the target is insightful for data analysis.

The following example is based on the California Housing dataset from Scikit-learn, and it employs linear regression to predict housing prices in California. The example also tries to determine which variables influence the result more, so the example standardizes the predictors.

```python
from sklearn.datasets import fetch_california_housing
import pandas as pd

def load_california_housing_data():
    dataset = fetch_california_housing()
    X = pd.DataFrame(data=dataset.data,
                     columns=dataset.feature_names)
    y = pd.Series(data=dataset.target, name="target")
    return X, y

X, y = load_california_housing_data()
```

The regression class in Scikit-learn is part of the `linear_model` module. As demonstrated in Chapter 12, you can set up a pipeline that can scale the variables and pass them to the model immediately afterward:

```python
from sklearn.linear_model import LinearRegression
from sklearn.preprocessing import StandardScaler
from sklearn.pipeline import Pipeline

regression = Pipeline(steps=[
    ('scaler', StandardScaler()),
    ('model', LinearRegression())])

regression.fit(X, y)
```

Now that the algorithm is fitted, you can use the score method to report the R^2 measure, which is a measure that ranges from 0 to 1 and points out how using a particular regression model is better in predicting y than using a simple mean would be. (The act of *fitting* creates a line or curve that best matches the data points provided by the data; you fit the line or curve to the data points in order to perform various tasks, such as predictions, based on the trends or patterns produced by the data.) You can also see R^2 as being the quantity of target information explained by the model (the same as the squared correlation), so getting near 1 means being able to explain most of the y variable using the model.

Here is the code used to access the score() method, which is used to report the R^2 measure:

```python
score = regression.score(X, y)
print(f"{score:.3f}")
```

Here is the resulting R^2 score:

```
0.606
```

In this case, R^2 on the previously fitted data is about 0.606, a good result for a simple model. You can interpret the R^2 score as the percentage of information present in the target variable that has been explained by the model using the predictors. A score of 0.606, therefore, means that the model has fit about 60 percent of the information you wanted to the model and prediction, and that a residual 40 percent of it remains unexplained.

REMEMBER

Calculating R^2, as well as any other predictive performance score, on the same set of data used for training is considered reasonable only when using linear models because of their simplicity. However, as a general rule, in data science and machine learning, it's always the correct practice to test scores on data that has not been used for training. More complex algorithms, compared to linear regression, have the tendency to memorize the data rather than truly learn from it, resulting in a phenomenon known as overfitting. Overfitting can lead to excessively high scores that may not accurately reflect the model's true performance.

To understand what drives the estimates in the multiple regression model, you have to look at the `coefficients_` attribute, which is an array containing the regression coefficients. The coefficients are the numbers estimated by the linear regression model to effectively transform the input variables in the formula into the target y prediction. In the following code snippet, the `zip` function will generate an iterable of both variable names and coefficient values, and you can print it for reporting.

```
for feature, coefficient in zip(X.columns,
                                regression['model'].coef_):
    print(f"{feature:12}: {coefficient:>7.3f}")
```

The reported variables and their rounded coefficients (beta coefficient values, or slopes, as described in the "Defining the family of linear models" section, earlier in this chapter) are

```
MedInc      :    0.830
HouseAge    :    0.119
AveRooms    :   -0.266
AveBedrms   :    0.306
Population  :   -0.005
AveOccup    :   -0.039
Latitude    :   -0.900
Longitude   :   -0.871
```

In terms of absolute values, the coefficients that are most noteworthy are MedInc (median income in an area), Latitude, and Longitude. This emphasis indicates that, according to the linear regression model, the location of your property in California and the income level of your neighbors play a significant role in estimating the value of your property.

Understanding limitations and problems

Although linear regression is a simple and effective tool for estimation, it has limitations that can impact its usefulness in certain cases, depending on the data. To determine whether these limitations are present, it's important to use some method to test its effectiveness. If you don't apply appropriate data-handling techniques (such as basic transformations, discussed here, or more advanced manipulations, as discussed in Chapter 19), you may encounter the following issues:

>> **Linear regression can model only numeric data as a target.** When modeling classes as response, you need to address the problem using a logistic regression, discussed in the next section.

>> **If data is missing and you don't deal with it properly, the model won't work at all.** Therefore, it is crucial to fill in the missing values beforehand by substituting them with a suitable value, such as the mean of that variable.

>> **As discussed in Chapter 16, outliers are quite disruptive to the machine learning model.** Linear regression tries to minimize the square value of the residuals, and outliers produce large residuals, forcing the algorithm to focus more on them than on the majority of regular points.

>> **The major limitation of linear regression is that it provides only a summation of terms,** which may not adequately capture the impact of variables that affect the outcome differently based on their values. This limitation makes it challenging to represent complex data situations with linear regression, which is better suited for simpler scenarios where the relationship between variables is more straightforward. For instance, the relation between the target and each predictor variable is based on a single coefficient, and there isn't an automatic way to represent complex relations like a parabola (there is a unique value of x maximizing y) or exponential growth. The only way you can manage to model such relations is to use mathematical transformations of your variables (and sometimes of your target) or add new variables. Chapter 19 explores both the use of complex transformations and the addition of new variables.

Moving to Logistic Regression

Linear regression is well suited for estimating values, but it isn't the best tool for predicting the class of an observation. In spite of the statistical theory that advises against it, you can actually try to classify a binary class by scoring one class as 1 and the other as 0. The results are disappointing most of the time, so the statistical theory wasn't wrong!

The fact is that linear regression works on a continuum of numeric estimates. However, in order to classify correctly, you need a more suitable measure, such as the probability of class ownership. Thanks to the following formula, you can transform a linear regression numeric estimate into a probability that is more apt to describe how a class fits an observation:

probability of a class = exp(r) / (1+exp(r))

r is the regression result (the sum of the variables weighted by the coefficients) and exp is the exponential function. exp(r) corresponds to Euler's number e elevated to the power of r. A linear regression using such a formula (also called a link function) for transforming its results into probabilities is a logistic regression.

Logistic regression is just part of a large number of extensions of the linear regression model, called the Generalized Linear Models (GLMs). *GLMs* are statistical models used to analyze data with a response variable that follows a particular probability distribution. Typical examples are binomial, Poisson, or gamma distribution. GLMs consist of three main components: a linear predictor; a probability distribution; and a link function that connects the linear predictor to the mean of the response variable. GLMs are widely used in various fields for predicting and understanding the relationship between variables in a flexible and interpretable way.

TIP

The Scikit-learn package offers a good choice of models that you can use for different problems in the same way as they were a linear regression model. You can explore the options at `https://scikit-learn.org/stable/modules/linear_model.html#generalized-linear-models`.

Applying logistic regression

Logistic regression is similar to linear regression, with the only difference being the target, which should contain integer values indicating the class relative to the observation. This example uses the Palmer Penguins dataset to demonstrate both the case of predicting two classes (called a binary prediction, one labeled as 0 and the other as 1) or multiple classes (a multiclass problem). The Palmer Penguins dataset is a widely used and popular dataset in the field of data science and machine learning. It contains measurements of various physical characteristics of penguin specimens collected from three different species of penguins: Adélie, Chinstrap, and Gentoo. The dataset is named after the Palmer Station, a research station located in Antarctica where the data was collected. You can download it directly from the internet using the following code:

```python
import pandas as pd

def load_palmer_penguins(only_numeric=True,
                         no_missing=True,
                         multiclass=True):
    url = "https://raw.githubusercontent.com/"
    url += "allisonhorst/palmerpenguins/main/"
    url += "inst/extdata/penguins.csv"
    numeric_features = ["bill_length_mm",
                        "bill_depth_mm",
                        "flipper_length_mm",
                        "body_mass_g"]
    categorical_features = ["island", "sex"]
    data = pd.read_csv(url)
    if no_missing:
        data = data.dropna()
    if multiclass:
        target = data.species.replace({'Adelie':1,
                                       'Gentoo':2,
                                       'Chinstrap':3})
    else:
        target = data.species.replace({'Adelie':1,
                                       'Gentoo':0,
                                       'Chinstrap':0})
    if only_numeric:
        return data[numeric_features], target
    else:
        return data[numeric_features +
                    categorical_features], target

X, y = load_palmer_penguins(only_numeric=True,
                            no_missing=True,
                            multiclass=False)
```

The following example fits a logistic regression model to determine whether a penguin is an Adélie or not and leaves the last example of the dataset apart for testing purposes:

```
from sklearn.linear_model import LogisticRegression

logistic = Pipeline(steps=[
    ('scaler', StandardScaler()),
    ('model', LogisticRegression())])

logistic.fit(X.iloc[:-1], y.iloc[:-1])

excluded_row = X.iloc[[-1]]
pred = logistic.predict(excluded_row)
proba = logistic.predict_proba(excluded_row)
print (f"Predicted class {pred[0]}, real class " +
        f"{y.iloc[-1]}")
print (f"with probability {proba[0, 0]:.3f}")
```

The preceding code snippet outputs the following result and probability, correctly verifying that the last example is not an Adélie penguin:

```
Predicted class 0, real class 0
with probability 0.987
```

In contrast to linear regression, logistic regression doesn't just output the resulting class (in this case, the class 0 – not an Adélie penguin) but also estimates the probability of the observation's being part of the predicted class. Based on the observation used for prediction, logistic regression estimates a probability of 99 percent of its being from class 0 — a very high probability, but not a perfect score, therefore leaving a slight margin of uncertainty.

TIP

Using probabilities lets you guess the most probable class of an example, but you can also order the predictions with respect to being part of that class. This is especially useful for medical purposes; for instance, ranking a prediction in terms of likelihood with respect to others can reveal which patients are most at risk of getting or already having a disease.

Considering the case when there are more classes

The previous problem, logistic regression, automatically handles a binary class problem (it started guessing whether a penguin is an Adélie). Most algorithms provided by Scikit-learn that predict probabilities or a score for class can automatically handle multiclass problems using two different strategies:

>> **One versus rest:** The algorithm compares every class with all the remaining classes, building a model for every class. If you have ten classes to guess, you have ten models. This approach relies on the OneVsRestClassifier class from Scikit-learn.

>> **One versus one:** The algorithm compares every class against every individual remaining class, building a number of models equivalent to $n * (n-1) / 2$, where n is the number of classes. If you have ten classes, you have 45 models: $10 * (10 - 1) / 2$. This approach relies on the OneVsOneClassifier class from Scikit-learn.

In the case of logistic regression, the default multiclass strategy is the one versus rest. The example in this section shows how to use both the strategies with the Palmer Penguins dataset, when the target is a number representing each of the three species. The following code loads the data in multiclass format and splits a part of it for testing purposes:

```
from sklearn.model_selection import train_test_split

X, y = load_palmer_penguins(only_numeric=True,
                            no_missing=True,
                            multiclass=True)
X_train, X_test, y_train, y_test = train_test_split(
    X, y, test_size=0.33, random_state=42)
```

Now it's time to evaluate the performance of both the one-versus-rest and the one-versus-one approaches. The following code trains two separate models and assesses their performance on the holdout dataset:

```
from sklearn.multiclass import OneVsRestClassifier
from sklearn.multiclass import OneVsOneClassifier
ovr = OneVsRestClassifier(logistic).fit(X_train, y_train)
ovo = OneVsOneClassifier(logistic).fit(X_train, y_train)
print('One vs rest accuracy: %.3f' % ovr.score(
    X_test, y_test))
print('One vs one accuracy: %.3f' % ovo.score(
    X_test, y_test))
```

The performances of the two multiclass strategies are

```
One vs rest accuracy: 0.973
One vs one accuracy: 0.982
```

The two multiclass classes, `OneVsRestClassifier` and `OneVsOneClassifier`, operate by incorporating the estimator (in this case, `LogisticRegression`). After incorporation, they usually work just like any other learning algorithm in Scikit-learn. Interestingly, the one-versus-one strategy obtained the highest accuracy thanks to its paired comparisons.

Making Things as Simple as Naïve Bayes

You may wonder why anyone would name an algorithm Naïve Bayes. The naïve part comes from its formulation; it makes some extreme simplifications to standard probability calculations. The reference to Bayes in its name relates to the Reverend Bayes and his theorem on probability. The Reverend Thomas Bayes (1701–1761) was an English statistician and a philosopher who formulated his theorem during the first half of the 18th century. The theorem was never published while he was alive. It has deeply revolutionized the theory of probability by introducing the idea of conditional probability — that is, probability conditioned by evidence.

Of course, it helps to start from the beginning — probability itself. *Probability* tells you the likelihood of an event and is expressed in a numeric form. The probability of an event is measured in the range from 0 to 1 (from 0 percent to 100 percent) and it's empirically derived from counting the number of times the specific event happened with respect to all the events. When you observe events (for example, when a feature has a certain characteristic), and you want to estimate the probability associated with the event, you count the number of times the characteristic appears in the data and divide that figure by the total number of observations available. The result is a number ranging from 0 to 1, which expresses the probability.

When you estimate the probability of an event, you tend to believe that you can apply the probability in each situation. The term for this belief is *a priori* because it constitutes the first estimate of probability with regard to an event (the one that comes to mind first). For example, if you estimate the probability of an unknown person's being a female, you may say, after some counting, that it's 50 percent, which is the prior, or the first, probability that you will stick with.

The prior probability can change in the face of evidence, that is, something that can radically modify your expectations. One possible example to demonstrate Bayes' theorem could be related to the probability of a person being a student based on whether they carry a backpack. For instance, assume that in the general population, 30 percent of people carry a backpack, while among students, 90 percent carry a backpack. If you encounter a person who is carrying a backpack, you may want to estimate from this evidence the probability that the person is a student.

This sounds like a predictive problem for Bayes' theorem, and in the end, this situation is really similar to predicting a categorical variable from data: You have a target variable with different categories, and you have to guess the probability of each category on the basis of evidence, the data. The Reverend Bayes provided a useful formula:

P(A|B) = P(B|A)*P(A) / P(B)

The formula looks like statistical jargon and is a bit counterintuitive, so it needs to be explained in depth. Reading the formula using the previous example as input makes the meaning behind the formula quite a bit clearer:

>> P(A|B) is the probability of being a student (event A) given that you carry a backpack (evidence B). This part of the formula defines what you want to predict. In short, it says to predict y given x, where y is an outcome (student or not) and x is the evidence (using a backpack).

>> P(B|A) is the probability of carrying a backpack if you are a student. In this case, you already know that it's 90 percent. In every data problem, you can obtain this figure easily by simple cross-tabulation of the features against the target outcome.

>> P(A) is the probability of being a student, a 20 percent chance in the population (a priori).

>> P(B) is the probability of carrying a backpack, which is 30 percent (another a priori).

TIP

When reading parts of the formula such as P(A|B), you should read them as follows: probability of A given B. The | symbol translates as *given*. A probability expressed in this way is a conditional probability, because it's the probability of A conditioned by the evidence presented by B. In this example, plugging the numbers into the formula translates into: 90% * 20% / 30% = 60%.

Therefore, getting back to the previous example, even if being a student is a 20 percent probability, just knowing evidence like carrying a backpack takes it up to 60 percent, which is a more favorable chance for the guess. In similar classification problems, gathering multiple pieces of evidence can raise the probability of making a correct prediction using Bayesian probabilities.

Finding out that Naïve Bayes isn't so naïve

Naïve Bayes, leveraging the simple Bayes' rule, takes advantage of all the evidence available to modify the a priori base probability of your predictions. Because your data contains so much evidence — that is, it has many features — the algorithm, based on a simplified Naïve Bayes formula, accumulates all the probabilities to derive a confident prediction.

REMEMBER

As discussed in the "Guessing the number: linear regression" section, earlier in this chapter, summing variables implies that the model takes them as separate and unique pieces of information. But this isn't true in reality, because applications exist in a world of interconnections, with every piece of information connecting to many other pieces. Using one piece of information more than once means giving more emphasis to that particular piece.

Because you don't know (or simply ignore) the relationships between each piece of evidence, you may wonder if it's correct to just plug all evidence into a Naïve Bayes algorithm. Actually, the simple and naïve move of throwing everything that you know at the formula works well indeed in many occurrences, and many studies report good performance despite the fact that you make a bold assumption. Here are some of the ways in which you commonly see Naïve Bayes effectively used:

» Building spam detectors (catching all annoying emails in your inbox)

» Sentiment analysis (guessing whether a text contains positive or negative attitudes with respect to a topic, and detecting the mood of the speaker)

» Text-processing tasks such as spell correction, or guessing the language used to write or classify the text into a larger category

Naïve Bayes is also popular because it doesn't need much data to work. In addition, it can naturally handle multiple classes. With some slight variable modifications (transforming them into classes), it can also handle numeric variables. Scikit-learn provides three Naïve Bayes classes in the `sklearn.naive_bayes` module:

» `MultinomialNB`: Assigns probabilities based on the presence of a feature in the data. It is often used to make predictions on textual data problems, after having transformed the text into a bag of words, as explained in Chapter 8.

» `BernoulliNB`: Assigns a different probability when the feature is present than when it's absent, which is different from multinomial Naïve Bayes. It also penalizes the absence of a feature. In fact, it treats all features as binary variables (the Bernoulli distribution is typical of binary problems). It's versatile for tasks like text classification and fraud detection.

» `GaussianNB`: Defines a version of Naïve Bayes that expects a normal distribution of all the features. Hence, this class is suboptimal for textual data in which words are sparse (use the multinomial or Bernoulli distributions instead). If your variables are numeric ones, this version is the best choice.

Predicting text classifications

Naïve Bayes is particularly popular for document classification because it doesn't need many documents to perform sufficiently well in a problem. In textual problems, you often have myriads of features involved, one for each word spelled correctly or incorrectly. Sometimes the text is associated with other nearby words in *n-grams*, that is, sequences of consecutive words. Naïve Bayes can quickly learn the patterns from the textual features and provide fast predictions.

This section tests text classifications using the binomial and multinomial Naïve Bayes models offered by Scikit-learn. The examples rely on the 20newsgroups dataset, which contains a large number of posts from 20 kinds of newsgroups. The dataset is divided into a training set, for building your textual models, and a test set, which is composed of posts that temporarily follow the training set. You use the test set to test the accuracy of your predictions:

```
import numpy as np
from sklearn.datasets import fetch_20newsgroups
from sklearn.feature_extraction.text \
    import CountVectorizer
import sklearn.feature_extraction.text as txt
from sklearn.naive_bayes import BernoulliNB, MultinomialNB
from sklearn.metrics import accuracy_score

newsgroups_train = fetch_20newsgroups(
    subset='train', remove=('headers', 'footers',
                            'quotes'))
newsgroups_test = fetch_20newsgroups(
    subset='test', remove=('headers', 'footers',
                           'quotes'))
```

After loading the two sets into memory, you instantiate the two Naïve Bayes models by setting their alpha values, which are useful for avoiding a zero probability for rare features (a zero probability would exclude these features from the analysis). You typically use a small value for alpha, as shown in the following code:

```
bernoulli_nb = BernoulliNB(alpha=0.01)
multinomial_nb = MultinomialNB(alpha=0.01)

multinomial_vectorizer = CountVectorizer(
    stop_words='english', binary=False)
binary_vectorizer = CountVectorizer(
    stop_words='english', binary=True)
```

In this example, CountVectorizer converts a collection of text documents into a numerical matrix. When used with the parameters stop_words set to 'english' and binary set to false, CountVectorizer removes common English stop words (such as *a, the, in,* and so on) from the text, converts the text to lowercase, and counts the frequency of occurrence of each word in the text documents.

```
train_targets = newsgroups_train.target
test_targets = newsgroups_test.target

multinomial_X = np.abs(
    multinomial_vectorizer.fit_transform(
        newsgroups_train.data))
multinomial_Xt = np.abs(
    multinomial_vectorizer.transform(
        newsgroups_test.data))
binary_X = binary_vectorizer.fit_transform(
    newsgroups_train.data)
binary_Xt = binary_vectorizer.transform(
    newsgroups_test.data)
```

After transforming the text, you can train the two classifiers and test them on the test set, which is a set of posts that haven't been involved in the training. The test measure is accuracy, which is the percentage of right guesses that the algorithm makes.

```
multinomial_nb.fit(multinomial_X, train_targets)
bernoulli_nb.fit(binary_X, train_targets)

for name, model, data in [
    ('BernoulliNB', bernoulli_nb, binary_Xt),
    ('MultinomialNB', multinomial_nb, multinomial_Xt)]:
    accuracy = accuracy_score(
        y_true=test_targets, y_pred=model.predict(data))
    print(f"Accuracy for {name}: {accuracy:.3f}")
```

The reported accuracies for the two Naïve Bayes models are

```
Accuracy for BernoulliNB: 0.567
Accuracy for MultinomialNB: 0.653
```

You may notice that it won't take a long time for both models to train and report their predictions on the test set. Consider that the training set is made up of more than 11,000 posts containing 300,000 words, and the test set contains about 7,500 other posts.

```
print(f'training posts: {len(newsgroups_train.data)}')
D = {word: True for post in newsgroups_train.data
     for word in post.split(' ')}
print(f'training words: {len(D)}')
print(f'test posts: {len(newsgroups_test.data)}')
```

Running the code returns all these useful text statistics:

```
training posts: 11314
training words: 300972
test posts: 7532
```

Learning Lazily with Nearest Neighbors

K-Nearest Neighbors (KNN) is not about building rules from data based on coefficients or probability. KNN works on the basis of similarities. When you have to predict something like a class, your best approach may be to find the most similar observations to the one you want to classify or estimate. You can then derive the answer you need from the similar cases.

Observing how many observations are similar doesn't imply learning something, but rather measuring. Because KNN isn't learning anything, it's considered lazy, and you'll hear it referenced as a lazy learner or an instance-based learner. The idea is that similar premises usually provide similar results, and it's important not to forget to get such low-hanging fruit before trying to climb the tree!

The algorithm is fast during training because it has to memorize only data about the observations. It actually performs more calculations during predictions. When there are too many observations, the algorithm can become slow and memory consuming. You're best advised not to use it with big data or it may take almost forever to predict anything! Moreover, this simple and effective algorithm works better when you have distinct data groups without too many variables involved because the algorithm is also sensitive to the curse of dimensionality.

The *curse of dimensionality* happens as the number of variables increases. Consider a situation in which you're measuring the distance between observations and, as the space becomes larger and larger, it becomes difficult to find real neighbors — a problem for KNN, which sometimes mistakes a far observation for a near one. Rendering the idea is just like playing chess on a multidimensional chessboard. When playing on the classic 2-D board, most pieces are near, and you can more

```
```

easily spot opportunities and menaces for your pawns when you have 32 pieces and 64 positions. However, when you start playing on a 3-D board, such as those found in some sci-fi films, your 32 pieces can become lost in 512 possible positions. Now just imagine playing with a 12-D chessboard. You can easily misunderstand what is near and what is far, which is what happens with KNN.

There are ways to enhance KNN's ability in detecting similarities between observations by removing redundant information and simplifying the data dimensionality using data reduction techniques, as explained in Chapter 14.

Predicting after observing neighbors

For an example showing how to use KNN, you can start with the digit dataset (as found in Chapters 12, 14, and 15). KNN is particularly useful, just like Naïve Bayes, when you have to predict many classes, or in situations that would require you to build too many models or rely on a complex model.

```
import matplotlib.pyplot as plt
from sklearn.datasets import load_digits
from sklearn.model_selection import train_test_split

digits = load_digits()
X_train, X_test, y_train, y_test = train_test_split(
    digits.data, digits.target,
    test_size=0.33, random_state=42)
```

KNN is an algorithm that's quite sensitive to outliers. Moreover, you have to rescale your variables and remove some redundant information. In this example, rescaling is not necessary because the data represents pixels, which means that it's already scaled and constrained in a range of values.

You can avoid the problem with outliers by keeping the neighborhood small — that is, by not looking too far for similar examples because outliers by definition lie further apart other observations.

In the following code snippet, you instantiate and train your KNN classifier by using a neighborhood (n_neighbors of 5 cases):

```
from sklearn.neighbors import KNeighborsClassifier
knn = KNeighborsClassifier(n_neighbors=5, p=2)
knn.fit(X_train, y_train)
```

KNN uses a distance measure to determine which observations to consider as possible neighbors for the target case. You can easily change the predefined distance using the p parameter:

>> When p is 2, use the Euclidean distance (discussed as part of the clustering topic in Chapter 15).

>> When p is 1, use the Manhattan distance metric, which is the absolute distance between observations. In a 2-D square, when you go from one corner to the opposite one, the Manhattan distance is the same as walking the perimeter, whereas Euclidean is like walking on the diagonal. Although the Manhattan distance isn't the shortest route, it's a more realistic measure than Euclidean distance, and it's less sensitive to noise and high dimensionality.

The Euclidean distance is the commonly used measure, but sometimes it can give you worse results, especially when the analysis involves many correlated variables. The following code shows that the analysis seems fine with it.

```
print('Accuracy: %.3f' % knn.score(X_test, y_test) )
print(f"Prediction: {knn.predict(X_test[-15:,:])}")
print(f"Actual:     {y_test[-15:]}")
```

The code returns the accuracy and a sample of the predictions you can compare with the actual values in order to spot differences:

```
Accuracy: 0.993
Prediction: [2 1 1 2 2 4 8 7 5 8 8 9 4 9 0]
Actual:     [2 1 1 2 2 4 8 7 5 8 8 9 4 9 0]
```

Choosing your k parameter wisely

A critical parameter that you have to define in KNN is k. As k (the number of neighbors checked to determine the classification of a specific query point) increases, KNN considers more points for its predictions, and the decisions are less influenced by noisy instances that could exercise an undue influence. Your decisions are based on an average of more observations, and they become more solid. When the k value you use is too large, you start considering neighbors that are too far, sharing less and less with the case you have to predict.

It's an important trade-off. When the value of k is less, you consider a more homogeneous pool of neighbors but can more easily make an error by taking the few similar cases for granted. When the value of k is more, you consider more cases at a higher risk of observing neighbors that are too far or that are outliers. Getting back to the previous example with digit dataset, you can experiment with changing the k value, as shown in the following code:

```
for k in [1, 3, 5, 7, 10, 50, 100]:
    kNN = KNeighborsClassifier(n_neighbors=k)
    kNN.fit(X_train, y_train)
    test_score = kNN.score(X_test, y_test)
    print(f"k= {k:3} \t accuracy= {test_score:.3f}")
```

After running this code, you get an overview of what happens when k changes, and can determine the value of k that best fits the data:

```
k=   1          accuracy= 0.985
k=   3          accuracy= 0.990
k=   5          accuracy= 0.993
k=   7          accuracy= 0.990
k=  10          accuracy= 0.983
k=  50          accuracy= 0.929
k= 100          accuracy= 0.899
```

Through experimentation, you find that setting n_neighbors (the parameter representing k) to 5 is the optimum choice, resulting in the highest accuracy. Using just the nearest neighbor (n_neighbors =1) isn't a bad choice, however, setting the value above 5 returns decreasing results in the classification task.

TIP

As a rule of thumb, when your dataset doesn't have many observations, set k as a number near the square root of available observations. However, there is no general rule, and trying different k values is always a good way to optimize your KNN performance. Always start from low values and work toward higher values.

IN THIS CHAPTER

» Learning about overfitting and underfitting

» Choosing the right metric to monitor

» Cross-validating the results

» Selecting the best features for your model

» Optimizing hyperparameters

Chapter **18**

Performing Cross-Validation, Selection, and Optimization

This chapter is about how machine learning algorithms learn, and it explores some methods for making them learn better. Machine learning algorithms can indeed learn from data. For instance, the four algorithms presented in the previous chapter, although not complex, can effectively estimate a class or a value after being presented with examples associated with outcomes. It is all a matter of learning by *induction*, which is the process of extracting general rules from specific examples. From childhood, humans commonly learn by seeing examples, deriving some general rules or ideas from them, and then successfully applying the derived rule to new situations as we grow up. For example, if we see someone being burned after touching fire, we understand that fire is dangerous, and we don't need to touch it ourselves to know that.

Currently, machine learning algorithms can't fully match human learning abilities. However, the knowledge they acquire can be highly advantageous for some assignments. To improve the situation, a human detects issues in the machine learning process and then provides methods for overcoming any issues, which are the two main focuses of this chapter. Learning by example using machine algorithms has pitfalls. Here are a few issues that might arise:

>> There aren't enough examples to endorse a rule, no matter what machine learning algorithm you are using.

>> The machine learning application is presented with the wrong examples and consequently cannot define suitable rules.

>> Even when the model sees enough correct examples, it may still struggle to understand the underlying rules because they are just too complicated for the model to comprehend.

It's important to consider these pitfalls as you read through this chapter because they affect your machine learning experience. The quantity of data, its quality, and the characteristics of the learning algorithm decide whether a machine learning application can generalize well to new cases. If anything is wrong with any of them, the resulting model will suffer serious limits. As a data science practitioner, you must recognize and learn to avoid these types of pitfalls in your data science experiments.

REMEMBER

You don't have to type the source code for this chapter manually; using the downloadable source is a lot easier (see the Introduction for download instructions). The source code for this chapter appears in the P4DS4D3_18_Performing_Cross_Validation_Selection_and_Optimization.ipynb file.

Pondering the Problem of Fitting a Model

Providing a model with examples is commonly referred to as *training* or *fitting data* to the model. Fitting a model implies learning from data a representation of the rules that generated the data in the first place. From a mathematical perspective, fitting a model is analogous to guessing an unknown function of the kind you faced in high school, such as $y=4x^2+2x$, just by observing its y results. Therefore, under the hood, you expect that machine learning algorithms generate math formulations by guessing how reality works based on the examples provided.

Determining the validity of such formulations is typically outside the realm of data science, and often the most practical approach is to test whether a working model can be constructed using the data. What is most important is that models work by producing exact predictions. To summarize, as a data scientist, you should always strive to approximate the real, unknown functions underlying the problems you face using the best information available. The result of your work is evaluated based on your capacity to predict specific outcomes (the target outcome) given certain premises (the data) thanks to a useful range of tools (the machine learning algorithms).

Linear regression is presented as a simple formula (y = bx + a) earlier in Chapter 17. It can approximate training data well, even if it's not linear. As with linear regression, all other machine learning algorithms have an internal formulation themselves and some, such as neural networks, even require that you define their formulation from scratch. The linear regression's formulation is one of the simplest ones; formulations from other learning algorithms can appear quite complex. You don't need to know exactly how they work. You just need to have an idea of how complex they are, whether they represent a line or a curve, and how they can respond to outliers or noisy data. When planning to learn from data, you should address the following problematic aspects based on the formulation you intend to use:

>> Whether the learning algorithm is the best one to approximate the unknown function that you imagine behind the data you're using. In order to make such a decision, you must consider the learning algorithm's formulation performance on the data at hand and compare it with other, alternative formulations from other algorithms.

>> Whether the specific formulation of the learning algorithm is too simple, with respect to the hidden function, to make an estimate (this is called a bias problem).

>> Whether the specific formulation of the learning algorithm is too complex, with respect to the hidden function to be guessed (leading to the variance problem).

REMEMBER

Not all algorithms are suitable for every data problem. If you don't have enough data or the data is full of noisy information, it may be difficult for some formulations to figure out the real function.

Understanding bias and variance

If your chosen learning algorithm can't learn properly from data and isn't performing well, the cause is bias or variance in its estimates:

>> **Bias:** Given the simplicity of formulation, your algorithm tends to overestimate or underestimate the real rules behind the data and is systematically wrong in certain situations. Simple algorithms have high bias; having few internal parameters, they tend to represent only simple formulations well.

>> **Variance:** Given the complexity of formulation, your algorithm tends to learn too much information from the data and detect rules that don't exist, which causes its predictions to be erratic when faced with new data. You can think of variance as a problem connected to memorization. Complex algorithms can memorize data features thanks to the algorithms' high number of internal parameters. However, memorization doesn't imply any understanding about the rules.

Bias and variance depend on the complexity of the formulation at the core of the learning algorithm with respect to the complexity of the formulation that is presumed to have generated the data you are observing. However, when you consider a specific problem using the available data rules, you end up having either high bias or variance when

>> **You have few observations.** Simpler algorithms perform better, no matter what the unknown function is. Complex algorithms tend to learn too much from data, and then output inaccurate estimates.

>> **You have many observations.** Complex algorithms tend to reduce variance. The reduction occurs because sophisticated data requires complex algorithms to learn all its nuances. However, this works only if the complex algorithm isn't too complicated for the data.

>> **You have many variables.** Provided that you also have many observations, simpler algorithms tend to find a way to approximate even complex hidden functions.

Defining a strategy for picking models

When faced with a machine learning problem, you usually know little about the problem and don't know whether a particular algorithm will manage it well. Consequently, you don't really know whether the source of a problem is caused by bias or variance — although you can usually use the rule of thumb that if an algorithm is simple, it will have high bias, and if it is complex, it will have high variance. Even when working with common, well-documented data science applications, you'll notice that what works in other situations (as described in academic and industry papers) often doesn't operate very well for your own application because the data is different.

You can summarize this situation using the famous no-free-lunch theorem of the mathematician David Wolpert: Any two machine learning algorithms are equivalent in performance when tested across all possible problems. Consequently, it isn't possible to say that one algorithm is always better than another; it can be better than another one only when used to solve specific problems. You can view the concept in another way: For every problem, there is never a fixed recipe! The best and only strategy is to try everything you can and verify the results using a controlled scientific experiment. Using this approach ensures that what seems to work is what really works and, most important, what will keep on working with new data.

At this point, you must consider a critical, yet underrated, aspect to ensure the success of your data project. For a best model and greatest results, it's essential to define an *evaluation metric* that distinguishes a good model from a bad one with respect to the business or scientific problem that you want to solve. In fact, for some projects, you may need to avoid seeing *negative cases* (ones where the evaluation metric shows a bad model) as if they are *positive cases* (ones where the evaluation metric shows a good model); for others, you may want to absolutely spot all the positive ones; and for still others, all you need to do is order them so that positive ones come before the negative ones so that you don't need to check them all.

By picking an algorithm, you automatically also pick an optimization process ruled by an evaluation metric that reports its performance to the algorithm so that the algorithm can better adjust its parameters. For instance, when using a linear regression, the metric is the mean squared error given by the vertical distance of the observations from the regression line. Therefore, it's automatic, and you can more easily accept the algorithm performance provided by such a default evaluation metric.

Apart from accepting the default metric, some algorithms do let you choose a preferred evaluation function or even allow you to create a custom one. In most cases, however, when you can't point out your favorite evaluation function, you can still influence the existing evaluation metric by appropriately fixing some of its hyperparameters, thus optimizing the algorithm indirectly for another, different, metric.

Scikit-learn offers access to a wide range of measures for both classification and regression problems. The `sklearn.metrics` module allows you to call the optimization procedures using a simple string or by calling an error function from its modules. Table 18-1 shows the measures commonly used for regression problems.

TABLE 18-1

Regression Evaluation Measures

Callable String	Function
mean_absolute_error	sklearn.metrics.mean_absolute_error
mean_squared_error	sklearn.metrics.mean_squared_error
r2	sklearn.metrics.r2_score

The r2 string specifies a statistical measure for linear regression called R^2 (R squared). It expresses how the model compares in predictive power with respect to a simple mean. Machine learning applications seldom use this measure because it doesn't explicitly report errors made by the model, although high R^2 values imply fewer errors; more viable metrics for regression models are the mean squared errors and the mean absolute errors.

Squared errors penalize extreme values more, whereas absolute error weights all the errors the same. So it's really a matter of considering the trade-off between reducing the error on extreme observations as much as possible (squared error) or trying to reduce the error for the majority of the observations (absolute error). The choice you make depends on the application. When extreme values represent critical situations for your application, a squared error measure is better. However, when your concern is to minimize the common and usual observations, as often happens in forecasting sales problems, you should use a mean absolute error as the reference. The choices even apply to complex classification problems, as you can see in Table 18-2.

TABLE 18-2 ## Classification Evaluation Measures

Callable String	Function
accuracy	sklearn.metrics.accuracy_score
precision	sklearn.metrics.precision_score
recall	sklearn.metrics.recall_score
f1	sklearn.metrics.f1_score
roc_auc	sklearn.metrics.roc_auc_score

Accuracy is the simplest error measure in classification, counting (as a percentage) how many of the predictions are correct. It takes into account whether the machine learning algorithm has guessed the right class. This measure works with both binary and multiclass problems. Even though it's a simple measure, optimizing accuracy may cause problems when an imbalance exists between classes. For example, it could be a problem when a class is frequent or preponderant, such as in fraud detection, where most transactions are actually legitimate with respect to a few criminal transactions. In such situations, machine learning algorithms optimized for accuracy tend to guess in favor of the preponderant class and be wrong most of time with the minor classes, which is an undesirable behavior for an algorithm that you expect to guess all the classes correctly, not just a few selected ones.

Precision and recall, and their conjoint optimization by F1 score, can solve problems not addressed by accuracy. Precision is about being precise when guessing. It tracks the percentage of times, when forecasting a class, that a class was right. For example, you can use precision when diagnosing cancer in patients after evaluating data about their exams. Your precision in this case is the percentage of patients who really have cancer among those diagnosed with cancer. Therefore, if you have diagnosed ten ill patients and nine are truly ill, your precision is 90 percent.

You face different consequences when you don't diagnose cancer in a patient who has it or you do diagnose it in a healthy patient. Precision tells just a part of the story, because there are patients with cancer that you have diagnosed as healthy, and that's a terrible problem. The recall measure tells the second part of the story. It reports, among an entire class, your percentage of correct guesses. For example, when reviewing the previous example, the recall metric is the percentage of patients that you correctly guessed have cancer. If there are 20 patients with cancer and you have diagnosed just 9 of them, your recall will be 45 percent, which isn't acceptable performance.

When using your model, you can be accurate but still have low recall, or have a high recall but lose accuracy in the process. Fortunately, precision and recall can be maximized together using the F1 score, which uses the formula $F1 = 2 *$ $(precision * recall) / (precision + recall)$. Using the F1 score ensures that you always get the best precision and recall combined.

Receiver Operating Characteristic Area Under Curve (ROC AUC) is useful when you want to order your classifications according to their probability of being correct. Therefore, when optimizing ROC AUC in the previous example, the learning algorithm will first try to order (sort) patients starting from those most likely to have cancer to those least likely to have cancer. The ROC AUC is higher when the ordering is good and low when it is bad. If your model has a high ROC AUC, you need to check the most likely ill patients. Another example is in a fraud-detection problem, when you want to order customers according to the risk of them producing a fraudulent transaction. If your model has a good ROC AUC, you need to check just the riskiest customers closely.

Dividing between training and test sets

Having explored how to decide among the different error metrics for classification and regression, the next step in the strategy for choosing the best model is to experiment and evaluate the solutions by viewing their ability to generalize to new cases. As an example of correct procedures for experimenting with machine learning algorithms, begin by loading the California housing dataset used in previous chapters:

```python
from sklearn.datasets import fetch_california_housing
import pandas as pd

def load_california_housing_data():
    dataset = fetch_california_housing()
    X = pd.DataFrame(data=dataset.data,
                     columns=dataset.feature_names)
    y = pd.Series(data=dataset.target, name="target")
    return X, y

X, y = load_california_housing_data()
print(X.shape, y.shape)
```

The goal is to be able to predict the price of a house in a given neighborhood. The output shows that the dataset contains 20640 observations and 8 features. The target is a price measure, and because it's common in house evaluation to look for how neighboring estates are valued, you decide to use a k-nearest neighbor algorithm (KNN) and to optimize the result using the R squared. The objective is to ensure that a KNN is a good model for the dataset and to quantify how good it is (which lets you compare it with alternative models).

```python
from sklearn.neighbors import KNeighborsRegressor

knn_model = KNeighborsRegressor(n_jobs=-1)
knn_model.fit(X, y)

r2 = knn_model.score(X, y)

print(f"R-squared value: {r2:.2f}")
```

The resulting mean square error generated by the commands is

```
R-squared value: 0.47
```

After having fitted the model with the data (which is called the training data because it provides examples to learn from), the score evaluation method, applied to the same data used for training, reports the data fitting error. An R squared value of 0.47 tells us that almost half the information in the data can be represented by the model but it's calculated directly on the training set, so you can't be sure the model will work as well with new data (machine learning algorithms are both good at learning and at memorizing from examples).

Ideally, you need to perform a test on data that the algorithm has never seen in order to exclude any memorization. Only in this way can you discover whether your algorithm will work well when new data arrives. To perform this task, you wait for new data, make the predictions on it, and then compare the predictions to reality. However, performing the task this way may take a long time and could become both risky and expensive, depending on the type of problem you want to solve using machine learning (for example, some applications such as cancer detection can be incredibly risky to experiment with because lives are at a stake).

Luckily, you have another way to obtain the same result. To simulate having new data, you can divide the observations into test and training cases. It's quite common in data science to have a test size of 20–30 percent of the available data and to train the predictive model using the remaining 70–80 percent. Here is an example of how you can achieve data partitioning in Python:

```
from sklearn.model_selection import train_test_split

X_train, X_test, y_train, y_test = train_test_split(
    X, y, test_size=0.20, random_state=0)

print(f"Training set shape: {X_train.shape}")
print(f"Testing set shape: {X_test.shape}")
```

The code prints the resulting shapes of the training and test sets, with the former being 80 percent of the initial dataset size and the latter just 20 percent:

```
Training set shape: (16512, 8)
Testing set shape: (4128, 8)
```

The example separates training and test X and y variables into distinct variables using the train_test_split() function. The test_size parameter indicates a test set made of 20 percent of the available observations. The function always chooses the test sample randomly. Now you can use the training set for training:

```
from sklearn.metrics import mean_squared_error

knn_model.fit(X_train, y_train)

preds_train = knn_model.predict(X_train)
preds_test = knn_model.predict(X_test)

test_mse = mean_squared_error(y_true=y_test,
                              y_pred=preds_test)
print(f"Train mean squared error: {train_mse:.5f}")
```

This time, you evaluate the mean squared error instead of the R squared. The output shows the training set's mean squared error:

```
Train mean squared error: 0.73442
```

At this point, you use the model to predict on the test set:

```
test_mse = mean_squared_error(y_true=y_test, y_pred=preds_test)
print(f"Test mean squared error: {test_mse:.5f}")
```

The code reports a test error of 1.11733, which is higher than what you obtained as a training error:

```
Test mean squared error: 1.11733
```

What a difference, indeed! Somehow, the estimate on the training set was too optimistic. However, although using the test set, is more realistic in error estimation, it really makes your result depend on a small portion of the data. If you change that small portion, the test result may also change. That's a common problem with machine learning algorithms. You know that each algorithm has a certain bias or variance in predicting an outcome. The problem is that you can't estimate its impact for sure because the training performances are always too optimistic and misleading, and by using a test set, you may get different results depending on what sample you use.

Using training data is always unsuitable when evaluating algorithm performance because the learning algorithm may actually predict the training data better than any test set. This is especially true when an algorithm has strong memorization capabilities because of its complexity. In this case, you can expect a lower error when predicting the training data, which means that you get an overly optimistic result that doesn't compare it fairly with other algorithms (which may have a different bias/variance profile), nor are the results useful for this example's evaluation. By using the test data, you actually reduce the number of training examples (which may cause the algorithm to perform less well), but in exchange, you get a more reliable and comparable error estimate, though an uncertain and variable one.

Cross-Validating

If test sets provide unstable results because of sampling, the solution is to systematically sample a certain number of test sets and then average the results. That gets you more stable results. Averaging multiple observed measures is a statistical approach, and that's the basis of cross-validation. The recipe is straightforward:

1. **Divide your data into folds.**

   Each *fold* is a container that holds an even distribution of the cases, usually 10, but fold sizes of 3, 5, and 20 are viable alternative options.

2. **Hold out one fold as a test set and use the others as training sets.**

3. **Train and record the test set result.**

   If you have little data, it's better to use a larger number of folds, because the quantity of data and the use of additional folds positively affects the quality of training.

4. **Perform Steps 2 and 3 again, using each fold in turn as a test set.**

5. **Calculate the average and the standard deviation of all the folds' test results.**

   The average is a reliable estimator of the quality of your predictor. The standard deviation will tell you the predictor reliability (if it is too high, the cross-validation error could be imprecise). Expect that predictors with high variance will have a high cross-validation standard deviation.

Even though this technique may appear complicated, Scikit-learn handles it using the functions in the sklearn.model_selection module.

Using cross-validation on k folds

To run cross-validation, you first have to initialize an iterator. KFold is the iterator that implements k folds cross-validation. There are other iterators available from the sklearn.model_selection module, mostly derived from the statistical field, but KFold is the most widely used in data science practice.

KFold requires you to specify the n_splits number (the number of folds to generate), and indicate whether you want to shuffle the data (by using the shuffle parameter). As a rule, the higher the expected variance, increasing the number of splits improves the mean estimate. It's a good idea to shuffle the data because ordered data can introduce confusion into the learning processes for some algorithms if the first observations are different from the last ones.

After setting KFold, call the cross_val_score function, which returns an array of results containing a score (from the scoring function) for each cross-validation fold. You have to provide cross_val_score with your data (both X and y) as an input, your estimator (the regression class), and the previously instantiated KFold iterator (as the cv parameter). In a matter of a few seconds or minutes, depending on the number of folds and data processed, the function returns the results. You average these results to obtain a mean estimate, and you can also compute the standard deviation to check how stable the mean is.

```
from sklearn.model_selection import cross_val_score, KFold
import numpy as np

cv = KFold(n_splits=10, shuffle=True, random_state=0)
scores = cross_val_score(knn_model, X, y, cv=cv,
    scoring='neg_mean_squared_error', n_jobs=-1)
mean_mse = np.mean(np.abs(scores))
std_mse = np.std(scores)

print(f"cv mean squared error: {mean_mse:.5f} std:
    {std_mse:.5f}")
```

Here is the result:

```
cv mean squared error: 1.10818 std: 0.02739
```

TIP

Cross-validating can work in parallel because no estimate depends on any other estimate. You can take advantage of the multiple cores present on your computer by setting the parameter n_jobs=-1 or you can set n_jobs=-2 in order to use all your CPU cores but one.

Sampling stratifications for complex data

Cross-validation folds are decided by random sampling. Sometimes it may be necessary to track if and how much of a certain characteristic is present in the training and test folds to avoid malformed samples. For instance, in the California housing dataset, latitude and longitude point out different areas in California. This information is important to understand the value of the house and determine whether people would like to spend more for it. You can see the effect of geographical coordinates using the following code:

```
import matplotlib.pyplot as plt
import pandas as pd

plt.hexbin(X.Longitude, X.Latitude, C=y, gridsize=50,
           cmap='Oranges')
cb = plt.colorbar()
cb.set_label('Median House Value')
plt.xlabel('Longitude'); plt.ylabel('Latitude'); plt.show()
```

The code will plot a heatmap of real estate values through California, represented in Figure 18-1, highlighting more expensive areas along the cost.

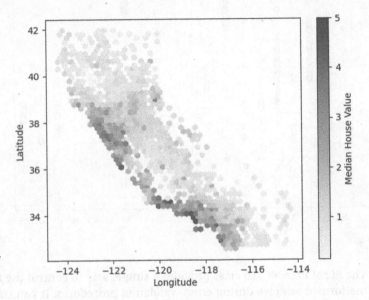

FIGURE 18-1:
Spatial
distribution of
house prices in
California.

Using cluster analysis, as explained in Chapter 15, you can segment the coordinates into homogeneous areas that you can test for their average housing value:

```
from sklearn.cluster import KMeans
coordinates = X[["Latitude","Longitude"]]
clustering = KMeans(n_clusters=20, n_init=10,
                    random_state=0)
clustering.fit(coordinates)
area = clustering.predict(coordinates)
df_area = pd.DataFrame({"area": area, "median_house_value": y})
df_area.boxplot("median_house_value", by="area");
```

A boxplot, represented in Figure 18-2, reveals how house prices are indeed varied in California due to the location.

In similar situations, when a characteristic is rare or influential, you can't be sure when it's present in the sample because the folds are created in a random way. Having too many or too few of a particular characteristic in each fold implies that the machine learning algorithm may derive incorrect rules.

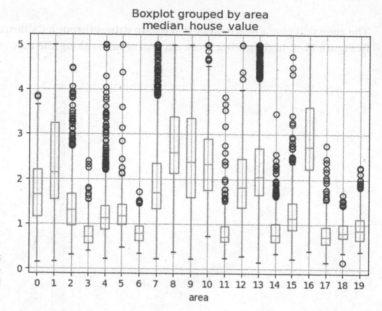

Boxplot grouped by area
median_house_value

FIGURE 18-2:
Boxplot of house
prices, grouped
by clusters.

The StratifiedKFold class provides a simple way to control the risk of building malformed samples during cross-validation procedures. It can control the sampling so that certain features, or even certain outcomes (when the target classes are extremely unbalanced), will always be present in your folds in the right proportion. You just need to point out the variable you want to control by using the y parameter, as shown in the following code.

```
from sklearn.model_selection import StratifiedKFold
from sklearn.metrics import mean_squared_error

skf = StratifiedKFold(n_splits=10, shuffle=True,
                      random_state=0)
scores = list()

for train_index, test_index in skf.split(X, area):
    X_train, X_test = X.iloc[train_index], \
        X.iloc[test_index]
    y_train, y_test = y[train_index], y[test_index]
    knn_model.fit(X_train, y_train)
    y_pred = knn_model.predict(X_test)
    scores.append(mean_squared_error(y_true=y_test,
                                     y_pred=y_pred))

print('%i folds cv mean squared error: %.5f std: %.5f' %
      (len(scores),np.mean(np.abs(scores)),
       np.std(scores)))
```

The result from the ten-fold stratified cross-validation is

```
10 folds cv mean squared error: 1.09899 std: 0.04505
```

Although the validation error is similar, by controlling the latitude and longitude variables, you can be more confident that training and validation samples are more homogeneous.

Selecting Variables Like a Pro

Selecting the right variables can improve the learning process by reducing the amount of noise (useless information) that can influence the learner's estimates. Variable selection, therefore, can effectively reduce the variance of predictions. To use just the useful variables in training and leave out the redundant ones, you can use these techniques:

>> **Univariate approach:** Select the variables most related to the target outcome.

>> **Forward or backward approach:** Keep only the variables that you can add or remove from the learning process without damaging its performance.

The following sections depend on a couple of variables, as shown here (which are follow-ons of previous sections):

```
df_area = pd.get_dummies(area, prefix="area")
df_X = pd.concat([X, df_area], axis=1)
```

The meaning of these variables will become clearer as the following sections progress; just know that you need to define them to make the code functional for now.

Selecting by univariate measures

If you decide to select a variable by its level of association with its target, you can refer to different metrics depending on whether your problem is a regression or classification. The available metrics for association are

>> `f_regression` or `r_regression`: Used only for numeric targets and based on linear regression performance.

» `f_classif`: Used only for categorical targets and based on the Analysis of Variance (ANOVA) statistical test.

» `chi2`: Performs the chi-square statistic for categorical targets, which is less sensitive to the nonlinear relationship between the predictive variable and its target.

TIP

When evaluating candidates for a classification problem, `f_classif` and `chi2` tend to provide the same set of top variables. It's still a good practice to test the selections from both the association metrics.

The regression example tests each feature's predictive power by testing its correlation with the target. The `r_regression` command will extract this information for each feature all simultaneously:

```
from sklearn.feature_selection import r_regression
correlations = r_regression(df_X, y)
for n, s in zip(df_X.columns, correlations):
    print(f"F-score: {s:+2.3f} for feature {n}")
```

The code will print each feature accompanied by its target correlation.

Using the correlation as a selection measure (higher absolute values signal more association of a feature with the target variable) helps you to pick the most important variables for your machine learning model, but you should watch out for these possible problems:

» Some variables with high association could also be highly correlated, introducing duplicated information, which acts as noise in the learning process.

» Some variables may be penalized, especially binary ones (variables indicating a status or characteristic using the value 1 when it is present, 0 when it is not).

Apart from applying a direct selection of the top correlations, Scikit-learn provides some helper functions. SelectPercentile (https://scikit-learn.org/stable/modules/generated/sklearn.feature_selection.SelectPercentile.html) can rank the best variables to make it easier to decide at what percentile to exclude a feature from participating in the learning process. The class SelectKBest (https://scikit-learn.org/stable/modules/generated/sklearn.feature_selection.SelectKBest.html) is analogous in its functionality, but it selects the top k variables, where k is a number, not a percentile.

TIP

The univariate selection process can give you a real advantage when you have a huge number of variables to select from and the other methods turn computationally infeasible. The best procedure is first to reduce the value of Select Percentile by half or more of the available variables, and then to proceed using a more precise method such as a forward or backward greedy selection.

Employing forward and backward selection

Forward and backward feature selection are two common techniques used in machine learning to select the most relevant features that contribute to the prediction of a target variable. Forward and backward feature selection techniques choose features based on how they work together, instead of just looking at each feature individually. In forward feature selection, the algorithm starts with an empty set of features and iteratively adds one feature at a time that improves the performance of the model. In contrast, backward feature selection begins with a full set of features and removes one feature at a time until the model's performance does not improve.

The provided SequentialFeatureSelector (https://scikit-learn.org/ stable/modules/generated/sklearn.feature_selection.Sequential FeatureSelector.html) by Scikit-learn allows you to set the direction of your search: forward if you are looking for a minimal set of features; backward if you want to just remove the non-useful features and have a set that's as complete as possible. Here is an example of using forward feature selection with our California housing data:

```
from sklearn.feature_selection \
    import SequentialFeatureSelector

selector = SequentialFeatureSelector(
    estimator=knn_model,
    direction='forward',
    cv=3,
    scoring='neg_mean_squared_error',
    n_features_to_select=14
)

selector.fit(df_X, y)
feature_mask = selector.support_
selected = [feature for feature,
            support in zip(df_X.columns,
                           feature_mask) if support]
print(f"Selected features: {selected}")
```

Using the forward procedure to select the best features for our model will take some time, but it helps us find a list of features that work the best for predicting outcomes:

```
Selected features: ['MedInc', 'HouseAge', 'AveRooms',
 'AveBedrms', 'AveOccup', 'area_0', 'area_3', 'area_4',
 'area_5', 'area_8', 'area_10', 'area_14', 'area_17',
 'area_19']
```

The next experiments found in the sections that follow try to improve the model's settings using the features chosen in the forward procedure. This is just like what would happen in a real project.

Pumping Up Your Hyperparameters

As a last example for this chapter, you can see the procedures for searching for the optimal hyperparameters of a machine learning algorithm to achieve the best possible predictive performance. Actually, much of the performance of your algorithm has already been decided by

>> **The choice of the algorithm:** Not every machine learning algorithm is a good fit for every type of data, and choosing the right one for your data can make the difference.

>> **The selection of the right variables:** Predictive performance is increased dramatically by feature creation (newly created variables are more predictive than old ones) and feature selection (removing redundancies and noise).

Fine-tuning the correct hyperparameters could provide even better predictive generalizability and pump up your results, especially in the case of complex algorithms that don't work well using the out-of-the-box default settings.

REMEMBER

Hyperparameters are parameters that you have to decide on yourself, because an algorithm can't learn them automatically from data. As with all other aspects of the learning process that involve a decision by the data scientist, you have to make your choices carefully after evaluating the cross-validated results.

The Scikit-learn `sklearn.model_selection` module has a section specializing in hyperparameters optimization. It contains a few utilities for automating and simplifying the process of searching for the best values of hyperparameters. The code in the following paragraphs illustrates the correct procedures, starting from reprising the initial KNN model.

TIP

Grid searching is easy to perform as a parallel task because the results of a tested combination of hyperparameters are independent from the results of the others. Using a multicore computer at its full power requires that you change n_jobs to –1 when instantiating any of the grid-search classes from Scikit-learn.

Implementing a grid search

The best way to verify the optimal hyperparameters for an algorithm is to test them all and then pick the combination with the highest score. This means, in the case of complex settings of multiple parameters, that you have to run hundreds, if not thousands, of slightly differently tuned models. *Grid searching* is a systematic search method that combines all the possible combinations of the hyperparameters into individual sets. It's a time-consuming technique. However, grid searching provides one of the leading ways to optimize a machine learning application that could have many working combinations, but just a single best one. Hyperparameters that have many acceptable solutions (called *local minima*) may trick you into thinking that you have found the optimal solution when you could actually improve their performance.

In the example for demonstrating how to implement a grid search effectively on the California housing dataset, you reprise the previously seen algorithm, the KNN classifier:

```
knn_model = KNeighborsRegressor(n_jobs=1)
```

The KNN classifier has quite a few hyperparameters that you can set for optimal performance:

>> The number of neighbor points to consider in the estimate

>> How to weight each of them

>> What metric to use for finding the neighbors

Using a range of possible values for all the parameters makes it apparent that you're going to test a large number of models. Specifically, the total number of evaluation models in this case is the product of the number of parameters, which is 8, 2, and 3, resulting in 48:

```
param_grid = {'n_neighbors': [1, 3, 5, 7, 10, 25, 50, 100],
              'weights': ['uniform', 'distance'],
              'metric': ['euclidean', 'manhattan',
                         'cosine']}
```

To set the instructions for the search, you build a Python dictionary whose keys are the names of the parameters, and the dictionary's values are lists of the values you want to test. For instance, the example shows a list of values for the hyperparameter n_neighbors, which is used in sequence during the grid search. Before starting, you also determine the cross-validation score using a *vanilla model*, a model with the following default parameters:

```
from sklearn.model_selection import cross_val_score

score_metric = 'neg_mean_squared_error'
scores = cross_val_score(
    knn_model, X=df_X.loc[:, feature_mask], y=y,
    cv=10, scoring=score_metric, n_jobs=-1)
baseline_score = np.mean(np.abs(scores))
print(f"Baseline with default parameters: {baseline_score:.3f}")
```

You take note of the result to determine the increase provided by optimizing the parameters:

```
Baseline with default parameters: 0.538
```

Using the mean squared error metric, the example first tests the baseline, which consists of the algorithm's default parameters (also clarified when instantiating the classifier variable with its class). Now the search locates a better set of hyperparameters using a tenfold cross-validation:

```
from sklearn.model_selection import GridSearchCV

search = GridSearchCV(
    estimator=knn_model, param_grid=param_grid,
    scoring=score_metric, n_jobs=-1, refit=True,
    return_train_score=True, cv=10)
search.fit(df_X.loc[:, feature_mask], y)
```

After being instantiated with the learning algorithm, the search dictionary, the scoring metric, and the cross-validation folds, the GridSearch class operates with the fit() method. Optionally, after the grid search ends, it refits the model with the best found parameter combination (refit=True), allowing it to immediately start predicting by using the GridSearch class itself. Finally, you print the resulting best parameters and the score of the best combination:

```
print(f"Best parameters: {search.best_params_}")
best_score = abs(search.best_score_)
```

```
print(f"CV mean squared error of best parameters:
    {best_score:.3f}")
```

Here are the printed values:

```
Best parameters: {'metric': 'cosine', 'n_neighbors': 50,
                        'weights': 'distance'}
CV mean squared error of best parameters: 0.481
```

When the search is completed, you can inspect the results using the `best_params_` and `best_score` attributes. The best squared error found was 0.481, an improvement over the initial baseline. To better understand how the optimization works with respect to the number of neighbors used by your algorithm, you can launch a Scikit-learn class for visualization. The `validation_curve` method gives you detailed information about how `train` and `validation` behave when used with different `n_neighbors` hyperparameters.

```
from sklearn.model_selection import validation_curve

tuned_model = KNeighborsRegressor(**search.best_params_,
                                    n_jobs=-1)

train, test = validation_curve(tuned_model,
    df_X.loc[:, feature_mask], y,
    param_name='n_neighbors', param_range=range(10, 101, 10),
    cv=3, scoring=score_metric, n_jobs=-1)
```

The `validation_curve` class provides you with two arrays containing the results arranged with the parameters values on the rows and the cross-validation folds on the columns:

```
import matplotlib.pyplot as plt

mean_test = abs(np.mean(test, axis=1))
x_ticks_labels = range(10, 101, 10)
x_ticks_values = range(0, len(x_ticks_labels))
plt.plot(x_ticks_values, mean_test, 'bD-.',
        label='Cross-validation')
plt.grid()
plt.xlabel('Number of neighbors')
plt.xticks(x_ticks_values, x_ticks_labels)
plt.ylabel('Mean squared error')
plt.legend(loc='upper right', numpoints=1); plt.show()
```

Projecting the row means creating a graphic visualization, as shown in Figure 18-3, which helps you understand what is happening with the learning process.

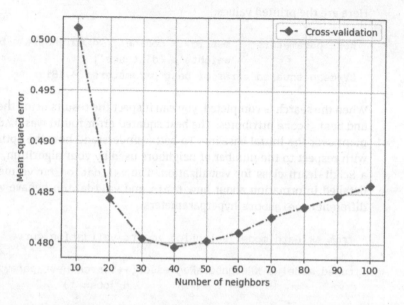

FIGURE 18-3:
Validation curves.

You can obtain an important piece of information from the visualization. The mean squared error tends to decline with more neighbors up to 40; then it starts increasing slowly. As with many hyperparameters in machine learning, n_neighbors has a sweet spot. This pattern happens frequently, and sometimes hyperparameters even interact between themselves; only certain combinations unlock the best score for your model.

TIP

It's part of the data science process to query, test, and query again. Even though Python and its packages offer you many automated processes in data learning and discovering, it is up to you to ask the right questions and to check whether the answers are the best ones by using statistical tests and visualizations.

Trying a randomized search

Grid searching provides an exhaustive examination of data, but it's also a time-consuming activity. It's prone to overfitting the cross-validation folds when you have few observations in your dataset and you extensively search for an optimization. You have options other than grid searching. As an experimental option, you also can try HalvingGridSearchCV (https://scikit-learn.org/stable/modules/generated/sklearn.model_selection.HalvingGridSearchCV.html).

HalvingGridSearchCV is a hyperparameter optimization technique that uses an iterative process to search for the best hyperparameters by repeatedly evaluating subsets of randomly selected hyperparameters. It discards underperforming subsets and continues with the best ones until a set of optimal hyperparameters is found. Here is our example:

```
from sklearn.experimental import enable_halving_search_cv
from sklearn.model_selection import HalvingGridSearchCV

search = HalvingGridSearchCV(
    estimator=knn_model, param_grid=param_grid,
    scoring=score_metric, n_jobs=-1, refit=True,
    return_train_score=True, cv=10, factor=2,
    max_resources='auto', aggressive_elimination=True,
    random_state=42)

search.fit(df_X.loc[:, feature_mask], y)
print(f"Best parameters: {search.best_params_}")
best_score = abs(search.best_score_)
print(f"CV mean squared error of best parameters: "
      f"{best_score:.3f}")
```

In a fraction of the time, the code returns the very same result from the standard grid search:

```
Best parameters: {'metric': 'cosine', 'n_neighbors': 50,
                  'weights': 'distance'}
CV mean squared error of best parameters: 0.481
```

Grid searching is like fishing with a large net. But there's a smarter way. Start with a large net with loose meshes to find where the "fish" (optimal hyperparameter values) are. Then, use a smaller net with tight meshes to catch the "fish" in those areas. This is a Scikit-learn experimental feature as of this writing, but we expect it to become part of the Scikit-learn package in the near future.

Another interesting alternative option is to try a randomized search. In this case, you define a grid search to test only some of the combinations, picked at random. Even though it may sound like betting on blind luck, a randomized search is actually quite useful because it's efficient — if you pick enough random combinations, you have a high statistical probability of finding an optimum hyperparameter combination, without risking overfitting at all. For instance, in the previous example, the code tested 48 different models using a systematic search, but using a randomized search, you can reduce the number of tests to just ten tests!

Using a randomized search is straightforward. You import the class from the `grid_search` module and input the same parameters as the `GridSearchCV`, adding a `n_iter` parameter that indicates how many combinations to sample. As a rule of thumb, you choose from a quarter or a third of the total number of hyperparameter combinations:

```
from sklearn.model_selection import RandomizedSearchCV

param_grid = {'n_neighbors': range(1, 100),
              'weights': ['uniform', 'distance'],
              'metric': ['euclidean', 'manhattan', 'cosine']}

random_search = RandomizedSearchCV(estimator=knn_model,
    param_distributions=param_grid, n_iter=10, cv=10,
    scoring=score_metric, refit=True, random_state=0, n_jobs=-1)

random_search.fit(df_X.loc[:, feature_mask], y)
print(f"Best parameters: {random_search.best_params_}")
best_score = abs(random_search.best_score_)
print(f"CV mean squared error of best parameters: "
    f"{best_score:.3f}")
```

Having completed the search using the same technique as before, you can examine the outputted best scores and best hyperparameters:

```
Best parameters: {'weights': 'distance',
'n_neighbors': 37, 'metric': 'cosine'}
CV mean squared error of best parameters: 0.480
```

From the reported results, it appears that a random search can actually obtain even better results compared to a much more CPU-expensive exhaustive grid search.

Chapter **19**

Increasing Complexity with Linear and Nonlinear Tricks

revious chapters introduce you to some of the simplest, yet effective, machine learning algorithms, such as linear and logistic regression, Naïve Bayes, and K-Nearest Neighbors (KNN). At this point, you can successfully complete a regression or classification project in data science. This chapter explores more complex and powerful machine learning techniques, including the following: reasoning on how to enhance your data; improving your estimates by regularization; and learning from big data by breaking it into manageable chunks.

This chapter also introduces you to the support vector machine (SVM), a powerful family of algorithms for classification and regression. The chapter touches on neural networks as well. Both SVMs and neural networks can tackle the most difficult data problems in data science. However, neural networks and tree ensembles have overtaken SVMs as the state-of-the-art predictive tool. Decision trees, random forests, and other tree-like structures are covered in a progressively more complex manner in Chapter 20, "Understanding the Power of the Many." Neural networks have a long history, but in the last few years, they have improved by giant leaps to the point of becoming incredible and indispensable tools for prediction and generation of images and text. Given the complexity of both regression and classification using advanced techniques, quite a few pages of this chapter are devoted to SVM and some to neural networks, but increasing your understanding of both strategies is definitely worth the time and effort.

REMEMBER

You don't have to type the source code for this chapter manually; using the downloadable source is a lot easier (see the Introduction for download instructions). The source code for this chapter appears in the P4DS4D3_19_Increasing_Complexity.ipynb file. You can also plot some of the complex drawings illustrating SVM algorithms by running the code in the P4DS4D3_19_Representing_SVM_boundaries.ipynb source file.

Using Nonlinear Transformations

Linear models, such as linear and logistic regression, actually sum the values of your features (after having weighted them by some learned coefficients) and provide a simple but effective model. In most situations, they offer a good approximation of the complex reality they represent. Even though they're characterized by a high bias, using a large number of observations can improve the estimates of their coefficients and make them more performant when compared to complex algorithms.

However, they can perform better when solving certain problems if you pre-analyze the data using the Exploratory Data Analysis (EDA) approach. After performing the analysis, you can transform and enrich the existing features by

>> Creating new features based on your understanding of the problem. This operation is called *feature engineering*.

>> Linearizing the relationships between features and the target variable using transformations that increase their correlation and make their cloud of points in the scatterplot more similar to a line.

>> Making variables interact by multiplying them so that you can better represent their conjoint behavior.

>> Expanding the existing variables using the polynomial expansion in order to represent relationships more realistically (such as ideal point curves, when there is a peak in the variable representing a maximum, akin to a parabola).

Doing variable transformations

An example is the best way to explain the kind of transformations you can successfully apply to data to improve a linear model. The example in this section, and the "Regularizing Linear Models" and "Fighting with Big Data Chunk by Chunk" sections that follow, relies on the California housing dataset. The problem relies on regression, and the data originally has seven variables to explain the median house values for California districts. Here is the code to download the dataset on your notebook:

```python
from sklearn.datasets import fetch_california_housing
import pandas as pd

def load_california_housing_data():
    dataset = fetch_california_housing()
    X = pd.DataFrame(data=dataset.data,
                     columns=dataset.feature_names)
    y = pd.Series(data=dataset.target, name="target")
    print(dataset.DESCR)
    return X, y

X, y = load_california_housing_data()
```

After downloading the dataset, the code prints a verbose description of the dataset.

TIP

You can find out more details about the meaning of the variables present in the California housing dataset by reading the description returned by the code. It will explain the meaning of the variables in the dataset and provide some historical background about the data itself.

To begin with the data transformation process, you can start feature engineering new variables based on your understanding of the problem. First, you clip any outlying value among the average number of household members (AveOccup) to a maximum of 100. Second, you compute new metrics based on the average number of individuals per room or per bedroom, as well as the same ratios but considering the overall population. Finally, you calculate the ratio between the number of bedrooms and the total number of rooms.

```python
X["AveOccup"] = X["AveOccup"].clip(upper=100)
X['AveOccupRooms'] = X['AveOccup'] / X['AveRooms']
X['AveOccupBedrms'] = X['AveOccup'] / X['AveBedrms']
X['Rooms_capita'] = X['Population'] / X['AveRooms']
X['Bedrms_capita'] = X['Population'] / X['AveBedrms']
X['Bedrms_pct'] = X['AveBedrms'] / X['AveRooms']
```

When it comes to improving the performance of your machine learning model, feature engineering plays a crucial role. This process involves creating new variables that enhance how the model learns from data. Additionally, you can also enhance the existing variables by applying certain functions that transform them into more useful representations.

Logarithmic transformation can help in such situations. However, your values should range from zero to one (as with percentages) as demonstrated in this example. In other cases, other useful transformations for your x variable could include $x**2$, $x**3$, $1/x$, $1/x**2$, $1/x**3$, and $sqrt(x)$. The key is to try them and test the result. As for testing, you can use the following script as an example for testing a logarithmic transformation on one of the features from the dataset:

```
import numpy as np
from sklearn.feature_selection import f_regression

single_variable = X["AveOccup"].values.reshape(-1, 1)
F, pval = f_regression(single_variable, y)
print(f'F score for the original feature {F[0]:.1f}')

F, pval = f_regression(np.log1p(single_variable),y)
print(f'F score for the transformed feature {F[0]:.1f}')
```

The code prints the F score, a measure to evaluate how predictive a feature is in a machine learning problem, both the original and the transformed feature. The score for the transformed feature is a great improvement over the untransformed one.

```
F score for the original feature 275.8
F score for the transformed feature 1434.7
```

The F score is useful for variable selection. You can also use it to assess the usefulness of a transformation because both f_regression and f_classif are themselves based on linear models, and are therefore sensitive to every effective transformation used to make variable relationships more linear.

Creating interactions between variables

When performing a weighted summation using all the features, the model responds independently to changes in each variable, without considering their interactions with other variables. In statistics, this type of model is referred to as a *main effects model* because it considers only the individual effects of each feature, treating them as standalone elements.

REMEMBER

The Naïve Bayes classifier makes a similar assumption for probabilities, and it also works well with complex text problems.

Even though machine learning works by using approximations and a weighted sum of a set of variables can produce predictions that work well in most situations, sometimes you may miss an important part of the picture. You can easily catch this problem by depicting the variation in your target associated with the conjoint variation of two or more variables in two simple and straightforward ways:

>> **Existing domain knowledge of the problem:** For instance, in the car market, having a noisy engine is a nuisance in a family car but considered a plus for sports cars (car aficionados want to hear that you have an ultra-cool and expensive car). By knowing a consumer preference, you can model a noise level variable and a car type variable together to obtain exact predictions using a predictive analytic model that guesses the car's value based on its features.

>> **Testing combinations of different variables:** By performing group tests, you can see the effect that certain variables have on your target variable. Therefore, even without knowing about the relationship between noisy engines and sports cars, you could have caught a difference in the average of preference level when analyzing your dataset split by type of cars and noise level.

The following example shows how to automatically test and detect interactions in the California housing dataset. You start creating a pipeline that puts together a StandardScaler and a LinearRegression. In this way, all the features are standardized, meaning they have zero mean and standard deviation one, before being processed by the algorithm. Afterward, you compute the mean squared error (MSE) using a tenfold cross-validation:

```
from sklearn.linear_model import LinearRegression
from sklearn.preprocessing import StandardScaler
from sklearn.pipeline import Pipeline
from sklearn.model_selection  import \
    cross_val_score, KFold

regression = Pipeline([("scaler", StandardScaler()),
                       ("model",LinearRegression())])
crossvalidation = KFold(n_splits=10, shuffle=True,
                        random_state=1)
```

```
baseline = np.mean(cross_val_score(
    regression, X, y,
    scoring='neg_mean_squared_error',
    cv=crossvalidation))
print(f'Baseline MSE: {abs(baseline):.3f}')
```

After completing the instructions, the code prints the baseline MSE value, which is calculated using the mean of the cross-validation scores:

```
Baseline MSE: 0.507
```

The idea now is to try to add one different interaction term, given by the multiplication of two existing variables, and check whether the MSE diminishes. Less MSE means an improvement because it corresponds to the quantity of errors the model contains. The fewer errors, the better. First, you need to compute the interactions between features. Polynomial features with degree 2 are created for the selected features using PolynomialFeatures. The interaction_only parameter is set to True to include only interaction terms, and include_bias is set to False to exclude an additional interaction term.

```
from sklearn.preprocessing import PolynomialFeatures

poly = PolynomialFeatures((2, 2), interaction_only=True,
                          include_bias=False)
features = ["MedInc", "HouseAge", "Population",
           "AveRooms", "AveBedrms", "AveOccup"]
poly.fit(X[features])
interactions = pd.DataFrame(
    poly.transform(X[features]),
    columns=poly.get_feature_names_out(features))
```

After all these instructions are completed, you can check the shape interactions DataFrame containing the interactions terms:

```
print(interactions.shape)
```

The print instructions reports having being created 15 interaction terms.

```
(20640, 15)
```

At this point, for each interaction term, you concatenate the existing features with the interaction term and compute the MSE error again using the same cross-validation procedure as before:

```
for col in interactions:
    Xt = pd.concat([X, interactions[col]], axis=1)

    test = np.mean(cross_val_score(
        regression, Xt, y,
        scoring='neg_mean_squared_error',
        cv=crossvalidation))
    if test > baseline:
        print(f"adding interaction {col} improves " +
              f"MSE to {abs(test):0.3f}")
```

If the resulting MSE is better than the baseline, the code prints the interaction terms and reports the improved score:

```
adding interaction MedInc HouseAge improves MSE to 0.504
adding interaction MedInc Population improves MSE to 0.500
adding interaction MedInc AveRooms improves MSE to 0.501
adding interaction MedInc AveBedrms improves MSE to 0.506
adding interaction MedInc AveOccup improves MSE to 0.507
adding interaction HouseAge Population improves MSE to 0.506
adding interaction Population AveOccup improves MSE to 0.490
```

The most effective interactions terms are those that multiply Population with AveOccup and MedInc with Population, implying that there is a much different impact on the median house value for California districts depending on the combination of these variables. They certainly would make an important addition to the model.

Regularizing Linear Models

Instead of looking for specific interactions and selectively adding them to your model, you could have just computed all the possible interactions and added them to your model. But there can be a problem with doing that. Linear models have a high bias, but as you add more features, more interactions, and more transformations, they start gaining adaptability to the data characteristics and memorizing power for data noise, thus increasing the variance of their estimates. Trading higher variance for less bias isn't always the best choice, but, as mentioned earlier, sometimes it's the only way to increase the predictive power of linear algorithms.

You can introduce L1 and L2 regularization as a way to control the trade-off between bias and variance in favor of an increased generalization capability of the model. When you introduce one of the regularizations, an additive function that depends on the complexity of the linear model penalizes the optimized cost function. In linear regression, the cost function is the squared error of the predictions, and the cost function is penalized using a summation of the coefficients of the predictor variables.

If the model is complex but the predictive gain is little, the penalization forces the optimization procedure to remove the useless variables, or to reduce their impact on the estimate. The regularization also acts on highly correlated features — attenuating or excluding their contribution, thus stabilizing the results and reducing the consequent variance of the estimates:

>> **L1 (also called Lasso):** Shrinks some coefficients to zero, making your coefficients sparse. It performs variable selection.

>> **L2 (also called Ridge):** Reduces the coefficients of the most problematic features, making them smaller, but seldom equal to zero. All coefficients keep participating in the estimate, but many become small and irrelevant.

REMEMBER

You can control the strength of the regularization using a hyperparameter, usually a coefficient itself, often called alpha. When alpha approaches 1.0, you have stronger regularization and a greater reduction of the coefficients. In some cases, the coefficients are reduced to zero. Don't confuse alpha with C, a parameter used by LogisticRegression and by support vector machines, because C is 1/alpha, so it can be greater than 1. Smaller C numbers actually correspond to more regularization, exactly the opposite of alpha.

TIP

Regularization works because it is the sum of the coefficients of the predictor variables, therefore it's important that they're on the same scale or the regularization may find it difficult to converge, and variables with larger absolute coefficient values will greatly influence it, generating an infective regularization. It's good practice to standardize the predictor values or bind them to a common min-max, such as the [-1,+1] range. The following sections demonstrate various methods of using both L1 and L2 regularization to achieve various effects.

Relying on Ridge regression (L2)

The first example uses the L2 type regularization, reducing the strength of the coefficients. This example uses all the original features, the features engineered and interactions built as part of the previous examples. The Ridge class implements L2 for linear regression. Its usage is simple; it presents just the parameter alpha to fix. Ridge regression performs better when applied to features that have been rescaled or standardized. If the features are not rescaled, it can take a longer time for the regression to converge and reach a solution. To address this issue, the example sets up a pipeline that includes the StandardScaler along with our model. This approach of using a pipeline with feature scaling will be applied to all regularized linear models we present, because they share the same problem.

```
from sklearn.model_selection import GridSearchCV
from sklearn.linear_model import Ridge

Xt = pd.concat([X, interactions], axis=1)

ridge = Pipeline([("scaler", StandardScaler()),
                  ("model",Ridge())])
search_grid = {'model__alpha': np.logspace(-6, 4, 20)}
search = GridSearchCV(estimator=ridge,
                      param_grid=search_grid,
                      scoring='neg_mean_squared_error',
                      refit=True, cv=crossvalidation)
search.fit(Xt, y)
print(f'Best parameters: {search.best_params_}')
score = abs(search.best_score_)
print(f'CV MSE of best parameters: {score:.3f}')
```

After searching for the best alpha parameter, the resulting best model is

```
Best parameters: {'model__alpha': 263.6650898730355}
CV MSE of best parameters: 0.499
```

TIP

A good search space for the alpha value is in the range np.logspace(-6,4,20). Of course, if the resulting optimum value is on one of the extremities of the tested range, you need to enlarge the range and retest.

Using the Lasso (L1)

The second example uses the L1 regularization, the Lasso class, whose principal characteristic is to reduce the effect of less useful coefficients down toward zero. This action enforces sparsity in the coefficients, with just a few having values above zero. The class uses the same parameters of the Ridge class that are demonstrated in the previous section.

```
from sklearn.linear_model import Lasso
from warnings import simplefilter
from sklearn.exceptions import ConvergenceWarning
simplefilter("ignore", category=ConvergenceWarning)
```

```
lasso = Pipeline([("scaler", StandardScaler()),
                  ("model",Lasso(selection='random'))])
search_grid = {'model__alpha': np.logspace(-6, 4, 20)}
search = GridSearchCV(estimator=lasso,
                      param_grid=search_grid,
                      scoring='neg_mean_squared_error',
                      refit=True, cv=crossvalidation)
search.fit(Xt, y)
best_alpha = search.best_params_
print(f'Best parameters: {search.best_params_}')
score = abs(search.best_score_)
print(f'CV MSE of best parameters: {score:.3f}')
```

In setting the Lasso, the code uses a random approach for its optimization
(selection='random'). The resulting mean squared error obtained is lower than
it is using the L2 regularization:

```
Best parameters: {'model__alpha': 0.004832930238571752}
CV MSE of best parameters: 0.492
```

Leveraging regularization

Because you can choose the sparse coefficients resulting from a L1 regression as a
feature selection procedure, you can effectively use the Lasso class for selecting
the most important variables. By tuning the alpha parameter, you can select a
greater or lesser number of variables. In this case, the code sets the alpha parameter to about 0.005, obtaining a much simplified solution as a result:

```
selection = np.abs(
    search.best_estimator_["model"].coef_) > 0
print(Xt.columns[selection].tolist())
```

The simplified solution is made of a handful of interactions:

```
['MedInc', 'HouseAge', 'AveRooms', 'AveOccup', 'Latitude',
 'Longitude', 'AveOccupRooms', 'AveOccupBedrms',
 'Rooms_capita', 'Bedrms_capita', 'Bedrms_pct',
 'MedInc HouseAge', 'MedInc Population',
 'MedInc AveRooms', 'HouseAge Population',
 'HouseAge AveOccup', 'Population AveRooms',
 'Population AveOccup']
```

Combining L1 & L2: Elasticnet

L2 regularization reduces the impact of correlated features, whereas L1 regularization tends to select them. A good strategy is to mix them using a weighted sum by using the ElasticNet class. You control both L1 and L2 effects by using the same alpha parameter, but you can decide the L1 effect's share by using the l1_ratio parameter. Clearly, if l1_ratio is 0, you have a ridge regression; on the other hand, when l1_ratio is 1, you have a lasso.

```python
from sklearn.linear_model import ElasticNet

elastic = Pipeline([
    ("scaler", StandardScaler()),
    ("model", ElasticNet(selection='random'))])
search_grid = {'model__alpha': np.logspace(-6, 4, 20),
          'model__l1_ratio': [0.05, 0.10 ,0.25, 0.5,
                              0.75, 0.90, 0.95]}
search = GridSearchCV(estimator=elastic,
                      param_grid=search_grid,
                      scoring='neg_mean_squared_error',
                      refit=True, cv=crossvalidation)
search.fit(Xt, y)
print(f'Best parameters: {search.best_params_}')
score = abs(search.best_score_)
print(f'CV MSE of best parameters: {score:.3f}')
```

After a while, you get a result that's quite similar to L1's because L1 regularization is predominant on L2:

```
Best parameters: {'model__alpha': 0.004832930238571752,
                  'model__l1_ratio': 0.95}
CV MSE of best parameters: 0.493
```

Fighting with Big Data Chunk by Chunk

Up to this point, the book has dealt with small example databases. Real data, apart from being messy, can also be quite big — sometimes so big that it can't fit in memory, no matter what the memory specifications of your machine are.

WARNING

The Xt and y variables used for the examples in the sections that follow are created as part of the example in the "Creating interactions between variables" section, earlier in this chapter. If you haven't worked through that section, the examples in this section will fail to work properly.

Determining when there is too much data

In a data science project, data can be deemed big when one of these two situations occur:

>> It can't fit in the available computer memory.

>> Even if the system has enough memory to hold the data, the application can't elaborate the data using machine learning algorithms in a reasonable amount of time.

Implementing Stochastic Gradient Descent

When you have too much data, you can use the Stochastic Gradient Descent Regressor (SGDRegressor) or Stochastic Gradient Descent Classifier (SGDClassifier) as a linear predictor. The only difference with other methods described earlier in the chapter is that they actually optimize their coefficients using only one observation at a time. It therefore takes more iterations before the code reaches comparable results using a ridge or lasso regression, but it requires much less memory and time.

This is because both predictors rely on *Stochastic Gradient Descent (SGD)* optimization — a kind of optimization in which the parameter adjustment occurs after the input of every observation, leading to a longer and a bit more erratic journey toward minimizing the error function. Of course, optimizing based on single observations, and not on huge data matrices, can have a tremendously beneficial impact on the algorithm's training time and the amount of memory resources.

When using the SGDs, apart from different cost functions that you have to test for their performance, you can also try using L1, L2, and Elasticnet regularization just by setting the penalty parameter and the corresponding controlling alpha and l1_ratio parameters. Some of the SGDs are more resistant to outliers, such as modified_huber for classification or huber for regression.

REMEMBER

SGD is sensitive to the scale of variables, and not just because of regularization but also because of the way it works internally. Consequently, you must always standardize your features (for instance, by using StandardScaler) or you force them in the range [0,+1] or [-1,+1] using the MinMaxScaler as done in the example in this section. Failing to do so will lead to poor results.

TIP

When using SGDs, you'll always have to deal with chunks of data unless you can load all the training data into memory. To make the training effective, you should standardize by having the StandardScaler infer the mean and standard deviation from the first available data. The mean and standard deviation of the entire dataset is most likely different, but the transformation by an initial estimate will suffice to develop a working learning procedure.

```python
from sklearn.linear_model import SGDRegressor
from sklearn.preprocessing import MinMaxScaler
from sklearn.metrics import mean_squared_error
from sklearn.model_selection import train_test_split

scaling = MinMaxScaler(feature_range=(0, 1))
scaled_X = scaling.fit_transform(Xt)

X_tr, X_t, y_tr, y_t = train_test_split(scaled_X, y,
                                        test_size=0.20,
                                        random_state=0)
SGD = SGDRegressor(loss='squared_error',
                   penalty='l1',
                   alpha=0.00001,
                   max_iter=2000,
                   learning_rate="adaptive",
                   random_state=0)
SGD.fit(X_tr, y_tr)

score = mean_squared_error(y_t, SGD.predict(X_t))
print(f'test MSE: {score:.3f}')
```

The resulting mean squared error after running the SGDRegressor is

```
CV MSE: 0.494
```

In the preceding example, you used the fit() method, which requires that you preload all the training data into memory. You can train the model in successive steps by using the partial_fit() method instead, which runs a single iteration on the provided data, then keeps it in memory and adjusts it when receiving new data. The following example monitors the results obtained by the model during the iterations:

```python
SGD = SGDRegressor(loss='squared_error',
                   penalty='l1',
                   alpha=0.00001,
```

```
                    learning_rate="adaptive",
                    random_state=0)

improvements = list()

for z in range(2000):
    SGD.partial_fit(X_tr, y_tr)
    score = mean_squared_error(y_t, SGD.predict(X_t))
    improvements.append(score)

print(f'test MSE: {improvements[-1]:.3f}')
```

Having kept track of the algorithm's partial improvements during 2000 iterations over the same data, you can produce a graph that helps you understand the improvements shown in the following code. Note that you could have used different data at each step.

```
%matplotlib inline
import matplotlib.pyplot as plt

plt.figure(figsize=(8, 4))
plt.subplot(1,2,1)
range_1 = range(0,50,5)
score_1 = np.abs(improvements[0:100:10])
plt.plot(range_1, score_1,'o--')
plt.xlabel('Iterations up to 100')
plt.ylabel('Test mean squared error')
plt.subplot(1,2,2)
range_2 = range(100,2000,100)
score_2 = np.abs(improvements[100:2000:100])
plt.plot(range_2, score_2,'o--')
plt.xlabel('Iterations from 101 to 2000')
plt.show()
```

As shown in the first of the two panes in Figure 19-1, the algorithm initially starts with a high error rate, but it manages to reduce it in just a few iterations, usually 5–10. After that, the error rate slowly improves by a smaller amount with each iteration. In the second pane, you can see that after 1,500 iterations, the error rate reaches a minimum and starts fluctuating. At that point, you're starting to overfit because data already understands the rules, and you're actually forcing the SGD to learn more when nothing is left in the data other than noise. Consequently, it starts learning noise and erratic rules.

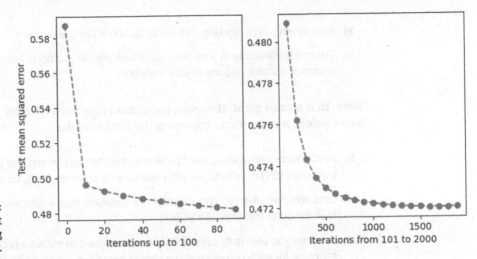

FIGURE 19-1:
A slow descent
optimizing
squared error.

TIP

Unless you're working with all the data in memory, grid-searching and cross-validating the best number of iterations will be difficult. A good trick is to keep a chunk of training data to use for validation apart in memory or storage. By checking your performance on that untouched part, you can see when SGD learning performance starts decreasing. At that point, you can interrupt iterating over the data (a stopping method known as early stopping).

Understanding Support Vector Machines

Support vector machines (SVM) are one of the most complex and powerful machine learning techniques in the data scientist's toolbox. However, since the recent success of neural networks, you usually find this topic solely in advanced manuals. In our opinion, you shouldn't turn away from this great learning algorithm. The Scikit-learn library offers you a wide and accessible range of SVM-supervised classes for regression and classification. When evaluating whether you want to try SVM algorithms as a machine learning solution, consider these main benefits:

>> Comprehensive family of techniques for binary and multiclass classification, regression, and novelty detection

>> Good prediction generator that provides robust handling of overfitting, noisy data, and outliers

>> Successful handling of situations that involve many variables

>> Effective when you have more variables than examples

>> Fast, when you're working with up to 10,000 training examples

>> Detects nonlinearity in your data automatically, so you don't have to apply complex transformations of your variables

Wow, that sounds great. However, you should also consider a few relevant drawbacks before you jump into importing the SVM module:

>> Performs better when applied to binary classification (which was the initial purpose of SVM), so SVM doesn't work as well on other prediction problems

>> Less effective when you have a lot more variables than examples; you have to look for other solutions like SGD

>> Provides you with only a predicted outcome; you can obtain a probability estimate for each response at the cost of more time-consuming computations

>> Works satisfactorily out of the box, but if you want the best results, you have to spend time experimenting in order to tune the many parameters

Relying on a computational method

Vladimir Vapnik and his colleagues invented SVM in the 1990s while working at AT&T laboratories. SVM gained success thanks to its high performance in many challenging problems for the machine learning community of the time, especially when used to help a computer read handwritten input. Today, data scientists frequently apply SVM to an incredible array of problems, from medical diagnosis to image recognition and textual classification. You'll likely find SVM quite useful for your problems, too!

REMEMBER

The code for this section is relatively long and complex. It appears in the P4DS4D4_19_Representing_SVM_boundaries.ipynb file, along with the outputs described in this section. You should refer to the source code to see how the code generates the figures in this section.

The idea behind SVM is simple, but the mathematical implementation is quite complex and requires many computations to work. This section helps you understand the technology behind the technique — knowing how a tool works always helps you figure out where and how to employ it best. Start considering the problem of separating two groups of data points. It's a classic binary classification problem in which a learning algorithm has to figure out how to separate one class of instances from the other one using the information provided by the data at hand. The first pane in Figure 19-2 shows a representation of a similar problem.

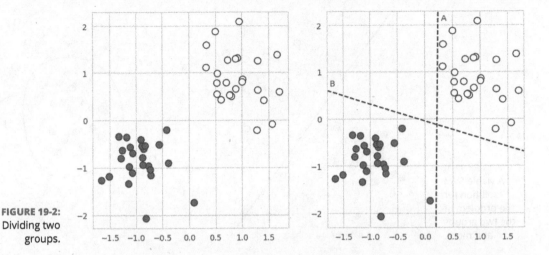

FIGURE 19-2:
Dividing two
groups.

If the two groups are separate from one another, you may solve the problem in many different ways just by choosing different separating lines. Of course, you must pay attention to the details and use fine measurements. Even though it may seem like an easy task, you need to consider what happens when the data changes, such as when you add more data points later. You may not be able to be sure that you chose the right separation line.

The second pane in Figure 19-2 shows two possible solutions, but even more can exist. Both chosen solutions are too near to the existing observations (as shown by the proximity of the lines to the data points), but there is no reason to think that new observations will behave precisely like those shown in the figure. SVM minimizes the risk of choosing the wrong line (as you may have done by selecting solution A or B from Figure 19-3) by choosing the solution characterized by the largest distance from the bordering points of the two groups. Having so much space between groups (the maximum possible) should reduce the chance of picking the wrong solution!

The largest distance between the two groups is the *margin*. When the margin is large enough, you can be quite sure that it'll keep working well, even when you have to classify previously unseen data. The margin is determined by the points that are present on the limit of the margin — the *support vectors* (the support vector machines algorithm takes its name from them).

You can see an SVM solution in the first pane in Figure 19-3. The figure shows the margin as a dashed line, the separator as the continuous line, and the support vectors as the circled data points.

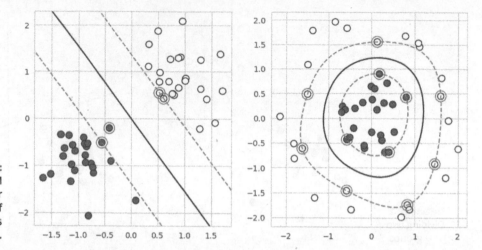

FIGURE 19-3:
A viable SVM
solution for
the problem of
the two groups
and more.

Real-world problems don't always provide neatly separable classes, as in this example. However, a well-tuned SVM can withstand some ambiguity (some misclassified points). An SVM algorithm with the right parameters can really do miracles.

REMEMBER

When working with example data, it's easier to look for neat solutions so that the data points can better explain how the algorithm works and you can grasp the core concepts. With real data, though, you need approximations that work. Therefore, you rarely see large and clear margins.

Apart from binary classifications on two dimensions, SVM can also work on complex data. You can consider the data as complex when you have more than two dimensions, or in situations that are similar to the layout depicted in the second pane in Figure 19-3, when separating the groups by a straight line isn't possible.

TECHNICAL
STUFF

In the presence of many variables, SVM can use a complex separating plane (the *hyperplane*). SVM also works well when you can't separate classes by a straight line or plane because it can explore nonlinear solutions in multidimensional space thanks to a computational technique called the *kernel trick*, a method used to bridge linearity and nonlinearity. (You can find a full discussion of the kernel trick at https://towardsdatascience.com/the-kernel-trick-c98cdbcaeb3f.)

Fixing many new parameters

Although SVM is complex, it's a great tool. After you find the most suitable SVM version for your problem, you have to apply it to your data and work a little to optimize some of the many parameters available and improve your results. Setting up a working SVM predictive model involves these general steps:

1. Choose the SVM class you'll use.
2. Train your model with the data.
3. Check your validation error and make it your baseline.
4. Try different values for the SVM parameters.
5. Check whether your validation error improves.
6. Train your model again using the data with the best parameters.

To choose the right SVM class, you have to think about your problem. For example, you could choose a classification (guess a class) or regression (guess a number). When working with a classification, you must consider whether you need to classify just two groups (binary classification) or more than two (multiclass classification). Another important aspect to consider is the quantity of data you have to process. After taking notes of all your requirements on a list, a quick glance at Table 19-1 will help you to narrow your choices.

TABLE 19-1   **The SVM Module of Learning Algorithms**

Class	Characteristic Usage	Key Parameters
sklearn.svm.SVC	Binary and multiclass classification when the number of examples is less than 10,000	C, kernel, degree, gamma
sklearn.svm.NuSVC	Similar to SVC	nu, kernel, degree, gamma
sklearn.svm.LinearSVC	Binary and multiclass classification when the number of examples is more than 10,000; sparse data	Penalty, loss, C
sklearn.svm.SVR	Regression problems	C, kernel, degree, gamma, epsilon
sklearn.svm.NuSVR	Similar to SVR	Nu, C, kernel, degree, gamma
sklearn.svm.OneClassSVM	Outliers detection	nu, kernel, degree, gamma

The first step is to check the number of examples in your data. Having more than 10,000 examples could mean slow and cumbersome computations, but you can still use SVM to obtain acceptable performance for classification problems by using sklearn.svm.LinearSVC. When solving a regression problem, you may find that the LinearSVC isn't fast enough, in which case you use a stochastic solution for SVM (as described in the sections that follow).

TIP

The Scikit-learn SVM module wraps two powerful libraries written in C, libsvm and liblinear. When fitting a model, there is a flow of data between Python and the two external libraries. A cache smoothes the data exchange operations. However, if the cache is too small and you have too many data points, the cache becomes a bottleneck! If you have enough memory, it's a good idea to set a cache size greater than the default 200MB (1000MB, if possible) using the SVM class' `cache_size` parameter. Smaller numbers of examples require only that you decide between classification and regression.

In each case, you'll have two alternative algorithms. For example, for classification, you may use `sklearn.svm.SVC` or `sklearn.svm.NuSVC`. The only difference with the Nu version is the parameters it takes and the use of a slightly different algorithm. In the end, it gets basically the same results, so you normally choose the non-Nu version.

After deciding on which algorithm to use, you find that you have a number of parameters from which to choose, and the C parameter is always among them. The C parameter indicates how much the algorithm has to adapt to training points. When C is small, the SVM adapts less to the points and tends to take an average direction, just using a few of the available points and variables. Larger C values tend to force the learning process to follow more of the available training points and to get involved with many variables.

The right C is usually a middle value, and you can find it after a bit of experimentation. If your C is too large, you risk *overfitting*, a situation in which your SVM adapts too much to your data and cannot properly handle new problems. If your C is too small, your prediction will be rougher and imprecise. You'll experience a situation called *underfitting* — your model is too simple for the problem you want to solve.

After deciding the C value to use, the important block of parameters to fix is kernel, degree, and gamma. All three interconnect and their value depends on the kernel specification (for instance, the linear kernel doesn't require degree or gamma, so you can use any value). The kernel specification determines whether your SVM model uses a line or a curve in order to guess the class or the point measure. Linear models are simpler and tend to guess well on new data, but they sometimes underperform when variables in the data relate to each other in complex ways. Because you can't know in advance whether a linear model works for your problem, it's good practice to start with a linear kernel, fix its C value, and use that model and its performance as a baseline for testing nonlinear solutions afterward.

Classifying with SVC

It's time to build the first SVM model. Because SVM initially performed so well with handwritten classification, starting with a similar problem is a great idea. Using this approach can give you an idea of how powerful this machine learning technique is. The example uses the digits dataset available from the module datasets in the Scikit-learn package. The digits dataset contains a series of 8-x-8-pixel images of handwritten numbers ranging from 0 to 9.

```
from sklearn import datasets
digits = datasets.load_digits()
X, y = digits.data, digits.target
```

After loading the datasets module, the load.digits function imports all the data, from which the example extracts the predictors (digits.data) as X and the predicted classes (digits.target) as y.

You can look at what's inside this dataset using the matplotlib functions subplot (for creating an array of drawings arranged in two rows of five columns) and imshow (for plotting grayscale pixel values onto an 8-x-8 grid). The code arranges the information inside digits.images as a series of matrices, each one containing the pixel data of a number.

```
%matplotlib inline

import matplotlib.pyplot as plt
for k, img in enumerate(range(10)):
plt.subplot(2, 5, k+1)
plt.imshow(digits.images[img],
         cmap='binary',
         interpolation='none')
plt.show()
```

The code displays the first ten numbers as an example of the data used in the example. You can see the result in Figure 19-4.

By observing the data, you can also determine that SVM could guess a particular number by associating a probability with the values of specific pixels in the grid. A number 2 could turn on different pixels than a number 1, or maybe different groups of pixels. Data science involves testing many programming approaches and algorithms before reaching a solid result, but it helps to be imaginative and intuitive in order to determine which approach to try first. In fact, if you explore X, you discover that it's made of exactly 64 variables, each one representing the grayscale value of a single pixel, and that you have plentiful examples — exactly 1,797 cases.

```
print(X[0])
```

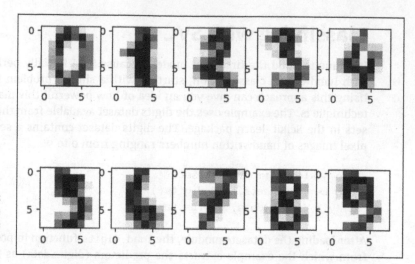

FIGURE 19-4:
The first ten
handwritten
digits from the
digits dataset.

The code returns a vector of the first example in the dataset:

```
[ 0.  0.  5. 13.  9.  1.  0.  0.  0.  0. 13. 15. 10. 15.
  5.  0.  0.  3. 15.  2.  0. 11.  8.  0.  0.  4. 12.  0.
  0.  8.  8.  0.  0.  5.  8.  0.  0.  9.  8.  0.  0.  4.
 11.  0.  1. 12.  7.  0.  0.  2. 14.  5. 10. 12.  0.  0.
  0.  0.  6. 13. 10.  0.  0.  0.]
```

If you reprint the same vector as an 8-x-8 matrix, you spot the image of a zero:

```
print(X[0].reshape(8, 8))
```

You interpret the zero values as the color white and the higher values as darker shades of gray:

```
[[ 0.  0.  5. 13.  9.  1.  0.  0.]
 [ 0.  0. 13. 15. 10. 15.  5.  0.]
 [ 0.  3. 15.  2.  0. 11.  8.  0.]
 [ 0.  4. 12.  0.  0.  8.  8.  0.]
 [ 0.  5.  8.  0.  0.  9.  8.  0.]
 [ 0.  4. 11.  0.  1. 12.  7.  0.]
 [ 0.  2. 14.  5. 10. 12.  0.  0.]
 [ 0.  0.  6. 13. 10.  0.  0.  0.]]
```

At this point, you might wonder what to do about labels. You can try getting a count of the labels using the unique function in the NumPy package:

```
np.unique(y, return_counts=True)
```

The output associates the class label (the first number) with its frequency and is worth observing (it is the second row of output):

```
(array([0, 1, 2, 3, 4, 5, 6, 7, 8, 9]),
 array([178, 182, 177, 183, 181, 182, 181, 179, 174, 180]))
```

All the class labels present about the same number of examples. That means your classes are balanced and the SVM won't be led to think that one class is more probable than any of the others. If one or more of the classes had a significantly different number of cases, you'd face an unbalanced class problem. An unbalanced class scenario requires you to perform an evaluation:

>> Keep the unbalanced class and get predictions biased toward the most frequent classes

>> Establish equality among the classes using weights, which means allowing some observations to count more

>> Use selection to cut some cases from the classes that have too many cases

TIP

An imbalanced class problem requires you to set some additional parameters. `sklearn.svm.SVC` has both a `class_weight` parameter and a `sample_weight` keyword in the `fit` method. The most straightforward and easiest way to solve the problem is to set `class_weight='balanced'` when defining your SVC and let the algorithm fix everything by itself.

Now you're ready to test the SVC with the linear kernel. However, don't forget to split your data into training and test sets, or you won't be able to judge the effectiveness of the modeling work. Always use a separate data fraction for performance evaluation or the results will look good at the start but turn worse when adding fresh data.

```
from sklearn.model_selection import train_test_split
from sklearn.model_selection import cross_val_score
from sklearn.preprocessing import MinMaxScaler
X_tr, X_t, y_tr, y_t = train_test_split(
    X, y, test_size=0.3, random_state=0)
```

The `train_test_split` function splits X and y into training and test sets, using the `test_size` parameter value of 0.3 as a reference for the split ratio.

```
scaling = MinMaxScaler(feature_range=(-1, 1)).fit(X_tr)
X_tr = scaling.transform(X_tr)
X_t = scaling.transform(X_t)
```

As a best practice, after splitting the data into training and test parts, you scale the numeric values, first by getting scaling parameters from the training data and then by applying a transformation on both training and test sets.

REMEMBER

Another important action to take before feeding the data into an SVM is scaling. *Scaling* transforms all the values to the range between −1 to 1 (or from 0 to 1, if you prefer). Scaling transformation avoids the problem of having some variables influence the algorithm (they may trick it into thinking they are important because they have big values) and it makes the computations exact, smooth, and fast.

The following code fits the training data to an SVC class with a linear kernel. It also cross-validates and tests the results in terms of accuracy (the percentage of numbers correctly guessed).

```
from sklearn.svm import SVC
svc = SVC(kernel='linear', class_weight='balanced')
```

The code instructs the SVC to use the linear kernel and to reweight the classes automatically. Reweighting the classes ensures that they remain equally sized after the dataset is split into training and test sets.

```
cv = cross_val_score(svc, X_tr, y_tr, cv=10)
test_score = svc.fit(X_tr, y_tr).score(X_t, y_t)
```

The code then assigns two new variables. Cross-validation performance is recorded by the `cross_val_score` function, which returns a list with all ten scores after a tenfold cross-validation (cv=10). The code obtains a test result by using two methods in sequence on the learning algorithm — `fit()`, that fits the model, and `score()`, which evaluates the result on the test set using mean accuracy (mean percentage of correct results among the classes to predict).

```
print(f'CV accuracy score: {np.mean(cv):.3f}')
print(f'Test accuracy score: {test_score:.3f}')
```

Finally, the code prints the two variables and evaluates the result. The result is quite good: 97.6 percent correct predictions on the test set:

```
CV accuracy score: 0.981
Test accuracy score: 0.976
```

You might wonder what would happen if you optimize the principal parameter C instead of using the default value of 1.0. The following script provides you with an answer, using `gridsearch` to look for an optimal value for the C parameter:

```
from sklearn.model_selection import GridSearchCV
svc = SVC(class_weight='balanced', random_state=1)
search_space = {'C': np.logspace(-3, 3, 7)}
gridsearch = GridSearchCV(svc,
                          param_grid=search_space,
                          scoring='accuracy',
                          refit=True, cv=10)
gridsearch.fit(X_tr,y_tr)
```

Using `GridSearchCV` is a little more complex, but it allows you to check many models in sequence. First, you must define a search space variable using a Python dictionary that contains the exploration schedule of the procedure. To define a search space, you create a dictionary (or, if there is more than one dictionary, a dictionary list) for each tested group of parameters. Inside the dictionary, you place the name of the parameters as keys and associate them with a list (or a function generating a list, as in this case) containing the values to test.

TIP

The NumPy `logspace()` function creates a list of seven C values, ranging from 10^{-3} to 10^3. This is a computationally expensive number of values to test, but it's also comprehensive, and you can always be safe when you test C and the other SVM parameters using such a range.

You then initialize `GridSearchCV`, defining the learning algorithm, search space, scoring function, and number of cross-validation folds. The next step is to instruct the procedure, after finding the best solution, to fit the best combination of parameters, so that you can have a ready-to-use predictive model:

```
cv = gridsearch.best_score_
test_score = gridsearch.score(X_t, y_t)
best_c = gridsearch.best_params_['C']
```

In fact, `gridsearch` now contains a lot of information about the best score (and best parameters, plus a complete analysis of all the evaluated combinations) and methods, such as `score`, which are typical of fitted predictive models in Scikit-learn.

```
print(f'CV accuracy score: {cv:.3f}')
print(f'Test accuracy score: {test_score:.3f}')
print(f'Best C parameter: {best_c:.1f}')
```

Here, the code extracts cross-validation and test scores, and outputs the C value related to these best scores:

```
CV accuracy score: 0.989
Test accuracy score: 0.987
Best C parameter: 10.0
```

The last step prints the results and shows that using a C=10.0 increases performance compared to before, both on the cross-validation and the test set.

Going nonlinear is easy

Having defined a simple linear model as a benchmark for the handwritten digit project, you can now test a more complex hypothesis, and SVM offers a range of nonlinear kernels:

>> Polynomial (poly)

>> Radial Basis Function (rbf)

>> Sigmoid (sigmoid)

>> Advanced custom kernels

Even though so many choices exist, you rarely use something different from the radial basis function kernel (rbf for short) because it's faster than other kernels and can approximate almost any nonlinear function.

TECHNICAL
STUFF

Here's a basic, practical explanation about how rbf works: It separates the data into many clusters, so it's easy to associate a response to each cluster.

The rbf kernel requires that you set the degree and gamma parameters besides setting C. They're both easy to set (and a good grid search will always find the right value).

The degree parameter has values that begin at 2. It determines the complexity of the nonlinear function used to separate the points. As a practical suggestion, don't worry too much about degree — test values of 2, 3, and 4 on a grid search. If you notice that the best result has a degree of 4, try shifting the grid range upward and test 3, 4, and 5. Continue proceeding upward as needed, but using a value greater than 5 is rare.

The gamma parameter's role in the algorithm is similar to C (it provides a trade-off between overfit and underfit). It's exclusive of the rbf kernel. High gamma values induce the algorithm to create nonlinear functions that have irregular shapes because they tend to fit the data more closely. Lower values create more regular, spherical functions, ignoring most of the irregularities present in the data.

Now that you know the details of the nonlinear approach, it's time to try rbf on the previous example. Be warned that, given the high number of combinations tested, the computations may take some time to complete, depending on the characteristics of your computer.

```python
from sklearn.model_selection import GridSearchCV

svc = SVC(class_weight='balanced', random_state=1)
search_space = [{'kernel': ['linear'],
                 'C': np.logspace(-3, 3, 7)},
                {'kernel': ['rbf'],
                 'degree':[2, 3, 4],
                 'C':np.logspace(-3, 3, 7),
                 'gamma': np.logspace(-3, 2, 6)}]
gridsearch = GridSearchCV(svc,
                          param_grid=search_space,
                          scoring='accuracy',
                          refit=True, cv=10,
                          n_jobs=-1)
gridsearch.fit(X_tr, y_tr)
cv = gridsearch.best_score_
test_score = gridsearch.score(X_t, y_t)
print(f'CV accuracy score: {cv:0.3f}')
print(f'Test accuracy score: {test_score:0.3f}')
print(f'Best parameters: {gridsearch.best_params_}')
print('Best parameters: %s' % gridsearch.best_params_)
```

Notice that the only difference in this script is that the search space is more sophisticated. By using a list, you enclose two dictionaries — one containing the parameters to test for the linear kernel and another for the rbf kernel. In this way, you can compare the performance of the two approaches at the same time. The code will take quite a while to run. Afterward, it will report to you:

```
CV accuracy score: 0.990
Test accuracy score: 0.993
Best parameters: {'C': 1.0, 'degree': 2, 'gamma': 0.1,
                  'kernel': 'rbf'}
```

The results confirm that rbf performs better. However, it's a small margin of victory over the linear models, gained at the expense of more complexity and computational time. In such cases, having more data available could help in determining the better model with greater confidence. Unfortunately, getting more data may be expensive in terms of money and time. When faced with the absence of a clear winning model, the best suggestion is to decide in favor of the simpler model. In this case, the linear kernel is much simpler than rbf.

Performing regression with SVR

Up to now, you have dealt only with classification, but SVM can also handle regression problems. Having seen how a classification works, you don't need to know much more than that the SVM regression class is SVR and there is an additional parameter to fix, epsilon. Everything else previous sections discussed for classification works precisely the same with regression.

This example uses a synthetic dataset, created by the make_regression() function in Scikit-learn. The underlying solution behind the data is made by combining three variables, but this example tries to confuse the algorithm by providing more irrelevant variables and adding plenty of noise to the values. In total, the dataset has 500 cases and 15 numeric variables (only three of which are meaningful for the solution).

```
from sklearn.model_selection import train_test_split
from sklearn.model_selection import cross_val_score
from sklearn.model_selection import GridSearchCV
from sklearn.preprocessing import MinMaxScaler
from sklearn.svm import SVR
from sklearn.datasets import make_regression

X, y = make_regression(n_samples=500,
                       n_features=15,
                       n_informative=3,
                       noise=10,
                       random_state=101)

X_tr, X_t, y_tr, y_t = train_test_split(X, y,
                                        test_size=0.3,
                                        random_state=0)
scaling = MinMaxScaler(feature_range=(-1, 1)).fit(X_tr)
X_tr = scaling.transform(X_tr)
X_t  = scaling.transform(X_t)
```

You'll try to guess the solution using SVR (epsilon-Support Vector Regression). In addition to C, kernel, degree, and gamma, SVR also has epsilon, as mentioned previously. *Epsilon* is a measure of how much error the algorithm considers acceptable. A high epsilon implies fewer support points, and a lower epsilon requires a larger number of support points. In other words, epsilon provides another way to trade off underfit against overfit.

As a search space for this parameter, experience tells you that the sequence [0, 0.01, 0.1, 0.5, 1, 2, 4] works quite fine. Starting from a minimum value of 0 (when the algorithm doesn't accept any error) and reaching a maximum of 4, you should enlarge the search space only if you notice that higher epsilon values bring better performance.

Having included epsilon in the search space and assigning SVR as a learning algorithm, you can complete the script. Be warned that, given the high number of combinations evaluated, the computations may take quite some time, depending on the characteristics of your computer.

```
svr = SVR()
search_space = [{'kernel': ['linear'],
                 'C': np.logspace(-3, 2, 6),
                 'epsilon': [0, 0.01, 0.1, 0.5, 1, 2, 4]},
                {'kernel': ['rbf'],
                 'degree':[2,3],
                 'C':np.logspace(-3, 3, 7),
                 'gamma': np.logspace(-3, 2, 6),
                 'epsilon': [0, 0.01, 0.1, 0.5, 1, 2, 4]}]
gridsearch = GridSearchCV(svr,
                          param_grid=search_space,
                          refit=True,
                          scoring= 'r2',
                          cv=10, n_jobs=-1)
gridsearch.fit(X_tr, y_tr)
cv = gridsearch.best_score_
test_score = gridsearch.score(X_t, y_t)
print(f'CV R2 score: {cv:.3f}')
print(f'Test R2 score: {test_score:.3f}')
print(f'Best parameters: {gridsearch.best_params_}')
```

The grid search may take a while on your computer. Even though the example uses all the computational power in your system (n_jobs=-1), the computer has to test quite a few combinations; for each kernel, you can figure out how many models it has to compute by multiplying the number of values it has to test for each parameter. For instance, for the rbf kernel, it has two values for degree, seven for C, six for gamma, and seven for epsilon, which equates to $2 * 7 * 6 * 7 = 588$ models, each one replicated 10 times (because cv=10). That is 5,880 models tested just for the rbf kernel. (The code also tests the linear model, which requires 420 tests.) Finally, you should get these results:

```
CV R2 score: 0.990
Test R2 score: 0.992
Best parameters: {'C': 100.0, 'epsilon': 0.5,
                  'kernel': 'linear'}
```

REMEMBER

Note that on the error measure, as a regression, the error is calculated using R squared, a measure in the range from 0 to 1 that indicates the model's performance (with 1 being the best possible result to achieve).

Creating a stochastic solution with SVM

Now that you're at the end of the overview of the family of SVM machine learning algorithms, you should see that they're a fantastic tool for a data scientist. Of course, even the best solutions have problems. For example, you might think that the SVM has too many parameters. Certainly, the parameters are a nuisance, especially when you have to test so many combinations of them, which can take a lot of CPU time. However, the key problem is the time necessary for training the SVM. You may have noticed that the examples use small datasets with a limited number of variables, and performing some extensive grid searches still takes a lot of time. Real-world datasets are much bigger. Sometimes it may seem to take forever to train and optimize your SVM on your computer.

A possible solution when you have too many cases (a suggested limit is 10,000 examples) is found inside the same SVM module, the LinearSVC class. This algorithm works only with the linear kernel, and its focus is to classify (sorry, no regression) large numbers of examples and variables at a higher speed than the standard SVC. Such characteristics make the LinearSVC a good candidate for textual-based classification. LinearSVC has fewer and slightly different parameters to fix than the usual SVM (it's similar to a regression class):

» C: The penalty parameter. Small values imply more regularization (simpler models with attenuated or set to zero coefficients).

» loss: A value of l1 (just as in SVM) or l2 (errors weigh more, so it strives harder to fit misclassified examples).

» penalty: A value of l2 (attenuation of less important parameters) or l1 (unimportant parameters are set to zero).

» dual: A value of true or false. It refers to the type of optimization problem solved and, though it won't change the obtained scoring much, setting the parameter to false results in faster computations than when it is set to true.

The `loss`, `penalty`, and dual parameters are also bound by reciprocal constraints, so please refer to Table 19-2 to plan which combination to use in advance.

TABLE 19-2

The Loss, Penalty, and Dual Constraints

Penalty	Loss	Dual
l1	l2	False
l2	l1	True
l2	l2	True; False

REMEMBER

The algorithm doesn't support the combination of `penalty='l1'` and `loss='l1'`. However, the combination of `penalty='l2'` and `loss='l1'` perfectly replicates the SVC optimization approach.

As mentioned previously, `LinearSVC` is quite fast, and a speed test against SVC demonstrates the level of improvement to expect in choosing this algorithm. Even this example uses a synthetic data example, this time for classification, thanks to Scikit-learn's `make_classification()` function:

```
from sklearn.datasets import make_classification
from sklearn.model_selection import train_test_split

X,y = make_classification(n_samples=500,
                          n_features=15,
                          n_informative=5,
                          random_state=101)
X_tr, X_t, y_tr, y_t = train_test_split(X, y,
                                        test_size=0.3,
                                        random_state=1)


from sklearn.svm import SVC, LinearSVC
svc = SVC(kernel='linear', random_state=0)
linear = LinearSVC(loss='hinge', max_iter=100_000,
                   random_state=0)

svc.fit(X_tr, y_tr)
linear.fit(X_tr, y_tr)
svc_score = svc.score(X_t, y_t)
libsvc_score = linear.score(X_t, y_t)
print(f'SVC test accuracy: {svc_score:.3f}')
print(f'LinearSVC test accuracy: {libsvc_score:.3f}')
```

The results are similar to SVC:

```
SVC test accuracy: 0.787
LinearSVC test accuracy: 0.787
```

After you create an artificial dataset using make_classfication(), the code obtains confirmation of how the two algorithms arrive at almost identical results. At this point, the code tests the speed of the two solutions on the synthetic dataset to understand how they scale to use more data:

```
import timeit
import numpy as np

X,y = make_classification(n_samples=10**3,
                          n_features=15,
                          n_informative=5,
                          random_state=101)
t_svc = timeit.timeit(
    'svc.fit(X, y)',
    'from __main__ import svc, X, y',
    number=3)
t_libsvc = timeit.timeit(
    'linear.fit(X, y)',
    'from __main__ import linear, X, y',
    number=3)
print(f'best avg secs for SVC: {np.mean(t_svc):0.1f}')
print(f'best avg secs for LinearSVC: '
      f'{np.mean(t_libsvc):0.1f}')
```

The example system shows the following result (the output of your system may differ):

```
best avg secs for SVC: 0.2
best avg secs for LinearSVC: 0.1
```

Clearly, given the same data quantity, LinearSVC is faster than SVC. However, it's important to understand what happens when you increase the size of the sample because what counts is how an algorithm scales when you increase the size of the problem. For example, here's what happens when you triple the size:

```
Avg time for SVC: 1.6 secs
Avg time for LinearSVC: 0.1 secs
```

The point here is that the time required for SVC grows much faster than that required by LinearSVC. This is because SVC requires nonlinearly more time to process the data provided, and the time will grow even more as the sample size increases. Here are the results when you have five times more data, highlighting even more differences:

```
Avg time for SVC: 984.9 secs
Avg time for LinearSVC: 5.5 secs
```

Using SVC with large amounts of data soon becomes unfeasible; LinearSVC should be your choice if you need to work with large data amounts. Yet, even if LinearSVC is quite fast at performing tasks, you may need to classify or regress millions of examples. You need to know whether LinearSVC is still a better choice. You previously saw how the SGD class, using SGDClassifier and SGDRegressor, helps you implement an SVM-type algorithm in situations with millions of data rows without investing too much computational power. All you have to do is to set their loss to 'hinge' for SGDClassifier and to 'epsilon_insensitive' for SGDRegressor (in which case, you have to tune the epsilon parameter).

Another performance and speed test makes the advantages and limitations of using LinearSVC or SGDClassifier clear:

```
from sklearn.datasets import make_classification
from sklearn.model_selection import train_test_split
from sklearn.model_selection import cross_val_score
from sklearn.svm import LinearSVC
import timeit

from sklearn.linear_model import SGDClassifier
X, y = make_classification(n_samples=10**5,
                           n_features=15,
                           n_informative=10,
                           random_state=101)
X_tr, X_t, y_tr, y_t = train_test_split(X, y,
                                        test_size=0.3,
                                        random_state=1)
```

The sample now is quite big — 100,000 cases. If you have enough memory and a lot of time, you may even want to increase the number of trained cases or the number of features and more extensively test how the two algorithms scale with even bigger data.

```
linear = LinearSVC(penalty='l2',
                   loss='hinge',
```

```
                    dual=True,
                    random_state=101)
linear.fit(X_tr, y_tr)
score = linear.score(X_t, y_t)
t = timeit.timeit("linear.fit(X_tr, y_tr)",
        "from __main__ import linear, X_tr, y_tr",
        number=1)
print(f'LinearSVC test accuracy: {score:.3f}')
print(f'Avg time for LinearSVC: {np.mean(t):.1f} secs')
```

On the test computer, LinearSVC completed its computations on all the rows in about 4.2 seconds:

```
LinearSVC test accuracy: 0.796
Avg time for LinearSVC: 4.2 secs
```

The following code tests SGDClassifier using the same procedure:

```
sgd = SGDClassifier(loss='hinge',
                    penalty='l2',
                    alpha=0.1,
                    max_iter=1000,
                    shuffle=True,
                    random_state=101)
sgd.fit(X_tr, y_tr)
score = sgd.score(X_t, y_t)
t = timeit.timeit("sgd.fit(X_tr, y_tr)",
                "from __main__ import sgd, X_tr, y_tr",
                number=1)
print(f'SGDClassifier test accuracy: {score:.3f}')
print(f'Avg time for SGDClassifier: {np.mean(t):.1f} secs')
```

SGDClassifier instead took about a fraction of the time for processing the same data and obtaining a comparable score:

```
SGDClassifier test accuracy: 0.796
Avg time SGDClassifier: 0.2 secs
```

TIP

Increasing the n_iter parameter can improve the performance, but it proportionally increases the computation time. Increasing the number of iterations up to a certain value (that you have to find out by test) increases the performance. However, after that value, performance starts to decrease because of overfitting.

Playing with Neural Networks

Starting with the idea of reverse-engineering how a brain processes signals, researchers based neural networks on biological analogies and their components, using brain terms such as *neurons* and *axons* as names. However, you'll discover that neural networks resemble nothing more than a sophisticated kind of linear regression because they are a summation of coefficients multiplied by numeric inputs. You also find that neurons are just where such summations happen.

Even if neural networks don't mimic a brain very well (they're arithmetic), these algorithms are extraordinarily effective against complex problems such as image and sound recognition, or machine language translation. They also execute quickly when predicting, if you use the right hardware. Well-devised neural networks use the name *deep learning* and are behind powerful tools like Siri and other digital assistants, along with more astonishing machine learning applications, such as ChatGPT (https://chat.openai.com/), as well.

Running deep learning requires special hardware (a computer with a GPU) and installing special frameworks such as Keras and TensorFlow (https://www.tensorflow.org/), MXNet (https://mxnet.apache.org/), Pytorch (https://pytorch.org/) or Chainer (https://chainer.org/). This book doesn't delve into complex neural networks but does explore a simpler implementation offered by Keras and TensorFlow instead; that implementation allows you to create neural network quickly and compare them to other machine learning algorithms.

Understanding neural networks

The core neural network algorithm is the neuron (also called a unit). Many neurons arranged in an interconnected structure make up the layers of a neural network, with each neuron linking to the inputs and outputs of other neurons. Thus, a neuron can input features from examples or from the results of other neurons, depending on its location in the neural network.

Contrary to other algorithms, which have a fixed pipeline that determines how algorithms receive and process data, neural networks require you to decide how information flows by fixing the number of units (the neurons) and their distribution in layers. For this reason, setting up neural networks is more an art than a science; you learn from experience how to arrange neurons into layers and obtain the best predictions. In a more detailed view, neurons in a neural network take many weighted values as inputs, sum them, and provide the summation as the result.

REMEMBER

A neural network can process only numeric, continuous information; it can't process qualitative variables (for example, labels indicating a quality such as red, blue, or green in an image). You can process qualitative variables by transforming them into a continuous numeric value, such as a series of binary values.

Neurons also provide a more sophisticated transformation of the summation. In observing nature, scientists noticed that neurons receive signals but don't always release a signal of their own. It depends on the amount of signal received. When a neuron in a brain acquires enough stimuli, it fires an answer; otherwise, it remains silent. In a similar fashion, neurons in a neural network, after receiving weighted values, sum them and use an activation function to evaluate the result, which transforms it in a possibly nonlinear way. For instance, the activation function can release a zero value unless the input achieves a certain threshold, or it can dampen or enhance a value by nonlinearly rescaling it, thus transmitting a rescaled signal.

Each neuron in the network receives inputs from the previous layers (when starting, it connects directly with data), weights them, sums them all, and transforms the result using the activation function. After activating, the computed output becomes the input for other neurons or the prediction of the network. Consequently, given a neural network made of a certain number of neurons and layers, what makes this structure efficient in its predictions is the weights used by each neuron for its inputs. Such weights aren't different from the coefficients of a linear regression, and the network learns their value by repeated passes (iterations or epochs) over the examples of the dataset.

Classifying and regressing with neurons

This example uses Keras, which is now part of the TensorFlow framework. There are instructions for installing TensorFlow on your system at https://docs. anaconda.com/free/anaconda/applications/tensorflow/ if you're working with Anaconda. You may need to ask an administrator to perform the installation for you if you don't have administrator privileges on your host machine. You need to have TensorFlow 2.0 or above installed, which you can check in Jupyter Notebook using the following code:

```
import tensorflow as tf
print(tf.__version__)
```

In addition to TensorFlow version 2.0 and above, Google has integrated the Keras package with Colab. Keras serves as a tool for constructing complex neural networks through a series of straightforward commands. What sets Keras apart is its ability to simplify the creation of deep learning applications, making it accessible to a wide range of users. Originally developed as an independent package by Francois Chollet, Keras has gained significant popularity over time, favored by practitioners, due to its intuitive and user-friendly nature. It effectively simplifies the complexities associated with TensorFlow, offering a performing solution.

Unlike other machine learning algorithms, the construction of neural networks for classification and regression tasks does not involve distinct sets of commands. Instead, the key differences reside in the output neurons of the network and the choice of loss function utilized to optimize the neural network's outcomes. Hence, this demonstration delves into a single example for classification, but it can also apply to a regression problem, with just a few tweaks. The example uses the handwritten digits dataset as an example of multiclass classification. It starts by importing the necessary packages, in particular all the building blocks necessary for Keras to build the neural network, loading the dataset into memory, and splitting it into a training and a test set (as the chapter has done when demonstrating support vector machines):

```python
import numpy as np
from sklearn.model_selection import train_test_split
from sklearn.preprocessing import MinMaxScaler
from sklearn.datasets import load_digits
from keras.models import Sequential
from keras.layers import Dense, Dropout
from sklearn.preprocessing import MinMaxScaler
from sklearn.model_selection import train_test_split
from sklearn.datasets import load_digits

X, y = load_digits(return_X_y=True)
X_train, X_test, y_train, y_test = train_test_split(X, y,
    test_size=0.2, random_state=0)
```

Preprocessing the data to feed to the neural network is an important aspect because the operations that neural networks perform under the hood are sensitive to the scale and distribution of data. Consequently, it's good practice to normalize the data by putting its mean to zero and its variance to one, or to rescale it by fixing the minimum and maximum between −1 and +1 or 0 and +1. Experimentation shows which transformation works better for your data, though most people find that rescaling between −1 and +1 works better. This example rescales all the values between −1 and +1:

```python
scaler = MinMaxScaler(feature_range=(-1, 1))
X_train = scaler.fit_transform(X_train)
X_test = scaler.transform(X_test)
```

Regarding the target, neural networks require each terminal neuron to make a prediction, which can take the form of a numeric value or probability. The neuron accomplishes the prediction by utilizing activation functions, which transform the input within the neuron. For example, in a classification task, neurons with a sigmoid transformation are employed as they produce values between zero and one, representing probabilities. In the case of multiclass classification, one approach involves encoding the classes using one-hot encoding (which is reviewed in Chapter 12 and you can find explained in detail at https://www.geeksforgeeks. org/ml-one-hot-encoding-of-datasets-in-python/) and assigning a separate neuron with sigmoid activation to predict the probability for each class. The class with the highest probability is then considered the winner among the others. The following code just transforms your target classes for train and test sets into a matrix of one-encoded values:

```
num_classes = 10
y_train = np.eye(num_classes)[y_train]
y_test = np.eye(num_classes)[y_test]
```

The next step involves constructing the architecture of the neural network and training it using the training data. This process employs the Keras Sequential API. It begins by initializing an empty network and subsequently adds layers of neurons progressively, starting from the top, where the data is inputted, and moving toward the bottom, where the results are obtained. This example incorporates two layers consisting of 64 and 32 neurons respectively, activated by the ReLU function. The activation function enables the network to learn nonlinear patterns. Each of these layers is followed by a dropout layer, which serves as a regularization technique to prevent overfitting, avoiding excessive adaptation to the data. The network concludes with a layer containing the probabilities for the classes, from which the winning class will be determined. To determine the outcome, the softmax activation function is employed in the final layer.

```
model = Sequential()
model.add(Dense(64, activation='relu', input_shape=(64,)))
model.add(Dropout(0.2))
model.add(Dense(32, activation='relu'))
model.add(Dropout(0.2))
model.add(Dense(num_classes, activation='softmax'))
```

Now, the code proceeds to compile the model to configure it for training. The loss parameter is specified as categorical_crossentropy, which is the appropriate loss function for tackling multi-class classification problems. For optimization, the optimizer parameter is set to Adam, a widely used algorithm known for its efficiency. Furthermore, the metrics parameter is set to accuracy, enabling the monitoring of the model's accuracy during the training process. When fitting the model, the code iterates over the data 50 times, processes the data in batches of 32 examples each, and utilizes the test data to provide progress updates:

```
model.compile(loss='categorical_crossentropy',
              optimizer='adam', metrics=['accuracy'])
history = model.fit(X_train, y_train, epochs=50,
                    batch_size=32,
                    validation_data=(X_test, y_test))
```

During the training process, you will receive updates and guidance regarding the progress made:

```
Epoch 32/50
45/45 [==============================] - 0s 3ms/step - loss:
   0.0752 - accuracy: 0.9812 - val_loss: 0.0843 - val_accuracy:
   0.9778
```

The script notifies you about the completion of a specific number of iterations, referred to as epochs, during which it processed a certain number of data batches. The script provides information on the loss and evaluation metrics for both the training data and the test data. By plotting this information, it's possible to assess how well the model learned to generalize by examining its performance on the test data, in comparison to its fit on the training data.

When the script has completed, you can check how it finally performs on the test data:

```
loss, accuracy = model.evaluate(X_test, y_test)
print('Test accuracy score:', accuracy)
```

The script also confirms the performance of the model:

```
12/12 [==============================] - 0s 2ms/step -
loss: 0.0832 - accuracy: 0.9750
Test accuracy score: 0.9750000238418579
```

In addition, you can visualize the entire training process:

```
import matplotlib.pyplot as plt

train_loss = history.history['loss']
val_loss = history.history['val_loss']

# Plot the training and validation loss over epochs
epochs = range(5, len(train_loss) + 1)
plt.plot(epochs, train_loss[4:], 'b',
         label='Training loss')
```

```
plt.plot(epochs, val_loss[4:], 'r',
        label='Validation loss')
plt.axvline(x=val_loss.index(min(val_loss)),
        color='r', linestyle='--')
plt.title('Training and Validation Loss')
plt.xlabel('Epochs')
plt.ylabel('Loss')
plt.legend()
plt.show()
```

You can see the output in Figure 19-5.

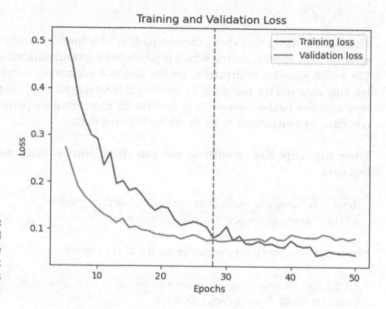

FIGURE 19-5: The training and test scores of the neural network as it learns from data.

Looking at the figure, it is evident that the training loss consistently decreased over time, which is a common pattern observed in neural networks that are either appropriately sized or oversized for a given problem. Such networks have a tendency to extract increasingly fine-grained details from the data, potentially even memorizing it. However, what's more noteworthy is the behavior of the test data, which is not being used during the training process but is used only for prediction purposes. The test loss gradually decreases until it reaches a minimum, after which it begins to deteriorate due to overfitting. The red dashed line indicates that the minimum loss was achieved prior to the end of the training. In neural networks, monitoring the model's performance and deciding when to stop training is a crucial factor for achieving a well-performing predictor model.

IN THIS CHAPTER

» Understanding how a decision tree
works

» Using Random Forest and other
bagging techniques

» Taking advantage of the best
performing ensembles by boosting

Chapter 20

Understanding the Power of the Many

I n this chapter, you go beyond the single machine learning models you've seen
until now and explore the power of *ensembles*, which are groups of models that
can outperform single models. Ensembles work like the collective intelligence
of crowds, using pooled information to make better predictions. The basic idea is
that a group of simple algorithms can produce better results than a single well-
trained model.

Maybe you've participated in one of those games that ask you to guess the number
of sweets in a jar at parties or fairs. Even though a single person has a slim chance
of guessing the right number, various experiments have confirmed that if you
take the wrong answers of a large number of game participants and average them,
you can get close to the right answer! Such incredible shared group knowledge
(also known as the wisdom of crowds) is possible because wrong answers tend to
distribute around the true one. By taking a mean of these wrong answers, you get
almost the right answer.

In data science projects involving complex predictions, you can leverage the wisdom of various machine learning algorithms and become more precise and accurate at predictions than you can when using a single algorithm. This chapter
creates a process you can use to leverage the power of many different algorithms
to obtain a better single answer.

REMEMBER

You don't have to type the source code for this chapter manually; using the downloadable source is a lot easier (see the Introduction for download instructions). The source code for this chapter appears in the P4DS4D3_20_Understanding_the_Power_of_the_Many.ipynb file.

Starting with a Plain Decision Tree

Decision trees have long been part of data mining tools. The first models date well before the 1970s. Since then, decision trees have enjoyed popularity in many fields because of their intuitive algorithm, understandable output, and effectiveness with respect to simple linear models. With the introduction of better-performing algorithms, decision trees slowly went out of the machine learning scene for a time, blamed for being too easy to overfit, but they came back in recent years as an essential building block of ensemble algorithms. Today, tree ensembles such as Random Forest or Gradient Boosting Machines are the core of many data science applications and are considered to be state-of-the-art of machine learning tools.

Understanding a decision tree

The basis of decision trees is the idea that you can divide your dataset into smaller and smaller parts using specific rules based on the values of the dataset's features. When dividing the dataset in this way, the algorithm must choose splits that increase the chance of guessing the target outcome correctly, either as a class or as an estimate. Therefore, the algorithm must try to maximize the presence of a certain class or a certain average of values in each split.

As an example of an application and execution of a decision tree, you could try to predict the likelihood of passenger survival from the RMS Titanic, the British passenger liner that sank in the North Atlantic Ocean in April 1912 after colliding with an iceberg. Quite a few datasets are available on the web that pertain to this tragedy at sea. Most notable among them is the one on the Encyclopedia Titanica website (https://www.encyclopedia-titanica.org), which contains articles, biographies, and data. Another is a Kaggle data science competition that has involved tens of thousands of enthusiastic participants (https://www.kaggle.com/c/titanic).

Many Titanic tragedy datasets differ in the data they contain. This chapter's example relies on the Titanic dataset freely granted for use by the Department of Biostatistics at the Vanderbilt University School of Medicine and available for download at https://github.com/lmassaron/datasets/blob/master/titanic.csv. This dataset features 1,309 recorded passengers with full stats. You don't find any of the crew in the dataset because the records focus on the paying passengers to determine whether surviving the disaster is a matter of luck or the place passengers were found on the ship at the time of the collision. The survival rate among passengers was 38.2 percent (500 of 1,309 passengers lost their lives). Based on the passengers' characteristics, the decision tree determines the following:

>> Being male changes the likelihood of survival, lowering it from 38.2 percent to 19.1 percent.

>> Being male, but being younger than 9.5 years of age, raises the chance of survival to 58.1 percent.

>> Being female, regardless of age, implies a survival probability of 72.7 percent.

Using such knowledge, you can easily to build a tree like the one depicted in Figure 20-1. Such visualization (and the visualization of the Mushroom dataset found later in the chapter) is possible because of the dtreeviz package developed by Prof. Terence Parr from San Francisco University (https://parrt.cs.usfca.edu) and Prince Grover, of the same faculty. If you are interested in creating visualizations of your decision trees, you can get the package and installation guidance at https://github.com/parrt/dtreeviz and read about the development and the functioning of the package in Prof. Parr's blog entry, "How to visualize decision trees," at https://explained.ai/decision-tree-viz.

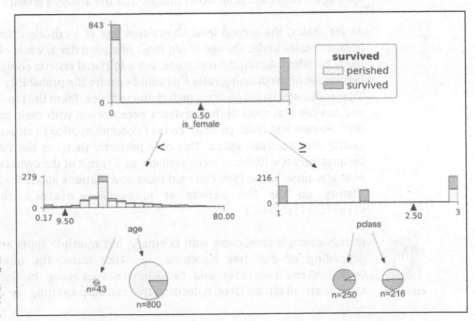

FIGURE 20-1: A tree model of survival rates from the Titanic disaster.

Notice that the visualized tree looks upside down (with the root at the top and all the branches spreading out from there). It starts at the top using the entire sample. Then it splits on the gender feature, creating two *branches*, one that turns into a *leaf*. A leaf is a terminal segmentation. The diagram classifies the leaf cases by using the most frequent class or by calculating the base probability of cases with the same features as the leaf probability. The second branch is further split by age.

To read the nodes of the tree, consider that the topmost node begins by reporting the rule used to split that node into all the following nodes. You have to start from the top. The tree shown in Figure 20-1 implies that gender is the best predictor, and on the top node, the is_female variable is in vertical, stacked bars. The left bar is for males and the right bar is for females. At a first glance, you can see that, proportionally, females had a higher survivability because the survived share (the light-green area, which doesn't show in color in the printed book) mostly occupies all the area of the bar.

The tree splits this node in half, separating males from females. You can read the rest of the story told by the tree by observing what happens on the next level. On the second level of the tree representation, on the right, you find a node consisting only of females, and the stacked bars reveal a key insight: almost all the female first- and second-class passengers survived, and about half of the female third-class passengers perished. This insight enables the tree to develop a first rule: Women in first and second class can be classified as survivors because that status is highly likely. As for third class, survival is uncertain, and the tree would need to split again to extract some other insight that the analysis doesn't include.

As for males, the second level shows that age is a criterion that discriminates because males under the age of ten most likely survived, while older males most likely perished. Again, the tree stops, but additional criteria could provide a more precise set of partitioning rules that could explore the probability of surviving the Titanic disaster based on one's own characteristics. From the top-level tree splits, you can see that most of the survivors were women with their children based on the "women and children first" code of conduct applied in situations when life-saving resources are scarce. This code perfectly matches the *Titanic*'s situation because very few lifeboats were available as a result of the owners' belief that the boat was unsinkable. (You can read more speculations about the lifeboats on the History on the Net website at https://www.historyonthenet.com/the-titanic-lifeboats.)

REMEMBER

In this example tree, every split is binary, but multiple splits are also possible, depending on the tree algorithm. In Scikit-learn, the implemented class DecisionTreeClassifier and DecisionTreeRegressor in the sklearn.tree module are all binary trees. A decision tree can stop splitting the data when

» There are no more cases to split, so the data appears as part of leaf nodes.

» The rule used to split a leaf has fewer than a predefined number of cases. This action keeps the algorithm from working with leaves that have little representation in general or are more specific than the data you're analyzing, thus preventing overfitting (see Chapter 18) and variance of estimates.

» One of the resulting leaves has fewer than a predefined number of cases — another sanity check for avoiding inferring general rules without the confidence provided by a good sample size.

TIP

Decision trees tend to overfit the data. By setting the right number for splits and terminal leaves, you can reduce the variance of the estimates. Depending on your starting sample size, a limit of 30 cases is usually a good choice.

Apart from being intuitive, and easy to understand and represent (depending on how many branches and leaves you have in your tree), decision trees offer another strong advantage to the data science practitioner — they don't require any particular data treatment or transformation because they model any nonlinearity using approximations. In fact, they accept any kind of variable, even categorical variables encoded with arbitrary codes for the represented classes. In addition, decision trees handle missing cases. All you need to do is to assign missing cases an unlikely value, such as an extreme or a negative value (depending on your data distribution of non-missing cases). Finally, decision trees are also incredibly resistant to outliers.

Creating classification trees

Data scientists call trees that specialize in guessing *classes* (the attributes, qualities, or traits that identify groups) classification trees; trees that work with estimation instead are known as regression trees. Here's a classification problem: trying to predict the likelihood of a mushroom being edible or poisonous based on its appearance. This is based on a dataset freely available on OpenML (https://www.openml.org/search?type=data&status=active&id=24) that describes mushrooms in terms of their physical characteristics and classifies them as poisonous or edible. On OpenML, you can find a complete description of the recorded characteristics. The records are drawn from *The Audubon Society Field Guide to North American Mushrooms* (1981), and they are in the public domain thanks to the donation of Jeff Schlimmer.

```
from sklearn.datasets import fetch_openml
import pandas as pd

def load_mushroom_data():
    features, target = fetch_openml(
```

```
          data_id=24, return_X_y=True, as_frame=True)
    X = pd.get_dummies(features)
    y = (target == "p").astype(int)
    return X, y
X, y = load_mushroom_data()
```

After loading the data into X, which contains predictors, and y, which holds the classifications (1 for poisonous, 0 for edible), you can define a cross-validation for checking the results using decision trees:

```
from sklearn.model_selection import cross_val_score
from sklearn.model_selection import KFold
crossvalidation = KFold(n_splits=5,
                        shuffle=True,
                        random_state=0)
```

Using the DecisionTreeClassifier class, you define max_depth inside an iterative loop to experiment with the effect of increasing the complexity of the resulting tree. The expectation is to reach an ideal point quickly and then witness decreasing cross-validation performance because of overfitting:

```
import numpy as np
from sklearn import tree
for depth in range(1,10):
    tree_classifier = tree.DecisionTreeClassifier(
        max_depth=depth, random_state=0)
    if tree_classifier.fit(X,y).tree_.max_depth < depth:
        break
    score = np.mean(cross_val_score(tree_classifier,
                                    X, y,
                                    scoring='accuracy',
                                    cv=crossvalidation))
    print('Depth: %i Accuracy: %.3f' % (depth,score))
```

The code will iterate through deeper trees until the tree won't expand anymore, and then the code will report the cross-validation score for accuracy:

```
Depth: 1 Accuracy: 0.887
Depth: 2 Accuracy: 0.954
Depth: 3 Accuracy: 0.984
Depth: 4 Accuracy: 0.991
Depth: 5 Accuracy: 0.999
Depth: 6 Accuracy: 0.999
Depth: 7 Accuracy: 1.00
```

TECHNICAL STUFF

Note that the downloadable source includes some additional code that isn't covered in the chapter due to space limitations. Reviewing this code will help you understand the example better. This code also works together to produce Figure 20-2.

The best solution is a tree with seven splits, but you could probably stop with five splits and accept a minimal risk of eating something not edible. There is some additional code in the downloadable source to display the results in a graphic format. Figure 20-2 shows the complexity of the resulting tree with depth five, which provides another insightful visualization obtained using the dtreeviz package. Visualizing helps show that the tree is not balanced in the way it grew, and the presence of certain characteristics help you quickly figure out whether a mushroom is edible. Other characteristics make things more uncertain and necessitate a longer scrutiny. For instance, if the mushroom has no odor and its spores are green, you are 100 percent certain that the mushroom is poisonous, and you don't need any other evidence.

Creating regression trees

Just as you use a classification tree for a classification problem in the previous section, you can model a regression problem by using the DecisionTreeRegressor class. This example solves a regression problem using the California Housing dataset (you first use this dataset in the "Defining applications for data science" section of Chapter 12). When dealing with a regression tree, the terminal leaves offer the average of the cases as the prediction output. Here is the code to obtain the data:

```
from sklearn.datasets import fetch_california_housing
import pandas as pd
```

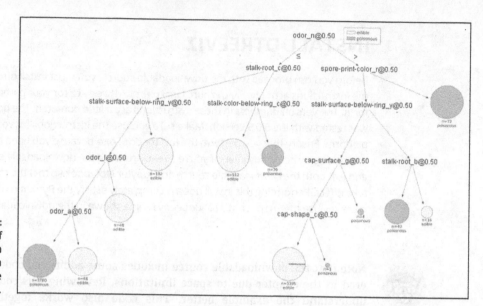

FIGURE 20-2:
A tree model of
the Mushroom
dataset using a
depth of five
splits.

```
def load_california_housing_data():
    dataset = fetch_california_housing()
    X = pd.DataFrame(data=dataset.data,
                     columns=dataset.feature_names)
    y = pd.Series(data=dataset.target, name="target")
    return X, y
```

You can now build the regression tree on the data:

```
from sklearn.tree import DecisionTreeRegressor

X, y = load_california_housing_data()
regression_tree = tree.DecisionTreeRegressor(
    min_samples_split=30, min_samples_leaf=10,
    random_state=0)
regression_tree.fit(X,y)
score = np.mean(cross_val_score(regression_tree,
                X, y,
                scoring='neg_mean_squared_error',
                cv=crossvalidation))
print('Mean squared error: %.3f' % abs(score))
```

The cross-validated mean squared error for the California Housing dataset is

```
Mean squared error: 0.367
```

Getting Lost in a Random Forest

Random Forest is a classification and regression algorithm developed by Leo Breiman and Adele Cutler that uses a large number of decision tree models to provide precise predictions by reducing both the bias and variance of the estimates. When you aggregate many models to produce a single prediction, the result is an *ensemble of models*. Random Forest isn't just an ensemble model; it's also a simple and effective algorithm to use as an out-of-the-box algorithm. It makes machine learning accessible to non-experts. The Random Forest algorithm uses these steps to perform its predictions:

1. Create a large number of decision trees, each one different from the other, based on different sets of observations and variables:

    a. Bootstrap the dataset of observations for each tree, sampled from the original data with replacement. The same observation can appear multiple times in the same dataset.

    b. Randomly select and use only a part of the variables for each tree.

2. Estimate the performance for each tree using the observations excluded by sampling (the Out Of Bag, or OOB, estimate).

3. Obtain the final prediction, which is the average for regression estimates or the most frequent class for prediction, after all the trees have been fitted and used for prediction.

You can reduce bias by using these steps, because the decision trees have a good fit on data and, by relying on complex splits, can approximate even the most complex relationships between predictors and predicted outcome. Decision trees can produce a great variance of estimates, but you reduce this variance by averaging many trees. Noisy predictions, due to variance, tend to distribute evenly above and below the correct value that you want to predict — and when averaged together, they tend to cancel each other, leaving, as a result, a more correct average prediction.

Making machine learning accessible

Leo Breiman derived the idea for Random Forest from the *bagging technique*, which is described in detail at https://blog.paperspace.com/bagging-ensemble-methods/ as a method for aggregating multiple versions of a predicted model. Scikit-learn has a bagging class for both regression (BaggingRegressor) and classifying (BaggingClassifier) that you can use with any other predictor you want to choose from the Scikit-learn modules. The max_samples and max_features parameters let you decide the proportion of cases and variables to sample (not bootstrapped, but sampled, so you can use a case only once) for building each model of the ensemble. The `n_estimators` parameter decides the total number of models in the ensemble. Here's an example that loads the German Credit Data (https://archive.ics.uci.edu/ml/datasets/Statlog+%28German+Credit+Data%29) dataset that classifies a bank's customers, described by a set of attributes, as good or bad credit risks. Credit risk classification is a common risk management activity in banking and finance. The dataset was donated in 1990s by Professor Dr. Hans Hofmann from Hamburg University.

```python
import numpy as np
import pandas as pd


def load_german_credit_data():
    url = "https://archive.ics.uci.edu/ml/ "
    url += " machine-learning-databases"
    url += "/statlog/german/german.data-numeric"
    col_names = [
        "checking_account", "duration", "credit_history",
        "credit_amount", "savings_account",
        "employment_duration", "personal_status",
        "residence_duration", "property", "age",
        "other_installment_plans", "number_credits",
        "people_liable", "telephone", "foreign_worker",
        "purpose_car_new", "purpose_car_used",
        "other_debtors_none",
        "other_debtors_coapplicant",
        "housing_rent", "housing_own",
        "job_unskilled_non_resident",
        "job_unskilled_resident", "job_employee",
        "credit_risk"]
    df = pd.read_csv(
        url, header=None, names=col_names,
        delim_whitespace=True)
    X = df.iloc[:, :-1]
    y = (df.iloc[:, -1] == 2).astype(int) # 2 = "Bad"
    return X, y

X, y = load_german_credit_data()
```

The example then fits the classification model using bagging:

```python
from sklearn.ensemble import BaggingClassifier
from sklearn.tree import DecisionTreeClassifier
from sklearn.metrics import roc_auc_score
```

```
from sklearn.model_selection import cross_val_score
from sklearn.model_selection import KFold

tree_classifier = DecisionTreeClassifier(random_state=0)
crossvalidation = KFold(
    n_splits=5, shuffle=True, random_state=0)
bagging = BaggingClassifier(tree_classifier,
                            max_samples=0.7,
                            max_features=0.7,
                            n_estimators=300,
                            random_state=0)
scores = np.mean(cross_val_score(bagging, X, y,
                                 scoring='roc_auc',
                                 cv=crossvalidation))
print(f'ROC-AUC: {scores:.3f}')
```

Here's the cross-validated ROC-AUC, a metric ranging up to 1.00 for perfect classifiers. It evaluates whether the riskier cases are assigned to higher probabilities:

```
ROC-AUC: 0.795
```

In bagging, as in Random Forest, the more models in the ensemble, the better. Here are some issues to consider:

>> You run little risk of overfitting because every model is different from the others, and errors tend to spread around the real value.

>> Adding more models adds stability to the result, but on the other hand, creating the model takes longer.

>> It permits estimation of variable importance while taking the presence of all the other predictors into account. In this way, you can determine which feature is important for predicting a target given the set of features that you have.

>> You can use the importance estimate as a guideline for variable selection.

REMEMBER

In contrast to single decision trees, you can't easily visualize or understand Random Forest, making it act as a black box (a *black box* is a transformation that doesn't reveal its inner workings; all you see are its inputs and outputs). Given its opacity, importance estimation is the only way to understand how the algorithm works with respect to the features.

Importance estimation in a Random Forest is obtained in a straightforward way. After building each tree, the code fills each variable in turn with junk data, and the example records how much the predictive power decreases. If the variable is important, crowding it with casual data harms the prediction; otherwise, the predictions are left almost unchanged and the variable is deemed unimportant.

Working with a Random Forest classifier

The example Random Forest classifier keeps using the previously loaded German Credit Data:

```
from sklearn.ensemble import RandomForestClassifier
from sklearn.model_selection import cross_val_score
from sklearn.model_selection import KFold

crossvalidation = KFold(
    n_splits=5, shuffle=True, random_state=0)
random_forest = RandomForestClassifier(n_estimators=300,
                                        random_state=0)
score = np.mean(cross_val_score(random_forest, X, y,
                                scoring='roc_auc',
                                cv=crossvalidation))
print(f'ROC-AUC: {scores:.3f}')
```

The cross-validated ROC-AUC score reported by this code for the Random Forest is equivalent to the bagging method tested in the previous section:

```
ROC-AUC: 0.795
```

Just setting the number of estimators is sufficient for most problems you encounter, and setting it correctly is a matter of using the highest number possible given the time and resource constraints of the host computer. You can demonstrate this by calculating and drawing a validation curve for the algorithm.

```
from sklearn.model_selection import validation_curve

param_range = [50, 150, 300, 600, 900, 1200, 1800,
               2400, 3000, 3600]
crossvalidation = KFold(
    n_splits=5, shuffle=True, random_state=0)
random_forest = RandomForestClassifier(
    n_estimators=300, n_jobs=-1, random_state=0)
train_scores, test_scores = validation_curve(
    random_forest, X, y, param_name='n_estimators',
    param_range=param_range, cv=crossvalidation,
    scoring='roc_auc')
```

```
mean_test_scores = np.mean(test_scores, axis=1)
for i, score in enumerate(mean_test_scores):
    print(f"n_estimators: {param_range[i]:4}, " +
          f"ROC-AUC score: {score:.3f}")
```

The code will print the results, and you can visualize them better in a plot depicting the progress of the evaluation metric, the ROC-AUC score, with respect to the hyperparameter controlling the number of trees used in the ensemble. This plot is called a validation plot:

```
import matplotlib.pyplot as plt

plt.plot(param_range, mean_test_scores,
         'bo-', label='CV score')
plt.xlabel('Number of Estimators')
plt.ylabel('ROC-AUC Score')
plt.title('Random Forest Validation Curve')
plt.legend(loc='lower right')
plt.grid(True)
plt.show()
```

Figure 20-3 shows the results provided by the preceding code. The more estimators, the better the results. However, at a certain point the gain becomes minimal and it makes little sense to add so many more trees for so little gain.

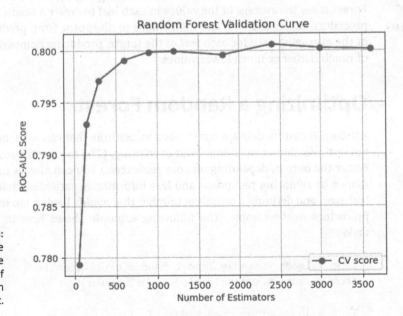

FIGURE 20-3: Verifying the impact of the number of estimators on Random Forest.

Working with a Random Forest regressor

RandomForestRegressor works in a similar way as the Random Forest for classification, using exactly the same parameters. The following code tests it on the
California Housing dataset:

```
from sklearn.ensemble import RandomForestRegressor
from sklearn.model_selection import cross_val_score, KFold

X, y = load_california_housing_data()
rf_regressor = RandomForestRegressor(
    n_estimators=300, random_state=0)
cv = KFold(n_splits=5, shuffle=True, random_state=0)
scores = cross_val_score(
    rf_regressor, X, y, scoring='neg_mean_squared_error',
    cv=cv)
mean_mse = abs(scores.mean())
print(f"Mean squared error: {mean_mse:.3f}")
```

Here is the resulting cross-validated mean squared error:

```
Mean squared error: 0.252
```

REMEMBER

The Random Forest uses decision trees. Decision trees segment the dataset into
small partitions, called leaves, when estimating regression values. The Random
Forest takes the average of the values in each leaf to create a prediction. Using this
procedure causes extreme and high values to disappear from predictions because
of the averaging used for each leaf of the forest, producing damped values instead
of much higher or much lower values.

Optimizing a Random Forest

Random Forest models are out-of-box algorithms that can work quite well without optimization or worrying about overfitting. (The more estimators you use, the
better the output, depending on your resources.) You can always improve performance by removing redundant and less informative variables, fixing a minimum
leaf size, and defining a sampling number that avoids having too many correlated
predictors in the sample. The following example shows how to perform these
tasks:

```
from sklearn.ensemble import RandomForestClassifier
from sklearn.model_selection import KFold

X, y = load_german_credit_data()
crossvalidation = KFold(
```

```
    n_splits=5, shuffle=True, random_state=0)
clf = RandomForestClassifier(random_state=0)
scorer = "roc_auc"
```

Using the German Credit Data and a first default classifier, you can optimize both max_features and min_samples_leaf. When optimizing max_features, you use preconfigured options (None for all features, sqrt or log2 functions applied to the number of features) and integrate them using small feature numbers and a value of 1/3 of the features. Selecting the right number of features to sample tends to reduce the number of times when correlated and similar variables are picked together, thus increasing the predictive performances.

There is a statistical reason to optimize min_samples_leaf. Using leaves with few cases often corresponds to overfitting to very specific data combinations. You need to have at least 30 observations to achieve a minimal statistical confidence that data patterns correspond to real and general rules:

```
from sklearn.model_selection import GridSearchCV

max_features = [X.shape[1] // 3, "sqrt", "log2", None]
min_samples_leaf = [1, 10, 30]
n_estimators = [50, 100, 300, 500, 1000]
search_grid = {
    "n_estimators": n_estimators,
    "max_features": max_features,
    "min_samples_leaf": min_samples_leaf}
search_cv = GridSearchCV(
    estimator=clf,
    param_grid=search_grid,
    scoring=scorer,
    cv=crossvalidation)
search_cv.fit(X, y)

best_params = search_cv.best_params_
best_score = search_cv.best_score_
print(f"Best parameters: {best_params}")
print(f"Best score: {best_score}")
```

The best parameters and best accuracy obtained are then reported, highlighting that the parameters to act on is the number of trees:

```
Best parameters: {'max_features': 8, 'min_samples_leaf': 1,
                  'n_estimators': 1000}
Best score: 0.8008907775588991
```

Boosting Predictions

Gathering different tree models is not the only ensemble technique possible. In fact, another machine learning technique, called *boosting*, uses ensembles effectively. In boosting, you grow many trees sequentially. Each tree tries to build a model that successfully predicts what trees that were built before it weren't able to forecast. The technique pools subsequent models and uses a weighted average or a weighted majority vote on the final prediction.

The following sections present two boosting applications: AdaBoost (Adaptive Boosting) and gradient boosting machines. You can use all boosting algorithms for both regression and classification. The examples in these sections start working with classification using the German Credit Data.

If you have already prepared the function `load_german_credit_data`, you just need to reassign the X and y variables as follows:

```
X, y = load_german_credit_data()
```

Knowing that many weak predictors win

`AdaBoostClassifier` fits sequential weak predictors. It's used by default when working with decision trees, but you can choose other algorithms by changing the `base_estimator` parameter. Weak predictors are usually machine learning predictors that don't perform well because they have too much variance or bias, so they perform slightly better than chance. The classic example of a weak learner is the decision stump, which is a decision tree grown to only one level. Usually, decision trees are the best-performing option in boosting, so you can safely use the default learner and concentrate on two important parameters to obtain good predictions: `n_estimators` and `learning_rate`.

`learning_rate` determines how each weak predictor contributes to the final result. A high learning rate requires few `n_estimators` before converging to an optimal solution, but it likely won't be the best solution possible. A low learning rate takes longer to train because it requires more predictors before reaching a solution. In addition, it also overfits more slowly.

TIP

In contrast to bagging, boosting can overfit if you use too many estimators. A cross-validation is always helpful in finding the correct number, keeping in mind that lower learning rates take longer to overfit, so picking an almost optimal value using a loose grid search is easier.

```
from sklearn.ensemble import AdaBoostClassifier
from sklearn.model_selection import cross_val_score, KFold
from sklearn.metrics import roc_auc_score

ada = AdaBoostClassifier(
    n_estimators=1000, learning_rate=0.01, random_state=0)
cv = KFold(n_splits=5, shuffle=True, random_state=0)
roc_scores = cross_val_score(
    ada, X, y, scoring='roc_auc', cv=cv)
mean_score = roc_scores.mean()
print(f'ROC-AUC score: {mean_score:.3f}')
```

After running the code, you get the cross-validated ROC-AUC score:

```
ROC-AUC score: 0.774
```

This example uses the default estimator, which is a full-blown decision tree. If you'd like to try a stump (which needs more estimators), you should instantiate the AdaBoostClassifier with base_estimator=DecisionTreeClassifier (max_depth=1).

Setting a gradient boosting classifier

The Gradient Boosting Machine (GBM) performs much better than the AdaBoost boosting technique, the first boosting algorithm ever created. In particular, GBM uses an optimization computation for weighting the subsequent estimators. As with the example in the preceding section, the following example uses the German Credit Data and explores some extra parameters available in GBM:

```
from sklearn.ensemble import GradientBoostingClassifier
from sklearn.model_selection import cross_val_score
from sklearn.model_selection import KFold

X, y = load_german_credit_data()
crossvalidation = KFold(
    n_splits=5, shuffle=True, random_state=0)
gbc = GradientBoostingClassifier(
    n_estimators=300, subsample=1.0, max_depth=2,
    learning_rate=0.1, random_state=0)
crossvalidation = KFold(
    n_splits=5, shuffle=True, random_state=0)
score = np.mean(cross_val_score(
    gbc, X, y, scoring='roc_auc', cv=crossvalidation))
print(f'ROC-AUC: {score:.3f}')
```

Apart from the learning rate and the number of estimators, which are key parameters for optimal learning without overfitting, you must provide values for subsample and max_depth. subsample introduces subsampling into the training (so that the training is done on a different dataset every time), as is done in bagging. max_depth defines the maximum level of the built trees. It's usually a good practice to start with three levels, but more levels may be necessary for modeling complex data.

On the very same problem you tested before, the GradientBoostingClassifier results in the following accuracy score after running the code:

```
ROC-AUC: 0.784
```

Running a gradient boosting regressor

Creating a gradient boosting regressor doesn't present particular differences from creating the classifier. The main difference is the presence of multiple loss functions that you can use (contrast this with GradientBoostingClassifier, which has only the deviance loss, analogous to the cost function of a logistic regression). The following example tests it on the California Housing dataset:

```
from sklearn.ensemble import GradientBoostingRegressor
from sklearn.model_selection import cross_val_score, KFold

X, y = load_california_housing_data()
gbr = GradientBoostingRegressor(
    n_estimators=1000, subsample=1.0, max_depth=3,
    learning_rate=0.01, random_state=0)
cv = KFold(n_splits=5, shuffle=True, random_state=0)
mse = np.mean(cross_val_score(
    gbr, X, y, scoring='neg_mean_squared_error', cv=cv))
print(f"Mean squared error: {abs(mse):.3f}")
```

After running the code, you get the mean squared error for the regression, which is worse than the corresponding one by a Random Forest:

```
Mean squared error: 0.285
```

The example trains a GradientBoostingRegressor using the default ls value for the loss parameter, which is analogous to a linear regression. Here are some other choices:

>> quantile: This guesses a particular quantile that you specify using the alpha parameter (usually it's 0.5, which is the median).

>> lad (least absolute deviation): This choice is highly robust to outliers; it tends to ordinally rank the predictions correctly.

>> huber: This creates a combination of ls and lad. It requires that you fix the alpha parameter.

Using GBM hyperparameters

GBM models are quite sensitive to overfitting when you have too many sequential estimators and the model starts fitting the noise in the data. It's important to check the efficiency of the coupled values of the number of estimators and the learning rate. The following example uses the California Housing dataset and tries to improve the previous score:

```
from sklearn.model_selection import KFold
from sklearn.model_selection import GridSearchCV

X, y = load_california_housing_data()
crossvalidation = KFold(
    n_splits=5, shuffle=True, random_state=0)
gbr = GradientBoostingRegressor(
    n_estimators=1000, learning_rate=0.01,
    random_state=0)
search_grid = {'subsample': [1.0, 0.9, 0.7],
               'max_depth': [2, 3, 4, 5, 6]}
search_func = GridSearchCV(
    estimator=gbr, param_grid=search_grid,
    scoring='neg_mean_squared_error',
    cv=crossvalidation)
search_func.fit(X, y)
best_params = search_func.best_params_
best_score = abs(search_func.best_score_)
print(f'Best parameters: {best_params}')
print(f'Best mean squared error: {best_score:.3f}')
```

Optimization may take some time because of the computational burden required by the GBM algorithms, especially if you decide to test high values of max_depth.

TIP

A good strategy is to keep the learning rate fixed and try to optimize subsample and max_depth with respect to n_estimators (keeping in mind that high values of max_depth usually imply a lesser number of estimators). After you find the optimum values for subsample and max_depth, you can start searching for further optimization of n_estimators and learning_rate.

After running the optimization, you can examine the resulting best mean squared error (which is much better now than those of Random Forest) and notice how it improved running the algorithm by the default parameters. Gradient Boosting always requires some parameter tuning in order to return the best results:

```
Best parameters: {'max_depth': 6, 'subsample': 0.7}
Best mean squared error: 0.220
```

Using XGBoost

XGBoost is a versatile and scalable machine learning algorithm that was originally developed as a command-line tool by Tianqi Chen and has since been enhanced with a Python wrapper. XGBoost supports multiple programming languages, including Python, R, Java, Scala, Julia, and C++. It can be utilized on a single machine with multithreading, as well as on Hadoop and Spark clusters. You can find more information about XGBoost on its website: `https://xgboost.readthedocs.io/en/latest/` and also instructions on how to install it on various systems at `https://xgboost.readthedocs.io/en/latest/install.html`. For Python usage the fastest ways are using pip or conda:

```
pip install xgboost
conda install -c conda-forge py-xgboost
```

The interesting fact about XGBoost is that its name stands for eXtreme Gradient Boosting, indicating that the algorithm working under the hood is a bit different, and faster performing, than the gradient boosting offered by Scikit-learn. That's also the reason that XGBoost has gained much popularity in data science competitions such as Kaggle (`https://www.kaggle.com/`) and the KDD Cup. The following example shows how it performs on the problems found earlier in this chapter, starting with the German Credit Data:

```
import xgboost as xgb
from sklearn.model_selection import cross_val_score, KFold

X, y = load_german_credit_data()

cv = KFold(n_splits=5, shuffle=True, random_state=0)

params = {'n_estimators': 800, 'subsample': 0.7,
          'max_depth': 2, 'learning_rate': 0.015,
          'random_state': 0,
          'objective': 'binary:logistic',
          'eval_metric': 'auc'}
```

```
gbc = xgb.XGBClassifier(**params)

score = np.mean(cross_val_score(
    gbc, X, y, scoring='roc_auc', cv=cv))

print(f'ROC-AUC: {score:.3f}')
```

Here are the results for the ROC-AUC score:

```
ROC-AUC: 0.801
```

The following example tests XGBoost on the California Housing Dataset regression problem:

```
import xgboost as xgb
from sklearn.model_selection import cross_val_score, KFold

X, y = load_california_housing_data()

xg_reg = xgb.XGBRegressor(
    n_estimators=900, subsample=0.8, max_depth=5,
    learning_rate=0.07, random_state=0)

cv = KFold(n_splits=5, shuffle=True, random_state=0)

mse = np.mean(cross_val_score(
    xg_reg, X, y, scoring='neg_mean_squared_error',
    cv=cv))

print(f"Mean squared error: {abs(mse):.3f}")
```

Also in this case, the results are the best obtained so far:

```
Mean squared error: 0.200
```

The impressive results are due to the fact that, if tuned using the right parameters, XGBoost can outpace all the other algorithms seen so far in the book.

6

The Part of Tens

Chapter **21**

Ten Essential Data Resources

I n reading this book, you discover quite a lot about data science and Python. Before your head explodes from all the new knowledge you gain, it's important to realize that this book is really just the tip of the iceberg. Yes, there really is more information available out there, and that's what this chapter is all about. The following sections introduce you to a wealth of data science resource collections that you really need to make the best use of your new knowledge.

In this case, a resource collection is simply a listing of really cool links with some text to tell you why they're so great. In some cases, you gain access to articles about data science; in other cases, you're exposed to new tools. In fact, data science is such a huge topic that you could easily find more resources than those discussed here, but the following sections provide a good place to start.

REMEMBER

As with anything else on the internet, links break, sites go out of business, and new sites take their place. If you find that a link is broken, please let me know about it at John@JohnMuellerBooks.com.

Discovering the News with Reddit

The data science field changes constantly for a number of reasons, including the addition of new algorithms and techniques, as well as the use of ever-larger datasets from an increasingly diverse set of sources. Consequently, you need a news source, such as the data science area of Reddit (https://www.reddit.com/r/datascience/) to obtain the latest information and stay ahead of your competitors. These blog posts often contain the latest techniques as well, ensuring that after you get up to speed on data science, you can stay that way. In addition, you find topics that are essential for your career, such as finding the range of data science salaries. This site also provides Python-specific information at https://www.reddit.com/r/python/ (which is a private community that you have to sign up to join) and data science news at https://www.reddit.com/r/datasciencenews/.

Getting a Good Start with KDnuggets

Learning about data mining and data science is a process. KDnuggets breaks down the learning process into a series of steps at https://www.kdnuggets.com/faq/learning-data-mining-data-science.html. Each step gives you an overview of what you should be doing and why. You also find links to a variety of resources online to make the learning process considerably easier. Even though the site emphasizes the use of R, Python, and SQL (in that order) to perform data science tasks, the steps will actually work for any of a number of approaches that you might take.

REMEMBER As with any other learning experience, a procedure like the one shown on the KDnuggets site will work for some people and not others. Everyone learns a little differently. Don't be afraid to improvise. The resources on this site might provide insights into other things that you can do to make your learning process easier.

Locating Free Learning Resources with Quora

Resisting the word *free* is really hard, especially when it comes to education, which normally costs many thousands of dollars. The Quora site at https://www.quora.com/What-are-the-best-free-resources-to-learn-data-science provides a listing of the best no-cost learning resources for data science.

Most of the links take on a question format, such as, "What are good ways to get started with data science for a complete novice?" The question-and-answer format is helpful because you might be asking the questions that the site answers. The resulting list of sites, courses, and resources are introductory, for the most part, but they are a good way to get started working in the data science field.

TIP

A few of the links go to prestigious institutions such as Harvard. The link gives you access to course materials such as lecture videos and blackboards. However, you don't get the actual course free of charge. If you want the benefits of the course, you still need to pay for it. Even so, just by viewing the course materials, you can obtain a lot of useful data science knowledge.

Gaining Insights with Oracle's AI & Data Science Blog

Major vendors can offer you significant amounts of useful information. Of course, you need to keep the source of this information in mind because it can be quite biased; pointing out vendor products (as an example) in favor of a more balanced view that includes all available products. The Oracle AI & Data Science Blog (https://blogs.oracle.com/ai-and-datascience/) provides you with a considerable amount of information — everything from the latest data analysis techniques to the methods you can use to reduce costs. In addition, you find category-specific information based on

>> Best practices

>> Data science education

>> Use cases

>> Data science as a platform

Accessing the Huge List of Resources on Data Science Central

Many of the resources you find online cover mainstream topics. Data Science Central (https://www.datasciencecentral.com/) provides access to a relatively large number of data science experts who tell you about the most obscure facts of data science. One of the more interesting blog posts appears at `https://www.datasciencecentral.com/how-ai-is-revolutionizing-change-data-capture/`.

This resource tells you about Change Data Capture (CDC) and methods of enhancing the capture of changes to databases using AI. The nice thing about this post is that it's succinct and doesn't bury you in detail that you might not want until you know that the techniques will actually work for your organization. Most of the posts follow this same format, which means that you can gain an overview of a considerable number of topics in a short period of time.

Discovering New Beginner Data Science Methodologies at Data Science 101

One of the major problems with becoming a data scientist is that many sites assume that you already are one or that you have a significant level of training in some related field. The result is a really high wall that exhausts many aspiring new data scientists before they even begin learning about the trade. Data Science 101 (`https://ryanswanstrom.com/datascience101/`) isn't like most sites. You find all sorts of materials that can help you become a data scientist even if your current level of knowledge leaves something to be desired when visiting those other sites. The information is also quite varied; you'll find resources of this type:

>> Blog posts

>> Learning resources

>> Videos

>> Academic papers

Obtaining the Most Authoritative Sources at Udacity

Even with the right connections online and a good search engine, trying to find just the right resource can be hard. U Climb Higher has published a list of 24 data science resources at `https://blog.udacity.com/2014/12/24-data-science-resources-keep-finger-pulse.html` that's guaranteed to help keep your finger

Index

D

N

Naïve Bayes algorithm, 317–322, 355
  text classification prediction, 320–322
  uses for, 318–319
National Institute of Standards and Technology (NIST), 152, 426
Natural Language Processing (NLP), 133
ndarray structure, 96–97, 153, 267, 296
n-dimensional array manipulation, 29
neighborhoods
  defined, 288
  k-nearest neighbors, 322–325
NetworkX library
  directed graphs, 198
  graph data, 139–141
  overview, 31–32
  undirected graphs, 196
neural networks, 329, 351, 385–390
  classification problems, 386–390
  deep learning, 385
  neurons, 385–386
  numeric values, 386
  overview, 385–386
  regression problems, 386–387
n-grams, 134–135, 138, 320
NIST (National Institute of Standards and Technology), 152, 426
NLP (Natural Language Processing), 133
NMF (Non-Negative Matrix Factorization), 266–268
"no free lunch" theorem, 308, 330
nodes
  adding to graphs, 196
  adjacency matrices, 138–139
  defined, 138, 195

nonlinear dimensionality reduction (manifold learning), 259–261
nonlinear transformations, 352–357
  interactions between variables, 354–357
  variable transformations, 353–354
Non-Negative Matrix Factorization (NMF), 266–268
nonparametric correlation, 244–246, 248
NoSQL databases, 99
notebooks
  Google Colab, 53–59
    creating, 54
    displaying table of contents, 66
    downloading, 59
    getting notebook information, 66–67
    opening, 54–55
    saving, 56–59
    sharing, 67–68
    storage locations, 55–59
    viewing, 66
  Jupyter Notebook, 44–47
    adding content to, 44–45
    creating, 44
    exporting, 45–46
    importing, 46–47
    removing, 46
novelty detection, 294–295
np.max() method, 153
np.min() method, 153
NumPy library
  aggregating data, 128
  arrays, 153–155, 219
  covariance and correlation, 243
  dimensionality reduction, 253–254
  documentation, 148
  identifying version of, 226

installing, 216
label count, 372
ndarray structure, 96–97, 153, 267, 296
overview, 29
pandas vs., 106–107
performance and speed issues, 219
random generator, 292
transformers returning features as, 210
trendlines, 185

O

objectify.parse() method, 101
object-oriented programming, 17
objects, 76–78
  help resources, 77–78
  properties and methods associated with, 78
  using magic functions with, 76–78
Olivetti faces dataset, 262, 428
omission, mistruths of, 146
one-hot encoding, 212, 388
OneHotEncoder() function, 207
OneVsOneClassifier class, 316–317
OneVsRestClassifier class, 316–317
online resources
  Advances in Neural Information Processing Systems, 424
  Anaconda, 36, 39–40
  AskSam, 97
  author's website, 411
  bagging technique, 399
  Basemap, 194
  bigml, 426
  Cartopy, 190, 193–194
  Chainer, 385
  ChatGPT, 385

About the Authors

Luca Massaron is a data scientist and a marketing research director who specializes in multivariate statistical analysis, machine learning, and customer insight, with more than a decade of experience in solving real-world problems and generating value for stakeholders by applying reasoning, statistics, data mining, and algorithms. From being a pioneer of web audience analysis in Italy to achieving the rank of top ten Kaggler on kaggle.com, he has always been passionate about everything regarding data and analysis and about demonstrating the potentiality of data-driven knowledge discovery to both experts and nonexperts. Favoring simplicity over unnecessary sophistication, he believes that a lot can be achieved in data science by understanding and practicing the essentials of it.

John Mueller is a freelance author and technical editor. He has writing in his blood, having produced 124 books and more than 600 articles to date. The topics range from networking to artificial intelligence and from database management to heads-down programming. Some of his current books include discussions of data science, data security, machine learning, and algorithms. His technical editing skills have helped more than 70 authors refine the content of their manuscripts. John has provided technical editing services to various magazines, performed various kinds of consulting, and writes certification exams. Be sure to read John's blog at http://blog.johnmuellerbooks.com/. You can reach John on the internet at John@JohnMuellerBooks.com. John also has a website at http://www.johnmuellerbooks.com/. Be sure to follow John on Amazon at https://www.amazon.com/John-Mueller/e/B000AQ77KK/.

Luca's Dedication

I would like to dedicate this book to my parents, Renzo and Licia, who both love simple and well-explained ideas and who now, by reading the book we wrote, will understand more of my daily work in data science and how this new discipline is going to change the way we understand the world and operate in it.

John's Dedication

This book is dedicated to all the people who help me each day — from the people at the café where I drink coffee to the guy who cuts my grass. I really couldn't make it without all these helpers, and it's my hope that they know how much I appreciate them.

Luca's Acknowledgments

My greatest thanks to my family, Yukiko and Amelia, for their support and loving patience.

John's Acknowledgments

Thanks to my wife, Rebecca. Even though she is gone now, her spirit is in every book I write, in every word that appears on the page. She believed in me when no one else would.

Rod Stephens deserves thanks for his technical edit of this book. He greatly added to the accuracy and depth of the material you see here. Rod often provides a different perspective on things, which I find helpful in making my books more rounded and appealing to a wider group of readers.

Matt Wagner, my agent, deserves credit for helping me get the contract in the first place and taking care of all the details that most authors don't really consider. I always appreciate his assistance. It's good to know that someone wants to help.

A number of people read all or part of this book to help me refine the approach, test scripts, and generally provide input that all readers wish they could have. These unpaid volunteers helped in ways too numerous to mention here.

Finally, I would like to thank Steve Hayes, Hanna Sytsma, Susan Christophersen, and the rest of the editorial and production staff.

Publisher's Acknowledgments

Executive Editor: Steve Hayes

Project Manager and Copy Editor: Susan Christophersen

Technical Editor: Rod Stephens

Production Editor: Pradesh Kumar

Cover Image: © filo/Getty Images